The Shell Global Scenarios to 2025

The future business environment: trends, trade-offs and choices

The first of these "possible futures" is called *Low Trust Globalisation.* This is a legalistic world where the emphasis is on security and efficiency, even if at the expense of social cohesion. The second, *Open Doors,* is a pragmatic world that emphasises social cohesion and efficiency, with the market providing "built-in" solutions to the crises of security and trust. The third, called *Flags,* is a dogmatic world where security and community values are emphasised at the expense of efficiency.

To create analytical clarity, the scenarios no longer tell particular "stories", but look at the interplay between the three essential forces and between the contrasted ways in which different groups can pursue their objectives. While they provide more complex and sometimes technical analyses

of our business environment, these scenarios are based on a map which provides a simple, unified context which I find very powerful to better understand the various conditions under which we may have to operate in different regions or in different circumstances. This helps to bring the scenarios close to the reality of business.

The power of shared insights, within Shell and globally

Within Shell, I think the imperative is to use this tool to gain deeper insights into our global business environment and to achieve the cultural change that is at the heart of our Group strategy. We face real challenges in the future, we will all need to be able to respond to changing circumstances

and make informed and rigorous judgements about our decisions: these scenarios and methodology will help us to do that better.

Within the global community, I also hope that they will have a wider resonance and I am encouraged by the reactions that a preview of this report elicited at the World Economic Forum in January 2005. *Shell Global Scenarios*, rightly, have an excellent reputation around the world. I know that they broaden one's mindset, stimulate discussions, both with colleagues and with the global community. We often contribute our scenario expertise to help identify and address challenges of common concern, such as those of sustainable development, long-term energy needs or, more recently, the fight against AIDS and for development in Africa.

I am looking forward to sharing new insights with partners, shareholders, the local communities in which we operate and our many other stakeholders.

The enhanced methodology on which the *Global Scenarios to 2025* are based reflects the talent of the Shell Scenario team led by Dr Albert Bressand and senior team leaders Peter Cornelius, Cho Khong, Norbert Roelofs, Wim Thomas, Angela Wilkinson —not forgetting Kamran Agasi and graphic designer Peter Grundy—as well as insightful contributions by external experts whom I want to acknowledge and to thank. This robust methodology will help us make further contributions to the wider debates about the fundamental questions that face us all.

STREAM

Contents

Scenarios of the 1990s. The dual crisis of security and trust. Forces that shape strategies and behaviours. The *Trilemma Triangle* framework.

Three plausible resolutions of the *Trilemma*, highlighting challenges of compliance, reputation and country risks.

Interactions between market, state and civil society. Economic policies, forces of integration and fragmentation. Economic growth and the energy scene in each scenario.

Capital markets, law and regulations, transaction costs, corporate governance. Demographic and economic baselines. Energy security and the energy-and-carbon industry. Climate change and biodiversity.

Building, creatively, on 30 years of *Shell Global Scenarios*

● **A new approach to scenarios emphasising continuity and flexibility for strategy work.**

Over the last three decades, Shell has developed *Global Scenarios* to cast light on the context in which the Group operates, to identify emerging challenges and to foster adaptability to change. These scenarios are used to help review and assess strategy.

The *Global Scenarios to 2025* released in 2005 build on this foundation to develop an enhanced, robust methodology that addresses a broader range of strategic and planning needs across the whole spectrum of relevant time horizons and contexts.

Hence the transition that has occurred from a three-year scenario cycle to an annual one. This will provide greater continuity while also enabling flexible contributions to Group processes for identifying critical risks and opportunities.

Continuity is based on a map, the *Trilemma Triangle*, which embodies both an analysis of key forces and a methodology to monitor the implications of these forces year after year.

Flexibility is based on the fact that this map is not limited to the three *Global Scenarios* themselves, but encompasses a far broader set of possible futures. This will lead to customised applications and to quicker updates. It will also help Shell make significant contributions to important debates in the world at large.

Cooperation with centres of excellence and contributions by eminent experts in the course of developing these scenarios reflect strong teamwork, within and beyond corporate boundaries.

TINA | The iconic worlds of the 2001 *Business Class* and *Prism* scenarios

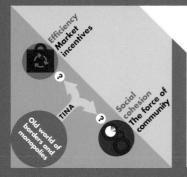

Previously, *Global Scenarios* explored the challenges of a globalising, deregulated, market-centric world...

During the 1990s, as market liberalisation accelerated, the *Shell Global Scenarios* explored the concept of "TINA"— There Is No Alternative—to increasing globalisation, the onrush of new technology and market liberalisation. The pairs of scenarios put forward in 1992, 1995 and 1998 all featured a market-centric world (*New Frontiers, Just Do It!* and *People Power*) as well as an alternative world giving more room to social and community aspirations.

This dilemma between efficiency on the one hand and values and social cohesion on the other still shaped the focal question behind the pair of 2001 Global Scenarios: *"will the resolution to dilemmas arising from globalisation be dominated by global elites or by the people of the heartlands?"*

The 2001 Global Scenarios — Business Class and Prism—drew striking and comprehensive implications of this analysis of globalisation, in an almost iconic manner:

Business Class offered a vision of "connected freedom" and greater economic integration. This was a world of efficiency, opportunities and high rewards for those who could compete and innovate successfully. Established authorities would be continually challenged and the power of nation states greatly reduced.

Prism highlighted the "connections that matter" and "multiple modernities" reflecting the influence of "heartlands" as opposed to "connected elites". The power of cultural values and belonging was stressed.

The tensions captured in 2001 remain valid, but societies also face more complex choices on the nature of regulation, the framework for corporate governance and welfare reforms. Conflicts over religion and values, shades of patriotic, populist and nationalist policies, and tensions between nations— including across the Atlantic— reflect greater divisiveness in the world.

Terrorism, insecurity, distrust

The dual crisis of security and market trust

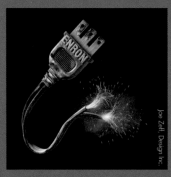

● **Disruption of both international security and trust in the marketplace highlight the importance of the role of the state.**

Two crises—in short, 9.11 and Enron—have unfolded since 2001, affecting national security and trust in the marketplace. Both have highlighted the vulnerability of our globalised world.

Western societies now expect the state to lead the restoration of physical security and market integrity. Middle Eastern, Asian, African and Latin American societies have heightened expectations of peaceful solutions to wars and to persisting poverty.

In addition to market incentives and community aspirations, this dual crisis brings into sharper focus a third force, namely the power of the state to regulate and to coerce.

This role involves both direct intervention—fighting terrorism and policing the market—and a more general emphasis on transparency, disclosure and good governance.

Society's heightened expectations accelerate the transformation of the state's agenda and methods. Because the new type of state acts in much closer synergy with the market (maximising opportunities for companies, individuals and civil society rather than welfare in general), this greater role of the state reinforces investors' power over value creation.

As a result, the *Global Scenarios to 2025* emphasise the importance of security concerns, legal and capital market cultures, and regulation.

• **Part 1** presents the *Trilemma Triangle*, the analytical framework developed to map relations between market participants, civil society and states.

• **Part 2** presents the *Global Scenarios to 2025* themselves. A selection of '*Trilemmaps*' then summarises implications of the *Global Scenarios* for key aspects of our global business environment.

• **Part 3** analyses critical trends common to all scenarios, first on the international scene (emphasising the US, China, the EU, India and Africa), then in matters of demography, and patterns of economic growth. It concludes by focusing on energy security and the move towards an "energy-and-carbon" industry.

2025

the Trilemma Triangle

The three forces ... the *Trilemma Triangle* ... the "two wins–one loss" areas

Forces

Market incentives

Coercion, regulation

The force of community

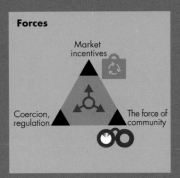

Points on the map show complex trade-offs...

...as competing forces pull toward the three triangle apexes

Objectives

Efficiency

Security

Social cohesion

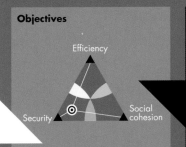

One of the three "two wins—one loss" areas

The *Global Scenarios to 2025* explore the three forces of market incentives, communities, and coercion or regulation by the state.

The three forces drive towards different objectives: efficiency, social cohesion and justice, and security. While societies often aspire to all three objectives, the forces display elements of mutual exclusiveness—one cannot be at the same time freer, more conformant to one's group or faith, and more coerced.

We explore the three dilemmas—a *Trilemma*—involved in the pursuit of these objectives. Hence the use of the *Trilemma Triangle* to map the interplay between market incentives, the force of community (aspirations to conform and

be listened to) and forces of regulation and coercion.

Trade-offs rather than utopias
The three corners, or apexes, would be tempting starting points for scenarios, as they would pit a market-centric world against society-centric and state-centric ones. In democratic market economies, however, such worlds are what Thomas Moore in 1516 called "utopias", worlds that can inspire but cannot exist.

We develop the new scenarios not at the apexes but in the areas of the *Trilemma Triangle* that capture the most plausible trade-offs between these diverse, complex objectives, namely the "two wins—one loss" areas in which forces combine to achieve more of two objectives. Each of

these areas embodies trade-offs acceptable to broader coalitions of actors than in the utopian worlds at the apexes.

Putting business relevance first leads to more complex, sometimes quite technical analyses of our business environment, as trade-offs reflect investor and customer expectations, corporate governance, legal cultures, regulatory integration or conflicts, policies and strategic choices. Yet this complexity is a source of critical strategic challenges, and the three scenarios capture plausible, coherent ways in which essential trade-offs will be arrived at.

Our framework also highlights transformations that will influence how various actors—whether

governments, NGOs or investors—can "play their cards" in pursuit of their objectives.

Limits and future developments
This *Jet Stream* report does not seek to provide answers to all questions that may affect the Group, and even less to list all events that could introduce change. Nonetheless, it is a cornerstone in a more comprehensive risk-assessment effort.

Jet Stream forces establish contexts, and our framework helps us to analyse in other work how such contexts can be modified by external shocks such as major wars, regional crises, radical climate change or major pandemics like AIDS.

Key to these *Global Scenarios* are the legal environment, the market culture, the global forces of integration and fragmentation and—more generally—the complex interplay between the three forces. These factors shape how different societies, and the global community, strive towards all three objectives of efficiency, social justice and security.

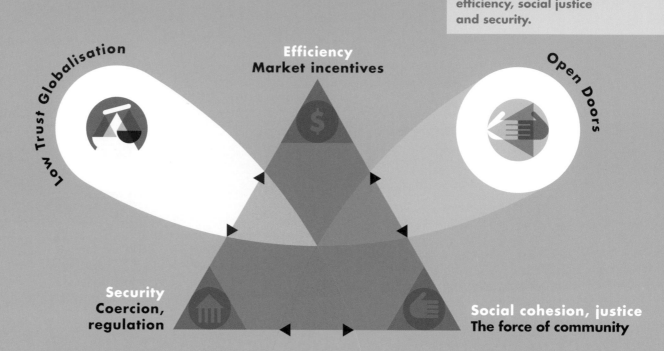

Low Trust Globalisation

Open Doors

Efficiency
Market incentives

Security
Coercion,
regulation

Social cohesion, justice
The force of community

Flags

**Part 2
the Three
Global
Scenarios
to 2025**

Chapter 3

Chapter 4

Chapter 5

Low Trust Globalisation

Open Doors

Flags

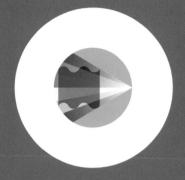

a legalistic, "prove it to me" world

a pragmatic, "know me" world

a dogmatic, "follow me" world

The absence of market solutions to the crisis of security and trust, rapid regulatory change, overlapping jurisdictions and conflicting laws lead to intrusive checks and controls, encouraging short-term portfolio optimisation and vertical integration. Institutional discontinuities limit cross-border economic integration. Complying with fast-evolving rules and managing complex risks are key challenges.

"Built-in" security and compliance certification, regulatory harmonisation, mutual recognition, independent media, voluntary best-practice codes, and close links between investors and civil society encourage cross-border integration and virtual value chains. Networking skills and superior reputation management are essential.

Zero-sum games, dogmatic approaches, regulatory fragmentation, and national preferences, conflicts over values and religion give insiders an advantage and put a brake on globalisation. Gated communities, patronage and national standards exacerbate fragmentation, and call for careful country-risk management.

Trilemm ▲ps

Scenario	Security	Trust
	Checks and Controls	Rules-based
	Precautionary Principle	Voluntary codes
	Gated communities	Community-based loyalty

Trilemmap 1: Resolution of the dual crisis

Scenario	Drivers	Disclosure	Business Impact
	Investors	Financial	"Bolt-on"
	Investors and civil society	Financial and global value reporting	"Built-in"
	National stakeholders	Financial and impact on local communities	Hybrid

Trilemmap 5: Transparency and disclosure process

● **Differences between the three scenarios are captured in *Trilemmaps* which compare specific features of our business environment.**

In this report, we share a select number of the implications we have derived from the *Trilemma Triangle* framework regarding our global business environment. Such analysis starts with the contrasted resolutions of the dual crisis of security and trust, a foundation for many other developments.

Investors' attitudes
Differences in investors' attitudes can be captured in the contrasts between "Exit", "Voice" and "Loyalty" (a trilogy of conflict-resolution behaviours that we describe): while investors in *Low Trust Globalisation* will "vote with their feet", they will be more inclined to voice their concerns in *Open Doors*. As transparency and alternatives are limited, *Flags* is a world of "home bias" and of high, even if constrained, loyalty.

The twin logic of compliance and reputation
The strategy and behaviour of companies are influenced by complex combinations of **regulations**, **compliance** mechanisms (whether through courts, arbitration or bargaining), and of **transparency** and **disclosure** requirements either through the law or through voluntary codes. For instance, the extent to which disclosure will have to cover non-financial performance differs significantly across scenarios: while the "triple bottom line" approach—financial, social and environmental— prevails in *Open Doors*, where civil society groups work closely with investors, measures of non-financial performance focus on local issues in *Flags* (air and water pollution, impact on jobs…).

In *Low Trust Globalisation*, financial reporting is complex and contentious enough for companies to "stick to the rules" and limit their disclosure to mandatory standards.

What type of regulatory integration?
We explore how regulators would interact across borders, and how this would impact business. We see a strong contrast between regulatory competition in *Low Trust Globalisation*, a clear dominance of national regulation in *Flags*, and regulatory "co-opetition"—a combination of in-depth cooperation and of competition to attract investors and companies—in *Open Doors*.

Executive Summary

Part 2
Chapter 6
market-level
tools

legal,
regulatory
and market
environments

... global civil society ... Kyoto ... internet governance ... corporate governance codes ...

Scenario	Instruments	Cross-border dynamics
	'Private attorneys general'	Regulatory competition
	Voluntary best practices	Regulatory co-opetition
	Command and control	Fragmented national regulations

Trilemmap 6: **Legal and regulatory integration**

Scenario	Drivers	Key CG risks	Instruments
	Institutional investors	Legal	Detailed rules
	Investors and stakeholders	Reputational	Comply-or-explain codes
	National champions	Loss of control	Stringent domestic laws

Trilemmap 13: **Corporate governance (CG) cultures**

Trilemmaps are building blocks that can be mobilised for market-level applications, such as risk assessment or project evaluation.

Our intention, in this report, is not to be exhaustive but simply to illustrate how the analytical framework behind the *Global Scenarios to 2025* lends itself to in-depth, customised strategic analysis.

Competitive assets
Trilemmaps are also used to explore key dimensions of corporate competitive strategies, in light notably of the nature and the level of transaction costs to be expected in each scenario. The differing incentives to outsource or to integrate vertically are among the points we discuss.

The emerging global civil society
The ways in which a "global civil society" can continue—or fail—to emerge in critical fields are also illustrated.

The *Trilemmaps* that we present focus on relations between NGOs, companies and government, as well as on the ways in which Internet governance is likely to evolve as governments seek to reassert control. Trends in civil society are also relevant the concluding chapter on biodiversity and the post-Kyoto regulatory framework to deal with climate change.

Corporate governance
How institutional investors and other actors influence the corporate governance agenda can also be analysed in the framework of the *Trilemma Triangle*. This leads us to contrast, for instance, how three major types of risks that the Boards of global companies have to consider would be prioritised and addressed:

Low Trust Globalisation is characterised by a combination of a very strong role for institutional investors and a legalistic approach to rules and compliance. Mandatory standards, systematic rating and disclosure reflect—and further reinforce—the overall climate of distrust. **Legal risk** is very high, and D&O (Directors and

Officers) insurance reaches staggering heights.
In *Open Doors*, by contrast, stakeholders have a major voice as well, and often work in cooperation with investors and regulators. The capacity to understand and evaluate different market cultures is high, and trust is reflected in comply-or-explain codes. Board evaluation is emphasised. Legal risk is moderate, but **reputational risk** matters a lot.

Flags sees political considerations interfering with a patchwork of stringent national rules, further encouraging the "home bias" in investment portfolios. **Loss of control** risk is very high, as groups with good connections and national champions can weaken the rule of law.

... the US financial and innovation global hub ... the Chinese manufacturing hub ... Indian democracy ... EU regional clout ...

● **Part 3 looks at how power affects scenario outcomes and at how critical energy and environment challenges can be met.**

US leadership

The differential in long-term growth potential between the US on the one hand, and Europe and Japan on the other (approximately 3% against 2% and 1%, respectively), means that trade with, and foreign direct investment into and out of, the US have become central to further integration patterns within the OECD. Global governance meanwhile reflects an overarching US influence.

In addition to its economic, financial and demographic importance, the US is also playing an increasingly central role in legal and regulatory terms. US legal concepts and regulatory standards are adopted or imitated, and US courts are increasingly involved in settling international disputes.

European and Japanese "soft power"

European contributions to global governance, like the "mutual recognition" concept, embody a more decentralised view of global integration. Europe has demonstrated very significant "soft power", pre-empting conflicts over minorities in Central Europe and facilitating political change in Turkey or Ukraine. Yet the role of "soft power" is dependent on the broader global context.

Forums like the International Organisation of Securities Commissions (IOSCO) or the International Accounting Standards Board (IASB) foster convergence among domestic jurisdictions, with the US a key player and the EU quite often able to leapfrog.

Chinese benchmarks

The combination of currently cheap labour costs, market size and rapid technological modernisation makes China the world's manufacturing hub, redefining the terms of global competition. Having rapidly modernized its regulatory framework by embracing WTO-endorsed rules, China is now facing a broader governance challenge, whether at corporate or at public level, which will condition its further success.

Against this background, global governance will differ widely in our three scenarios, ranging from rejuvenated multilateralism in *Open Doors* to coalitions of the willing in *Low Trust Globalisation* and an inter-national rather than global order in *Flags*.

Executive Summary

Part 3
Our Global
Business
Environment

Chapter 8
African futures

... trans-Atlantic relations ... the Middle East peace process ... AIDS ... conditionality and development ...

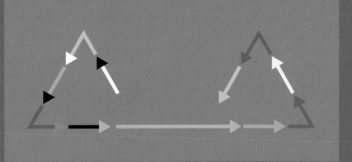

● European integration, the Middle East and the African development challenge.

The Middle East
Open Doors offers hopeful prospects for the Middle East as the Iraqi situation is internationalised and new reforming groups offer alternatives to authoritarianism and fundamentalism. Development fosters security, opening new possibilities of trans-Atlantic cooperation in the region.

In *Low Trust Globalisation*, strong regimes address social needs, helped by high oil prices, but there is little incentive to reform and fundamentalism appeals to disenfranchised groups. The US maintains a regional presence, with a low profile. *Flags* sees a turbulent Middle East, driven by conflict. Low oil prices provide additional incentives to attempt cautious reform, but this is bitterly

contested. Groups unite against common enemies rather than for common objectives.

India out of China's shadow
Is India set to emulate China's rise to become a global player? India can combine "soft power" — witness Bollywood's global success—with regional "hard power". Yet the IT services sector is not a broad enough base to achieve full-scale modernisation, when agriculture still occupies more than half the working population but accounts for only 22% of GDP. The complexity of Indian democracy—reflecting political coalitions based on ethnicity, caste and language— makes policy reform less strikingly effective than in China, but may well provide a more stable foundation for success.

African futures
For Africa also, *Open Doors* is more favourable as the international community takes a long-term view on trade, foreign aid and the fight against AIDS. Conditionality is based on fundamental principles (human rights but also Kyoto implementation for EU donors and Christian values for US ones). *Low Trust Globalisation* sees an emphasis on access to resources, the fight against corruption and efforts to deal with failed states on an emergency basis. *Flags* is about "strong men", patronage, national efforts to combat AIDS, war against terror and bilateral deals.

... private actors coercing through courts ... states using the market ... investors seeking alignment ...

How the *Trilemma* is resolved infuences the strategies open to states, civil society, companies and investors.

● **How power translates into law, how key actors play their cards, alone or in alliances...**

The *Global Scenarios to 2025* are about the dynamics of change as shaped by the three forces, by the actors behind them, and by the objectives they point toward.

In addition to international trends reflecting changes fostered by US power and by the rise of China, each of the three scenarios explores transformations in the set of incentives, constraints and instruments for key actors. Of particular importance are the globalisation of the legal scene, the gradual transformation of the ways in which states exercise power, and the importance of corporate governance for value creation but also as part of investor efforts to seek greater alignment on the part of their companies.

Global legal forum shopping

By seeking a judgement against another party, civil society groups or investors can mobilise the coercive power of the courts to redress their losses or advance their interests. Investor activism, "legal forum shopping" and the adoption of new business models by law firms give US courts a global appeal and reach.

Market States

Contrary to predictions by many "business gurus", the state does not wither away. Rather, the gradual transition from the Nation State to a Market State model implies a redefinition of states' fundamental promises, towards maximisation of opportunities for companies, investors, civil society and citizens rather than of the Nation's welfare.

Investors seeking alignment

In the wake of the Enron crisis, institutional investors scrutinise how companies create or destroy value. Rating agencies and a whole "trust value-chain", reinforced by NGOs and "ethics watchers", help them align companies with mandatory or "comply-or-explain" standards.

Corporate governance is an essential lever in investors' hands as they seek stronger alignment. It is also critical to a company's capacity to anticipate and address risks, and is increasingly reflected in its market valuation. Convergence towards Anglo-Saxon standards of corporate governance is a key aspect in the further globalisation of capital markets.

Chapter 11
**economic
baselines**

**Chapter 10
demography
and
migrations**

... demographics and migration ... productivity differentials and border discontinuities shaping economic growth ...

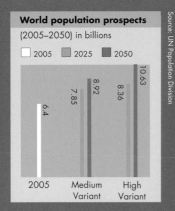

World population prospects
(2005–2050) in billions
☐ 2005 ▨ 2025 ▨ 2050

Source: UN Population Division

6.4 — 2005
7.85 — Medium Variant
8.92
8.36 — High Variant
10.63

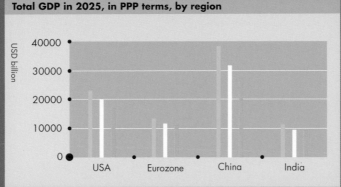

Total GDP in 2025, in PPP terms, by region

USD billion

40000
30000
20000
10000
0

USA   Eurozone   China   India

Source: Shell estimates

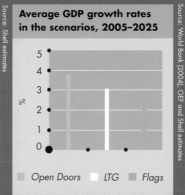

**Average GDP growth rates
in the scenarios, 2005–2025**

%

5
4
3
2
1
0

▨ Open Doors   ☐ LTG   ▨ Flags

Source: World Bank (2004), OEF and Shell estimates

● **By 2025, the level of global economic prosperity is 40% higher in *Open Doors* than in *Flags*.**

As well as bringing to light qualitative changes in the business environment, the *Global Scenarios to 2025* enable us to identify the quantitative trends ahead. These trends—including economic growth, demand for energy and pace of change— are strongly influenced by demography and migrations.

International migrations will be the aspect of demographic change most influenced by the set of incentives and constraints captured in the *Trilemma Triangle*. *Open Doors* differs from the other two by the importance of knowledge sharing and off-shoring opportunities that can make up for the "youth and brain drain" prominent in *Flags* and *Low Trust Globalisation*. In the latter, migrations are limited to meet labour market needs.

Productivity and growth
Economic growth rates range from 2.6% per annum in *Flags* to 3.8% in *Open Doors*. These growth differentials are largely explained by levels of productivity growth and border discontinuities.

In *Open Doors*, technological progress is rapid thanks to substantial R&D efforts conducted in a cooperative environment within one set of global Intellectual Property (IP) rules. With trade barriers progressively dismantled, and the hurdle of institutional discontinuities diminishing, foreign trade expands rapidly. Financial markets are more integrated, fostering the efficient allocation of capital on a global scale.

In *Low Trust Globalisation*, trade integration also increases, albeit along a flatter path due to security concerns and continuing institutional differences across borders. IP regimes differ, and knowledge dissemination is hampered by legal and security considerations.

A very different pattern develops in *Flags*, where national barriers undermine collaborative research efforts across borders and impede the wider distribution of technological innovations. Markets remain fragmented, and high domestic savings are required in order to finance investments.

Re-linking, energy security, carbon

... demand elasticity ... technology ... investment ... consumer–producer dialogue ...

ENERGY

World total primary energy growth vs GDP growth

Source: IMF/IEA/Shell estimates

- GDP
- Energy
- — Ratio

GDP and Energy Year-on-Year Growth

6% · 5% · 4% · 3% · 2% · 1% · 0

1.4 · 1.2 · 1.0 · 0.8 · 0.6 · 0.4 · 0.2 · 0.0

1966-70   1971-75   1976-80   1981-85   1986-90   1991-95   1996-00   2001-05e

CLIM▲TECHANGE

The triple discontinuity

The energy scene is being transformed under the impact of a triple discontinuity reflecting qualitative changes in the three forces at the apexes of the *Trilemma Triangle*. On the market side, three decades of 'delinking' of economic growth and energy consumption are giving way to strong 'relinking' as the largest share of new demand comes from developing economies. Forces of coercion and regulation, meanwhile, reflect a new awareness that energy supply will come from unconventional energy sources and from more challenging regions. Growing concerns over detrimental climate change make carbon management a pillar of the emerging energy-and-carbon industry.

Relinking

Already in 2001–2004 China accounted for 40% of new oil demand. With a car fleet expected to grow from 20 million cars in 2005 to 150–180 million in 20 years, and with massive increases in power generation, the Chinese energy mix—with coal in any case still the dominant source—and the policies China may adopt to achieve energy efficiency will have major impacts on global demand patterns.

Energy security

With investment needs assessed at USD 16 trillion over three decades, critical uncertainties are not only about the regions in which energy companies will be able to invest; they also cover which types of technology will be developed, either as a result of market forces or in conjunction with ambitious national or international technology programmes like fuel cell cars or new types of nuclear power plants.

Encouraging such investments will be part of the determined, and possibly anxious, search for energy security. However, such security can be sought through bilateral deals, point-to-point pipelines and allocating priority to indigenous sources—as in *Flags*—or through international cooperation as in *Open Doors*. In the latter, we see the IEA, China, India and OPEC engaged in a policy dialogue that would cover the development and use of strategic reserves as well as of spare production capacities.

Some of the same ingredients would also be present in *Low Trust Globalisation*, but with strategic reserves and spare capacities used in a much more divisive context, and with investment encouraged within narrower bilateral or regional preferential agreements.

The energy-and-carbon industry

The third discontinuity, relating to carbon emissions, is both less visible as the full impact of carbon emissions will only be felt in several decades, and more radical because the CO_2 concentration in the atmosphere is already half as high as it would be if our planet had continued on the natural cooling trend that began 10,000 years ago. Scientific evidence is still debated, but the US National Academy of Sciences and the IPCC concur that man is now co-responsible for the state of the planet, irrespective of current political doctrines.

Chapter 13
climate change and biodiversity

Jet Stream

Open Doors

Trilemmaps

Low Trust Globalisation

Flags

Climate change
While people are more inclined to address climate change issues in *Open Doors*, this is also the scenario in which CO_2 emissions increase most rapidly as a result of higher economic growth and of the absence of security-driven investment in indigenous renewable energy sources. The long-term trajectory leading to a stabilisation of CO_2 at 550 ppm is crossed towards the end of the next decade—except if carbon sequestration is pursued very actively, which would be the case if worrisome signals of detrimental change or scientific certainty also crossed a major threshold.

Low Trust Globalisation, paradoxically, could see faster progress towards carbon efficiency as a result of a different set of policies aimed at energy efficiency, conservation and development of renewables, notably wind. Major nuclear power generation programmes are also conceivable. Where the scenario differs from *Open Doors* is in the more hesitant development of emission trading schemes as called for under the Kyoto Protocol. While the EU would try to incentivise developing countries to join, the US would stay outside, even if states like California took far-reaching measures of their own.

Flags would see a patchwork of national approaches, a number of which would place a high value on environmental and climate objectives. Here also the search for energy self-reliance would have positive implications in terms of carbon efficiency.

The Kyoto Protocol
In all scenarios, the implementation of the Kyoto Protocol in February 2005 will have taken users and producers through a 'cognitive threshold': who emits what, and what rights and risks are being created, becomes explicit knowledge.

Whether this awareness leads to action will vary widely across the policies and corporate scenarios. But carbon atoms now carry a price tag. The 'invisible' has become 'visible' and the price mechanism is at work, with major developments conceivable. Our scenario period is indeed the time when the energy-and-carbon industry comes of age.

Biodiversity
Environmental issues are, of course, not limited to climate change. Biodiversity is an issue for which the energy-and-carbon industry will be expected to play a prominent role, for the sake of the communities in which it operates. Building on work by the IUCN and other organisations, we identify different types of policies that would be pursued in each scenario.

Of special interest is the shift from the still relatively abstract notion of "biodiversity" to the concept of "ecosystem services" that could be expected in *Open Doors*: providing specific resources such as fresh water, protecting natural barriers e.g. against floods, and providing cultural and aesthetic benefits could indeed be among the "win–wins" that would put market forces more effectively at the service of human development and aspirations.

TRIANGLE

RILEM

Describing the forces that shape the global business environment, Part 1 opens with the dual crisis of security and trust in the marketplace, highlighting the role of the state in attempts to resolve them.

The *Trilemma Triangle* is introduced as a tool for organising our thinking on key drivers and critical uncertainties. It provides a robust analytical framework for mapping out the interplay between market incentives, the force of community and the power of the state to regulate and to coerce.

Part 1

Forces of Change and Analytical Framework

► **"** The **World Trade Center**, in this uniquely international city, was home to men and women of every faith from some 60 nations. This was an attack on all humanity ••• if the world can show that it will carry on, that it will persevere in creating a stronger, more just, more benevolent and more genuine international community across all lines of religion and race, then terrorism will have failed. **"** Kofi A. Annan, Secretary-General of the United Nations, September 21, 2001.

► **"** Corporate reputation is fortunately re-emerging out of the ashes of the **Enron** debacle as a significant economic value. Corporate governance has doubtless already measurably improved as a result of this greater market discipline in the wake of recent events. **"** Alan Greenspan, Chairman of the Federal Reserve Board, March 26, 2002.

Chapter 1
The dual crisis of security and trust

The dual crisis of security and trust has fundamentally challenged the visions of the world presented in the 2001 Shell scenarios *Prism* and *Business Class*. Today, companies and individuals are seriously concerned for their physical security and anxious about the future—how will violence reshape the global landscape? Meanwhile, the hopes that millions placed in the market in the 1990s have been tempered by the emergence of major disillusionment: people lack trust in companies and are concerned for the security of their welfare, jobs, assets or pensions. Such anxieties reinforce questions that existed before these events and that our framework would have had to address in any case. How these difficulties are to be resolved, and with what implications for the role of the state and the nature of governance, is a question of fundamental importance behind the *Global Scenarios to 2025*.

"Security" has many dimensions. In Latin America, the "poverty trap", environmental degradation and sometimes personal security are the most prominent concerns; in Africa, civil war, AIDS, the lack of safe water sources, and extreme poverty are the true faces of the security challenges.[1] In Europe, concerns over data privacy and episodes like the panic over mad cow disease have contributed to a pervasive sense of insecurity, as have worries about job security. In Russia, concerted campaigns of terror, linked to the war in Chechnya, highlight the regional complexities—some would say ambiguities—of the global "war on terror". In the US, terrorism is unambiguously viewed as the main security threat, and even remote communities have been affected by the apprehensive mood. In Hamilton, Ohio, the greatly expanded homeland security budget has been employed on *"bomb-unit trucks, decontamination tents, anthrax test kits, X-ray scanners and advanced communication equipment"*, for fear that the precautions now taken in large US cities would *"inadvertently herd the terrorists toward heartland America."*[2] Even technology is not fully secure, as viruses, "spam" and "physhing" have demonstrated the way in which the Internet, and other essential IT-controlled infrastructures, can be paralysed, abused or undermined.

In the present *Jet Stream* perspective we focus on five security issues of prime importance: terrorism, stability in the Middle East, nuclear proliferation, failed states, and energy supply. The working of the international system will be of particular importance in determining how security is sought in these various domains.

We then turn our attention to the modern world's "third great wave of distrust"—which echoes earlier "waves of distrust" in the 1930s and 1960s. The links between international security and trust in institutions and the market lead us to speak of one "dual crisis" of security and trust.

We emphasise especially how investors, concerns about distrust in the market place give added weight to the corporate governance agenda, in developed as well as in emerging economies.

1

"Human security means freedom from pervasive threats to people's rights, their safety or even their lives", quoted in *Empowering People at Risk*, Helsinki Process Track Report, Finnish Ministry for Foreign Affairs, 2005.

2

Brian Knowlton, "Letter from America", *International Herald Tribune*, August 27, 2004.

The 9.11 Commission Report: US strategy and diplomacy in the age of terror—a brief summary

What gives rise to terrorism?
In its summer 2004 report, the National Commission on Terrorist Attacks Upon the United States sees the new threat from Islamist terrorists as characterised not by conflict across borders, but by political and economic "fault lines" within societies which ensure that a minority is receptive to Bin Laden's message at a time when *"few tolerant or secular Muslim democracies provide alternative models for the future."*

As such, the report recommends a two-pronged "global strategy". First, the US must directly combat the terrorist threat through a series of immediate diplomatic and strategic priorities. Second, it must engage in a long-term struggle to prevent the growth of Islamist terrorism.

Immediate priorities— combating the terrorists
The report recommends that the US utilises *"all elements of national power"* in attempting to eliminate terrorist sanctuaries, including working with other countries. Three countries are identified as particularly important in this strategy: Pakistan, Afghanistan and Saudi Arabia.

Pakistan's poverty, corruption and ineffective government are recognised as creating opportunities for terrorist activity. In the past, the US had three problems with Pakistan: its cooperation with the Taliban, its slow progress towards democracy, and nuclear proliferation concerns. The report recommends that, as long as President Musharraf *"stands for enlightened moderation"*, the US must maintain its current level of military and economic assistance to Pakistan.

Some warn that **Afghanistan** is *"near the brink of chaos"*. Warlords control much of the country, the Taliban and Al Qaeda have regrouped, the narcotics trade is booming and economic development is a *"distant hope"*. The report recommends that the US and others make a *"long-term commitment to a secure and stable Afghanistan"*. This strategy should involve not simply security work, but efforts to restore the rule of law and extend the authority of the new government, enabling them to *"improve the life of the Afghan people"*.

Saudi Arabia, in this report, is noted as a *"problematic ally"* in efforts to combat Islamist terrorism. Al Qaeda has been able to raise funds in the country as some Wahhabist organisations have been exploited by extremists. While Saudi Arabia is criticised in America,

the report stresses that the kingdom faces major political and security challenges, and endorses friendly, constructive relations. It recommends that the problems in the US–Saudi relationship are confronted openly, and that the relationship should be based on more than oil: on a shared commitment to promoting tolerance and *"political and economic reform"*.

Long term— preventing the growth of Islamist terrorism
The report also recommends that the US engage in a struggle to *"defeat an ideology, not just a group of people"*. First, it should act in a way which offers *"moral leadership"* and a commitment to *"treat people humanely [and] abide by the rule of law"*—including in relations with governments that do not always respect these principles. Second, the US should realise that perceptions of its actions influence popular opinion in the world. This should be taken into account when formulating foreign policy, particularly in relation to Israel–Palestine. Popular perceptions of the US are also influenced by the media, and the report suggests that more resources be devoted to broadcasting, and in scholarship, exchange and library programmes— i.e. means of communicating America's humane values. It also advises that the US promote development in the Muslim

world through, for example, free trade agreements and providing funding for schools. *"Terrorism is not caused by poverty,"* the Commission concludes, yet *"when societies break down, and countries fragment, the breeding grounds for terrorism are created."*

While not endorsing or contradicting Bush administration policies, the Commission does not shy away from the more controversial multilateral dimension of foreign policy, which is reported to have come as some surprise to the Bush administration. On several fronts the report calls for international cooperation, with both Muslim countries and non-Muslim countries. It calls for the development of a comprehensive coalition strategy on combating terrorism, and on determining humane standards for the treatment of terrorist prisoners. The report also suggests that efforts be made on nuclear proliferation—to develop a legal regime to enable the capture, interdiction and prosecution of nuclear smugglers. Non-NATO members such as Russia and China should be encouraged to participate in the Proliferation Security Initiative (on the interdiction of WMD shipments) and the US should renew its commitment to ensuring that the WMDs spread across the former Soviet Union are secured under the Cooperative Threat Reduction Program.

1.1

The security crisis: terrorism, the Middle East, nuclear proliferation, failed states and energy security

Terrorism and the war against terror

9.11 and the series of attacks in Africa, Asia and Europe, compounded by the fear of nuclear terrorism, have created a climate of deep insecurity, with implications well beyond the military and diplomatic sphere. Popular perceptions are dominated by anxiety; for many, the fear of a "clash of civilisations" has replaced hope for the emergence of a democratic, market-friendly and peaceful world order—the hope for an "end of history".[1]

Terrorism will remain a major threat, both in the Middle East and in the Western countries. This will have important implications for economic activities globally, not just in some regions or hot spots. Ensuring the security of trade now involves protecting against direct attacks on the means of transport as well as ensuring the efficient and coordinated real-time workings of the complex web of supply chains on which the global economy depends. The risk that nuclear devices might be hidden in a container is taken very seriously and has led the US to promote a major Safe Trade initiative. Yet the very concept of a "war on terror" can be a source of insecurity: its target is not an enemy that can be defeated, but hatred itself, a hatred with complex roots, leading to totalitarian attitudes and to violence divorced from any focused call for change—hence the far-reaching strategy advocated in the US by the bipartisan Commission on 9.11. The Commission's report, in terms reminiscent of more troubled times, calls on the US *"to defeat an ideology, not just a group of people"* (see box).

Instabilities in the Middle East

The war in Iraq is perceived by many as the first link in a potentially longer chain of upheavals and conflicts in the Middle East. Coalition forces in Iraq are engaged in a "battle for hearts and minds" in which devastating firepower can be a source of moral vulnerability. The images of some coalition soldiers holding Iraqi prisoners in humiliating or excruciating conditions will have a lasting impact in the Arab world and beyond, just as images of the Vietnam War were influential in shaping opinion on that conflict. In its *Strategic Balance*

report of May 2004, the International Institute for Strategic Studies (IISS) draws alarming conclusions, suggesting that the first year of war in Iraq increased, rather than decreased, the level of the terrorist threat. A panel of former senior US officials, business leaders and academics, convened by the CSIS under the chairmanship of former U.S. Secretary of Defense William S. Cohen, highlights how the crises of trust and security (as we refer to them here) are intertwined in the Middle East. Observing that *"an overwhelming number of leaders we talked to believed that the United States is engaged in a war with the Arab world or Islam itself"*, they deplore that *"U.S.– Arab relations are at their lowest point in generations…Fear, anger, and frustration between Arabs and Americans are creating a dangerous trust gap that is growing wider every day[2]"*.

While the Oslo peace process is now a distant memory, progress towards a peaceful and democratic Middle East is slow. The building of a wall across Cisjordania is dampening the hopes for universal harmony that emerged after the fall of the Berlin wall. The stability of Saudi Arabia is a direct target of Al Qaeda acts of terror. Reforms of the educational systems and debates on the role of women outside the home, combined with one of the world's highest population growth rates, are illustrative of the development challenges that must be met in the Arabian peninsula.

Nuclear proliferation

The fight against nuclear proliferation has met with some success—such as Libya's "return to the fold". But, by and large, the decision by India and Pakistan to develop nuclear forces and the far-reaching black-market network put in place by Abdul Qadeer Khan to sell enrichment technology and nuclear bomb design have put an end to an era of relative success for the UN Non-Proliferation Treaty. The development of nuclear arsenals may soon become an inevitable aspect of regional rivalries—as well as a guarantee some states may seek to protect themselves against "coalitions of the willing" intent on promoting regime change.

The decision of the G-8 countries, at the Sea Island summit of June 2004, to tighten export rules regarding the enrichment of uranium is a promising step towards the level of nuclear containment and discipline that analysts such as Graham Allison have called for.[3] Yet a

1

Samuel Huntington, *The Clash of Civilisations and the Remaking of World Order*, Simon & Schuster, New York, 1996; Francis Fukuyama, *The End of History and the Last Man*, NY Free Press, 1992.

2

From Conflict to Cooperation: Writing a New Chapter in U.S.- Arab Relations, A Report of the CSIS Advisory Committee on U.S. Policy in the Arab World, Project Director: Jon B. Alterman, Centre for Strategic and International Studies (CSIS), Washington, D.C., 2005, pp. vii–viii.

3

Graham Allison, *Nuclear Terrorism: The Ultimate Preventable Catastrophe*, Times Books, July 2004.

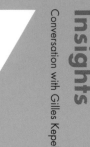

Gilles Kepel is Professor and Chair of Middle East Studies at the Institut d'Etudes Politiques in Paris and the author of *Jihad: The Trial of Political Islam*, Harvard University Press, 2002, and of *The War for Muslim Minds: Islam and the West*, Harvard University Press, 2004. Conversation conducted by Albert Bressand in London, November 2004.

Al Qaeda and the war for Muslim minds

You emphasise the importance of Cold War thinking both in the Neocons' approach to the Middle East and in Bin Laden's and Al Qaeda's strategy. Why is there that symmetry?

Gilles Kepel: Bin Laden and his mentor Ayman al-Zawahiri developed their "global jihad" strategy after the defeat of the Soviets in Afghanistan in 1989. They convinced themselves that the Muslim freedom fighters involved in the conflict had been the primary cause of this unprecedented victory over a superpower, rather than an instrument in the hands of the world's other superpower. They saw their victory as the fulfilment of divine providence and had little doubt that they could recommit themselves to wreaking havoc on the US, as "knights under the Prophet's banner", to use the title of Zawahiri's most important work.

Meanwhile, Neocons in the US, centred around Albert Wohlstetter and Paul Wolfowitz, were also exhilarated by the fall of the Soviet Union, and were advocating the pursuit of a morally determined foreign policy. Huntington's clash of civilisations theory indicated a set of parallels between the dangers of communism and those of Islam that gave them the feeling that they could transpose the conceptual tools and the policy approaches

designed for the Cold War and apply them to this new threat.

Al Qaeda usually evokes images of strength and terror, but your analysis of Al Qaeda's "global jihad" emphasises the weakness of their position in the Muslim community...

GK: The devastating attacks on US, Israeli and other Western targets that Al Qaeda embarked on after 1992 were attempts to resolve a major problem that had stymied Islamist radicals since the early 1980s, namely their inability to mobilise popular support in favour of an Islamic state to replace the established Middle Eastern regimes that they refer to as the "nearby enemy". Indeed, a deep fear of isolation runs through Zawahiri's texts such as *Knights under the Prophet's Banner* in which he advocates an alliance between jihadists and the two "liberated" countries of Afghanistan and Chechnya.

Who are the suicide bombers and martyrs?

GK: While acts of terror do reflect frustration from a movement incapable of truly mobilising the Arab masses, they also reflect an escalating strategy intended to resonate first among potential candidates for martyrdom.

These militants must combine a rational mindset and the technical training that a Western education can provide with an alternative mindset that infuses suicide attacks with metaphysical meaning and value. Al Qaeda has been more effective at recruiting and motivating this vanguard than at reaching out to the broader *ummah*— the Muslim community that Zawahiri often depicts as passive and devoid of conscience.

Would you say that the strategy Zawahiri designed for Al Qaeda is inspired by religion?

GK: I would rather describe this strategy as grounded in *realpolitik*, as it appears to follow Machiavelli more closely than religious principles. It starts from the view that a *"universal battle"* is under way as the US, Israel, the UN, humanitarian NGOs, corrupt Muslim leaders, multinationals as well as communication systems and media are seen to form a grand coalition against Islam. Second, it advocates turning some of these forces, such as the Internet and satellite television, against these enemies, as well as mobilising *"young combatants carrying out jihad"*. Last, it advocates a military strategy based on terrorising *"Americans and Jews"* through spectacular actions that would create support within the Muslim world. This

is about military strategy, not religion. Creating support for this strategy in the *ummah* has been most difficult. In the late 1990s, while the Oslo peace process seemed to be on track, Zawahiri emphasised Afghanistan, Chechnya and Saudi Arabia but this did not mobilise the support expected. Then, as the second *intifada* began, Al Qaeda's ideologues borrowed from Hezbollah strategy in Lebanon. They chose to emphasise the Palestinian struggle and the political language —certainly not a religious one—of suicide attacks.

You refer to the Oslo peace process as a "utopian scenario". Are "realistic scenarios" about the Middle East only violent ones?

GK: I detect a strong feeling in Washington that the "war on terror" policy—which proved useful in winning the election on November 2, 2004— does not provide a satisfying way out of the Middle East quagmire. I expect some reassessment of the US policy regarding Palestine—Israel, now that the Arafat era has come to an end. The US has to win the war for Muslim minds if it wants Arab civil societies to mobilise significantly against jihad-inspired terrorism. This is going to be one of the major challenges of the new US administration—on top of military action.

former Assistant Secretary of Defense in the Reagan administration can still lament that *"the danger of nuclear weapons falling into the wrong hands"* has increased rather than decreased. Lawrence Korb goes on to deplore the fact that the *"reciprocal bargain"*, which made the UN Non-Proliferation Treaty a success, has been undermined—notably by US efforts to develop nuclear "bunker busters" and "mini-nukes", its willingness to use nuclear weapons against non-nuclear states, its opposition to inspections as part of the Fissile Material Cutoff Treaty and its decreased funding for the Nunn-Lugar Cooperative Threat Reduction Initiative. This latter programme has deactivated more than 6500 nuclear warheads in the former Soviet Union but many more thousands are still not properly secured.[1]

Clearly, the 1990s' hope of a peaceful world system exposed only to local conflicts has receded. We turn to Gilles Kepel (see box) to discuss how the fight for the soul—in his book, the Muslim soul—can degenerate into rejection, terror and war. In the words of Jeffrey Garten, Dean of the Yale School of Management, to a Shell audience, the world may be *"only one major act of terror away from a radical shift in the nature of international relations that would put national security above any other objective"*.

Failed states and the resource curse

Meanwhile, lawlessness and the collapse of state structures in some regions have given warlords and traffickers safe havens from which new perils might emerge. "*Failed states*," argues former Assistant Secretary of State for Africa Chester Crocker, "*have become sufficiently common that the leading nations must find a way to authorise and conduct de facto trusteeships.*"[2] Failure to build a peaceful, democratic Afghanistan, or failure to prevent African nations from disintegrating—like Sierra Leone, Liberia, Somalia and Ivory Coast, among others—could have far-reaching consequences.

Far from easing the path of development, natural resources—whether diamonds, minerals or hydrocarbons—can accelerate the disintegration of the state, as private armies take control, or fight for a wealth that detracts from long-term development efforts. Botswana, a major diamond producer, is one of the few exceptions to what is often referred to as the resource curse.

> ‘ **Countries often end up poor because they are oil rich.** ,

In the words of Nancy Birdsall and Arvind Subramanian, "*countries often end up poor because they are oil rich.*"[3] Two-thirds of the 34 "oil-rich" countries (meaning countries for which oil and natural gas constitute at least 30% of total exports) are not democratic. In most cases, these countries have weak or non-existent political and economic institutions. This is because there is no incentive in oil-rich countries to use resources efficiently, or for citizens to call for accountability, as tax payers usually do. Hence Birdsall and Subramanian's conclusion that "*the irony of the resource curse is that good government and strong institutions require that the raising of public resources be costly.*" When governments derive revenues from natural resource rents they are living "*in a dangerous supply-sider's paradise*".[3]

Of course, other factors can contribute to the inadequacy of institutions. The UN Development Programme's *Human Development Report 2002* provided an in-depth analysis of how the lack of a free press and the low status of women can further hinder the emergence of the institutions and governance processes that are essential to sustainable value creation and development. Democracy and development indeed go together, and finding the appropriate manner to foster both simultaneously, in keeping with the fundamental values of each culture, will be a fundamental challenge throughout the time horizon of our *Global Scenarios*.

1

Lawrence J. Korb, "Bush's Policy Endangers US Security", *International Herald Tribune*, August 9, 2004.

2

Chester A. Crocker, "Engaging Failing States", *Foreign Affairs*, September/October 2003, p. 41.

3

Nancy Birdsall and Arvind Subramanian, "Escaping the Oil Curse: Saving Iraq From its Oil", *Foreign Affairs*, July/August 2004.

Insights
By Rodney Craig

Rodney Craig is Defence Analyst, specialising in maritime issues, at the International Institute for Strategic Studies (IISS) in London. Gratitude goes to **Simon Cotton**, an Oxford graduate and an intern with the PXG team, and to **Tim Huxley** from the IISS.

Threats to maritime trade: old and new

Piracy

The main threat to maritime security in peacetime used to be piracy—an illegal act such as theft committed on the high seas, as opposed to territorial seas where national law applies. Pirates continue to present a threat today, with worldwide attacks rising dramatically since the early 1990s. Pirates employ modern tools, such as high-powered boats and automatic weapons, and can quickly overpower today's lean-manned merchant vessels if insufficient countermeasures are in place. Low freeboard vessels—for example, laden tankers—are particularly vulnerable.

Ironically, the international law of the sea (UNCLOS) and the legal status of territorial seas often give pirates the legal loopholes they need to operate. Criminal activities that occur across different jurisdictions require a coordinated international response, which is often lacking. However, pirates are invariably shore-based, need to dispose of stolen goods, and are deterred by the prospect of arrest. As such, strong national laws can go some way to counter the threat of piracy.

Terrorism

Terrorism has recently emerged as a new and dangerous menace to maritime trade. Although attacks were previously sporadic, the Achille Lauro in 1985 being a prominent example, recent years have seen the attacks on the USS Cole in 2000 and the tanker MV Limburg in 2002. The danger of Al Qaeda and other groups using ships as a target or tool will exist for the foreseeable future.

In addition, the rise in piracy attacks demonstrates that there are security vulnerabilities that could be exploited by terrorists. Tankers will continue to be of interest to terrorist groups, whether the aim is to destroy the cargo, discharge crude off an economically sensitive coast, or sink a ship in a strategic choke point. Perhaps more dangerously, fundamentalist terrorist groups such as Al Qaeda are likely to hijack a ship as part of a suicide mission.

Mutilateral responses

Counter-terrorist measures must necessarily stress prevention and therefore multilateral responses are particularly important. There are several models on which to base such approaches. In the Caribbean, the US Navy and Coastguard combine with other naval forces and shore-based authorities in drug interdiction operations (DIOPS). In the Iran–Iraq "Tanker War" (1980–89), Western navies protected own-flagged vessels through the Straits of Hormuz, with logistic support from friendly littoral states.

The Malacca Strait testing ground

The Malacca Strait has traditionally been a piracy hotspot: it and the waters of Indonesia together accounted for one-third of piracy attacks worldwide in 2003. Various initiatives have been attempted to combat attacks in this region, which are committed by organised criminal gangs, but could potentially be carried out by terrorists. External powers have proposed different solutions to the problem.

Although Japan's proposal for a "Regional Coast Guard body" has met some resistance, Japan has conducted bilateral naval exercises with states in the region, and negotiations continue between ASEAN, Japan, China and other regional powers towards forming a Regional Cooperation Agreement on Anti-Piracy in Asia (ReCAAP).

US proposals for a Regional Maritime Security Initiative (RMSI) initially faced opposition from Malaysia and Indonesia. However, following the IISS Asian Security Conference, and US Admiral Thomas B. Fargo's visit to Malaysia in July 2004, all nations now appear committed to addressing the issue along firmly multilateral lines. In late July, the first Malacca Strait Coordinated Patrol (MALSINDO) was conducted, employing maritime forces from Malaysia, Indonesia and Singapore, each in their own territorial waters. The weakest link in the chain remains Indonesia. It is unlikely that its maritime defence budget will rise, and as long as law enforcement remains inadequate, piracy and the threat of terrorism will be a problem. In addition, a legal framework is required to allow a "hot handover" from one state's forces to another when suspect vessels are being pursued across borders, if regional cooperation is to be effective.

Energy supply security

The Bush administration's National Energy Policy of May 2001 already emphasised that energy security must be a priority of US trade and foreign policy—as further discussed in chapter 12.

The rising costs of finding new reserves, the huge investment needs, the likelihood that non-OPEC oil production will plateau soon, and China's rapidly rising imports have all exacerbated concerns about energy security, contributing to higher prices. Recent blackouts on both sides of the Atlantic, as well as in Argentina and Brazil, have prompted a fresh look at market liberalisation and regulation. Whereas the EU Gas Directives of 1998 and 2003 were driven primarily by concerns about enhancing market efficiency, the EU strategy now gives recognition to energy security and to the role of trade and foreign policy in achieving it.[1]

Physical threats—such as terrorists attacks on Iraqi and Saudi terminals—exacerbate energy security concerns. Maritime security is also a growing concern as an increasing level of piracy makes new terrorist threats quite credible (see box). The efforts by China to build or secure deep-harbour facilities in Gwadar (Pakistan) and in Myanmar reflect worries about the security of the sea lanes, through which 40% of the world's oil passes—as well, possibly, as about US naval patrols in the Indian Ocean.[2]

Uncertain cooperation, rising nationalism

How states will cooperate, bilaterally or multilaterally, will affect how these sources of insecurity can develop. Recent trends have been mixed, at best, with acrimonious relations and the loss of a sense of common purpose to some degree offsetting the end of the major ideological divides. While membership of organisations such as the OECD, the World Trade Organisation (WTO) or the EU has been expanded, recent years have also seen nationalist trends reawaken or rise in most parts of the world, including in Europe —where half a century of integration has made possible the first almost-borderless region in recent history. While "nationalism" is widely denounced, few see their own "patriotism" in the same light. Religion, similarly, can be a source of new divides, depending on whether faiths are affirmed with tolerance or with an overriding sense of having a monopoly on the truth.

> **The rising costs of finding new reserves, the huge investment needs, the likelihood that non-OPEC oil production will plateau soon and China's rapidly rising imports have all exacerbated concerns about energy security.**

1

"Natural gas supply for the EU in the short and medium term", Clingendael Energy Programme, The Hague, March 2004.

2

Nayan Chanda, "China's Sea Strategy: The Dragon Swims Again", *International Herald Tribune*, April 12, 2005.

1.2
The world's third great wave of distrust

1

Daniel Yankelovich,

Making Trust a

Competitive Asset,

Viewpoint Learning,

New York, May 2003.

2

For a discussion of the

negative effects that the

litigation culture may

have, see Philip Howard's

The Collapse of the

Common Good, How

America's Lawsuit Culture

Undermines our Freedom,

Ballantine Books,

January 2002.

The other dimension of the "dual crisis" is what has been called, with reference to the 1930s and 1960s, "*the world's third great wave of distrust*".[1] How trust will or will not be restored is a key consideration in our *Global Scenarios*.

The disillusion that followed the bursting of the Internet bubble and major corporate governance failures, exemplified by Enron's bankruptcy, cast a thick and potentially lasting cloud of distrust over the market. Mutual funds trusted by millions of savers, companies with household names, star analysts, auditors and blue-blooded investment banks and insurance companies have been found in breach of fiduciary duties. Well-known CEOs have been prosecuted and sometimes imprisoned by regulators. While market forces continue to gather momentum, recent opinion polls show an all-engulfing wave of distrust towards corporations as well as governments and parliaments. Yet this distrust coexists with growing use of market mechanisms by individuals (e.g. to cater for their pensions) and by states. As a greater role of market forces combines with higher distrust for what globalisation brings about, one should not be surprised to witness what pollsters and analysts Steve Rosell and Dan Yankelovich call "*punitive attitudes*" from investors as well as "*the emergence of integrity as a significant competitive factor*" for companies.[1]

In continental Europe, distrust is reinforced by worries regarding food safety, technology and high unemployment. German public opinion, for instance, does not share Chancellor Schröder's trust in pro-market reform of the welfare state: measures taken to promote inclusion of all in the labour market are perceived as exacerbating, rather than reducing, social exclusion. In France, the pro-market agenda that had gone hand in hand with European integration is now the main reason why support for the latter flounders. In Latin America, a general loss of confidence in institutions has led to large efforts to organise independently of them. In Asia, optimism is more widespread, but continued "policy lending" and non-performing loans (officially at 24% of assets but probably closer to 50% in China) suggest that markets cannot be trusted

Trust in institutions to operate in society's best interests

Little/no trust — A lot/some trust

Institution	Little/no trust	A lot/some trust
Armed forces	26	69
NGOs	32	59
UN	34	55
Religious institutions	38	57
WTO	39	44
Government	47	50
Press/media	47	49
Trade unions/labour	45	47
World Bank	41	43
IMF	41	39
Global companies	48	39
Large national companies	52	42
Parliament/Congress	51	38

100   0   100

Source: Gideascan, 2003 Proportional Global Ratings (n=36,000 across 47 countries) 2002

to have fully overcome the shortcomings in governance that led to the 1997 Asian crisis.

Litigation and "law as a business"
The third wave of distrust is also reinforced by independent developments in the legal arena that make litigation more pervasive and legal forum shopping a global trend. In continental Europe and Asia, economic liberalisation has undermined the role of the state as the natural allocator of rights and arbiter of disputes: the shift towards a market-centric culture of contracts makes litigation a more normal course than used to be the case. In the US, law has clearly become a business, a trend that can be traced back to the watershed 1985 Supreme Court ruling *Piper vs. New Hampshire*. In the ruling, Mr. Piper, a lawyer, was vindicated in his right to practice law in New Hampshire while not residing there. From then on, lawyers would be treated as professionals among others—like barbers or architects—rather than like judges or governors. Law firms pursue business aggressively, amalgamating if necessary hundreds and thousands of smaller claims which may generate huge triple-damage compensation. Under the doctrine of Private Attorneys General, law firms are seen indeed as serving the broader public interest in fraud discovery, irrespective of who ends up being compensated for the fraud discovered.[2]

The crisis of trust fostering investor activism on corporate governance

In the past, with the notable exception of a handful of public, mostly US pension funds such as Calpers, institutions and their asset managers have largely been passive, absentee owners of companies. In the aftermath of the crisis of trust that we have described, institutions are increasingly becoming *engaged shareowners,* whether because of a heightened perception of investor risk or because they find themselves under pressure from regulators, NGOs or their own clients. Corporate governance, in many ways, is the instrument of this reaffirmation of the power of company owners.

Corporate governance, *"a term that did not exist in the English language until twenty years ago,"*[1] now features prominently in public policy debates and is increasingly reflected in companies, valuations. In the words of Deutsche Bank, *"corporate governance is a component of the equity risk… a company's operating performance, however attractive in the short term, risks being undermined if the CG foundations are weak."*[2] In a nutshell, investors fear that a company's weak governance will lead to loss of shareholder value because it allows the people in control of day to day operations (whether management or controlling shareholders) to either :
• let the quality of management and/or the business deteriorate, or
• expropriate value from non-controlling investors to the profit of insiders.

Over 10 years, well-governed US companies across a wide range of sectors have seen an average valuation 8% greater than their badly governed peers. Recent studies in Europe have yielded similar results.[3] Studies in emerging markets like Korea or Russia found an even higher correlation between corporate governance and a company's valuation.

Well-governed companies in countries with weak, low-trust institutional environments command even higher premiums than companies in high-trust (mostly large OECD) markets. A much cited McKinsey survey has found that global institutional investors (the group surveyed managing more than USD 1.2 trillion of assets) will pay a premium for well-governed companies that ranges from 12% in the UK to over 40% in Indonesia.[4]

As a result, investors are increasingly adjusting fundamental valuations for Corporate Governance risk: Deutsche Bank has come out with a specific portfolio product that links Corporate Governance to fundamental research, and the FTSE is creating a Corporate Governance global index to allow other asset managers to do the same.

Research by Nestor Advisors shows that, among the 50 biggest pension funds in the world, 24 have explicit governance codes that set norms for their investee companies and impose obligations on the asset managers that they hire. Similarly, 20 of the top 30 global asset managers—with USD 8 trillion under management—have explicit governance codes for their investee companies that guide their proxy/ voting policies.

Meanwhile, some institutional investors, especially public and trade union pension funds, are aligning themselves increasingly with NGOs and civil society groups to demand clear corporate policies—to be determined by the top managers—on the criteria and processes that a company uses to make decisions. As a result, value creation and the affirmation of values are increasingly intertwined as reporting extends from the financial realm to the "triple bottom line" of economic performance, sustainable development and social responsibility—the latter including labour practices and community development.

An important issue over our scenario period is how the growing role of hedge funds may change the manner in which investors mobilise the corporate governance agenda to achieve their investment objectives.

1

Luigi Zingales,

"Corporate Governance",

The New Palgrave Dictionary

of Economics and the Law,

P. Newman, ed., Macmillan,

New York, 1998.

2

"Corporate Governance:

Implications for Investors",

Deutsche Bank Global Equity

Research, April 1, 2004.

3

Amra Balic,

"Transparency, Disclosure

and Audit", in *Governance*

and Risk, George Dallas,

ed., McGraw Hill, 2004,

pp. 86-110.

4

McKinsey & Company,

"Global Investor Opinion

Survey: Key Findings",

2002.

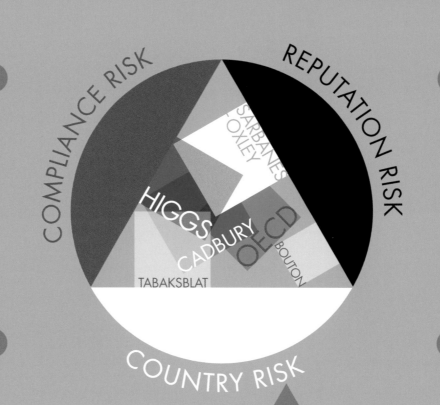

Institutional investors

Corporate Governance is an essential determinant of value creation by companies, as well as a tool in the hands of investors, notably institutional investors, to achieve tighter alignment

Rating agencies

Media

COMPLIANCE RISK

REPUTATION RISK

SARBANES OXLEY

HIGGS

CADBURY

OECD

BOUTON

TABAKSBLAT

Regulators

Issue groups

COUNTRY RISK

Three distinct risk environments—which the three Global Scenarios will make clear—centred respectively on compliance to strict rules, reputation stemming from respecting broader principles, and the patchwork of country rules and risks.

Constituencies

1.3
Security, regulation and corporate governance: the essential role of the state

The "dual crisis" of security and trust, and the responses it has elicited, have reinforced the need to challenge the bipolar structure behind the Shell *Global Scenarios* of the 1990s. The interplay between market efficiency and the force of community (or, in EU language, aspirations for "social cohesion") has not lost its vigour, but a third force must be acknowledged as similarly important—that of coercion and regulation by the state.

A security-conscious world
People have turned to the state to provide security on the international scene, at home and in the marketplace, and states have responded: Germany and Japan have overcome their deep opposition to sending troops abroad; NATO has broadened its theatre to encompass the whole world; and the US has put the war on terror at the centre of its foreign policy. China, meanwhile, is forging new relationships with key oil-producing states while the EU moves to implement an Emissions Trading Scheme intended to reduce the risk of catastrophic climate change. Most states have tightened supervision over banks, companies and intermediaries.

How effective governments can be is open to question, adding to the climate of uncertainty. Guantanamo Bay, fingerprinting, the interception of communications by intelligence agencies under the "Echelon" programme, or simply the creation of national identity cards in countries used to driving licences elicit much vocal opposition. Yet few doubt that, in this security-conscious and distrustful world, governments, so often derided as part of the problem in the 1990s, have to be part of the solution. The US elections of 2004 saw President Bush and Senator Kerry compete in large part on how good a Commander in Chief they would be.

Meanwhile, various forms of authoritarian systems remain present, and doubts increase that the appeal of Western-style democracy will lead to their transformation.

The stronger (self-)regulatory hand
In the marketplace, the role of the state has clearly ceased to retreat as bruised investors call for standards of transparency and good governance to be substantially upgraded. The rising investor worries about corporate governance that we just discussed are leading to new regulations and much stricter enforcement. Indeed, strict regulations and good corporate practices appear as two sides of the same coin: transparency and disclosure have come to the forefront as *"leading indicators of a company's overall governance standards"* and now play *"a crucial role in the capital allocation process"*.[1] Voluntary codes—in the Cadbury report tradition—still play an important role, witness the recent Higgs report and Bouton report in the UK and France, but binding norms, like in the 2004 Tabaksblat corporate governance code in the Netherlands, in the French *Loi sur la Sécurité Financière* of July 2003, in the EU draft directive on mandatory audit committees or in the mandatory Chinese Corporate Governance Code, are becoming common.[2]

The Sarbanes-Oxley watershed
The depth and scope of disclosure requirements are increasing substantially. Not only are financial performance indicators scrutinised, with International Accounting Standards (IAS/IFRS) bringing Europe and Australia into the world of "fair value" and "mark-to-market" volatility, but distrustful investors also demand the full picture of risks, vulnerabilities and internal control. The Sarbanes-Oxley Act and new listing requirements imposed by NASDAQ and the New York Stock Exchange are striking examples of standards that establish tighter links between what companies used to consider to be matters of internal organisation and what they must now disclose in order for the market to trust valuations of their assets.

A number of professions now see their practices scrutinised and codified through hardline regulations. Auditors are now regulated, rather than self-regulated, in the US as well as in the EU. Self-regulation of rating agencies has been found by the SEC and EU authorities still to be appropriate. By contrast, information brokers are now under increased scrutiny in the US as waves of identity thefts illustrate the weakness of self-regulation as compared to the strict regulatory framework in place in the EU.

1

George Dallas, "Country Influences on Individual Company Governance", in: *Governance and Risk, op. cit*, pp. 138–163.

2

Derek Higgs, "Review of the role and effectiveness of non-executive directors", Report to the Chancellor of the Exchequer, January 2003. "Pour un meilleur government des entreprises cotées", Daniel Bouton, MEDEF, September 23, 2002. "The Dutch corporate governance code: principles of good corporate governance and best practice provision", Report of the Tabaksblat Committee, December 9, 2003. "Principles for the corporate governance of listed companies", China Securities Regulatory Commission & State Economic and Trade Commission (jointly), 2002.

Focus

The Global Opacity Index

The Global Opacity Index, a project developed by former Harvard Business Review editor Joel Kurtzman and supported by the PricewaterhouseCoopers Endowment for the Study of Transparency and Sustainability, provides an estimate of the adverse effects of opacity on the cost and availability of capital in 48 countries.

The index draws upon 65 objective variables from 41 sources, including the World Bank, the IMF, and individual countries regulators. The index offers a composite "O-Factor" ranking for each country. These rankings make use of opacity data in the following five areas that affect capital markets:
1 corruption in government bureaucracy;
2 laws governing contracts or property rights;
3 economic policies (fiscal, monetary, and tax-related);
4 accounting standards; and
5 business regulations.

Together, these create the acronym **CLEAR (Corruption, Legal, Economic, Accounting, Regulatory). Opacity in any of these areas will raise the cost of doing business as well as curtail the availability of funds.**

In order to estimate the real-world costs associated with opacity, an interest-rate premium equivalent is calculated, which shows the opacity risk premium/discount that US-based investors demand with regard to investments abroad. Previously, the degree of opacity was also expressed in terms of tax equivalents, showing the economic costs of opacity as if it were a hidden tax.

According to the 2004 estimates, Indonesia suffers from the highest degree of opacity, with an overall "O-Factor" of 59 out of 100. Indonesia is the worst performer not only among the 11 countries listed in the table, but also among all 48 economies covered by the Global Opacity Index. The costs are substantial. Reducing the level of opacity in Indonesia to that of the US (used as the benchmark in 2004) is estimated at an improvement of 854 basis points in terms of the country's opacity risk premium. In Venezuela, the second worst performer in terms of opacity, the interest rate premium equivalent is estimated at 656 basis points.

There is irony in these findings. Many emerging market economies are eager to provide tax incentives to boost investment, often by offering tax concessions to attract foreign direct investment. The interest equivalent perspective implies that a reduction in opacity can essentially substitute for such incentives. To put it differently, domestic reforms that reduce opacity may be as effective as a tax cut in boosting domestic investment and attracting foreign direct investment—without sacrificing tax revenues. These results are largely consistent with tax equivalent calculations made in 2001 for 35 economies. For instance, it was calculated that reducing the level of opacity in China to that in Singapore (the benchmark country in 2001) was equivalent to lowering the corporate income tax rate in China by 46% in terms of the cost of doing business. In Russia, the second worst performer in the 2001 index, the tax equivalent was estimated at 43%.

Opacity and interest-rate equivalent, 2004

Country	Opacity factor	Interest-rate equivalent (%)
Finland	13	-1.83
UK	19	-0.44
USA	21	0.00
Brazil	40	4.29
Mexico	44	5.01
Russia	46	5.64
India	48	6.09
Nigeria	49	6.12
China	50	6.49
Venezuela	51	6.56
Indonesia	59	8.54

Doing Business in 2004. *Understanding Regulation*, The World Bank, Washington, DC; see also D. Kaufmann, A. Kraay and M. Mastruzzi, *Governance Matters III: Governance Indicators 1996–2002*, Draft: http://www.worldbank.org/wbi/governance/pdf/govmatters3.pdf.

L. F. Klapper and I. Love, "Corporate Governance, Investor Protection, and Performance in Emerging Markets," *Journal of Corporate Finance*, March 2004.

McKinsey & Company, *"Global Investor Opinion Survey: Key Findings"*, 2002.

In this more demanding context, transparency for companies now involves far more than merely opening one's books. A recent publication for Standard & Poor's highlights its role as a tool, for companies as well as for investors, to reflect four sources of value: financial performances, the business models behind them, the commitments that a company has been able to develop, and the corporate governance mechanisms that enable them to preserve integrity and to continuously improve on all these fronts.[1]

Governance and opacity: emerging markets and the trust barrier

Emerging economies face a very real distrust barrier, which fast economic growth and high foreign-exchange reserves cannot mask. The fact, for instance, that the incipient Chinese equity market has achieved negative results over a five-year boom period reflects investors' disappointment at losses rooted in governance and opacity issues.[2]

Once taboo, the word "corruption" has found its way into official reports. Joel Kurtzman and the PwC Endowment for Transparency and Sustainability have developed a Global Opacity Index that combines five sources of legal uncertainty and distrust, among which is corruption in government bureaucracy. The index is then used to compute the cost that lack of transparency represents, expressing it as the equivalent of an additional interest-rate premium over low-risk investment in US Treasury bills (see box). McKinsey & Company have expressed the same costs as the level of hidden "tax" that opacity represents for companies operating in a given country. With Singapore as the world's benchmark in 2001, this implicit tax reached 15% for Mexico, 25% for Brazil and a striking 43% for Russia.

Two decades ago, such matters concerned mostly official lenders and specialist investors. Over our scenario time horizon, as cross-border investment is an option to be considered—if not adopted—in all scenarios, they increasingly become the concern of mainstream investors and pensioners. According to the US Bureau of Economic Analysis' *Survey of Current Business*, the amount of corporate stock ownership of US entities outside the US increased from less than USD 300 billion in 1993 to almost USD 2 trillion in 2003. With memories of the Asian crisis still lingering, it is no surprise that emerging markets and resource-rich countries are now assessed by investors and by companies in ways that reflect the growing importance attached to transparency and governance. As Michael Johnston of Capital Group, by far the largest investor in emerging markets, explains, "*...such countries are home to most of the world's population. It is expected that over the next 20 years, these countries will constitute two-thirds of the world's economic growth. Given the fact that most of this growth will come from commercial enterprise not state-directed enterprise, corporate governance issues in emerging markets become critically important to this nexus of growth.*"[3]

The quality of corporate governance at company level and the quality of public governance—the institutional and regulatory framework within which companies operate and the effectiveness and integrity of the state behind them—will be essential in establishing trust with a larger base of investors.[3] The quality of the legal system plays a particularly important role, with strong investor protection laws a precondition for broader and deeper capital markets as well as for a more dispersed shareholder base and a more efficient allocation of capital across firms.

Altogether, the full integration of emerging economies into the global economy will occur at a rate that reflects not only their economic performances but the depth of trust that they establish in their governance and related systems.

1

Albert Bressand and Catherine Distler, eds. *Enhanced Transparency: Meeting European Investors' Needs*, a PROMETHEE report for Standard & Poor's, Paris, 2003.

2

"Angry Exchanges: Woes of China's Stock Market Amplify Investors Fury", *The Wall Street Journal Europe*, April 21, 2005.

3

Michael J. Johnson, "Portfolio Investment in Emerging Markets: An Investor's Perspective", in *Corporate Governance and Capital Flows in a Global Economy*, Peter K. Cornelius and Bruce Kogut, eds., Oxford University Press, 2003.

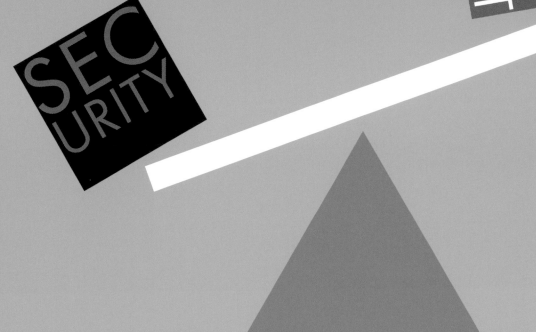

Chapter 2
Mapping complex trade-offs: the *Trilemma* dynamics

The dual crisis of security and trust highlights certain continuities and changes in the relations between state, the economy and society. In this respect, bringing the state back into the picture is only the beginning. Mapping the possible transformations in our global business environment calls for a precise tool that can be, at the same time, generic enough to be open to transformations still to come, and discriminating enough to have identified the changes that will really matter.

To this effect we have developed a two-dimensional analytical tool, the *Trilemma Triangle*. This tool captures essential trade-offs across the full range of economic, political and social objectives. At its core are three types of forces: market incentives, the force of community and of the values that hold groups together ("social cohesion"), and coercion and regulation by the state. The emphasis is on the incentives, power relations and coalition opportunities that shape the choices that investors, companies, civil society and policymakers are presented with.

This chapter presents, first, the 'focal question' behind the *Global Scenarios* (section 2.1) and the *Trilemma Triangle* analytical framework (section 2.2). It then explains how we have identified *Global Scenarios* that are not "inspiring stories" or "utopias" but business-related environments (section 2.3), concluding with the three *Global Scenarios to 2025* (section 2.4).

2.1
The focal question for the *Global Scenarios to 2025*

The force of coercion by the state, which the dual crisis of security and trust has highlighted, can either reinforce or undermine the other forces of market incentives and aspirations to social cohesion which previous *Shell Global Scenarios* focused upon. Hence our *Global Scenarios to 2025* are shaped by three key drivers:
- market incentives,
- the force of community (which we also refer to as aspirations to social cohesion and justice), and
- coercion and regulation by the state.

The three objectives with which these three forces are commonly identified are efficiency, fairness (or 'justice' or 'social equity') and security, respectively. While societies may prioritise one objective, most favour achieving all three. Yet the three forces on which the achievement of these objectives depends display strong elements of mutual exclusiveness. One cannot be moved at the same time towards greater "individualism", conformity and coercion.

Indeed, the policy-making process—and, more generally, the political process—in democratic countries reflects these elements of mutual exclusion. The policies that push towards greater efficiency are, in general, promoted by actors opposed to government intervention and reluctant to endorse generous social programmes. Similarly, the social equity agenda is often seen by public opinion as setting limits on deregulatory moves and higher military budgets. Meanwhile, coercive states are willing to forego some of the benefits of market forces, and concerns for national security are typically presented as taking precedence over efficiency and social cohesion.

In reality, what emerges from these competing forces is not any one absolute world, of "efficiency", "social justice" or "security", but a set of political and economic trade-offs. These trade-offs are embedded in the critical policies, regulations, strategies and interlocking mutual expectations that influence our business environment. The focal question for the *Global Scenarios* can thus be summarised: **how will the triple dilemma, or *Trilemma*, of efficiency, social justice and security be resolved in a globalised world?**

▶ **S**tressing that our business environment will not be a utopia but a world which is influenced by complex trade-offs embedded in policies, strategies and expectations, we are faced with a stark question:

How will the *Trilemma* ～ or "triple-dilemma" ～ between efficiency, social justice and security be resolved in a globalised world **?** The answer to this question is the starting point in our exploration of the predetermined trends, strategic uncertainties and long-term partial equilibria that lie at the heart of the *Global Scenarios to 2025* **...**

2.2
A map of policy trade-offs and social choices

To represent this *Trilemma* we focus not on the objectives themselves—as most societies aspire to achieving all three—but on the forces that pull a given group towards a particular combination of the objectives. In other words, the objectives are always desired but the type of policies, regulations and strategies through which they are pursued can differ widely, creating very contrasted business environments. The map that we have designed, the *Trilemma Triangle*, is intended to capture the full range of the combinations of the three forces—market incentives, coercion and social aspirations—that shape these environments. This map can be applied not only at the global *Jet Stream* level as it is in this report, but also at the level of a country, of a market (e.g. the global LNG market or the global bond market) or, more generally, of any community that is bound together by elements of economic, social and political organisation.

Effectively, previous *Global Scenarios* explored part of this map as they focused on the tensions between market incentives, on the one hand, and aspirations to social cohesion and values on the other. The *Trilemma Triangle* provides a far more comprehensive map of the many "possible futures" that can result from behaviours and strategies in our business environment as influenced by market incentives, public opinion, and forces of coercion and regulation. It also positions the *Shell Global Scenarios vis à vis* traditional economic forecasts to help identify which forces these forecasts take or do not take into consideration (e.g. do they cover possible changes in regulation or in social aspirations?).

Each point on the map represents a unique trade-off between the three objectives (e.g. "more or less emphasis on security as compared to efficiency and social cohesion"). Our map, therefore, reflects considerations similar to those that led Harvard Professor Dani Rodrik[1] to introduce the "Rodrik triangle" to explore relations of mutual exclusivity between the forces of "global integration", "democracy" and "nation states". Like him, we stress that one cannot achieve the three objectives completely and simultaneously (a world that is totally efficient, cohesive and secure). Where the Rodrik triangle focuses on absolutes that are achieved or not ("democracy", "sovereignty" and "global integration"), our approach captures the different degrees to which the three objectives of efficiency, social cohesion and security are achieved through different combinations of the three forces.

Adopting this robust mapping tool is a key step in moving from *Global Scenarios* that are entirely rewritten every three years to a framework for analysis that we can continue to use over time to map key changes, across various time horizons. This mapping tool can also be used to contrast different business environments—for instance, those encountered in Europe or the US, in the Middle East or Russia.

Actors, objectives and forces: three interrelated but distinct analytical layers
The *Trilemma Triangle* differs from a more usual trilogy of Market, Society and State defined in terms of actors.

Simplified views tend to equate markets with pure money incentives and states with coercive forms of intervention. Yet market participants ("the Market") react not only to market incentives but also to forces of coercion. The latter can be enabling (buyers can be coerced to pay for what they bought, market abuses can be punished) or restricting (e.g. interest payments can be forbidden in certain countries, certain types of information or services cannot be provided, genetically modified organisms cannot be sold...). Similarly, the state, as we shall describe, can act through market incentives as well as through coercion and regulation (see p. 62.) States can also become "failed states", leaving the power to coerce in the hands of warlords and mafias who bring it to bear on market interactions. By focusing on the forces that shape behaviours and expectations, rather than actors, the *Trilemma Triangle* enables us to cover these various complexities within one analytical framework.

1

Dani Rodrik,

"How Far will Economic

Integration Go?",

*Journal of Economic

Perspectives*,

Winter 2000.

We also sought inspiration

from Robert Mundell's

work on the triangle of

mutual incompatibility

between full capital

mobility, independent

national monetary policy

and fixed exchange rates.

The three forces

As political symbols emphasise absolutes
- **the nation,**
- **social justice,**
- **free markets,**

it is tempting to create scenarios at the apexes...
Yet the three forces are always present, interacting in far more complex ways. Hence our focus on trade-offs and choices...

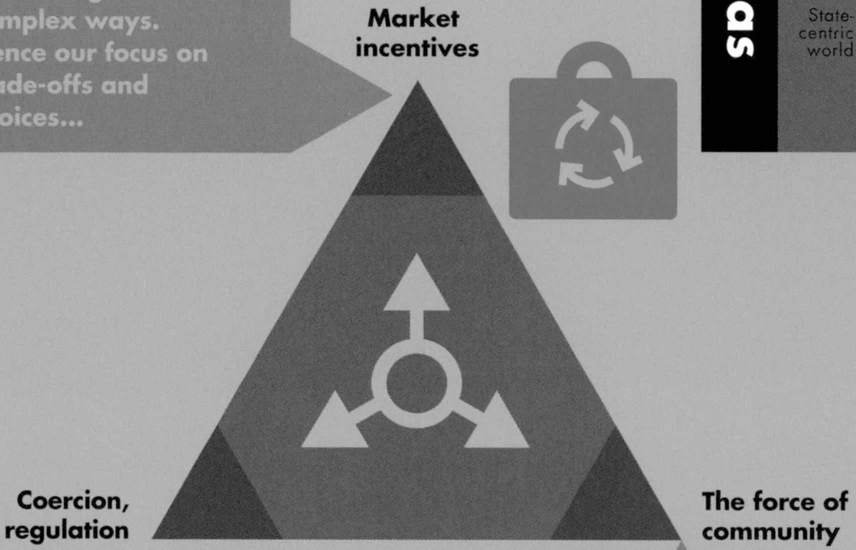

Market incentives

Coercion, regulation

The force of community

Utopias

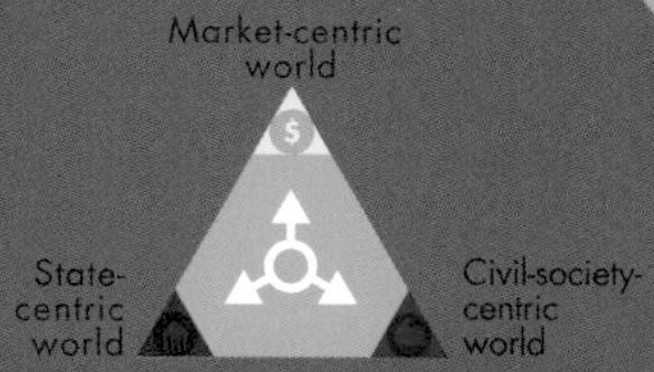

Market-centric world

State-centric world

Civil-society-centric world

• **Aspirations to social cohesion and justice:**
How people relate to one another and their natural environment, and find meaning in the world, depends on their culture, history and beliefs. Fairness, for instance, may be about things as different as equal opportunities, wealth redistribution or respect for religious norms embedded in the Bible or the Koran.

Part 1
Forces of Change and Analytical Framework
1 The dual crisis of security and trust
2 The *Trilemma dynamics*

2.3

From utopias to the more plausible "two wins–one loss" scenario contexts

When faced with several forces to consider, it is natural to consider each one in turn. This is indeed what the previous *Shell Global Scenarios* did in describing market-centric and society-centric worlds. Yet no force ever exists in isolation: even if more appealing to the corporate mind, the world of pure market is no more likely than the world of pure government. Indeed, each of the apexes can be associated with a "utopia". The term "utopia", coined by Thomas Moore[1] in 1516, refers to a world that does not, indeed cannot, exist but tells us about fundamental forces, hopes or fears governing behaviour.

The first utopia on our map lies in the upper part of the triangle and corresponds to a world entirely governed by market forces: while acknowledging that no such world can exist, it remains essential to reflect on how it would operate, something that *2001 Business Class* did very clearly. The second utopia, in the lower right corner of the triangle, could be either a set of different communities each living according to its faith or values (multiple modernities", or a perfectly cohesive society—for instance, a global community governed by egalitarian and ecological values and using world resources sustainably for the benefit of all (in the tradition of Club of Rome reports). *2001 Prism* captured important aspects of this world as it emphasised the role of values. The third utopia is a state-centric world, as idealised by both communist and welfare state advocates. It has not been illustrated in a *Shell Global Scenario* since the *1992 Barricades*, a world in which globalisation and market liberalisation would be rejected in the hope of protecting the social *status quo*—rather as French society rejects the idea of competition within its public services. Yet, as we stressed, the contemporary state discharges its role through a variety of means, including through the market, in ways that defy straightforward apology or rejection.

Analysts and political philosophers have carried out useful interpretations of such utopias, and political leaders will remain informed by them.[2] However, to better address the complex decisions that a global company must take, we break away from the tradition of offering these utopias as guiding scenarios. Understanding what trade-offs will really shape our global business environment calls for an exploration of the regions that lie away from the apexes, governed by more complex or nuanced forces. Our *Global Scenarios* need to be internally coherent, challenging, contrasted and easy to communicate—like previous Shell scenarios—but they should also address the political economy of global and social relations in its full complexity.

Indeed, the communities in which Shell companies work will pursue many difficult trade-offs between competing objectives: e.g. safety vs. innovation, right-to-know vs. privacy rights, freedom vs. security, and equity vs. efficiency. To prepare for contrasted yet plausible business environments, we need to anticipate the complex decisions that can be taken at the interface between these forces.

Institutional discontinuities

In addition, as a group operating in more than 100 countries, we must remember that such decisions, taken in the framework of different market and legal cultures, can feed conflicts over jurisdictions, reinforcing what economists call *institutional discontinuities*.

How these conflicts are resolved, what trade-offs are arrived at—in the market as well as in politics and society—how these trade-offs are translated into legislation, or embedded in cultural expectations, and what institutional discontinuities are created or bridged as a result of conflict and convergence among countries… such are the essential questions that will shape our global business environment.

1

Sir Thomas Moore, in *Utopia* (1516), described a perfect world at peace, in which each citizen worked for the common welfare and had access to the wealth created by everybody.

2

For axiomatic utopias, see respectively Kenichi Ohmae, *The Borderless World: Power and Strategy in the Interlinked Economy*, William Collins, London, 1990; Jan Tinbergen (coordinator) for the Club of Rome, *RIO Report: Reshaping the International Order*, Dutton, New York, 1976; and the dystopia of George Orwell, *Nineteen Eighty Four*, Harcourt, Brace & Co., New York, 1949.

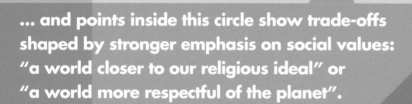

Points inside this circle represent trade-offs that are shaped by stronger market forces than today: "more globalisation"...

starting from the centre of the triangle "where we are now"

... and points inside this circle show trade-offs shaped by stronger emphasis on social values: "a world closer to our religious ideal" or "a world more respectful of the planet".

One of the three "two wins–one loss" areas, indicating a plausible equilibrium

Efficiency

Security

Social cohesion

Points on the map show complex policy trade-offs and social choices, as competing forces pull towards the three triangle apexes

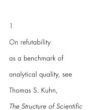

"Win–wins" and negotiated compromises

Having identified fundamental forces that can shape strategies, and searching for more realistic perspectives than the "utopias" can offer, we are looking for the more plausible equilibrium states that emerge when interacting forces achieve some kind of lasting balance and coherence.

This approach directs the spotlight to three zones on the map (see diagrams p. 44 for an explanation of the geometry and its meaning). We call them "two wins–one loss" zones because they represent a balance that could be created (in a democratic society, at least). "Win-wins" satisfy a broad, lasting coalition of at least two groups in corporate, state or civil society—combining, for instance, social progress with freer markets, or freer markets with a massive security effort to protect the homeland and defeat forces of evil. Actors seeking to achieve objectives different from those captured in the win–win still have influence, but they must negotiate from a weaker position, which may lead them towards making appropriate compromises with the stronger players.

On the "right side" of the triangle, for instance, the state does not wither away. It seeks power and legitimacy in closer alignment either with groups in society—endorsing social consensus in legislation—or with investors and companies—achieving its objectives through market incentives, within a pro-business regulatory framework. Similarly, on the "left side", NGOs have more difficulty being heard and may seek to align themselves with state or corporate institutions, or they may retrench in a more dogmatic affirmation of their faiths and values. In this sense, our enhanced scenario methodology also covers the power relationships, the "games" being played among actors, and the coalition strategies leveraging their power, as opposed to the absolutes to which these actors are attracted.

With these game theory and policy process considerations built into the *Trilemma* framework, we identify these "two wins–one loss" zones as the most plausible contexts in which to develop the *Global Scenarios*. These scenarios, as we shall see, embody distinct approaches to solving the dual crisis of security and trust, with major implications for the energy scene.

Before presenting the scenarios, let us stress that the *Trilemma Triangle* map is not limited to these three scenarios, as it positions them within a spectrum of other possible futures. This allows us to position and discuss, for example, more violent world futures, such as a *Prism with Guns* (see chapter 5). This greater depth and coverage is made possible by the *Trilemma Triangle* behind the scenarios and by the three-tier combination of *Jet Stream*, of "*Weather Systems*", and of crises to be analysed in *Navigation*. It enables us to support medium-term scenarios and conduct project-specific risk assessment and strategy work. Our methodology could also find applications in the design of Risk Policy & Guidelines and in supporting tools. We use it internally, for instance, to test the robustness of the high-energy-price reference case that our *Global Scenarios* suggest.

Previous bipolar approaches had the appeal of simplicity: the new triangular map puts business relevance first. It highlights distinct consequences for a global company of different resolutions to the dual crisis of security and trust through dynamic assessments of how various groups pursue their diverse objectives, cooperatively as well as in opposition to one another. For all their complexities, the three *Global Scenarios to 2025* correspond to three contrasting business environments, with clear-cut differences for, notably, transparency, risk and reputation management, compliance, joint ventures and corporate finance.

Domain of validity and limits of our framework

A rigorous analytical framework leading to refutable analyses,[1] our *Trilemma Triangle* has a finite domain of validity. Certain developments must be analysed separately. First among them are "acts of God", transformations in our natural environment such as a new form of pandemic or a major disruption in the earth's climate as envisioned in the film *The Day after Tomorrow*. How policymakers, investors and companies would respond can, however, be analysed in our framework.

Finally, it should be noted that the framework presented here would need to be adapted to fit the realities of certain political cultures around the world, a task we can undertake as appropriate.

1

On refutability as a benchmark of analytical quality, see Thomas S. Kuhn, *The Structure of Scientific Revolutions*, University of Chicago Press, 1962.

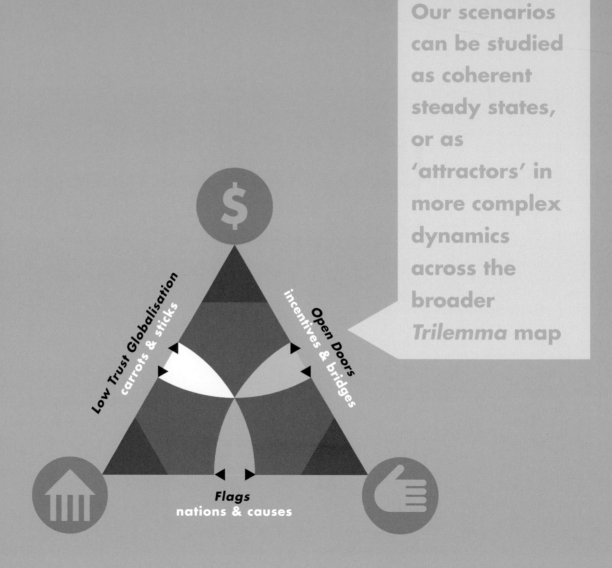

Low Trust Globalisation
carrots & sticks

Open Doors
incentives & bridges

Flags
nations & causes

Our scenarios can be studied as coherent steady states, or as 'attractors' in more complex dynamics across the broader *Trilemma* map

2.4
The three *Global Scenarios to 2025* and predetermined trends: a preview

As shown on the map, and as described in Part 2 of this report, the three *Global Scenarios* developed in the "two wins–one loss" regions of the *Trilemma Triangle* are:
* **Low Trust Globalisation:** a world of heightened globalisation *and* more coercive states and regulators ("Carrots and Sticks");
* **Open Doors:** a world of heightened globalisation *and* more cohesive civil societies ("Incentives and Bridges");
* **Flags:** a world in which values are affirmed in a more dogmatic, zero-sum game manner, *and* in which states try to rally divided societies around the flag ("Nations and Causes").

Each of the three forces (market incentives, the force of community, and coercive power of the state) plays a central role in two scenarios, and a subordinated, yet significant, role in a third. Emphasising plausible trade-offs rather than extremes, the *Global Scenarios to 2025* help us to understand how the impact of one force (e.g. market incentives) will be modified by each of the other two forces, leading to very different legal and business contexts. We see this in the real world where market forces can express themselves in the cohesive context of Norway just as much as in the coercive context of China; or where coercion by the state can take the form of the Sarbanes-Oxley legislation in the US, as well as of direct intervention by the Kremlin in the selection of governors for the various regions of the Russian Federation.

The combination of forces behind each scenario has enough coherence to be lasting. Yet, even the most stable configurations (e.g. "the cold war", "it's the economy, stupid!"…) come to an end, and the *Trilemma Triangle* can also be used to analyse the more complex dynamics of change that ensues.

Predetermined trends
While the positioning of the *Global Scenarios* on the *Trilemma Triangle* map enables us to analyse the nature of fundamental trade-offs, another essential pillar for development of the scenarios involves identifying "predetermined trends"—trends present in all scenarios.

> ‘ **The three Global Scenarios to 2025 are not "stories" but stable solutions to the Trilemma, also reflecting predetermined trends in the way each type of actor can influence outcomes.** ’

Such trends are analysed in Part 3 of this report. The first such trend concerns the geography of globalisation and the role of the US and China as agents of change. Three other trends reflect qualitative changes in the methods employed by actors associated with the triangle "apexes" in influencing the resolution of the *Trilemma*. These trends are: how civil society groups and market players can act through the courts; how states can use market forces; and how investors can have a stronger influence on the nature of corporate governance. Last but not least, demographic trends as well as major trends at work in our natural environment (especially the risks to biodiversity and to the earth's climate) have far-reaching implications in all three scenarios, in ways that vary from one to another as we analyse in Parts 2 and 3.

Rather than "stories", the new *Shell Global Scenarios* describe the three "two wins–one loss" zones in the *Trilemma Triangle* that capture plausible long-term trade-offs and equilibria.

Each *Global Scenario* is first summarised ("The scenario in a nutshell") before the interplay between market participants, civil society and states is presented in greater detail (the "*Trilemma* relations"). We then look successively at economic policies, at forces of integration and fragmentation that affect globalisation patterns, and at implications for economic growth. We then conclude with a first level of implications for the energy scene.

Laying out the incentive systems and constraints that shape behaviours and decisions, the three *Global Scenarios* also provide starting points for further exploration of global trends and of specific business environments, which we do in *Trilemmaps* such as those presented in chapter 6.

Obviously, as always, these scenarios are not forecasts but plausible, alternative futures.

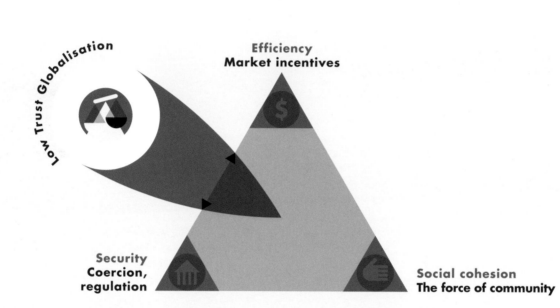

Low Trust Globalisation

Efficiency
Market incentives

Security
**Coercion,
regulation**

Social cohesion
The force of community

Part 2

The Three Global Scenarios

3 *Low Trust Globalisation*

4 *Open Doors*

5 *Flags*

6 *Trilemmaps*

Low Trust Globalisation

The scenario in a nutshell: "Carrots and Sticks"
In *Low Trust Globalisation*, globalisation carries on, but the world does not evolve towards a *laissez-faire* economy as Shell canvassed in *2001 Business Class*, or previously in *People Power, Just Do It! and New Frontiers*. Market incentives are at work in all aspects of the economy and society, but so are efforts to deal with insecurity and distrust.

Trust is not restored, at least not through the operation of the market. Investors, customers and companies deploy significant energy to protect themselves against the misdeeds, or potential failings, of others. This is a world in which redress is sought in court, and regulators frequently step in to impose discipline.

Transparency, a *leitmotif* of this scenario, is equated with disclosure procedures that are mandatory, complex and costly. Barriers to entry are high, debt financing is preferred to equity financing, and new norms of "extended producer responsibility" emerge. Companies are held responsible for upstream (supplier) impacts as well as for downstream (customer) effects. They therefore seek control over the full supply chain through vertical and horizontal integration. Demarcating the boundaries of different jurisdictions, institutional discontinuities remain significant impediments to deeper economic integration. Generating higher transaction costs than within a domestic economy, such discontinuities serve to segment markets in much the same way as trade barriers. One example is contract enforcement, which remains much more problematic across national boundaries than it does domestically. Competition laws, which cover notably M&As, continue to differ significantly between the EU, the US and emerging countries.

The state plays a major role in providing security to the nation and in overseeing the process whereby trust in the market is preserved through satisfactory opportunities to seek redress for market abuses or dysfunctions. This involves a stronger coercive and discretionary power for the state and the independent regulatory agencies. Regulators themselves are not fully trusted, however, and they must demonstrate that they take the interests of investors, minority shareholders, customers and other stakeholders into proper consideration. Far from engaging in a "race to the bottom", they are aware that distrust in the marketplace, along with international insecurity, will foster a "flight to quality", in which firms and individuals are attracted to regimes with strong and efficient regulatory frameworks. "Regulation-light" offshore jurisdictions are publicly criticised and, if need be, blacklisted.

In this context, regulators must also adopt a "transparency" model. Environmental agencies, for example, will identify key metrics such as air and water pollution levels, and will track indicators that provide a way to gauge the severity of problems. More generally, in this increasingly data-intensive world, benchmarking and quantitative performance measurement are used by governments, regulators and companies. The media, which tend to focus on scandals and breaches of faith as well as on corporate performances, add to this climate of unforgiving scrutiny.

Altogether, dealing with regulatory and compliance risks is an essential part of successful corporate strategies.

The scenario in
a nutshell

51

By Tim Huxley

Insights

Tim Huxley is Senior Fellow for Asia-Pacific Security and the editor of Adelphi Papers at the International Institute for Strategic Studies (IISS) in London.

When security concerns reshape market liberalisation patterns: insights from the energy sector

Two decades of market liberalisation

Liberalisation of the gas and power sector has been a recurring theme around the world since the mid-1980s. In terms of governance and ownership, liberalisation has proceeded along two different paths:

• in an economy dominated by private ownership, the traditional US approach has been to regulate the activities of the oil and gas sector closely;

• in contrast, the European approach has been dominated by the privatisation of state-owned utility companies, or the removal of national or regional monopolies in the supply of gas and power.

Five important lessons learned from both these approaches have been:

• **Transparency** in terms and conditions of access to pipeline/storage facilities is key for system efficiency.

• Pipelines and related facilities are generally **natural monopolies** and some form of tariff, access and investment regulation is necessary to prevent market abuse or failure.

• Effective **unbundling** of pipeline/ storage and supply/trading activities is crucial to ensuring non-discriminatory third-party access and efficient regulation.

• Dialogue between regulatory authorities, transmission system operators, gas suppliers and traders,

consumers, network users and gas exchanges is useful in preventing **regulatory failure**.

• Responsibility for regulation needs to be clearly defined and vested in an appropriate state institution, **independent** of market players.

The independent regulator has emerged as the "agent of the public good", charged with ensuring even-handed implementation of energy policy and intervention in the event of market failures. Aspects related to the latter have prompted regulation specifying the appropriate rate of return for natural monopolies and the protection of consumers from monopoly abuse, while encouraging timely industry development.

Regulatory failures

Nevertheless, regulatory failures have happened over the past 10 years, notably in:

• **Inappropriate market models:** market design and complexity may result in the type of failure apparent in the California power market.

• **Regulatory capture:** market players may achieve sufficient scale to become, in effect, self-regulating, the more so if the regulatory authority lacks sufficient power to assert itself.

• **Unbalanced regulatory objectives:** for example, a short-term focus on reduction of energy costs to end-consumers, overlooking long-term investment requirements in infrastructure development and environmental objectives.

A new focus on energy security

Governments, regulators and industry have learned from the past: now there appears to be a growing tendency to develop predictable regulation in dialogue with all stakeholders and to ensure a level playing field for competition. Also key is the provision of timely investments for new infrastructure and sensible levels of system redundancy for ensuring energy security. Pragmatic approaches for new infrastructure, such as temporary derogation from third-party access, have recently become acceptable for regulatory and competition authorities. In the US, this trend reflects

a longer-term need to attract new gas supplies through new LNG import terminals. In the EU, there is a growing feeling of vulnerability as a lack of interconnection capacity between member states, notably in the electricity sector, as well as between the EU and major resource holders for gas, stands in the way of ensuring diversity of supply.

To most governments and consumers, continuity in energy supply has become far more important than additional short-term gains that could accrue from liberalising markets without taking security concerns into account. The recent energy blackouts across the world have refocused government policy on the social, political and economic costs of failure, and have put regulators under more pressure to deliver the new policy objectives of energy security to ensure economic growth and social cohesion. This has been done with significant, although incomplete, international cooperation. Hence the *Low Trust Globalisation* flavour of many recent developments.

Part 2

The Three Global Scenarios

3 Low Trust Globalisation

4 Open Doors

5 Flags

6 Trilemmaps

3.1
The market, civil society and the state in *Low Trust Globalisation*

Low Trust Globalisation, situated on the left side of the *Trilemma Triangle* map, is a world in which economic integration proceeds further, without the market delivering a full solution to the dual crisis of security and trust. As a result, the pressure for global-scale regulation mounts but is met by a patchwork of often conflicting rules. Regulation becomes not only more complicated but also multi-tiered. National governments apply numerous standards and rules, but so too do local and state/provincial authorities—consistent with a market-driven spirit of decentralisation. As regulation demands multiply and become more divergent, multinational companies press for the harmonisation of standards. Some even seek stronger international governance processes and institutions as a way to promote consistency in rules and requirements and thus smooth market access. Where the need for intervention is inescapably trans-border, because the underlying problems cannot be handled on a country-by-country basis, a new international layer of regulation emerges, even if painfully. Adoption of common accounting standards is a good example.

Regulatory competition and flight to quality
Simultaneously, a competitive dynamic emerges among governmental entities. Countries, as well as the states and provinces within larger nations, vie for investment, jobs and new enterprises. "Regulatory competition" is a powerful disciplinary mechanism, and results not in a "race to the bottom", but in a combination of respect for market forces and efficient intervention on the part of regulators and the state. In a world of ever more mobile capital and versatile corporations, authorities who neglect the possibility of market failure find themselves under significant political and economic pressure, as do those who regulate in a heavy-handed or cumbersome way.

While internalising externalities is considered appropriate (e.g. by applying the "polluter pays" principle), governments often prefer the higher degree of control associated with taxes. In the environmental realm, where market mechanisms such as pollution fees are preferred, these wide differences in normal approaches result in a myriad of incompatible regulations. The Kyoto Protocol is not significantly strengthened in subsequent revisions (see chapter 13); the US stays out and, while the EU endeavours to incentivise China into joining, many European companies denounce Kyoto as a major competitive disadvantage.

Market liberalisation continues
A greater and more visible role for government in a low-trust environment does not mean a return to direct involvement in economic activity—through, for example, state-owned companies, taxation and higher public spending (other than defence spending). While bursts of coercive and discretionary regulation capture the headlines, the thrust of state intervention is market-friendly.

The transition from Nation States towards Market States (as described in chapter 9) accelerates and the use of incentives is critical to state action, even if it is only one of the tools states can use. Financial engineering is not discouraged, and regulators are not surprised that they sometimes need to step in to correct the problems that this creates.

Governments serve two key functions:
• First, whereas certain security support functions have already been outsourced to the private sector, national security remains the most important public good. As serious terrorist threats continue to exist, the provision of security, both internally and internationally, remains likely to interfere with market operations.
• Second, as markets fundamentally rely on trust, a good they believe they cannot provide themselves, governments put in place institutions and regulations to ensure that markets function efficiently. Although intended to be market-friendly, there is a danger that an increasingly complex regulatory framework undermines private risk-taking.

Ad hoc and conflicting policies to restore security and trust
Traditional politics is continued in *Low Trust Globalisation*, in the sense that the fundamental domestic political debate is over where the boundaries of the state should effectively be. On the one hand, there is a drive to ensure security through regulation, and on the other there are concerns over market efficiency. The drive towards globalised markets is moderated by a degree of *dirigisme*, justified in the name of security and protection for society.

Trilemma **relations**

53

Signposts

1

Allen T. Cheng, "Some see legal dysfunction; others say China is playing fair," *International Herald Tribune*, August 30, 2004.

2

"Cadbury chief slams investor groups for lack of openness", *Financial Times*, April 22, 2005.

Glaxo, Europe's largest drug maker, in August 2004 gave up a fight to protect a key ingredient in Avandia, its top diabetes treatment, a month after China revoked the local patent for Viagra, the world's best-selling impotence treatment.

"It isn't hard to find loopholes in Chinese patents held by overseas drug makers," said Xu Guowen, a Beijing lawyer who led the Viagra and Avandia cases. "All I need is to find one weakness and I can break your patent."

"Rather than wilfully infringe the patents, as Chinese firms have notoriously done in the past, these firms have mounted what appears to be a legal challenge," said Professor Mueller at the University of Pittsburgh. "The US wants other countries to play by our intellectual property rules; that seems to be exactly what is taking place here."[1]

Costs of complying with Sarbanes-Oxley lead a number of non-US companies to consider delisting from US exchanges. However, those companies will still have to comply with US reporting requirements if they have more than 300 US investors (a rule currently under review by the SEC).

Goldman Sachs is hired to help UK-based media group ITV – with no US listing – buy out US shareholders whose stake does not exceed 175,000 at a 15% premium (plus USD 500) in order to fall below the 300 US trigger. The company is also seeking a change in its articles of association so that it has a power of sale of stock if it seems that the number of shareholders will again exceed 300.

Vivendi is the first company to apply for the new tax status that is reserved for multinational corporations headquartered in France.

Under the new "consolidated global profit tax", international corporations can use past losses at unprofitable divisions to offset future earnings at profitable units in which they own at least a 50% stake. In exchange for its newly favourable tax status, Vivendi has promised the government that it will help create new jobs over the next five years in several French regions that are struggling with high unemployment.

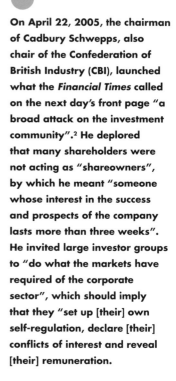

On April 22, 2005, the chairman of Cadbury Schwepps, also chair of the Confederation of British Industry (CBI), launched what the *Financial Times* called on the next day's front page "a broad attack on the investment community".[2] He deplored that many shareholders were not acting as "shareowners", by which he meant "someone whose interest in the success and prospects of the company lasts more than three weeks". He invited large investor groups to "do what the markets have required of the corporate sector", which should imply that they "set up [their] own self-regulation, declare [their] conflicts of interest and reveal [their] remuneration.

Part 2

The Three Global Scenarios

3 Low Trust Globalisation

4 Open Doors

5 Flags

6 Trilemmaps

Greater tolerance of strong states

Countries like Russia, China or Venezuela find this context a hospitable environment in which they can defend their statist stances without appearing anachronistic. Yet their policies give too much discretionary power to the state to be representative of the norm in *Low Trust Globalisation*. In the key countries that set what we call *Jet Stream* contexts, there is, in many instances, a clear trade-off between the needs of open markets and the regulatory requirements of the state, leading to a search for balance between the two.

Much of the actual overseeing is, in practice, delegated to regulated private sector entities, such as accountants, audit firms and rating agencies. The regulatory environment mandates transparent competition between these service providers, and adamantly seeks to prevent or punish major conflicts of interest.

"Law is a business"

Unsure of its own capacity to monitor the marketplace, the state also relies on civil lawsuits among market participants as an essential tool in the fraud discovery mechanism, making the "private attorneys general" US doctrine a key pillar of regulatory enforcement globally. More generally, the trends in US legal culture acquire global relevance. Even more than in any other scenario, "law is a business" (in the words of Philip Bobbitt), and law firms continue to develop the wherewithal to conduct long, protracted legal actions profitably.

Pressure on companies in *Low Trust Globalisation* comes not only from government and from other market participants, but also from an ever more demanding set of confrontational civil society actors operating under the banner of "corporate social responsibility". While this scenario is located in the part of the *Trilemma Triangle* where aspirations to social cohesion take second place to the market and to the state, civil society groups do not stand idle in *Low Trust Globalisation*. NGOs of all kinds—consumer advocates, community organisations and environmental groups—insist upon more complete corporate reporting on a range of issues including pollution practices and results, investments in the communities where facilities are located, workplace conditions and wage levels. They often take their cases to the courts.

Published rankings identify leaders and laggards. And tremendous pressure is brought to bear on those whose performance is judged to be sub-standard.

BINGOs and GRINGOs: NGOs seek to overcome their limited clout

Yet the NGO movement also adapts to the reduced clout of stakeholders and many civil society groups, by seeking to influence events through alliances with investors or by lobbying governments to enact binding regulation in support of their values and causes. Governments and companies adapt to this changed context, and there is also a proliferation of what are mockingly referred to as GRINGOs (government-related NGOs), BINGOs (business-initiated NGOs) or RINGOs (religious NGOs, often with an ultra-conservative agenda).

Many signposts in our present business environment suggest clear trends towards *Low Trust Globalisation*, particularly when we look at the behaviours of intermediaries, courts, supervisors and NGOs. The efforts of Chinese lawyers and courts to identify legal shortcomings in the patents of foreign companies (over such flagship products as Viagra) is one such signpost (see box). So too are the ways in which the Public Company Accounting Oversight Board, which was established by Congress in 2002 after the Enron, Worldcom and Arthur Andersen fiascos, has begun to review how consistently the "Big Four" audit firms apply complex rules—to their clients and to themselves.

Trilemma **relations**

55

1

Clayton M. Christensen,

The Innovator's Dilemma:

When New Technologies

Cause Great Firms to Fail,

Harvard Business Press,

Cambridge, MA, 1997.

2

www.wolfsberg-principles.

com

Size, private equity and the global bond market

Competing in this world requires staying power and significant legal resources. The costs of complying with an increasingly stringent and complex set of corporate governance codes and regulations are high and rising. For example, Aegon, one of the world's largest insurance companies, estimates that it spent around USD 20 million in 2003, or about 1% of its earnings, in order to comply with Sarbanes-Oxley alone, on top of more than USD 10 million in other corporate governance costs. As costs of compliance become similarly significant in many other sectors, size is highly valued even if size, which suggests "deep pockets", is also an invitation to litigation.

Operating across complex regulatory frameworks, meeting the high costs of ever-evolving compliance processes, being prepared for lawsuits under US jurisdiction even when not operating in the US, and maintaining tight control over one's supply chain—only large companies can afford such prerequisites. Vertical and horizontal integration is then the way to preserve one's "licence to operate".

The equity markets are not embraced unreservedly, as they are in *Open Doors* (see next chapter), because investors fear the challenges that can arise from public listing. Indeed many medium-sized companies opt to de-list, or not to list, especially in the US. This is a world of very large bond issuers but also of private companies, private equity markets and financial engineering.

Disruptive innovation, hard-to-protect intellectual property rights, and public R&D

Markets, however, remain highly contestable and contested. Venture capitalists are at hand to fund the development of "disruptive technologies",[1] which have the potential to humble some of the larger, integrated corporate groups. Protecting one's intellectual property is often more a matter of discouraging law suits through the size and aggressiveness of one's legal skills than of achieving unchallengeable rights, often an elusive objective in this fast-moving, "disrespectful" world.

Research and development is important, with governments collaborating closely with universities and the private sector. New national research clusters emerge, such as those that already exist in Silicon Valley or Munich. With regulatory barriers to entry relatively high, and disruptive technologies notwithstanding, the bulk of R&D activity comes from large incumbents. Intellectual property rights enjoy strong protection. However, that protection is hard to extend across borders as it requires registering with each national patent office. Even the EU struggles to agree on a single Europe-wide patent regime, as a result of language-related issues. What is achieved comes short of a level playing field.

There are other reasons why innovation is less intense than it could be. Cross-country research networks remain limited in size and scope, and may even be actively discouraged in some sensitive areas. Even within national borders, a profound lack of trust prevents companies from sharing research outcomes. More generally, the diffusion of ideas is slowed down by suspicions of all types and by uncertainties as to what can safely be protected across borders. Foreign access to new security-sensitive technologies, such as computer encryption software, is highly restricted. Operating in China is no longer done without extensive legal preparation and safeguards.

Yet a more focused NGO community also helps shape important voluntary rules in critical fields. An early example was the anti-money-laundering guidelines ("Wolfsberg Principles"[2]) which were initiated by Transparency International in 2000. The principles, which were initially signed by 11 leading international banks, establish anti-money-laundering guidelines that are viewed as appropriate when dealing with clients in the global marketplace. The principles reinforce "know your customer" policies that pertain to relationships between high net worth individuals and private banking institutions. The tendency, however, is for such codes to be made compulsory, often through the extra-territorial reach of US courts and US laws.

The media and the risk of not being right

As reported by the media, news is often relatively dull in *Low Trust Globalisation*. Having to justify their opinions, and quite often being challenged to expose their sources in court, the media are concerned about presenting balanced and documented views, with emphasis on facts rather than judgements. Corporate performances and corporate scandals receive sustained attention, but disclaimers are part of every story. Some groups act as "watchdogs" to track the media's record on various issues and are ready to hold them accountable for distortions. The risk of not being right is high in what looks very much like an 'audit society'…

Part 2

The Three Global Scenarios

3 Low Trust Globalisation

4 Open Doors

5 Flags

6 Trilemmaps

3.2

Economic policies in *Low Trust Globalisation*

Fiscal conservatism and simplified tax structures

Consistent with a fundamentally market-oriented approach, *Low Trust Globalisation* witnesses a general suspicion of government spending. Tax systems are generally simple, with few loopholes. With the emphasis being on efficiency, the tax regime is not considered an appropriate instrument to achieve a more equal distribution of income. The degree of tax progressivity is limited, and some countries, in "a spasm of radical simplification"[1], follow the example of the Baltic countries and Russia, and choose to have flat tax rates. Tax avoidance is limited thanks to a strong tax administration and coercive international agreements. Budget deficits tend to be low, although defence spending may increase and lead in some countries to higher deficits.

Narrowly defined public goods

Public goods, namely goods that are not delivered in a satisfactory manner or quantity by the market, are very narrowly defined. For example, the supply of university education is largely left to the private sector, with the labour markets essentially determining the curriculum. More generally, the state prefers to act as a regulator in order to ensure that markets actually provide certain goods.

While some goods might be undersupplied because neither the state nor markets provide them, national security, perhaps the most fundamental public good, is supplied in abundance. That does not mean that we live in a perfectly safe world. On the contrary, continuous conflicts within and across borders as well as terrorist attacks ensure that there remains sufficient support for defence spending and for regulations that provide tighter security, even if they undermine market efficiency or intrude into people's lives.

Public investment is relatively high. In contrast, public consumption, e.g. in the form of public sector employment, is relatively low. Security issues play an important role in public procurement and projects. Private sector suppliers are carefully screened, with national champions being favoured and external competitors being excluded from bidding for sensitive projects. Although public and private investment is relatively high, current account imbalances remain

limited thanks to relatively high private sector savings for pension reasons. Reliance on capital inflows is reduced.

Transparent central banks and currency volatility

Central banks are generally independent. Yet central bank governors are incentivised to deliver low and stable inflation. Those who don't are held accountable. The minutes of policy sessions are published and decisions attributable to individual board members. Exchange rates are largely left to market forces. Currency pegs are rare and limited to countries with inconvertible currencies for capital transactions (like China at present). As a result, exchange rates fluctuate widely and at times may become seriously misaligned.

Efficient labour markets and "four pillars" pensions

Labour markets are largely efficient. Wage negotiations are decentralised, ensuring that wage increases reflect productivity gains. Of course differing wage increases lead to rising income disparities, both regionally and sectorally. However, higher wage growth attracts more workers, with both job-to-job mobility and regional mobility being high. Trade unions generally play a limited role in the wage-setting process. Nevertheless, they may represent an important voice in society and provide some checks and balances regarding government policies. Wage dispersion within companies remains large, but senior executives are under pressure to justify their large pay packages.

Equal opportunities matter more than equality of income, and absolute poverty more than inequality. The state provides minimum support on a strictly means-tested basis. Welfare reform combines company-specific provision and pressure on individuals to provide for themselves through private sector schemes, encouraged by fiscal incentives; an example would be four-pillars pensions, which combine public schemes, company-specific schemes, voluntary contributions and a flexible retirement age system. Such reforms proceed in a relatively abrupt and conflictual manner, as governments feel under high pressure to let market forces play a greater role.[1] The strict application of competition law further challenges their freedom to influence prices of medical services and pharmaceuticals. Hence, a series of technical reforms gradually diminish benefits without explicit political debate. The "European social model" is seen as increasingly hard to sustain, and societies are disillusioned about what politicians can achieve.

Economic policies

1

"The flat-tax revolution: towards simpler, fairer and better taxes", *The Economist*, April 16-22, 2005, pp. 9 and 63-65.

2

For details see "Ageing of the population: achievements and challenges, a report to Shell", Gregor Hochreiter, Jorgen Mortensen, Regina Sauto and Svetla Tsolova, Centre for European Policy Studies (CEPS), Brussels, March 2004. On *The Four Pillars* and the challenges of the future financing of pensions see the Geneva Association, www.genevaassociation.org, and *Itinéraire vers la retraite à 80 ans*, Orio Giarini, Economica, Paris, 2002.

Insights
By Ralph Welborn and Vince Kasten

Ralph Welborn and **Vince Kasten** are both Managing Partners of Unisys Corporation, USA, and authors of *The Jericho Principle: How Companies Use Strategic Collaboration to Find New Sources of Value*, John Wiley & Sons, Inc., 2003. They are actively involved in the "Safe Commerce" initiatives described here.

Safe commerce: securing the US trade routes

Ensuring safety and security has now become a top priority for the US government, other developed countries and supply-chain executives worldwide. Three related risks are seen as threatening the stability and even viability of global commerce and could make the present approach a permanent feature of a *Low Trust Globalisation* world:

1. Terrorism:
an act of terrorism, targeted at a commercial container or port, would have an economic impact many times larger than 9.11;

2. Government reaction:
the port closures and stringent import regulations resulting from an incident would bring global commerce to a halt;

3. Commercial viability:
in the words of one Fortune 30 executive whom we interviewed, "… *if an act of terrorism were committed on one of our containers, we believe it would be a company-ending event."*

As defined now by the US administration, "safe commerce" must meet the twin goals of a high degree of control over physical assets and information flow, and acceptable commercial costs. Yet a typical trade transaction, from source through destination, involves on average 25 different parties and 30 different documents, using policies, processes and technologies created in an era before end-to-end security was a concern. Security has traditionally focused on individual parties, with no single point of liability for an end-to-end trade transaction. In contrast, post 9.11 safe trade challenges involve:

• **Multiple participants and breakpoints**: Security of physical assets and information flow must be maintained across and within the many parties involved in a transaction.

• **Process, personnel and facility security**: Even with adaptive and robust technology solutions, ensuring the security of employees, processes and facilities remains a formidable task.

• **Jurisdictional complexity**: Global regulations, covenants or laws present an inconsistent—sometimes conflicting—environment for global commerce.

• **Cyber security**: The transactional, communication and data stores are not secure.

Operating a secure supply chain—one that meets governmental regulations and provides commercial benefits—demands an entirely new approach to conducting international trade. From the source manufacturer to the final destination, any Blueprint for Safe Commerce must:

• consist of inter-operating end-to-end processes, policies and technologies;

• incorporate standards, developed and accepted by industry and government, for technology, data security, policy and notifications;

• leverage existing infrastructures from ports, carriers and governmental agencies;

• provide continuous improvement measures.

The commercial impact and benefits (financial, legal, supply chain and risk mitigation) are so large that all parties in global commerce—governments, source manufacturers, logistics providers, warehouse operators, carriers and service providers—must take a proactive position in driving both regulations and industry standards across the value chain to enhance security, while improving the bottom line. A Safe Commerce Blueprint will see an increase in companies and government working together to create the necessary regulations, standards and infrastructure to "think through" and "take action" towards secure global commerce.

Part 2

The Three Global Scenarios

3 Low Trust Globalisation

4 Open Doors

5 Flags

6 Trilemmaps

3.3

Forces of global integration and fragmentation in *Low Trust Globalisation*

Global crisis management and competing global standards

As a consequence of the crises of security and trust in the market, a new form of global order arises in *Low Trust Globalisation*. Security concerns, previously limited to a country's sovereign domestic territory, become globalised, structured within global networks in which strong states such as the US assert their dominant power against the declining sovereignty of weaker states. Meanwhile, globalising markets become subjected to more interventionist government policies, not to the detriment of markets, but to provide those public goods that markets undersupply.

This new global order unleashes forces of integration and fragmentation which are unique to *Low Trust Globalisation*. Two sets of dynamics are at play. First, as powerful states perceive their security concerns to be globally integrated—notably in response to terrorism—sovereignty becomes a variable concept; the territorial notion of security is contested, with lesser states expected to comply with the security concerns of the major powers. At the same time, the reaction against terrorism carries a cost: it restricts market flows and also, possibly, feeds anti-globalisation sentiments. Secondly, globalising markets constrain policy choices for governments, who seek to intervene to support their respective national competitive advantages in global markets. And yet faced with the risk of provoking capital flight by mobile investors and producers, they also have to respond to the economic insecurities of their peoples.

These forces are evident in today's world. On security concerns, there is no global integrating framework. The US, Russia, China and the EU each have their own separate security assessments, but their security concerns come together in combating global terrorism in a range of other countries, where they see it as in their respective national interests to collaborate. On market concerns, only a few global institutional structures are developed to provide a framework for this buoyant yet fierce global competition. Few, however, does not mean none. Central bankers are at the centre of high-powered networks of regulators able to cooperate almost instantaneously when confronted with crises of global proportion. The Financial

Stability Forum—created in 1999 to bring together key central banks, securities market regulators and insurance regulators as well as the Bank for International Settlement (BIS), the IMF and the World Bank—develops further, with fully-fledged branches in Shanghai, Mexico City and Johannesburg. Significant financial crises do occur to keep the Forum on its toes. Meanwhile, ensuring that containers are not turned into terrorist weapons leads to a far-reaching set of technical measures to monitor the flows of goods entering the US and other vulnerable countries, making every shipment fully traceable (see box).

Large companies cannot afford to ignore transparency pressures from, notably, US pension funds and asset managers. The latter, however, resist efforts to disclose the identity of their own owners.

The recent decision by the SEC to require hedge funds to register illustrates an uneasiness about this lack of ownership transparency, an uneasiness which grows in *Low Trust Globalisation* as hedge funds become part of mainstream portfolios and as companies become distrustful of some opportunistic shareholders. US GAAP accounting standards become the *de facto* global reference. Nonetheless, the EU does come up with alternative regulation in fields such as competition law, privacy, data transfer, biotech, vehicle emissions and the workplace. Conflicts are thus frequent between the US and the EU. The latter is constrained by the need to achieve consensus among a sizeable majority of its 30-odd members.

Hesitant EU integration, opportunistic Russia and China

The EU sees its political integration process stall and possibly reverse. Its efforts to articulate a common vision of the world is overtaken by conflicting interests. A lack of trust in Brussels' capacity to deliver the proper set of incentives and/or coercion leads national governments to substitute a number of not always enlightened national measures in place of the much decried "EU Directives". Access to North American and Asian markets becomes an essential aspect of European policies, while creeping protectionism chips away at a number of the benefits of the internal market. While the British press frequently discusses the possibility of its collapse, the euro still remains the common currency of a majority of the EU countries, as the legal risks and economic costs of a nationalist move away from the Eurozone would be excessive.

Globalisation

59

By Philip Bobbitt

Insights

Philip Bobbitt, a member of the 2005 Shell scenario team, is Professor of Constitutional Law at the University of Texas. The following draws on his personal views as expressed in *The War on Terror*, Knopf, New York, forthcoming (late 2005).

What visionary leaders could do for the Middle East in a *Low Trust Globalisation* world

Although it was unheralded at the time, one important consequence of the regime change in Baghdad was its effect on the nuclear weapons programmes of the states in the region. Efforts in Iraq under Saddam Hussein to acquire WMDs also galvanised the efforts of other states in the region. Iran, which had negotiated with Russia to purchase a full fuel cycle capability, accelerated its programmes. Israel began pressing the US for a definitive change of regime in Iraq. Libya—in concert, it is rumoured, with other states in the region including Saudi Arabia—linked up with the clandestine A. Q. Khan network to purchase nuclear weapons technology.

The invasion of Iraq in 2003 complicated this situation. Iraq's effort to acquire nuclear weapons, which sooner or later would have borne fruit, was halted. Libya, which had been in diplomatic discussions on ways to lift the economic sanctions imposed for Libyan terrorism, decided to come clean and invited US inspectors to dismantle the Libyan facility. Iran's determination to press ahead with its programme initially faltered after the invasion of Iraq, which strengthened fears in Tehran that its hardline regime might be the next target of the Coalition. Iran seems to have redoubled its efforts, however, once the Coalition occupation met stiff resistance.

Israel meanwhile prepared a pre-emptive strike against the Iranian nuclear facilities, seeking to buy time much as it had in 1981 by destroying the French-built Osirak nuclear reactor before Saddam Hussein could accumulate enough fissile material to make weapons. A strike against Iran, however, was fraught with difficulty. Owing to the limited air refuelling capability of the Israelis and the distance to Iran, the US would inevitably be involved in any attack at a time when the American appetite for foreign adventures was waning and American status in the Muslim world had hit an all-time low. Unlike Osirak, Iranian sites were multiple and dispersed. Unlike the Iraqis, the Iranians had developed medium-range ballistic missiles that could target Israel's own nuclear facility at Dimona in retaliation for any pre-emptive attack.

A new approach to regional security?

It needn't end in conflict, however, because a way out for all parties was made possible by Saddam Hussein's removal.

Apart from reasons of prestige, domestic political manoeuvring, and a genuine desire to diversify its energy base in order to export gas and oil for hard currency, Iran sought nuclear weapons for three strategic reasons: to deter an Israeli nuclear threat arising from Iran's support for Hezbollah operations against Israel; to deter nuclear threats by its Arab neighbours, especially Iraq; and to deter a US-led invasion. These strategic requirements can be satisfied without Iranian nuclear weapons, now that the regional situation has dramatically changed.

If the US gave security guarantees to Israel as it has to Germany and Japan, this—coupled with advanced conventional systems whose accuracy give them a lethality that in military terms makes them as effective as nuclear systems—could lead to a negotiated dismantling of the Israeli arsenal. No state in the region remotely poses a conventional threat to Israel, nor could one in the foreseeable future.

But Iran could, by design or through the malice of a rogue mullah, give nuclear weapons to terrorists willing to die in order to destroy Israel once and for all. So an essential element in the Israeli renunciation of its nuclear weapons must be a mutual renunciation by Iran, with much enhanced transparency for verification. With Saddam Hussein gone from Iraq, no state in the region threatens Iran unless the US should decide to bring about a change in regime by force; this only makes sense if Iran continues to pursue the acquisition of nuclear weapons.

The break-up of the Libyan consortium of Arab states seeking a clandestine nuclear weapons programme, and Saddam Hussein's removal that catalysed that break-up, have made such a resolution possible—but only possible. It would take imaginative and courageous political leadership in several capitals to make this a reality. Otherwise, there will inevitably come a day of reckoning when more states in the world's least stable region acquire the world's most dangerous weapons.

Part 2
The Three Global Scenarios

3 Low Trust Globalisation

4 Open Doors

5 Flags

6 Trilemmaps

Russia is under less pressure than in the *Open Doors* scenario (see next chapter) to bring its own standards and practices in line with the EU—or for that matter the WTO —and the thrust for reform of the state is reduced. It pursues economic and administrative modernisation but political reform stalls.

China sees this legalistic world as an opportunity to achieve integration with the global market in ways that minimise foreign pressures and let her achieve some extra-territorial influence. The licensing processes needed to gain access to the Chinese market involve adherence to transparency rules on technology as well as on IP sharing rules that border on 'taxes payable in IP'. Most enterprises have little choice but to strengthen their legal defences and accept, but others see that they would put their own survival at stake and reassess the overall risk and reward equation for the Chinese market. Here again, coercion is applied under the umbrella of market incentives. This combination of strong market incentives and coercion typifies *Low Trust Globalisation* along with the skilful use of legal uncertainty, which emerges as a "speciality" of the Chinese in this scenario.

Realpolitik, and a de-nuclearised Middle East?
While this is a world that is neither idealistic nor trustful, *realpolitik*, combined with strong market incentives, can provide a good foundation for global governance. The threats of a nuclear arms race in the Middle East can be met, in this world, in ways different from a pre-emptive attack by US or Israeli forces on Iranian nuclear facilities. As described by Philip Bobbitt (see box), a combination of guarantees by the US, of economic and technical assistance by the EU, and of sober calculations in Tehran and Jerusalem could lead to Iran foregoing the development of WMDs and to Israel following "the South African route", a metaphor for dismantling nuclear capacities that have not been acknowledged but are known to exist.

Globalisation

> **The licensing processes needed to gain access to the Chinese market involve adherence to transparency rules on technology as well as on IP sharing rules that border on 'taxes payable in IP'.**

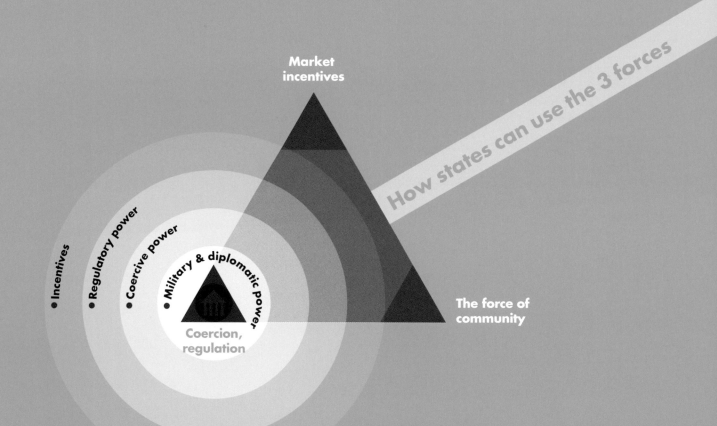

Market
incentives

How states can use the 3 forces

- Incentives
- Regulatory power
- Coercive power
- Military & diplomatic power

Coercion,
regulation

The force of
community

Part 2

The Three Global Scenarios

3 Low Trust Globalisation

4 Open Doors

5 Flags

6 Trilemmaps

Globalisation

Global commons: a narrow view

Against this background, international politics is far from harmonious, leaving little room for grandiose common objectives. As an alternative to fully developed international institutions, UN organisations and NGOs work closely with investors and with private charities to gather the necessary resources to pursue their aims. Protection of the global commons is only pursued to the extent that it does not conflict with major national interests. Issues such as pollution and global warming are dealt with on a crisis-by-crisis basis—resulting in high insurance premiums—rather than proactively. Conflicts over water develop— between, for example, the energy-rich, water-poor countries and the water-rich, energy-poor countries of central Asia—with no properly functioning regional or international frameworks in which to seek resolution.

Opportunistic alliances

On matters of war and peace, international alliances also tend to exhibit low trust. The creation of "coalitions of the willing" becomes an acceptable way of working on common problems, and this fosters opportunistic strategies as well as pragmatic solutions. Over the long term, the lack of broader principles of legitimacy tends to increase the costs and limit the efficiency of these pragmatic solutions.

While the US remains dominant, and the EU Common Foreign and Security Policy remains unambitious, China continues to develop a far-reaching network of implicit and explicit mutual obligations. This makes China an indispensable international partner on a broad range of issues, particularly because "coalitions of the willing" established by the US rest on only partial legitimacy. In the second half of the period, China expresses increasingly assertive views, whether on the resources of the South China Sea or on the need for Taiwan to fully integrate with the mainland. The expiration in 2012 of the ten-year agreement reached among ASEAN countries and China on November 4, 2002, to "exercise self-restraint" regarding territorial disputes in the South China Sea marks the beginning of increased tensions in the region.

Reduced aid, and cautious foreign investment in poorer countries

Economic support to developing countries is largely provided on a bilateral basis. While strategically important countries can count on unconditional support, non-strategic countries are supported, if at all, only under strict conditions. Performance criteria focus less on traditional macroeconomic indicators, as they do today under IMF-supported programmes, and more on governance issues. However, since overall development assistance is reduced, the incentive for governments in the developing world to support pro-business reforms is diminished. Importantly, there is less progress on trade issues.

Overall, the industrialised countries' commitment to development— encompassing aid, open borders, environment, foreign investment, migration and peace-keeping—slips from levels seen at the beginning of the 21st century. The "Millennium Development Goals"—an ambitious commitment by the 191 members of the UN to reduce by half the proportion of people living on less than one US dollar a day by 2015—are not being achieved. Foreign trade remains the single most important contributor to international development, despite relatively slow progress in trade liberalisation. Security concerns and peace-keeping tend to weigh more than development concerns in foreign aid. In contrast, migration diminishes in importance both relative to other North–South flows and in absolute terms.

A home bias exists with regard to foreign investment, reflecting institutional and jurisdictional discontinuities which prevent investors from fully exploiting potential diversification gains. These discontinuities heighten regulatory risks, in response to which companies also become more home-market-oriented, a number of medium-sized companies opting to de-list from US exchanges.

Foreign investment may be prohibited for security reasons. Trade sanctions are prevalent and imposed on any country that is perceived to pose a security threat. Export controls do not disappear, even if their scope tends to be limited. Companies and asset managers must ascertain for themselves that the countries in which they invest meet the acceptability criteria defined by those groups or countries with the capacity to sue or to coerce. Laws restricting outside investment have *de facto* global reach. If, for instance, a US company is not allowed to invest in a particular country, then any country which allows its companies to invest there may be subjected to economic sanctions. Trade and investment thus become more tightly integrated with foreign policy.

Since the terrorist attacks of 9.11 the US has imposed tight restrictions on immigration. Between 2001 and 2003, the number of non-immigrant visas issued fell by more than a third. Restrictions have even been imposed on citizens of countries that are part of the US Visa Waiver Program. From the end of October 2004, such persons have had to carry computer readable passports in order to enter the US under the programme and biometric passports will be required by 2006.

What has been the impact of these controls? According to the Travel Industry Association, the decline in international travel has cost the US economy USD15.3 billion between 2001 and 2004. A June 2004 report by the Washington-based consultancy firm the Santangelo Group concluded that, in the eight months to March 2004, US firms were hit by direct and indirect costs of USD 30.7 billion due to visa delays or denials.

Tight visa controls have had a particularly sharp impact on students travelling to the US to undertake study. According to the General Accounting Office (an agency of the US Congress), who randomly selected a sample of science-student visa applicants in mid-2003, the average time to process a visa application requiring a security review was 67 days. Another reason for delays is that most non-immigrant visa applicants, including students, now require an interview at a US consulate. Delays and difficulties in acquiring visas may be partly responsible for a fall in the number of students seeking to study in the US. A Council of Graduate Schools survey found that there was a drop of 32% in international applications to US universities between 2003 and 2004. Such trends could have an impact on the productivity of the US economy, as a significant proportion of US scientists and engineers are foreign-born.

International migration as an economic policy matter

Migration is restricted, ostensibly for security reasons, with tightened controls on the movement of people. Low levels of official immigration do not prevent illegal immigration from continuing to grow. Nevertheless, the UN forecasts, which anticipate a net inflow to Europe (excluding Eastern Europe) of more than 32 million people by 2050, or more than 650,000 per year, turn out to be over-generous. Similarly, net inflows to North America remain well below present UN forecasts of roughly 1.3 million people per year. While the migrant stock in the world's population continues to increase from an estimated 175 million in 2000, in relative terms it falls back from 2.9% to around 2.5%—its level in the mid-1970s.

With tight restrictions in place, the inflow of foreign workers remains much too small to offset the rapid decline in the workforce in countries such as Germany, Italy and Japan. While selective official immigration is allowed where skilled labour is seen by governments to aid national competitiveness—albeit only on a temporary basis—no "global labour market" emerges. In individual cases, migrant workers' remittances continue to play an important role, but, on a global scale, they fall short of developing countries' needs (see also chapter 10).

With many countries facing huge challenges with regard to their social security systems, portable pensions across borders remain a distant goal—even within the EU. The pension roadblock thus continues to undermine one of the main goals of the Union, namely to create a fully open and flexible labour market. The agreement to allow pension funds to operate on equal terms in all member countries by 2005 is as far as policymakers are willing to go. Needless to say, different regulations and tax treatments prevent international companies from setting up single global pension funds, which would allow employees to take their pensions across borders.

Part 2

The Three Global Scenarios

3 *Low Trust Globalisation*

4 *Open Doors*

5 *Flags*

6 *Trilemmaps*

3.4
Economic growth in *Low Trust Globalisation*

An important trait of the global economy in this highly regulated and controlled world is the gap between the potential for full trade integration and the actual level of movements of goods, financial assets and people.

Low Trust Globalisation is still a world in which trade between a US state and the neighbouring Canadian province or Mexican state remains far lower than between two domestic states or provinces. Investments—like people—travel, but following stringent rules and controls put in place to ensure transparency and to enhance security. Innovation is also not achieving its full potential: while much fundamental research is still conducted cooperatively, the increased institutional discontinuities and curtailed movement of goods and people limit the free movement of knowledge. Sensitivities about security put a lid on the sharing of information.

This departure from a fully efficient allocation of resources (e.g. goods, financial assets and people) as well as knowledge, as a result of institutional discontinuities, has a negative impact on productivity levels.

As a result, the average growth rate in *Low Trust Globalisation* is below 3% for the 2004–2015 period, after which it adjusts to around, or slightly above, 3% (real GDP at market rates). Europe is the area that suffers most. Growth rates stagnate around 2%, far from the levels achievable under full integration. The US adapts better, settling on growth levels in the 3% range, only slightly outperforming global growth levels.

Among the emerging markets, China and India are by far the most boisterous, with growth levels averaging 7.5% and 6.7% respectively. Still, this is roughly one percentage point lower than the average growth rates in the highest growth scenario, *Open Doors*. The reduction in trade levels takes its toll over growth rates in these two countries, the economies of which rely largely on exports to the US, Europe and Asia.

Brazil, Russia and Mexico are the emerging markets that suffer most in this scenario, mainly due to difficulties in integrating their economic systems into the highly regulated trade arena. In the financial markets, these countries tend to carry a significant risk premium: on average more than 300 basis points over US Treasury bonds, adding hindrance to economic growth. This is due to the limited role played by institutions like the IMF in maintaining stability in these markets. Nevertheless, real long-term interest rates are likely to be high even in the US: the model predicts that they will be slightly above 3% on average over the period of analysis (i.e. above 5% in nominal terms).

Some countries, such as China and India, will catch up in the scenario, thus reducing inequality between countries. Yet—at least in the short run—life is more difficult for the people at the bottom of the distribution ladder, as they have to rely on market forces to lift them out of poverty. This implies that inequality within countries is likely to increase in this scenario, with fewer opportunities for social mobility.

The economic environment briefly described here represents the baseline of the scenario. At this stage neither individual crises nor the business cycle have been taken into consideration modelling the growth pattern. Crises can then be superimposed onto the baseline to generate a full volatility profile.

Economic growth

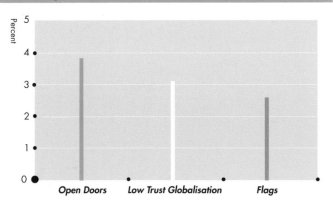

Economic growth in the three *Global Scenarios*

FOCUS

Energy security driving policies in *Low Trust Globalisation*: the EU signpost

1

Green Paper: Towards a European Strategy for the Security of Energy Supply, European Commision, Luxembourg, 2001.

California's energy crisis in 2000, and blackouts that have occurred since then in the US and Europe, are reminders that botched deregulation and privatisation of energy markets in pursuit of short-lived price benefits to consumers can lead to underinvestment in energy infrastructure.

Increasing import dependence from more challenging, less familiar non-OECD supply sources and the uncertainty over the estimated hydrocarbon reserves of these regions raise a number of concerns regarding energy use, mix and diversification in consuming nations.

More investment will be needed to produce and transport the volumes of hydrocarbons that will be needed in the future. This requires a reliable and equitable platform of cooperation, based on international law, between producers and consumers. In addition, it is clearly understood in this scenario that shipping, pipelines and transmission links are vulnerable to acts of sabotage and terrorism.

Developed as well as developing nations, in their roles as both consumers and producers of energy, are equally worried about energy security and its impact on their economies. The EU example is worth reflecting upon.

Future hydrocarbon supply becomes more risky

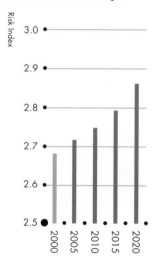

Source: WMRC and Shell estimates

The changing energy profile of the EU

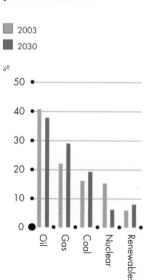

The European Commission's Green Paper on a European Strategy for Energy Security[1]

The Commission states that *"security of supply does not seek to maximise energy self-sufficiency or to minimise dependence, but aims to reduce the risks linked to such dependence."* But in achieving this objective, the following challenges arise:

• Hydrocarbon dependence is high in all sectors of the economy, and especially in transport.

• The expected fall in nuclear energy use will be to the detriment of energy security and greenhouse gas emissions.

• 45% of oil imports come from the Middle East and 40% of natural gas from Russia. This dependence calls for a strategy of geographical diversification. As Winston Churchill put it on the eve of World War II, *"safety and certainty in oil lie in variety and variety alone."*

• The liberalisation of the energy sector has led to a more competitive European internal market and is changing the competitiveness of coal, nuclear energy and renewables relative to natural gas and oil.

Because the EU has no major indigenous resources to draw upon, beyond nuclear and renewables, and because of the limited options that exist to diversify the supply of hydrocarbons, the EU recognises it will have to lay more emphasis on demand

policy. A real change in consumer behaviour is therefore called for, for example, via taxation to steer demand towards sustainable options such as renewables.

The Commission calls for the doubling of the share of renewables in energy supply from 6% to 12% by 2010. It also calls for steady increase in the percentage of biofuel in transportation fuels. It recommends financial measures, in the form of aid, tax incentives and financial support from profitable energies, such as oil and gas, to achieve these ambitious aims.

Progress that reinforces the impact of this strategy must be encouraged, notably by creating markets of a sufficient size for a new technology, and encouraging increased efficiency of engines and fuels.

The Green Paper also stresses that the Union needs a stronger mechanism to build up strategic stocks of oil and gas, and to open new import routes.

Interestingly, one can observe that the massive efforts called for to develop renewable energy sources will be more than offset—when it comes to energy self-sufficiency and to reduction in carbon emissions—by the planned decline in nuclear power generation.

Part 2
The Three Global Scenarios

3 Low Trust Globalisation

4 Open Doors

5 Flags

6 Trilemmaps

3.5

The energy scene in *Low Trust Globalisation*[1]

Low Trust Globalisation sees market forces and government regulation or coercion shaping the energy system. States use market incentives as much as possible to achieve their objectives, but they do not shy away from more coercive measures when higher order policy objectives are at stake. This is the case for energy security, an essential public good that looms large in this scenario.

Despite the general push for energy efficiency, strong growth in developing economies such as China, India and Brazil results in energy demand growth of about 2.3% per annum. Note that this is via 0.6% growth in developed economies and 3.5% growth in developing economies.

Security of supply, competition and energy conservation: the energy policy mix

In *Low Trust Globalisation*, the mix of market and coercive measures that is the hallmark of the scenario implies that many public goods such as energy security are delivered through market-oriented mechanisms but under strict government supervision.

Energy security is considered fundamental to both national security and domestic prosperity, and growing import dependency worries many states. Energy conservation and diversification of supply, in terms of geographical spread and energy mix, are also encouraged by policy and regulatory instruments. Greater interconnection between consumer and producer nations—meaning tighter economic interdependence as well as pipelines or power lines—is favoured to reinforce a sustainable basis for long-term stability and social cohesion. Governments agree to promote regional interconnectivity of gas and electricity networks, but shy away from full cross-border integration.

Recent EU policies are a good illustration of what can be expected in *Low Trust Globalisation*, and notably of the role of demand policies once policies to diversify supply reach their limits (see box).

Energy

> ❛ **Energy security must be a priority of US trade and foreign policy. We must look beyond our borders and restore America's credibility with overseas suppliers. In addition we must build strong relationships with energy-producing nations in our own hemisphere, improving the outlook for trade, investment, and reliable supplies.** ❜
>
> George W. Bush, May 2001

1

This section draws on the integrated perspective on energy, energy security and the energy-and-carbon industry which we present in the concluding chapters.

A stringent regulatory environment for energy

In *Low Trust Globalisation*, a stringent regulatory environment develops around the triple objectives of fostering competition, ensuring security of supply and protecting end-consumers. The short-term focus of markets leaves little room for maintaining backups in the energy system or the timely development of new infrastructure, which fosters further regulation. This regulation remains continuously in flux, with frequent ex-post adjustments by powerful regulators.

Convergence of regulatory standards is significant in certain regions, when it is supported by governments or industry as they pursue interconnection and efficiency. Environmental objectives become increasingly integrated into energy regulation, pushed by active NGOs and the media, who demand a larger role at the interface between government, the public and the market place.

Taxing times for the environment

A wide range of indigenous resources, especially renewables, see their production stimulated through tax incentives and market instruments. In some regions, coal or unconventional resources are increasingly used, in conjunction with developments in clean technology and CO_2 abatement programmes. Many countries pursue the reduction of national greenhouse gas emissions and encourage the development of alternative energy sources, notably wind and solar energy, as well as energy efficiency via hybrid and fuel cell vehicles. Yet there is little international coordination outside the EU.

International carbon permits are mistrusted and do not set a level playing field for a competitive industry between countries. Governments tend to prefer to use carbon taxes as a way of controlling demand and emissions; the more so as they also provide a welcome addition to the tax base. Trading in CO_2 permits continues, nevertheless, around the EU Emissions Trading Scheme (ETS). When regional expansion of such regimes occurs, it is through the grouping of national systems.

Complex energy markets

As a result of this combination of state control, stringent regulation and reliance on market forces, a full spectrum of market forms coexist—from fully liberalised to only partly liberalised. Uncertainties in the rules of market liberalisation and environmental regulation create delays and added costs. Large incumbent companies respond by integrating vertically and horizontally, within the limits set by competition law in their respective countries—with energy security often calling for more lenient applications of such limits.

National companies need to be competitive

National oil or energy companies (NOCs) are looked to by their governments to deliver energy security. *Low Trust Globalisation*, however, is a world in which they are increasingly held accountable to market principles, and the competition of international companies (IOCs) is encouraged—although not everywhere. In OPEC countries, IOCs and non-national NOCs are invited to bid for niche and non-strategic investments, usually under tough terms in an attempt to relieve budget pressures, secure demand and siphon international capital away from investments in non-OPEC countries.

Gas markets develop on a regional basis

Gas demand growth is strong at 3.1%—as in the other scenarios this is particularly true of the power sector. Gas is soon to overtake coal in the primary energy mix. Despite regional interconnection by pipelines and new LNG terminals, gas markets remain regional and tied in to long-term contracts, with only a limited spot market developing—except in the US.

In the US, in spite of an increasing focus on security of supply, concerns about physical security and environmental issues lead to greater regulatory and public scrutiny, slowing the progress of major new import projects. Despite growing challenges in meeting demand, and with higher costs of indigenous supply pushing up prices in real terms, there remains strong political and regulatory opposition to opening up new federal land to exploration in environmentally sensitive regions. Building new import facilities for LNG is not plain sailing either, but sufficient LNG import capacity is developed to allieviate the delays in access to indigenous resources.

The Three Global Scenarios

Part 2

3 *Low Trust Globalisation*

4 *Open Doors*

5 *Flags*

6 *Trilemmaps*

Energy

In the EU, the focus is on expanding and diversifying energy infrastructure. This is done by connecting member states' systems to enhance energy security, and by locking the Union in to major producing countries through infrastructure, with long-term supply contracts under competitive pricing mechanisms. Demand policies are tightened as the limits of supply diversification are reached (see box p. 66).

In Russia, an internal gas market develops with competitive pricing covering economic costs. A change in the law establishes the role of private Russian companies, giving them access to transmission and distribution networks. Nevertheless, Gazprom's role as monopolistic sales agent for all (new) Russian gas exports remains firmly established, under the Kremlin's control.

Similarly, China offers long-term bilateral deals for gas, but prefers pipeline gas over LNG. Markets throughout the value chain open up, but joint ventures with Chinese NOCs are still a precondition for participation.

Coal dominates the power market

Coal maintains its market share at around 23%. For countries like China that are rich in coal, this resource alleviates energy security concerns. However, in China, this results in major logistical problems—coal already absorbs 60% of Chinese rail freight traffic capacities. New clean technology (e.g. Integrated Gasification Combined Cycle (IGCC) and CO_2 sequestration) facilitates its use in the power sector, while Coal-to-Liquids (CTL) technology does so in the transport sector (see box p. 70).

More demand for renewables/indigenous resources develops, stimulated by government policy, particularly in Europe. Renewables grow by more then 10% per annum and gradually achieve close to 5% market share by 2025 in *Low Trust Globalisation*. After hydro, wind is the fastest growing renewable, followed by solar energy. Solar photovoltaic (PV) rapidly develops, at a rate of almost four times that of solar thermal, as PV provides extensive distributed and centralised power generation solutions. Ocean energy, predominantly from waves and tidal flows, sees increased installed capacity over this period.

> **Many countries pursue the reduction of national greenhouse gas emissions and encourage the development of alternative energy sources, notably wind and solar … Yet there is little international coordination outside the EU. Carbon taxes are preferred to carbon permits.**

Focus

1

Rob Routs, Executive
Director Downstream,
Royal Dutch/Shell Group,
"Seizing opportunities in
the future fuels market",
The National Ethanol
Conference, Arizona, 8th
February, 2005.

Gas to liquids

A major challenge in the development of energy resources is to unlock gas reserves that are far from the consumer markets. Building pipelines and developing Liquefied Natural Gas (LNG) are currently the two main ways to deliver gas. The conversion of Gas to Liquids (GTL) opens a third major avenue.

GTL technology makes possible the transformation of gas into liquid products that are more easily transported. The resulting products are of a high quality and can be used as a stand-alone fuel or blended with diesel, allowing use in unmodified vehicles and distribution via existing infrastructure. This eases introduction and contributes to security and diversity of supply.

The Fischer-Tropsch process

The Fischer-Tropsch process underpins all the "to-liquids" technologies (GTL, CTL, BTL). It was named after its inventors and was developed in Germany in the 1920s. It uses catalytic reactions to synthesise complex hydrocarbons from simpler organic chemicals. Resulting fuels ("liquid") are of high homogeneity and quality. GTL fuel, for instance, provides significantly lower emissions of local pollutants, such as particulates, carbon monoxide, hydrocarbons and nitrogen oxides, even when compared to sulphur-free diesel.

Fischer-Tropsch Process

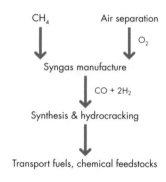

Coal to Liquids and Biomass to Liquids

Coal to Liquids (CTL) generates more CO_2 than GTL and may require CO_2 capture and sequestration to be compatible with CO_2 emissions objectives (see chapter 13). Biomass to Liquids (BTL) is still at an early stage of development. CTL and BTL will develop more quickly if increasing concerns about energy security make countries decide to maximise utilisation of their indigenous resources, as is the case in *Low Trust Globalisation* and *Flags*.

Shell's activities

Shell has pioneered the development of GTL technologies and has operated a medium scale 14,700 bbl/day GTL plant at Bintulu, Malaysia, since 1993. Retail sales of blended GTL fuel with standard diesel have been successfully launched by Shell in Asia and in Europe, contributing to reduced local emissions and to improved engine efficiency. A major Shell GTL project is now under way in Qatar. GTL is produced using the Shell patented Shell Middle Distillate Synthesis Process, a process that can equally be applied to coal and to biomass.[1]

Part 2

The Three Global Scenarios

3 Low Trust Globalisation

4 Open Doors

5 Flags

6 Trilemmaps

Nuclear power generation loses market share, as a result of unfavourable economics and government policies. These develop in response to public opposition. Alternative developments, however, are possible, depending on progress regarding waste disposal and on the development of third and fourth generation nuclear power plants.

The transportation sector fuels oil demand, but alternatives to oil develop

In *Low Trust Globalisation*, oil demand continues to grow at around 1.5% per annum. Oil remains the dominant global fuel, yet alternative fuels and improving energy efficiency, particularly in transport, eat into its market share.

Rapid growth in key emerging countries drives the world growth in transportation needs. Meanwhile, neither congestion charging nor innovative urban planning and transportation systems significantly reduce transportation growth in the developed world. Yet the steady gains in market share of hybrid and diesel-engine vehicles, supported by the use of biofuels, GTL and CTL, increase the oil efficiency of the transportation sector (see box).

Fuel cell vehicles are encouraged by governments, initially as environmentally friendly demonstrator projects. These projects boost confidence around refuelling and infrastructure issues, and this leads to growth in the use of fuel cells after 2010. The production of hydrogen and power from dirty coal is discouraged, as more environmentally friendly solutions are sought, such as from gas and renewables.

Cohesive, proactive OPEC

OPEC countries seek to reach their budget targets through a combination of higher prices and slight increases in production to accommodate the less disciplined members, even at the cost of stagnating market shares. The OPEC cartel is cohesive and perceived as proactive, and has its eye firmly on short-term income maximisation.

Russia does not join OPEC, but does act in accordance with its objectives, reinforcing the cartel's market power. The instruments for this implicit coordination are "high-level dialogues" and state control

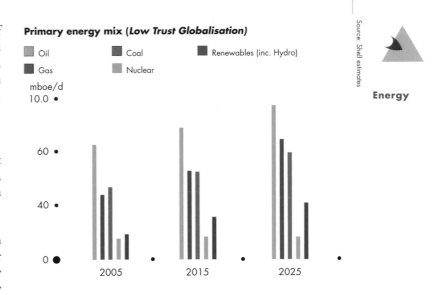

Primary energy mix (*Low Trust Globalisation*)

- Oil
- Gas
- Coal
- Nuclear
- Renewables (inc. Hydro)

mboe/d

Source: Shell estimates

Energy

over Russian exports via export infrastructure, licensing or other political means.

The US needs oil prices to stay high enough to stimulate indigenous oil and gas production, and does not object to OPEC's stance, so long as its own domestic economic growth remains strong.

A high-oil-price world

This scenario sees higher oil prices in real terms than in the past, and higher oil prices than the other two scenarios.

With these high oil prices, more expensive oil-producing areas can continue to be developed and non-OPEC supply growth initially leaves little room for OPEC growth. However, based on the currently known resource base, we can expect non-OPEC oil production growth to slow down and level off during the second decade. As a result, around 2010, OPEC market share and production begin to grow steadily. With a firmer grip on the market, OPEC members can aim for higher oil prices.

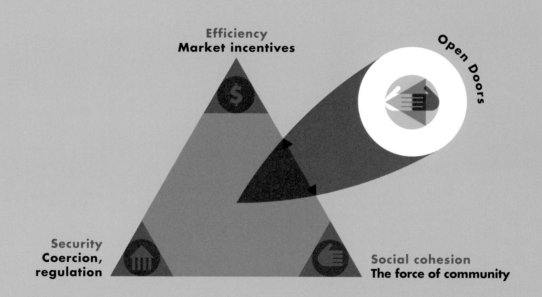

Efficiency
Market incentives

Open Doors

Security
**Coercion,
regulation**

Social cohesion
The force of community

Part 2
The Three Global Scenarios

3 Low Trust Globalisation

4 Open Doors

5 Flags

6 Trilemmaps

Chapter 4

Open Doors

The scenario in a nutshell: "Incentives and Bridges"

Open Doors, like *Low Trust Globalisation*, is a world in which globalisation progresses further. It is also a world in which civil societies in different countries are reassured that their fundamental values can be affirmed and strengthened, not only domestically but across borders, and in conjunction with market forces. However, for all its emphasis on web-like technologies, cooperative links, seamless transnational operations and citizens' empowerment, this is not a *laissez-faire* world.

The dual crisis of trust and security has been resolved, or rather kept in check, by the development of a web of security-enhancing and trust-building procedures—procedures which come "built-in" rather than "bolt-on", as is the case for both the other *Global Scenarios*. Security concerns are high and, while the emphasis is on prevention, efforts are made to keep checks and controls non-intrusive. The same is true in the marketplace, where appropriate credentials and reputation can ensure trust, and the transactional space is structured around procedures and interactions that take issues of security and integrity into consideration. Indeed, a whole industry is at work certifying, assessing and promoting trust-enhancing norms and initiatives. This "trust value-chain" smoothes the way for a sense of "global community".

A culture of open accountability

Many governance institutions behind *Open Doors* are of a private and voluntary nature. States and regulators, however, develop a special knack for fostering and channelling these private initiatives. Participation and the opportunity to be heard become widely accepted elements of good governance, in the corporate as well as governmental setting. The right to "voice"—to have one's concerns and values factored into a decision-making process—becomes a common norm among investors, consumers, civil society leaders and governments. A culture of accountability develops as the common reference for these hybrid (public and private) modes of governance.

Government welfare provision in *Open Doors* is based on redistributing opportunities rather than assets. It is focused, for instance, on retraining people who have fallen into unemployment, rather than on granting unemployment benefits indiscriminately. This involves more than a basic safety net, as society provides services to open the doors of the labour market to the unskilled. In *Open Doors*, it is often civil society organisations, in cooperation with companies and government agencies, that provide a number of public goods, with the aim, for instance, of overcoming social exclusion.

Civil society is also a source of supervision and screening, and assesses contributions by companies and government towards shared goals, as well as towards specific causes embraced by influential groups. Faith-based organisations (FBOs) play a large role in the process, notably in the US.

The scenario in a nutshell

1

Ralph Welborn and

Vince Kasten,

The Jericho Principle:

How Companies use

Strategic Collaboration

to Find New Sources

of Value, John Wiley &

Sons, Inc., New York,

April 2003.

2

Richard Normann,

Rafael Ramirez, *Designing*

Interactive Strategy: From

Value Chain to Value

Constellation, John Wiley

& Sons Ltd, Chichester,

October 30, 1998.

3

2003 Report on Socially

Responsible Investing

Trends in the US,

The Social Investment

Forum, 2004.

4.1

The market, civil society and governance
in *Open Doors*

A culture of openness, under strong media scrutiny

Companies, civil society organisations, faith-based organisations (FBOs) and governments work in an increasingly overlapping and integrated manner. Indeed, the closeness of their interactions, and the access they grant one another to their results, objectives and opinions, is why this world is perceived as one of *open doors*. This is a shareholders' and stakeholders' world in which participatory processes are widespread, principles of legitimacy widely shared and consensus valued. To find doors open, however, one must be ready to open one's own door—which can absorb time and resources. In defining "time to market", companies are well advised to include "time to consensus" and "time to implementation"!

While a number of groups take more restrictive views, a culture of openness is shared widely enough to provide the set of references needed for this more complex division of labour between market, civil society and state. The individual plays a central role, even though there are still precise rules and processes. This is a world of multiple identities and multiple "belonging". Companies are reconciled to the fact that they receive only partial loyalty from employees who are also members of FBOs, NGOs, civil groups and polling networks, each tracking good and bad governance. Yet openness and freedom are neither unchallenged nor unchecked. The media, themselves subject to scrutiny from society, play an essential part in empowering stakeholders to hold companies, governments, individuals—and even NGOs—accountable for the initiatives they take, or fail to take. Their role as the "fourth power" is one that leaders in all spheres take very seriously indeed.

Co-production, built-in trust mechanisms
and the "Jericho Principle"

"Built-in" rather than "bolt-on" technology plays a key role in automatic processes that ensure higher levels of security and trust. Smart bar codes, global tracking, databases and many other techniques are called upon to minimise interferences and delays. Similarly, legal techniques based on standardisation and mutual recognition ensure

that operations that occur across different jurisdictions are no more costly than those which occur in a single jurisdiction.

What Ralph Welborn and Vince Kasten call the "Jericho Principle"[1] is fully applicable to this scenario. Just as in the Biblical story when Joshua had trumpets played around the besieged city of Jericho and the walls fell, the barriers between companies, as well as across economies, have crumbled. People seek self-fulfilment as well as employability through horizontal links with peers, professional communities and other groups in society who share values and interests that are relevant to the workplace.

Companies display greater confidence, therefore, in entering joint ventures and in working as members of consortia. Inter-operability, partnering and virtual teams are increasingly common. Instead of the vertical and horizontal integration typical of *Low Trust Globalisation*, this is a world in which the "value web"[2] assumes its full meaning: co-production is a well-supported strategy for value maximisation. This in turn leaves greater room for new entrants and SMEs—as long as they can set up and manage the appropriate connections.

Investors and stakeholders resorting to "Voice"
as well as to "Exit"

Investors seek to maximise value over the long term and are prepared to give companies adequate time to restructure and implement value-maximising strategies. Hence the many forms of dialogue between organisations in which market participants need to engage. Here, too, the "co-production" of value brings together companies, investors, investment banks and NGOs. Establishing the right connection with investors has become standard practice for NGOs, many of which are staffed by executives seconded from private companies.

Ethical investing and Socially Responsible Investing (which accounted for 11% of assets under management in the US in 2003) continue to develop.[3] Corporate social responsibility matters to investors, for normative as well as functional reasons. This is part of a broader trend, not always a source of harmony, whereby personal accountability is high, with employees as well as employers taken to court. Companies need to be clear on their mission and on their values if they are to preserve employees' loyalty, develop customers' commitment, and

Part 2

The Three Global Scenarios

3 Low Trust Globalisation

4 Open Doors

5 Flags

6 Trilemmaps

Trilemma **relations**

retain their corporate identities. Reporting to the market goes beyond financial reporting to include significant voluntary disclosure, which is often done in conjunction with like-minded companies. The asset-management community is influenced by these many horizontal and professional networks in which reputations are tracked, checked and challenged. Security and trust, in other words, are "co-produced" between companies and investors, civil society and the market, employees and employers. Co-branding is highly developed, as reputation is systematically valued and leveraged.

Thus, compared with *Low Trust Globalisation*, *Open Doors* can be described as a more "ethical" world. This is not because people are fundamentally different in *Open Doors*, but because this scenario is in the part of the *Trilemma Triangle* in which values can be affirmed as part of pro-market "win–wins". In the absence of the overly legalistic mandatory requirements and regulations of *Low Trust Globalisation*, companies have wide discretion over the ethical choices they face.

Regulatory 'co-opetition'

In this world, 'regulatory co-opetition' emerges strongly—blending elements of competition and cooperation among regulators, as states endeavour to provide a better market environment globally. Regulatory negotiation is common as NGOs, industry groups and regulators work together to set standards.

With reputation a distinctive competitive asset, companies often find it to their business advantage to be out in front of the established requirements. With a prevailing social context that values good citizenship—and in order that a number of "open doors" do not close to them—many businesses voluntarily adopt high environmental, health and safety standards. A significant element of regulation centres on data production, disclosure and validation. Under this "information regulation" model, governments simply mandate (and audit) the publication of relevant data such as metrics of environmental performance. The market punishes those seen to be lagging.

Regulation is about processes and outcomes, rather than targets, which increases opportunities for differences to coexist in a spirit of mutual recognition.

A risk-averse world supported by the value chain of trust

Trust is restored not by regulatory fiat but as a result of a variety of private schemes to inspect and certify, label and advertise, and insure and remedy.

Insurance companies have clout and influence rivalling that of investment banks. A comprehensive regulatory framework is in place —this is not the Shell *Just Do It!* scenario of 1995 by any means— but it largely reflects demands and lobbying from social groups rather than the imposition of norms and standards by the state. Strict rules guarantee professional standards. Few projects are undertaken without a whole gamut of impact assessments and diligent checks being carried out. Identities are easy to ascertain, as trusted third parties keep records of who is really behind an "electronic address" or a corporate structure. Whether as employee, producer or even customer, one is accountable to these rules.

In this world, companies' reputations depend not on the decisions of courts, but on opinions in society. Customers, stakeholders and companies are inclined to rely on networks within which bad reputation is quickly spread on a peer-to-peer basis—on the model of the eBay "power seller" system.

Reputation management is key, therefore, and this leads companies to be more risk-averse. While the courts are used less aggressively than in *Low Trust Globalisation*, interest groups and transnational coalitions turn to them to affirm principles that they value, rather than to achieve specific monetary returns from legal action. States put strict limits on damages that can be awarded, and elaborate insurance schemes develop in the shadow of a widely applied precautionary principle as envisioned by the EU. Mediation and arbitration are valued alternatives to lawsuits. True, this implies accepting some risk that the other parties will not abide by the mediation, but that risk is partly kept in check by the cost that opportunistic behaviours would exact in this world.

Signposts

From municipal waste to multicultural banking: signposts towards an _Open Doors_ context

1
British economist James Tobin proposed the injection of "a grain of sand" in the wheels of potentially disruptive speculation, in the form of a tax on short-term cross-border capital flows. While Tobin himself disavowed the schemes proposed decades later by anti-globalisation movements, a "Tobin tax" is often presented as a way to fund development programmes while preventing speculators from thwarting government efforts to focus on long-term needs. In France, the ATTAC movement has successfully placed this proposal on the policy agenda as part of the G-8 Evian summit preparation process.

To reduce the amount of household waste that citizens generate (which in Europe is increasing by 10% every five years), the city of Zurich—as well as German cities like Dresden—combine market incentives, smart technology and municipal oversight.

The Zuri-Sack cost 5 Swiss Francs (USD 4.3) each, and they are the only accepted receptacle for trash disposal. Meanwhile smart codes and investigation systems for unidentified bags enable the city authorities to fine offenders. As a result of this typical _Open Doors_ approach, a well accepted one in German-speaking Europe, town dwellers have significantly reduced the burden they impose on municipal waste collection and processing capacities: the average Zurich family produces only one Zuri-Sack a week and municipal waste has decreased by 40% since 1992.

On October 6, 2004, the EU Commission released a report on Turkey's bid to join the EU that opened the way for Turkish accession negotiations to begin.

The report's recommendations were made after Turkey had implemented substantial legislative changes in order to meet EU standards on human rights, the rule of law and democracy. Turkey has also agreed not to incorporate some legal approaches derived from Islamic Sharia law into its civil code, most notably in relation to adultery.

On December 17, the European Council agreed that Turkey sufficiently fulfils the Copenhagen political criteria to open negotiations regarding its accession to the EU. Political leaders stress that this was a sign that people of different faiths can live in harmony and build a common destiny.

In a conference ahead of the UN General Assembly of September 2004, Brazilian president Lula da Silva and French president Jacques Chirac proposed that the USD 50 billion that UN officials believe is needed to tackle poverty could be financed by some form of global tax mechanism such as those advocated in a number of countries—on credit card purchases, airline tickets, arms sales or greenhouse gas emissions, for example. In the past, France has also promoted the idea that such a move could incorporate a "Tobin tax" on speculative capital movements.[1]

Speaking at Davos in January 2005, and at a Franco-Japanese economic forum in March 2005, President Chirac proposed the creation of a levy to finance the fight against AIDS. He suggested it could take the form of a tax on financial transactions or fuel for air and sea transport or flows of capital entering or leaving the tax havens. Another option, he suggested, would be to levy USD1 on every airline ticket.

The Western banking sector is building bridges in the financial world to gain greater access to the assets of Muslims. In accordance with Sharia law, which forbids a fixed rate of return on capital, a bank bases its operations on the sharing of investment risk with its customers. Several large multinational banks such as HSBC, Citigroup and UBS have Islamic subsidiaries and Singapore has announced intentions to promote Islamic banking products as part of its campaign to promote its status as a financial hub.

Part 2
The Three Global Scenarios

3 Low Trust Globalisation

4 Open Doors

5 Flags

6 Trilemmaps

The Precautionary Principle

Reflecting this search for "built-in" approaches to security, as well as the significant risk aversion of many, the Precautionary Principle with its bias toward the *status quo* is widely applied to provide people with a stronger feeling of security in a complex, open environment.

This trend is particularly noticeable in relation to environmental concerns and it acts as a disincentive for innovation, most notably in Europe. For example, food made from genetically modified organisms (GMOs) continues to be disfavoured by European consumers due to concerns about long-term implications, despite the fact that new bio-engineered crops have higher yields and permit less chemically-intensive agriculture. More generally, Europe continues to take the lead in affirming the privacy rights of individuals and in pursuing policies inspired by a strong sense of social cohesion.

Welfare reform: Market States with a Scandinavian touch

Europe also brings a market logic to bear on its reform of the welfare state. In relation to unemployment, people are 'incentivised' to find work, although it is also society's responsibility to ensure labour-market opportunities are available. The Monday Protests that greeted Chancellor Schröder's 2004 reform of unemployment benefits are a distant memory in Germany. The European Constitution, renegotiated after a first failed try in 2005, and its Charter of Fundamental Rights embody the combination of social cohesion and market principles that are characteristic of *Open Doors*, a scenario in which the Market States logic develops fully (see chapter 9).

Reform of the European welfare system follows the Scandinavian—rather than the Thatcherite—model. Olivier Blanchard's view on the European model—as articulated from MIT in 2004—is widely shared.[1] Europe is a competitive region, where high productivity per hour worked creates the resources to satisfy the demand for leisure and for social inclusion, as an integral part of what consumers and workers really aspire to rather than at the expense of competitiveness. Europe's success is seen as an example of the "win–win" approach that can overcome the tension between the need for welfare provision and the need for a productive and entrepreneurial society. More generally, the "third way"[2] remains an important approach in efforts to put market forces and incentives at the service of social objectives.

In the US, increased activities by FBOs, charities and single-issue groups provide an alternative way to achieve comparable levels of cohesion, with tax incentives redirected to support such organisations and behaviours.[3]

"Referendum world": *Open Doors* politics

Referendums are numerous, and the state is often called upon to forge common ground in debates that pit different groups within society against one another. Yet this can be done, in many cases, in a win–win mindset, as part of consensus-seeking processes. Consensus, however, is often sought on a case-by-case basis, leading to a patchwork of policies, despite the problems of such approaches as illustrated by the budget deficits of the early 2000s in California. In turn, this patchwork calls for new efforts to harmonise approaches, or at least to prevent differences from becoming barriers.

In societies with institutions and democratic cultures that are not consolidated, however, referendums may determine more ambivalent paths towards *Open Doors*. Latin American democratic systems, for example, show signs of persistent patron-styles of leadership. "Referendum politics"—the direct relationship between the leader or *caudillo* and the masses—which appears to offer a direct voice to citizens, may in fact reflect weak and by-passed political institutions, and may reinforce a political culture that is open to manipulation by rhetoric. *Open Doors* is therefore better defined, in this respect, as a world where consensus is achieved through meaningful and ongoing debates, in the context of a well-established democratic culture.

Tolerance

On the whole, politics in *Open Doors* is inclusive but complex as many groups and causes are vying for attention. The notion of "multiple modernities", which was central to the *2001 Prism Global Scenario*, can be used to describe the open spirit in which different values are affirmed as equally legitimate. The spirit of tolerance and the search for "win–win" solutions is a distinctive feature of *Open Doors*, as opposed to *Flags*.

1
Olivier Blanchard, "The Economic Future of Europe", Journal of Economic Perspectives, May 2004.

2
On the "third way" see notably Anthony Giddens, The Third Way: the Renewal of Social Democracy, Polity Press, 1998, and Ralf Dahrendorf, "The Third Way and Liberty: An Authoritarian Streak in Europe's New Center", Foreign Affairs, September/October 1999.

3
E.J. Dionne Jr. and John J. Dilulio Jr., eds., What's God Got To Do With the American Experiment?, Brookings Institution Press, 2000.

4.2

Economic policies in *Open Doors*

1

In September 1985, the G5 (US, UK, Japan, Germany, and France) decided at the Plaza in New York to intervene to lower the value of the overvalued dollar. In February 1986 the G7 (G5 + Italy and Canada) announced at the Louvre in Paris that they will intervene only to ensure international stability.

While endeavouring to smooth the business cycle, governments generally pursue a prudent policy stance. Built-in stabilisers are combined with discretionary spending programmes to cushion real activity and employment in times of economic slowdowns. Over the entire cycle, however, fiscal policy is generally aimed at achieving balanced budgets in order to avoid an excessive burden for capital markets, which could crowd out the private sector. Public investment is designed to be complementary to private investment, for example, by developing a well-functioning infrastructure and helping to provide a well-educated workforce. Inflation is kept low.

Countries have put in place a global financial architecture conducive to greater financial stability. When financial crises do emerge, countries are prepared to act collectively. Central banks do not attempt to completely smooth foreign exchange movements but act decisively to prevent misalignment with "Louvre" and "Plaza" type agreements.[1]

Broad public objectives, strong private involvement

At the national level, the distinction between public and private goods becomes increasingly blurred. Goods that were traditionally provided by the state are increasingly supplied by the private sector. At the same time, there is increasing recognition that at the regional and global scale certain goods, such as public health and knowledge, will remain undersupplied unless governments play an active role in their provision. The avoidance of unacceptably large divides both within and across countries is given high priority and, consistent with this policy objective, tax systems are generally progressive and redistributive.

While this is an economically benign world, it is a world in which crises can have a severe impact. Because the provision of welfare services is not centrally overseen, there is the potential for people to fall through the holes in the social safety net, particularly if they are poorly informed and do not know where to seek the services they require. However, NGOs and community-based organisations are seriously concerned about social exclusion and, assisted by government incentives or by business support, attempt to cover the holes in the social safety net and generate opportunities for people at the very bottom of the income distribution system.

In a world in which social cohesion and trust plays a fundamental role, inequality and relative poverty are issues of global concern—or in economists' terms, alleviating these problems is an "international public good".

Meeting the Millennium Development Goals is an objective widely supported by public opinion. FBOs—Christian, Muslim, Jewish and Hindu—are given a major role in this respect.

Gaps that widen, and gaps that close

Different concepts of fairness and justice are put forward—in terms of equality of outcomes or of opportunities, of needs or of access, between genders or between generations…

Views differ, sometimes very strongly, and a number of groups do not share the culture of openness and tolerance. On the whole, however, what develops is a common sense of global community.

Within Europe and the US, thanks to the political pressure of civil societies, inequality becomes less pronounced. However, in *Open Doors*, globalisation and integration penetrate further; in countries that are quickly industrialising, this implies higher inequality levels as skilled people move into the new upcoming sectors. In rapidly growing emerging markets, such as China and India, inequality may initially increase before slowly decreasing (towards 2020) just as it did in Western Europe after World War II.

All this notwithstanding, the number of people in absolute poverty continues to decrease drastically, thanks mainly to high and more inclusive growth in China and India.

Part 2
The Three Global Scenarios

3 Low Trust Globalisation
4 Open Doors
5 Flags
6 Trilemmaps

4.3
Forces of integration and fragmentation in *Open Doors*

In *Open Doors*, states are no longer the masters of all that they survey. Global governance is multi-layered. Markets, and hence business corporations, count. Society, and hence NGOs, count. States continue to matter as well, but they no longer have definitive solutions to economic and social problems. State authority diffuses downward, to a host of local institutions and NGOs, and upward to a series of international institutions with global remits. The latter, however, are not the standard international institutions of today; rather they are "born again" reformed global institutions, representing a wider scope of global interests, accountable through strict monitoring and evaluation processes, and committed to a range of open regimes to manage the international economy and to promote global welfare.

The world of *Open Doors* is far from the world of today. But there are signs of moves in this direction. There is the move of Ukraine's new government to rapidly integrate with global and regional European institutions and to win a formal declaration of market-economy status from the EU and from the US. There is the invitation from the EU to Turkey to start accession negotiations. There is growing discussion around the need to reform the UN to make it more representative of, and a more effective voice for, today's world. Meanwhile, the continuing balancing act of the Chinese communist regime to stem the voice of growing social unrest through maintaining the momentum of economic growth, and to do so by opening up the economy to the global market (what Scott Kennedy calls the "mandate of Mammon"[1]), suggests that any country, wherever it lies on our triangle, can be pulled towards an *Open Doors* world.

A multilateral world kept together by US "soft power"
In *Open Doors*, multilateralism is seen as an important tool in overcoming the *jurisdictional discontinuities* (differences in regulations between jurisdictions) that hamper free flows of people, information, capital, goods and services. In this world, 'free trade' encompasses regulatory rules, regional development policies and aid plans—as in the EU.

Multilateralism, however, is not divorced from the geopolitical power structure—the US engages in international negotiation precisely because this is to its advantage. For the US, it takes "*patience to work with allies and to bring out the best in international organisations*" but "*doing so also delivers great benefits: costs are shared, burdens distributed, legitimacy enhanced, diverse talents engaged. And everyone joins in wanting success.*"[2]

Economic policies
Globalisation

More generally, the US complements its use of military might and economic muscle with the application of what Joseph S. Nye calls "soft power" (see box overleaf). Soft power—the ability to co-opt support rather than coerce—can arise when a country is admired for its culture, ideals or policies. In *Open Doors*, this is increasingly important in dealing with transnational issues (i.e. terrorism, international crimes and the spread of infectious diseases) that require multilateral cooperation. Soft power enables the US to gain broad acceptance of its policies in areas where military and economic power are insufficient or inappropriate. More generally, successful societies assert influence globally as role models through the "soft power" they are able to wield.

Japan deploys soft power of its own, with Japanese popular culture—from mangas to pop songs—continuing to appeal to youth in Asia and even Russia. A peaceful solution for the Southern Kouril islands is found, allowing Japan and Russia to cooperate on larger, longer-term projects, notably in Eastern Siberia. History classes—in Osaka, Paris or Dallas—are seen as opportunities to compare and understand different cultural and national perspectives rather than to protect or affirm one's nation's feelings of unique destiny and exceptionalism.

Europe sees no problem in continuing to put soft power before military power, as the US shifts from a narrow concept of "burden sharing" on security matters to a broader view of international security that gives economic development and nation building an essential role.

Indeed, the EU model is emulated in a small number of regions where enough commonality of interest exists. In many respects, *Open Doors* looks like the globalised world that Jagdish Bhagwati and Martin Wolf defend in their recent books.[3]

1

Scott Kennedy, "Divining China's Future", *World Policy Journal*, vol. 21 no. 4, Winter 2004/05, p.82. Mammon was the Phoenician God of Commerce.

2

Madeleine K. Albright, "Bridges, Bombs, or Bluster?", *Foreign Affairs*, September/October 2003, p.18.

3

Jagdish Bhagwati, *In Defense of Globalization*, Oxford University Press, New York, 2004. Martin Wolf, *Why Globalization Works*, Yale University Press, New Haven, CT, 2004.

Joseph S. Nye , author of *Soft Power: The Means to Success in World Politics*, Public Affairs, March 2004, is Dean and Don K. Price Professor of Public Policy at the Kennedy School of Government, Harvard University. He served previously as Deputy Under Secretary of State in the Carter Administration, as Assistant Secretary of Defense for International Security in the Clinton Administration and as Chair of the National Intelligence Council. Discussion conducted by Albert Bressand in Cambridge, MA in Autumn 2004.

Soft power and the war on terror

Since the collapse of the Soviet Union, there is a widely held belief in the overwhelming power of the United States. How powerful is America?

Joseph S. Nye: Some claim that the US is the only superpower in a unipolar world. Yet the context is far more complex than first meets the eye. The agenda of world politics has become like a three-dimensional chess game. On the "top board", which represents a game of military might, the US is indeed the only superpower with global military reach, and it makes sense to speak of hegemony. However, on the middle board of inter-state economic issues, the distribution of power is multipolar. The US cannot obtain the outcomes it wants on trade, antitrust or financial regulation without the agreement of others. And on the bottom board of transnational issues such as terrorism, international crime and the spread of infectious disease, power is widely distributed and chaotically organised among state and non-state actors alike. This is very far from a unipolar world. This is the set of issues that is now intruding into the world of grand strategy.

Nevertheless, the current Administration still focuses almost entirely on the top board of military power. It mistakes the necessary for the sufficient and acts as a one-dimensional player in a three-dimensional game.

So what form of power should the US deploy in playing this three-dimensional game?

JSN: The solution of transnational issues requires other countries to cooperate with you. Their willingness to do so depends in part on their own self-interest, but also on the attractiveness of your position. Other countries may choose to follow you because they share your values and wish to emulate your example. This power to attract and persuade is what I call soft power. It co-opts people, rather than coerces them—to use the term in your *Trilemma Triangle*. It means you ensure convergence between what others want and what you want, and it reduces the need to use carrots to entice and sticks to force others to do what you want.

Hard power grows out of military and economic might. Soft power arises from the attractiveness of one's culture, ideals and policies. Hard power will always remain important in a world of nation states. Yet soft power is increasingly important in dealing with transnational issues that require multilateral cooperation and that involve civil society and transnational forces as well as states themselves.

You characterise terrorism as a "bottom board" issue. What new element does terrorism add to the analysis of power at the heart of your vision of the world?

JSN: Many Europeans properly point out that terrorism is nothing new. Yet two developments have made terrorism more lethal and more difficult to manage in the 21st century.

First, the working of our societies now depends on complex, highly technological systems that are also more vulnerable and fragile.

Second, progress democratises technology, and puts into the hands of deviant groups destructive capabilities that were once limited to governments and armies. The IT revolution allows these groups to become global in reach and organisation.

Putting together these developments, we can explain recent terrorism trends —trends which have resulted in a form of terrorism radically different from that of the IRA or ETA, and which looks set to continue.

So should the US be focusing more on employing soft power in its policies on preventing or dealing with terrorism, or is this a problem which requires hard power?

JSN: The paradox of American power in the 21st century is that world politics is changing in a way that makes it impossible for the strongest world power to achieve some of its key international goals alone.

Terrorists stand to gain recruits and popular support if the US underestimates the importance of soft power. Other countries and other causes also wield soft power in support of the hard power resources that they are able to deploy. Yet the US seems to be squandering its soft power, as recent opinion polls show that the rest of the world has an increasingly less favourable perception of American policies.

Wherever possible, the US should look to soft power as a way to gain broad acceptance and to legitimise its policies on terrorism and on other "bottom board" issues. Of course, this would be even more important in the scenario you call *Open Doors*.

Part 2

The Three Global Scenarios

3 Low Trust Globalisation

4 Open Doors

5 Flags

6 Trilemmaps

Globalisation

The Arab world and the pivotal role of Turkey

Success in the Middle East is critical for achieving the more peaceful global environment of *Open Doors*. The US takes the lead, making good on Madeleine Albright's recommendation of 2003: "*For years, Arab populations have received a distorted message from Washington: that the United States stands for democracy, freedom, and human rights everywhere except in the Middle East and for everyone except the Arabs. The time has come to erase that perception and the reality that too often lies behind it.*"[1]

It is in this context that the Turkish secularist model becomes more widely accepted among Muslim countries, even if it is not adopted in more than a few nations. Turkey, a full member of the EU, is a success story that a number of other countries want to emulate. Calls for democracy are no longer summarily dismissed by Middle Eastern public opinion as Western ploys to legitimise the power of foreign interest groups and exclude Islamic opposition from the democratic process. Gradually, extreme movements lose their appeal, and a "Marshall Plan for the Middle East" is launched by a large coalition of donors, first among which is the EU.

Co-regulation, co-sovereignty and the role of regional integration

This future is characterised by common approaches to regulation, often extending to co-regulation and even to some pooling of sovereignty when it is obvious that global approaches are in order. The Kyoto Protocol does not meet all expectations, but the periodic renegotiations provided for in the Protocol provide opportunities to correct and improve, this time with the US and China on board (see chapter 13). Chinese participation is secured in return for significant international aid—aid which is used to support energy efficiency policies. These policies are necessitated in China by resource shortages, pollution burdens and bottlenecks that occur in energy supply.

Significant elements of *co-regulation* and *co-sovereignty* are more easily achieved at the regional, rather than global, level as they imply developing regulations or standards in common (i.e. EU directives or OECD standards) and even pooling sovereignty on some matters (e.g. in relation to monetary policy).

The "ASEAN+3" forum provides Japan and China with a counterweight to the EU and NAFTA. The natural vehicles for Latin Americans and Africans to make their voices heard on the global scene are Mercosur and sub-regional African organisations such as the Economic Community of West African States (ECOWAS) and the Southern Africa Development Community (SADC) and to some extent the African Union, respectively.

The European Bank for Reconstruction and Development (EBRD) plays a critical role in bringing central Asia into the community of democratic nations. Its relationship with the EU, and its capacity to promote complex programmes in support of its mandate for democratisation, have been greatly strengthened.

The World Trade Organisation (WTO) finds new efficiency and legitimacy as an inter-regional forum in which these various groupings work towards an acceptable common framework for their respective regional undertakings, through global harmonisation when possible and through policy dialogue otherwise. Building on the Chiang Mai currency swap agreements of 2001, the ASEAN countries perceive national currencies as barriers to regional integration and as sources of vulnerability. As such, they find it advantageous to adopt a common currency by 2020.

The US is the key partner of these regional economic groups. It engages actively in this revised version of multilateralism, using the NAFTA and LAFTA regional agreements to reassess the relative costs and benefits of shared decision-making processes. The UN mystique of "one country, one vote" is abandoned in favour of global standard setting and inter-regional synergies. Voting arrangements are determined in light of what each country actually contributes over the long term, in contrast to UN as well as to unilateral approaches.

A rejuvenated trans-Atlantic relationship (a theme we develop in chapter 7) plays an important role in providing leadership to the set of interlocking institutions that contribute to global governance. The "G-2"—as the US and EU are then referred to—has achieved in-depth integration in the trade and investment fields, with common principles of competiton law and essential regulations, thanks to an in-depth consultation process (see box p.82).

1

Madeleine K. Albright,
op.cit., p. 13.

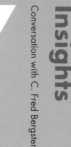

C. Fred Bergsten is Director
of the Institute for International Economics
in Washington D.C. and chairman
of the G-8 Preparatory Conference
that advises the annual G-8 Summits.

Europe–US relations in *Open Doors*: how the G-2 would work

You have been advocating the creation of a high-level, if possible informal, coordination mechanism between the US and the EU which you label the Group of Two (G-2). Assuming we are in *Open Doors*, what would the G-2 do?

C. Fred Bergsten: A functional G-2 would be pursuing two sets of objectives: a more effective relationship between Europe and the United States, and a more effective global economic order. The basic idea behind the G-2 is to create a mechanism that would strive constantly to achieve these two objectives, which are almost always compatible and indeed mutually reinforcing. Indeed, harmonious trans-Atlantic relations are a necessary condition for global stability as you envision in your *Open Doors* scenario

What aspects of the international economic agenda would be better addressed if your proposal were followed?

CFB: The issue areas that would be amenable to G-2 management include at least ten important ones: trade, competition policy, regulatory policy which includes corporate governance, macroeconomic policy, international monetary policy, international financial markets, energy, the environment, migration and global poverty.

The experience of APEC, which initially set out to be a sort of trans-Pacific G-2 (though without a cohesive Asian pillar), suggests that officials in almost every issue area will seek to organise their own consultative ties once a critical mass of other issue areas is reached—and especially if there is a "top-down" decision from the highest political levels to pursue the concept.

Obviously, a natural starting point is trade. While it already enjoys a high degree of G-2 interaction, there are key systemic issues that are not being addressed, such as the rapidly proliferating network of bilateral trade agreements in which the US and Europe both engage (something which could be addressed in a strengthened Article 24 in the WTO) and the need for a more coordinated response to the critics of globalisation. Europe and the US failed to prevent the WTO breakdown at Cancun.

Competition policy is probably one of the most important issue areas beyond trade itself. What type of cooperation would you see in this field?

CFB: Competition policy is another potentially fruitful area for G-2 management. If not quite as extensively as in trade, it is now well accepted that Europe, through the EU institutions, also plays a leadership role in competition policy, and hence provides a clear partner for the US.

Consultation is already extensive across the Atlantic. The GE–Honeywell dispute and disagreements over Microsoft, however, highlight the substantive importance of forging much closer trans-Atlantic agreement on both the philosophy and the procedures of antitrust prosecution. The rapid proliferation of new competition policies in numerous emerging market economies cries out for international leadership to minimise differences in both substance and process that could otherwise cause endless turmoil in future decades.

It should not be forgotten that this issue area became the focal point of much "trade conflict" between the US and Japan for most of the 1990s.

One 'policy instrument' could be the publication of an agreed, and even joint, procedure for addressing antitrust cases that would avoid both duplication and risk of inconsistent results. Another, as already proposed by the EU, would be the addition of this issue to the agenda of the Doha Round in an effort to start forging an agreed international template.

Competition policy is, of course, only one of many regulatory issues open to systematic G-2 management. The TransAtlantic Business Dialogue (TABD) has in fact pursued a number of such issues, seeking Mutual Recognition Agreements (MRAs) on the EU model. However, even these seemingly technical discussions have often broken down, for instance when the US Food and Drug Administration refused to accept European certifications.

Could energy policy be an important element in the G-2 agenda in an *Open Doors* world?

CFB: Energy policy is a critical issue where Europe and the United States have essentially "agreed to disagree" for some time.

Philosophies, policies and practices (at both corporate and personal levels) are dramatically different, and there are no serious efforts to reconcile them. American military might and strategic petroleum stockpiles have sufficed to avoid major trans-Atlantic problems *vis à vis* the oil markets in recent years; but the sharp conflict that flared after the first oil shock, and could have easily recurred in the context of the war in Iraq, should not be forgotten. Possible policy avenues include serious joint efforts to accelerate the commercialisation of low-carbon technology (e.g. in automobiles) and to commercialise non-carbon energy sources.

Part 2

The Three Global Scenarios

3 Low Trust Globalisation

4 Open Doors

5 Flags

6 Trilemmaps

Globalisation

Mobility

People become remarkably mobile, with no-frills airlines helping to define new global standards of openness and accessibility. In keeping with the "built-in" approaches to security of *Open Doors*, sharing of name-files among customs and police forces of different countries, as well as the use of biometrics, reduces the need for visas. The UK chooses to no longer exercise its many "opt-out" clauses in the EU, becoming party to trust-based schemes like Schengen—the EU agreement to eliminate border controls.

Co-production of public goods in a transnational civil society

Co-production is an essential concept not just in the economic sphere, but also in global politics, as key public goods are co-produced by countries or regions. Companies, NGOs, international organisations and governments find it natural to work together towards specific objectives and to "co-produce" essential services like education and health. Closer cooperation on regulation, and steps toward co-regulation, greatly facilitate such approaches. So does the transition toward Market States as analysed in chapter 9.

Faced with more empowered organisations and taxpayers, governments do not wither away: they organise themselves to make efficient use of lesser resources by engaging in appropriate partnerships, with private-sector organisations and/or with non-profit groups, depending on the issue at stake. International aid, for instance, is distributed by states jointly with NGOs and private companies. In these tripartite endeavours, NGOs provide primarily skills but also resources; companies provide mainly resources but also skills; and governments provide the basis of legitimacy as well as resources. Private money and private commitments are legitimately put at the service of public objectives.

Using "incentives" rather than coercion is a central feature of the way in which governments preserve an important role for themselves. For example, matching grants are put up to support private initiatives. Tax incentives, Public-Private Partnerships (PPPs) and cooperative R&D programmes are among the favourite tools of emerging Market States. Global energy companies see tax incentives and other instruments as resources that can be counted upon, provided the appropriate industry structure and governance standards are developed. This extends to Kyoto, or Kyoto-like, instruments that are created to enable the trading of emission rights.

This is indeed a transnational world, rather than merely an international one, in which the "public space" has become almost as globalised as the marketplace. Media, NGOs, political movements and the public do not express their views or confront one another on a domestic level but in a global public arena that gives McLuhan's metaphor of the "global village" a concrete meaning.[1]

National institutions find it to their advantage to join or set up transnational networks that give them the scope, reach and legitimacy on which their lasting success depends.

Decentralised global governance

Indeed, a pragmatic network of global institutions emerges to support this combination of global market and global civil society. Unlike what was envisioned in 1998 in a *Global Scenario* entitled *The New Game*, nothing like a world government takes shape. Rather, co-regulation, co-production of public goods and, at least at regional level, elements of co-sovereignty combine in more decentralised forms of global governance adapted to a world of Market States. Conventions make it easier to work across different jurisdictions, letting private actors select the legal regime under which they want to contract, thereby fostering a process of legal and regulatory convergence.

Nevertheless, some common institutions do develop, for instance to preside over the by-then-universal International Financial Reporting Standards (IFRS). The UN is encouraged to reform, and partially succeeds in overcoming bureaucratic tendencies. Most importantly, in keeping with the higher levels of trust achieved in *Open Doors, mutual recognition* gradually extends from the technical realm (covering electrical equipment, medical devices, pharmaceuticals, etc.) to the legal one.

1

Marshall McLuhan,

The Gutenberg Galaxy,

University of Toronto Press,

Toronto, 1962.

Insights

By Jenny B. White

Jenny White is Associate Professor of Anthropology, Boston University, author of *Islamist Mobilization in Turkey*, University of Washington Press, Seattle, 2002.

An alternative to radical Islamism? Turkey's new "Muslimhood" model

On November 3, 2002, the Justice and Development Party (AKP), the latest in a series of Islamist parties—its predecessors all banned by the state—won Turkey's national elections, sweeping most other established parties from the table. At the same time, AKP politicians and some intellectuals and theologians began to claim that religious radicalism, inspired by Arab Islam, which had guided many Turkish Islamists since the 1970s, had failed. "Islamism" has been replaced by "Muslimhood", a model in which religiosity is not part of political actors' identities in the public sphere. This novel definition of the "Muslim individual" in society, tempered by nationalism, constitutes a radical challenge to the thesis that, in Islam, religion and state are inseparable.

Living with secularism

The idea that a personal, individual Muslimhood can act in the political arena without contradicting its secular, liberal or pluralist nature is supported by a group of Islamic thinkers who have rejected Arab reformist Islam in favour of what they consider to be a Turkish brand of Islamic philosophy that they argue is more liberal and pluralist because it is based on Turkey's Central Asian, Sufi and Ottoman heritages. This model of an Islam that is both more personal and more public is rooted in recent social and political transformations.

The Turkish consumer society

Since the 1980s, Turkey has developed a consumer society in which identity can be demonstrated through purchased goods, and items are advertised by playing on identities. Market and media are wresting control over defining a "Muslim" away from the state and, to some extent, even away from Islamic groups and movements. Veiling has become a fashion industry with its own couture runway shows. Muslimhood has become a fashionable means of self-expression.

How tolerant a model?

The Muslimhood model, however, does not necessarily guarantee tolerance and liberalism. The divisiveness is expressed most obviously in a continuing battle over what constitutes public space and who controls what can and cannot appear there. At present, veiled women cannot attend university, work as civil servants or become members of parliament. Secularist government officials, including the president, avoid social functions that would be attended by the veiled wives of AKP officials. The secularist establishment model seems to imply that a modern, democratic system requires not just certain practices in the public arena, but also a certain kind of person. The Muslimhood model challenges this by asserting that a believing Muslim can be a secular politician, that their

qualities of personhood not only do not disqualify them from running the secular government machinery, but may even benefit the political realm by inserting personal ethics and a moral stance. Islam is a religion, a party is just a political institution, and secularism is just a style of management or a technology, as some high-level AKP members put it.

The EU accession beacon

A younger generation of politicians has supplemented patronage-based politics with a more participatory, populist grassroots political style. Market and media have created cross-currents of ideas and practices, uprooting previous meanings. Representatives of different views regularly debate such issues on television talk shows. The hope of European Union accession also drives the AKP government towards moderate, liberal reforms.

The Muslimhood model is a complex phenomenon, but fundamentally new and important. It may well hold a key for other Muslim societies to enable them to incorporate Islamic belief, practice and identity in a global, secular, democratic society.

For more information on religion and politics in Turkey:

Sibel Bozdogan and Resat Kasaba, eds., *Rethinking Modernity and National Identity in Turkey*, University of Washington Press, Seattle, 1997;

Heinz Kramer, *A Changing Turkey: The Challenge to Europe and the United States*, Brookings Institution Press, Washington, D.C., 2000;

David Shankland, *Islam and Society in Turkey*, The Eothen Press, Huntingdon, UK, 1999.

Part 2
The Three Global Scenarios

3 Low Trust Globalisation

4 Open Doors

5 Flags

6 Trilemmaps

Globalisation

The Global Environmental Mechanism (GEM)

Environmental pressures, most notably the need for a robust international response to the threat of catastrophic climate change, lead not to a Global Environmental Organisation but to the creation of a Global Environmental Mechanism (GEM)—a network-based institution with a small secretariat. The GEM draws on *ad hoc* groups of experts from governments, universities, research centres, NGOs and the private sector to address particular problems. Standards are set on a global scale but implemented by national authorities. The GEM also serves as a data, technology and policy clearing house providing an international mechanism for identifying "best practices" in response to pollution control and natural resource management issues.

Sovereignty, rights... and responsibilities

US visions of sovereignty, however, continue to differ from European ones, in line with America's history as a community of citizens with "inalienable rights" that they chose not to transfer to their own state. Even on such matters, however, *Open Doors* leads to a gradual blurring of the line between what are today sharply contrasted Anglo-Saxon and continental European political philosophies.

In a longer-term perspective, therefore, beyond the 2025 horizon of our *Global Scenarios*, the experience that states will have acquired of co-regulation and of using market incentives as part of a broad range of policies makes possible the emergence of what we call "a society of Market States". The constitutional order of such a "society" is one in which a number of sovereignty rights and responsibilities can be "traded" among states as part of broader contracts that also involve private and civil society actors and that govern the co-production of international and global public goods (see box pp. 86–87).

Regions where doors are not fully open...

Again, our *Jet Stream* context does not assume that all countries live under the same principles. *Weather Systems* are influenced but not determined by this global context. In particular, even in an *Open Doors* world, one needs to ask how the crisis of trust might be resolved in countries where the legitimacy of ruling regimes is in question and where social dissent is increasing.

As described by Boston University's Jenny White, this Turkish model suggests the compatibility of Islam and liberalism, based on an emerging definition of the "Muslim individual" in society, albeit tempered by nationalism (see box). It has allowed Turkey to incorporate Islamic belief, identity and practice in a globalised, secular and democratic society. In *Open Doors*, a less polarised Middle East and better living conditions will gradually reduce the attractiveness of fundamentalist schools of thought. One should remember, however, that Arab public opinion often still associates Turkey with the Ottoman empire, which implies that, even if she successfully integrates within the EU—a very likely prospect in *Open Doors*—Turkey is not necessarily seen as a role model...

Latin America must be analysed as a specific *Weather System*, as its democracies are not fully consolidated and see ongoing social mobilisation in demand of greater personal security and of economic and social equality.[1] Public trust in institutions and political parties is low, although the majority of the population continues to support democracy.[2] The narrow manner in which the "Washington consensus" has tended to be interpreted in the 1990s gives way to the more comprehensive approaches that put institutions at the centre, in the ways suggested notably by John Williamson who coined the term "Washington consensus".[3] These "social conflicts through voice" reflect unresolved tensions and struggles with outcomes depending upon the ability of governments and elites to respond in an *Open Doors* rather than *Flags* spirit...

Similarly, while we rule out *Open Doors* as a possible scenario for Russia by 2025, Russia is influenced by *Open Doors* developments, notably through tighter links with the EU which foster developments and economic diversification comparable to those taking place in Eastern and Central Europe. This does not mean that the differences in historic experience are abolished, and Russia continues to manage its relations with the external world in ways designed to promote respect for Russia as a major actor on the world scene. What changes, rather, is the greater role of transnational linkages in achieving such objectives.

1

George Philip,

Democracy in Latin America,

Polity Press, Cambridge,

MA, 2003.

2

See the "Latinobarometro" report

in *The Economist*,

August 14, 2004.

3

See Pedro-Pablo Kuczynski and

John Williamson, eds., *After*

the Washington Consensus:

Restarting Growth and Reform in

Latin America, IIE, 2003.

Insights

by Philip Bobbitt, Albert Bressand
and Peter Cornelius

Philip Bobbitt is Professor of
Constitutional Law at the University
of Texas. **Albert Bressand** is
the head of the Global Business
Environment department and of
the *Shell Global Scenarios* team.
Peter Cornelius is Group Chief
Economist at Royal Dutch Shell.

The *Open Doors* market in sovereignty rights and the emerging Society of Market States

1

Richard Cooper "A
Monetary System for the
Future", *Foreign Affairs*,
Fall 1984.

By 2025, an *Open Doors* world would have dealt with borders and conflicting jurisdictions to such an extent as to radically change the agenda for relations between states. Let us imagine therefore that we are in *Open Doors 2025*, at a time when the Royal Dutch Shell scenario team is working on its "2050 *Trilemmaps*". What sort of world order would states then be contemplating?

The trans-Atlantic dialogue after Mars and Venus

In all probability, Americans and Europeans would still differ, but not in the stark terms imagined by Robert Kagan when he pitted Mars against Venus. International security would be dealt with through a combination of military, economic and technical instruments, with Europe not a free rider but an essential contributor. Europeans would feel enough at ease in their well-integrated union to work actively towards sharing principles of co-regulation and co-sovereignty with the US and key partners. Not only would they hold annual conferences named after Richard Cooper on the need to adopt the globo as a single currency for the world[1] but, more seriously, they would invite other countries to reflect, in the Market State perspective by then very common, on how sovereignty rights can be "traded" for other public goods like assuaged climate change, a pacified Middle East

or the abolition of inhumane treatments beginning with capital punishment (a 2004 example of such "trading" is the way in which Turkey is invited today to trade its sovereign right to punish adultery along the Sharia principles to gain membership in the EU). Americans would still emphasise that rights are vested in the individual, and that states cannot "transfer" to some international entity what is merely in their custody. Yet a Market State environment would lend itself to a fruitful dialogue between these and other perspectives, with India in particular drawing on its own multicultural experience as a possible model for a federation of diverse communities.

A "Society of Market States" would then be discussed as a possible successor to the 1940s United Nations and to the 1920s League of Nations, with voting processes replaced by "markets for rights and responsibilities". The currency in such markets would not be money but limits on a state's sovereignty—such as accepting to reduce carbon emissions, increasing migration quotas or submitting to technical inspections of military or R&D facilities. Some countries would opt to stay out, but incentives to join would be high as states could acquire rights from other states in a simpler and faster manner than through intergovernmental negotiations. China would still be very reluctant to share sovereignty but would

be comfortable with a high degree of regulatory integration, in line with its rapid adoption of global best practices through its 2001 WTO accession. This changed approach to sovereignty reflects two major changes: different approaches to rights and responsibilities in general, and a different analysis of what is gained (or lost) by attributing an absolute, or very high, value to "sovereignty" over matters that can be influenced by several states and by private actors.

The rights revolution...and counter-revolution

As earlier *Shell Global Scenarios* observed, a counter-revolution was under way in the 1980s to the "rights revolution" that had dominated the preceding quarter century. From 1953 when the US Supreme Court handed down *Brown vs. the Board of Education* assuring the right to be free from race discrimination in public schools, and 1954 when the European Commission on Human Rights was established, the agenda of generating individual rights had dominated constitutional discourse. Workers' rights to strike had burgeoned, holding some societies like the UK virtual hostage. Patients' rights in societies like Canada drove the cost of health care to unprecedented percentages of GDP. The rights of free speech protected libellous journalists in the US and child pornographers in Europe... A communitarian critique

then arose, criticising the rights movement for demanding economically unsustainable welfare rights, and undermining family and social ties to civil society. A strident rhetoric of rights was indicted for justifying neglect of social responsibilities. More significantly, criticism of the rights revolution arose in East Asia where the notion of "Asian values" was juxtaposed to Western-style rights. As Lee Kuan Yew put it, Asians have *"little doubt that a society with communitarian values, where the interests of society take precedence over that of the individual, suits them better than the individualism of America."*

"Transparent sovereignty": rights that go with responsibilities

By the late 1990s, this debate had migrated to the discussion of the rights and responsibilities of states. Here the positions were reversed, only in part as a reflection of relative power: the US was demanding the highest recognition of the responsibilities of states and the greatest compromise of their autonomy on matters of security; Europe was taking a middle position, although some advocated "the right of interference" in the face of genocide; and the states of Asia were most insistent on non-interference with the sovereignty of states.

Americans began to distinguish between three views of state sovereignty: opaque sovereignty, a classical concept that holds that events within a state's borders are entirely internal matters, beyond the purview of other states; translucent sovereignty, a more recent result of the human rights movement, which holds that authoritative agencies like the UN Security Council can declare a state in violation of fundamental international norms—against genocide, for example—and forfeit the perpetrator's sovereignty; and transparent sovereignty, a largely American concept that, because a regime's sovereignty arises from its compact with its people and the society of states, sovereignty can be penetrated when a state commits widespread acts of violence against its own people, threatens its neighbours with aggression, or acquires WMD in violation of its agreements. States holding these views by 2005 on security issues, as seen from Washington, were China (opaque), France (translucent) and the US (transparent) and there was a risk that these three views would come into conflict, for instance in the fight against terrorism or money laundering. Hence increasingly pressing demands by the US that other states redefine their sovereignty rights under the constraint of "transparent sovereignty".

The European perspective on co-sovereignty

In the *Open Doors* world of 2025, Europeans would have no problem working with these American-born concepts of state responsibilities, as the debate would have moved beyond the stage when the US concept of "transparent sovereignty" would have been perceived as casting a veil over America's own lack of accountability. Rather than being limited to issues of international security, "transparent sovereignty" would extend to fields in which the US would have come to accept higher levels, and influence from other states, for instance through binding international dispute settlements as in WTO and NAFTA.

The discussion, after two decades of *Open Doors*, would centre on which set of universal rules could achieve "transparent sovereignty" by common agreement rather than through the coercion of power. The EU countries would have significant experience to share on how national parliaments and governments can create common binding legal instruments. They would advocate "global directives" patterned after the European directives behind the internal market. Such directives, adopted in strengthened forums like the "G-2", the "G-8" and the "G-G" bringing the various "Gs" together, would lay out the principles to which sovereign states would accept to be held accountable along the lines of "transparent sovereignty". A Court of Justice would be in a position not only to settle disputes on the interpretation of a set of binding treaties but also to apply fundamental principles accepted by several states to subjects not completely covered in treaties.

A Market State "infrastructure" for co-sovereignty

Market States are not states that have been downsized into market actors, but states that have upgraded their skills to use the market well. In this spirit, an *Open Doors* world could see the emergence of "markets in sovereignty rights" in which "pooling" of sovereignty could be done in the flexible manner of the market rather than through complex negotiations among governments. The ways in which Turkey has agreed to transfer sovereignty to the EU on issues like the penal system is an interesting model of how states can respond to incentives. *Open Doors* could see such trading of sovereignty rights on a much larger scale thanks to a global infrastructure for sovereignty pooling (GISP).

This infrastructure would not cover all domains but would have developed pragmatically as countries would have found it useful to deal with a number of cross-border or global issues in a more integrated manner. In the monetary field, a number of regional monetary unions would have paved the way for letting other countries bid for adjustments in another country's macroeconomic or exchange rate policies around common objectives and instruments. In the security field, a revamped UN would have a set of committed forces ready for deployment under the authority of an international common and control system, with countries ready to bid "international moral credits" for specific actions. Development aid would be managed mostly by multilateral agencies interacting directly with NGOs and governments with a legitimacy based on their technical expertise rather than a political oversight by member governments.

Obviously, back in 2005, such a world seems a bit out of touch with what is much more like a *Low Trust Globalisation* present context. Yet, in their own ways, both the US and the EU appear to be searching for some more effective way of dealing with the agenda of global interdependence, an agenda likely to expand well beyond national means to cope with it…

4.4

High economic growth, especially in emerging market economies

The concern for efficiency and the deepening of integration, in terms of the removal of institutional discontinuities, provides fertile ground for economic growth in *Open Doors*. This is matched by strong innovation thanks to the global flow of knowledge and research coordination in industry. Productivity growth is kept high by an increasingly mobile and trained workforce. Global GDP in *Open Doors* grows on average by 3.8% until 2025.

Reaping the benefits of increased and undisrupted trade with the fast-growing markets of particularly China and India, the US is able to maintain growth levels just short of 4% on a sustained basis, even though this is a gradual slow-down after the exceptional performance of 2004. Japan and Europe—even if with lower average growth rates—benefit even more in relative terms.

Having moved ahead with its "Lisbon plus" labour market and welfare state reform agenda, the EU reaches US growth levels by 2010. It then adjusts to an average of 2.8% over the following decade, considerably closing the GDP gap with the US by the end of the period under analysis. The emerging economies are the real winners in this scenario, with China growing at a staggering 8% per year on average, expanding the economy six-fold by 2025, and achieving a GDP of USD 8000 billion. This gargantuan creation of wealth substantially closes the GDP gap with the US, and pushes Chinese GDP past that of Japan by 2025. India is also a winner in this scenario. Even in per capita terms, India closes the gap with the US—between 2005 and 2025, Indian per capita income grows from 1/20th to 1/10th of the corresponding US figure.

Lower risk premiums, tighter certification processes
Financial markets are almost fully integrated and allocate capital to the highest-return projects. Governments are also increasingly good at creating financial instruments to strategically place their debt in the markets.

Emerging markets' risk premium is considerably lower than in the other scenarios, on average only 250 basis points over US Treasury benchmarks. This reflects the solidity of the international monetary system thanks to reformed and well-functioning international financial institutions, closely scrutinised by NGOs. The baseline for long-term US interest rates is also low in *Open Doors*, thanks to low risk premiums and a tight control over inflationary pressure. On average, bond yields are below 2% in real terms.

The economic environment described above represents the baseline of the scenario. Crises can then be superimposed to generate a full volatility profile. In the case of *Open Doors*, crises such as a deepening of the fiscal problems in the United States or a collapse of the Chinese banking system (as described in chapter 11) could be particularly disruptive given the importance of these two countries as engines of global growth.

Part 2

The Three Global Scenarios

3 Low Trust Globalisation

4 Open Doors

5 Flags

6 Trilemmaps

4.5
The energy scene in *Open Doors*

Open markets, "externalities priced in" and choice
Customers expect abundant, convenient and affordable energy. Open markets and free trade are seen as essential to achieving security of supply and it is left to the market to allocate resources in the most efficient way to satisfy demand. Price signals, therefore, play the key role in fostering appropriate responses from the market as well as from society, in support of key policy objectives like energy security. It is understood that prices have to reflect not only supply and demand but also the indirect implications of the production and consumption process on the environment and sustainable policy objectives (in economic jargon, prices must "internalise externalities"). This is done, notably, through the "polluter pays principle".

In addition, when both necessary and accepted by society, flexible tax structures reinforce the price signals—with the European gasoline taxes the clearest example. While possibly never adopting European style gasoline taxes, the US would adopt the recommendations of the Rocky Mountain Institute to "cross-tax or subsidise" each type of passenger car in order to reflect their relative energy efficiency.[1] Energy- (and carbon-) efficient cars would be subsidised to the same extent as energy-inefficient cars would be taxed without changing the total tax revenues levied by states and the federal government, and respecting fundamental consumer preferences between, for instance, SUVs and small cars. As described by its authors, this proposal is *"market-oriented without taxes, innovation-driven without mandates, not dependent on major (if any) national legislation, and designed to support, not distort, business logic"*: very much an *Open Doors* proposal indeed!

A regulatory environment with international coherence
Governments focus on ensuring competition and dealing with market failures when purely commercial approaches do not work. For example, antitrust authorities condone cooperative approaches if they also promote delivery of public goods by the private sector. Major new energy infrastructure projects are financed in a timely manner, facilitated by pragmatic and predictable market regulation and international legislation, for example the global adoption of the Energy Charter Treaty and Transit Protocol, as presently discussed between the EU and Russia.

Most of the time self-regulation is a key part of the regulatory approach—and it works to the extent that market participants see reputation as important to their long-term competitiveness. *Open Doors* is a world in which corporate best practices, voluntary codes and constant rating and screening by investors and NGOs promote responsible behaviours.

Under the same principle, recognising consumer value and best operating practices, groups of leading companies undertake voluntary emission reductions. The emergence of trading systems among groups of companies from different sectors provides a framework for change. Global trading in CO_2 is a natural development of national and regional systems (see box overleaf).

Competition and technology development
In niche markets, stationary fuel cells become increasingly popular. By 2015, they are providing reliable power and low-cost Combined Heat and Power (CHP) in major commercial buildings. As costs fall, more and more households also adopt them. Around 2015, fuel cell vehicles are introduced in fleets. At first, photovoltaic cells remain at a cost disadvantage, except for remote rural applications; however, as the demand for hydrogen increases after 2020, hydrogen generation using photovoltaic power and nuclear becomes more attractive. Hybrid vehicles are readily adopted in as much as the price signals—incorporating or not carbon-credit elements—make them competitive when assessed over their total life span.

A highly competitive energy market
Liberalisation continues apace, as markets become increasingly integrated and competitive. There is greater diversity of supply. Markets are highly transparent and liquid throughout the value chain, with strong links to financial and insurance markets, robust pricing systems and clear signals for system adjustment. This ensures that infrastructure gets built in time. Long-term contracts will still be important for the development of major new fields but spot markets (e.g. LNG) will develop as companies extract as much as possible from their assets.

Economic growth Energy

1

Winning the Oil Endgame: Innovation for Profits, Jobs, and Security, Amory B. Lovins, E. Kyle Datta, Odd-Even Bustnes, Jonathan G. Koomey and Nathan J. Glasgow; edited by Beatrice T. Aranow, preface by Mark Moody-Stuart, Rocky Mountain Institute, Snowmass, CO, 2004.

Emissions trading in *Open Doors*

There is growing acceptance that greenhouse gases (GHGs) from human activities are leading to changes in the global climate. However, what is the most efficient way of reducing emissions, considering that the full effects of man-made GHG emissions are not likely to be felt for decades? What will lead to the uptake of lower carbon technologies or more efficient energy use by consumers, in a world of uneven energy resource development and economic wealth?

One tool, which may lead to active management of emissions, is emissions trading. Such a tool is consistent with the *Open Doors* world, in which market mechanisms are explored to achieve social objectives in an efficient manner. Emissions trading allows one emitter to keep emitting above a certain limit if they buy enough credits from others who emit below this limit.

Cap and Trade

The Kyoto Protocol provides GHG reduction targets and allows the use of international emissions trading and other flexible mechanisms to achieve these targets at lowest cost.

Clean Development Mechanism and Joint Implementation

For example, the "Clean Development Mechanism" (for developing countries) and "Joint Implementation" (with other industrialised countries) allow governments to recognise business-initiated emission-reduction projects abroad that they can offset against their domestic target. The European Union's Emissions Trading Scheme (EU ETS) allows European companies to count credits from emission reduction projects around the world towards their obligations, to help achieve country-level GHG emission targets. This delivers an overall EU reduction of 8% in CO_2 emissions by 2012 relative to 1990 levels. In the first phase, the ETS coverage includes approximately 45% of EU CO_2 emissions relating to energy activities.

The success of trading systems will depend on the potential for effective and fair negotiations between parties to trade, which requires reaching shared agreement on the basic rules, guidelines and principles. The trading system depends on firms that emit above their allocated limit buying enough credits from others who emit below their limit. Careful definition of limits is required, along with regular review to ensure that overall improvements are achieved.

In the US, trading has primarily focused on NOx, VOC, SOx, CO and particulates. For example the US acid rain programme (established in 1990) achieves 30% reduction in sulphur dioxide emissions, with lower costs of implementation by:

• Setting limits for power plant sulphur dioxide emissions;

• Fixing the number of emission allowances available per year;

• Rigorously monitoring the emissions;

• Encouraging trading of allowances;

• Allowing companies to either reduce their emissions to allowance level or purchase spare allowances from other companies.

90

Part 2
The Three Global Scenarios

3 Low Trust Globalisation
4 Open Doors
5 Flags
6 Trilemmaps

IOCs and NOCs compete on a level playing field

Governments see open markets and free trade as the best assurances for security of supply and development of their natural resources. National energy companies will therefore have to compete on merit with international energy companies, or else see their role reduced to a non-operating vehicle, or even face being privatised. In the OPEC countries, IOCs and non-national NOCs are invited to facilitate high-cost investments under competitive terms, in order to relieve domestic budget pressures. However, OPEC NOCs remain firmly in place as keepers of the low-cost (swing) capacity.

The dash for gas in power and transportation

The use of natural gas for power generation and cars, via application of Gas to Liquids and fuel cells technology, expands rapidly at 3.5% per annum, encouraged by economics, convenience and environmental qualities. Coal production almost doubles by 2025, enabled by cleaner coal technologies, yet the market share of gas grows.

In the US, the political climate for the development of LNG import facilities is favourable, postponing the need to develop some of the higher-cost domestic gas sources after 2015.

The EU focuses on expanding, interconnecting and diversifying its energy infrastructure, linking the EU to its major energy partners efficiently. The harmonisation of operating practices and the strict enforcement of competition law go together with a pragmatic attitude to the large-scale horizontal consolidation of the midstream industry. In Russia, an internal market develops, where independents are given transparent access to transmission and distribution networks. Gazprom's role as monopolistic sales agent for gas is limited to exports gas. LNG exports are allowed by independents.

Fuelling a rapidly expanding industrial sector in the emerging markets, coal demand rises by 2.3% per year. With the internalisation of carbon cost, coal is relatively disadvantaged which in part limits its growth. Renewables continue to gain in importance, as people become more aware of environmental impacts, and the internalisation of carbon cost in fossil fuel use begins to ensure renewables can compete directly on cost. Renewables growth, year on year, is approximately 9%, which delivers a market share of 5%.

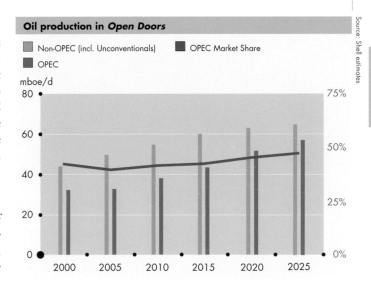

Oil production in *Open Doors*

Non-OPEC (incl. Unconventionals) — OPEC Market Share — OPEC

mboe/d

Source: Shell estimates

Energy

OPEC: Spare capacity is the Middle East only

Oil remains the dominant global fuel through to 2025, and demand growth is on average nearly 1.9% per annum. OPEC market share and production increase significantly. High growth and economic diversification mean that OPEC can afford loose cohesion, and only the core Middle East members retain any spare capacity.

Limited spare capacity breeds uncertainty and volatility. Middle East OPEC exploits this by being able to build new capacity quickly and placing additional volumes in the market at the highest premium. Mastering the volatility game is essential. Nevertheless, OPEC is careful not to impair demand growth coming predominantly from the developing nations: it does so by producing sufficient volumes to moderate the average oil price to a similar level to that in *Low Trust Globalisation,* which is overall more affordable as the world at large is richer in this scenario.

The highly volatile price environment causes non-OPEC producers to invest efficiently: relentless cost reduction is therefore a major concern for non-OPEC countries. At times the limits of growth are tested, when supply growth cannot keep pace with demand growth, causing high oil prices and continuously testing what the market can bear.

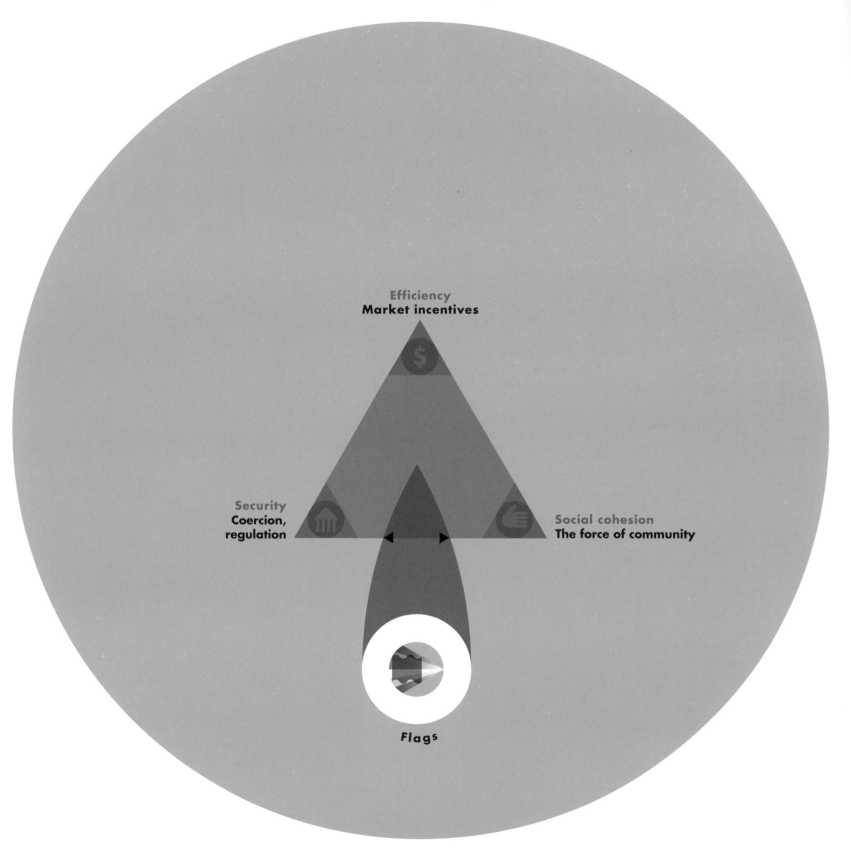

Part 2
The Three Global Scenarios

3 Low Trust Globalisation

4 Open Doors

5 Flags

6 Trilemmaps

Chapter 5
Flags

The scenario in a nutshell: "Nations and Causes"
Flags is a world in which national societies are split into diverse groups, and trust is fragmented. Efficiency takes a back seat to security and solidarity. Globalisation, while not necessarily opposed, often stalls. Distinct social groups, while tight-knit and highly trusting internally, are distrustful of outsiders. Governments aspire to overcome centrifugal forces, which could break the national community apart, and often promote nationalism and patriotism in the pursuit of social cohesion. Religious affiliations have a direct impact on political debate, and the US remains in the midst of a "new religious revival", a revival which Nobel economist Robert W. Fogel has called "its Fourth Great Awakening".[1]

The process of globalisation continues, but at a more measured pace, with a number of countries opting for some form of protection against what they see as the inherent dangers of international integration. There is more "grit" in the system—economic barriers are raised by governments, under the pressure of national civil society groups, to lessen the volatility of global economic flows and to limit exposure to external threats. Opportunities that could come from global integration are sometimes deliberately foregone in the interests of social stability or of national sovereignty.

Flags encompasses huge and potentially divisive variety in the way people see the world and what causes, religion or values they prioritise. Domestic politics plays a critical role, with different groups in society promoting their own causes or interests.

Zero-sum games
This is a world in which key countries are trying to re-articulate the fundamental political compromises and social contracts that shape their political systems. In keeping with the area of the *Trilemma Triangle* in which *Flags* is located, the transition to Market State proceeds more slowly, as differing political and religious values, and the unconstrained use of power, lock players into "zero-sum games".

Thus the structure of the state and conflict between values are fundamental to politics. Problems that could be addressed by resorting to the global market, as in *Open Doors* and *Low Trust Globalisation*, are often dealt with through national rules, which differ from country to country, and which form a global patchwork of regulations.

This scenario is a heterogeneous world of many different flags—of nations and causes, global crusades and local resistance, religion and patriotism. A key tension which characterises *Flags* is between internationalism and nationalism. The highly interconnected global elites have to pursue their transnational objectives in a divided world where sovereign national identities are emphasised.

More strikingly than *Low Trust Globalisation* and *Open Doors*, *Flags* is a world that necessarily encompasses very different sub-variants, some violent—depending on the ways in which terrorism evolves and key political and social divisions are shaped and addressed (see p. 96).

The scenario in
a nutshell

1

Robert W. Fogel,

*The Fourth Great Awakening
and the Future of Egalitarianism*,

University of Chicago Press,

Chicago, IL, 1999.

By Mark Valencia

Insights

Mark Valencia is a Senior Fellow at the East-West Center, Hawaii, with 25 years' experience and over 150 publications in maritime policy and international relations.

The South China Sea: nationalism and the potential for conflict

Six competing flags

The 40-odd Spratly Islands in the South China Sea are claimed wholly or in part by six governments: China, Taiwan, Brunei, Malaysia, the Philippines and Vietnam. Military forces of all but Brunei occupy the islands in a patchwork quilt pattern. To the north, the Paracel Islands are occupied by China, which seized them in 1974 from Vietnam, which still claims them. The islands are situated near strategic sea lanes and the surrounding seabed may harbour oil and gas. Occasional conflicts have erupted, such as those between China and Vietnam in 1988.

Diplomacy...

On November 4, 2002, ASEAN and China signed a Declaration on the Conduct of Parties in the South China Sea.

New achievements include a statement that the parties will refrain from any "action of inhabiting" uninhabited islands, and commitments to continued dialogue. It also reaffirms the parties' commitment to freedom of navigation in, and flight over, the South China Sea, and involves an implicit recognition by all claimants that competing claims will be resolved in accordance with international law, including the 1982 UN Convention on the Law of the Sea (UNCLOS). This is of particular significance because, under the UNCLOS, all of the maritime claims have weaknesses. Yet the Declaration is not a legally binding code of conduct.

... and gunboats

In February 2004, the Philippines undertook military exercises with the US in the South China Sea, apparently because of Manila's concern about the increasing number of visits by Chinese vessels to the Spratly Islands and the appearance of new Chinese markers on unoccupied reefs. Then on March 23, a Taiwanese speedboat landed and constructed a makeshift "bird-watching stand" on Ban Than Reef, leading Vietnam to protest at "an act of land-grabbing expansion that seriously violated Vietnam's territorial sovereignty".

As relations deteriorate between, for example, China and Vietnam or China and Taiwan, the disputes could flare up and even become the harbinger of worse to come.

The US, Japan and ASEAN containing China?

In a larger geostrategic context, it is quite clear that ASEAN, Japan or the US would never accept China's dominance of the area and its critical sea lanes. Japan has already arrogated to itself the duty of defending the sea lanes leading to Japan, and with US backing is trying to boost its relations with ASEAN as well as extend its presence through assistance on anti-piracy efforts.

Japan's initiative puts pressure on China to, at least, refrain from actions that would alter the *status quo* or alarm ASEAN. Meanwhile, most ASEAN countries remain somewhat suspicious of China's intentions in the South China Sea and generally accept the US military presence in the region.

A possible interim solution is joint development—claimants agreeing to set aside their jurisdictional claims and jointly explore and exploit any resources in the disputed area.

A *Flags* hand in an *Open Doors* glove?

China consistently proposes joint development for the Spratly area, but with a catch: the other claimants first have to recognise China's sovereignty. It is also not clear whether China is proposing joint development for areas that are clearly on others' legal continental shelves. Areas claimed by only two parties may be more congenial to joint development, such as that to the north of the Spratlys, which is claimed only by China and the Philippines. The *Open Doors* spirit may still prevail in this dispute, but nationalism is clearly on the rise and the multiple claims to much of the area are more in line with a *Flags* world.

Part 2
The Three Global Scenarios

3 Low Trust Globalisation

4 Open Doors

5 Flags

6 Trilemmas

5.1
Markets, civil society and governance in *Flags*

The competing claims of communities: local, national and international

Flags is a world of many different communities, each claiming the sole allegiance of its members. Reactions to globalisation vary enormously, and there is a search for new economic models including different varieties of hybrid capitalism combining Anglo-Saxon approaches with continental European or Asian practices that give an advantage to insiders and local players. Governments attempt to bind these diverse social groups together through state-guided national projects, with varying degrees of success. There is also a globalised cutting-edge elite, whose views and life-styles are cosmopolitan, and whose members connect closely with one another on a global stage. While this group contains some who espouse market capitalism and are often in conflict with what they see as errant governments, others see multinational corporations as part of the problem rather than of the solution.

There is no prevailing economic ideology (such as the Washington Consensus in *2001 Business Class*) to dictate "best policy".[1] Politics may have a strong populist tone, although this does not stop some governments from promoting pro-market reforms when other approaches have failed. The trade-offs that occur in the political arena and between politicians are more important in influencing outcomes than debate amongst those who formulate policy. Economic nationalism leads to a world of complex and heterogeneous national regulation, and there is debate on whether and to what extent economic "self-reliance" is important in a number of "strategic" sectors.

Command-and-control regulations

In the regulatory domain, these pressures translate into a world of demanding requirements and rules established by national authorities. Governments find themselves constantly fighting with distrust and needing to reassure the public about their capacity to provide security. Social legitimacy takes priority over market efficiency.

The trend towards economic-incentive-based regulations continues, but old-style "command-and-control" tactics still capture the imagination of governments. Standards that are relatively inflexible and widely divergent across jurisdictions translate into high compliance costs and significant non-tariff barriers to trade.

Media, tabloids and news that sell

The media continue to function as a watchdog for society in an often divisive climate. Reporting on scandals and abuses puts the "fourth power" in the position of regulation arbiter. Media scrutiny, however, focuses on political compromises and connections that distort markets, rather than on standards of social responsibility as is the case in *Open Doors*. Actually, this makes for more exciting news, even if readers realise that much of it is either commercially driven—the media "create" the news that sells—or one-sided.

Populist politics, protests and patronage

The state is central to domestic politics. States assert dominant identities that are often, but not always, nationalistic and sometimes narrowly ethnic. Within society many different ideas and political groupings contend for government support. This leads to populist politics, and may degenerate into a situation in which the ruling elite exercises patronage, handing out privileges to clients and supporters. In reaction, popular protest often turns violent with strikes and demonstrations, disaffected groups adamantly asserting their agendas.[2]

The role of the state as a provider of public goods makes the quality of governance and institutions a key parameter in this scenario.

In Latin America, for example, the variations in *Flags* will also be dependent on the capacity of institutions to enforce law, to reduce levels of political co-opetition and corruption, to articulate an effective and independent judiciary, and to develop professional administrative structures. These will be key elements of economic and social policies that people can see as contributing to social justice, with an overall impact on internal stability.[3]

In the EU, the capacity of the European parliament to provide an accepted forum as part of a broader 'European public space' is similarly important, the more so as a number of media groups do not shy away from xenophobia. The Indian Union is also severely tested as caste and local loyalties are emphasised.

Trilemma relations

1

See Pedro-Pablo Kuczynski and John Williamson, *op. cit.*

2

Amy Chua, *World on Fire: How Exporting Free Market Democracy Breeds Ethnic Hatred and Global Instability*, Doubleday, New York, 2003.

3

Mark Halle et al., *Trade, Aid and Security: Elements of a Positive Paradigm*, International Institute for Sustainable Development, Winnipeg, 2004.

Deportation, nationalism and terror: signposts towards a *Flags* context

Yusuf Islam—better known by his former name of Cat Stevens—who repeatedly denounced the terrorist attacks of 9.11 as an insult to Islam, was refused admission to the US after his name was discovered on a "watch list" during a trans-Atlantic flight in September 2004. The former pop singer, en route to Mexico, was deported. The US Department of Homeland Security claimed that his name had been on the watch list because some of his recent activities could "potentially be related to terrorism". The intelligence data that was used to support Islam's inclusion on the list was not shared with the public or with the singer. The Council on American-Islamic Relations deplored that the move sent the message that even moderate Muslims were being "treated like terrorists".

Widespread tensions emerged ahead of a national referendum on the use of hydrocarbons in Bolivia during July 2004. Farmers demanding infrastructure improvements in the east of Bolivia turned a pipeline valve off, halting gas exports to Argentina. While other protesters were setting up roadblocks around the country, in the Chaco region an indigenous group marched to La Paz to demand the cancellation of a gas field contract that had been granted to the Brazilian state oil company Petrobras.

Critics dismissed some of these actions as the work of the labour union federation Central Obrera Boliviana (COB), which saw the referendum as biased against the possibility of nationalisation in the hydrocarbon sector. Yet the protests also made clear to the government that in order to build a social consensus regarding future gas projects, the exploitation of Bolivia's most important natural resource would have to be seen to deliver real benefits for ordinary people.

Chinese and Indian National Oil Companies (NOCs) embark on major efforts to secure energy supply through long-term agreements with producing countries; aid and trade instruments are mobilised whilst return on investment is a secondary consideration.

Created in July 2004 within the CIA, on the recommendation of the 9.11 Commission, the National Counter-Terrorism Center (NCTC) released a preliminary report on April 27, 2005. It identified 651 "significant" terrorist attacks in 2004, with 1907 people killed—including the 190 victims of the March 11 Madrid train bombing, over 300 victims of the Beslan School terror act, and about 300 victims of violence related to the conflict between India and Pakistan.

A year ago, using a different typology, the State Department counted 208 attacks that killed 625 people, which at the time marked a 21-year high. Attacks by perpetrators against people of their own nationality, notably in Iraq, were not included at this stage.

Part 2
The Three Global Scenarios

3 Low Trust Globalisation
4 Open Doors
5 Flags
6 Trilemmaps

5.2
Opportunistic economic policies in *Flags*

When trust is fragmented, as it is in *Flags*, investors are naturally sceptical about global markets—they need to be enticed by high premiums to overcome their natural preference for domestic investment. This opens up opportunities for global arbitrage, not just by the financial community but also through the operations of multinational corporations, as assessments of the same risks can vary widely across countries and institutions. Not all actors are able to take advantage of such opportunities, even at high risk premiums.

Reacting to the failure of markets to meet social needs, states are proactive in regulating the market and in providing public goods and services. Governments are concerned to protect the consumer by setting safety standards on a wide range of products through regulation.

Special interest groups exert pressure for protectionist policies. Governments play along, sometimes agreeing with them, and at other times imposing liberal economic policies and partial reform of the welfare state in the interests of wider society.

Lower competitive pressures leave greater room for inflation, which is clearly higher and less homogeneous across countries than in the other scenarios. Central banks are less reluctant to let currencies devalue, with risks of overshooting and of beggar-thy-neighbour macroeconomic policies. As a consequence, anti-dumping and other "countervailing duties" flourish, introducing even higher unpredictability in trade.

Governments also have to place more debt on the markets as their expenditure rises to meet security needs and social demands. As a result, domestic interest rates tend to be high and the global sovereign debt market remains exposed to frequent crises.

Stop-and-go reform of the welfare state
Poverty alleviation measures are often "pro-poor", populist in inspiration rather than guided by "welfare state" approaches. There are strong social pressures to increase welfare spending, but governments also face political pressure to moderate tax rises. Some governments cave in, running up unsustainable fiscal deficits. Others successfully manage to square the circle by disbursing welfare benefits in a highly targeted and tightly controlled manner, and by stiffening welfare provision with a strong element of coercion designed to force people back to work. The large, emerging and modernising countries are better at setting up an efficient welfare infrastructure based on selective provision, though they too are squeezed by escalating social demands.

The multinational company in a nationalist world
Flags is an environment with many different, sometimes incompatible, national regulations. As a result, companies find it difficult to become truly global organisations and to operate throughout using one set of standards. They often have to compete against national champions, and find it hard to deliver global synergies and economies of scale, as they have to balance competing sets of country risks and opportunities. Wide-ranging regulatory requirements drive compliance costs up. In much of the modernising world, with its re-emergent nationalism, foreign companies have to work hard to gain and, more importantly, maintain the trust of local elites.

There are few global agreements regulating corporate operations. There are also few global standards for companies to measure their activities against, which means that their operations appear less transparent. This attracts a more aggressive approach from NGOs who see "facts on the ground"—or contradictions between companies' global and local behaviours. They go after companies in a more conflictive way and, unlike in *Open Doors*, they pay little attention to investors' views and interests.

Economic policies

Focus

Flags: variants in the spirit of the 2001 Prism Global Scenario

As stated earlier, the *Flags* scenario necessarily encompasses a number of diverse variants, with the potential for many different crises and outcomes. Several questions can be used to guide our thinking. How violent will the turbulences in *Flags* be? Will protests be peaceful, as in Seattle in 1999, more violent, as in Genoa in 2002, or will they result in outright episodes of terrorism? To what extent will these turbulences be confronted by democratic processes or through various forms of authoritarianism?

Some potential answers to these questions are captured here in three variants of *Flags* which draw on the *Prism* scenario of 2001. Again these are not forecasts but 'what-if?' explorations of more extreme parts of the *Trilemma Triangle* map.

Variant One:
Prism with Glasses

Flags captures a particular balance of forces between a strongly assertive state on one side and turbulent societies on the other. In *Prism with Glasses*, divided groups within society come to a realisation of their own interdependence ('glasses' is a reference to the pair of glasses that symbolised diversity of values in Prism 2001).

Efforts are made to preserve mutual respect between groups that differ fundamentally over concerns such as abortion, gay rights and religion. Governments increasingly seek cooperative solutions to these conflicts, to enable, in the language of the *2001 Global Scenarios*, "multiple modernities" to coexist.

After a period of instability when the old arrangements prove patently inadequate, a new "politics of invention" arises, involving interactions between states, NGOs, existing international institutions and societal groupings, some with a transnational reach.

Variant Two:
Dark Prism

Dark Prism is an authoritarian variant. Much of the modernising world sees a democratic breakdown and the western world retrenches into populist politics with Big Brother undertones.

China's economic development is not accompanied by political liberalisation but by assertive nationalism. Meanwhile, post-modern Western societies see the rise of New Right politics, which is welfarist, populist and embraces new technology. Technology, in fact, enhances the state's control over society—there is literally no place to hide.

"Two-tier" societies arise, in which governments look after the needs of mainstream citizens, while rigidly excluding social minorities and outsiders. Governments define their country's interests in a narrow, often confrontational, manner.

Variant Three:
Prism with Guns

Prism with Guns plays out the divisive element in *Flags*, with "us *versus* them" as the primary dynamic.

This is a globalised world where political authority has failed, leaving the power to coerce in the hands of charismatic leaders or even gangs. It is characterised by a hierarchy of violence, from local terrorism and civil conflicts to international wars fought over access to resources. Violence is dominated by global terrorism, a force that is *anomic*—divorced from social standards. The US is perceived as acting purely in its own, narrowly defined, self-interest, dividing world opinion and generating violent localised resistance.

Nuclear terrorism would take the world to an even more violent and coercive future (see Philip Bobbitt's 'catastrophic' scenarios on p.102).

Part 2

The Three Global Scenarios

3 Low Trust Globalisation

4 Open Doors

5 Flags

6 Trilemmaps

5.3
Forces of global integration and fragmentation in *Flags*

As Dani Rodrik has argued,[1] the increasing international economic integration engendered by globalisation contributes to domestic social disintegration. In *Flags*, this opens up deep fault lines in societies. The tensions that are released place governments under increasing pressure to restrain the flows of globalisation, so as to preserve what is often a very fragile 'social cohesion'. In practice, however, consumers continue to shop for cheap products, and globalisation proceeds but in a far more acrimonious context and more unevenly, creating an inherently unstable international system.

Flags is a world in which national identities are asserted, often as a substitute to an effective 'social contract' internally. Governments and people everywhere see no reason to actively pursue appropriate and responsible international roles; there is little enthusiasm for taking on the burdens that a globalised world imposes; on the contrary, blaming the foreigners—whether Central Americans, Ukranians, Turks or East Asian Chinese—is politically appealing. Public opinion in developed societies shows increasingly little interest or enthusiasm for activist foreign policies. Like domestic societies everywhere, the world too becomes divided and compartmentalised.

Signs of *Flags* pervade today's world. Most notably in East Asia, there is the resurgence of nationalism in China, in response to an increasing sense of loss of control by government over key social and political elements. This has led to rising tensions with Japan and the unanimous passing by the National People's Congress of an anti-secession law in March 2005, authorising the use of force in the event that Taiwan declares independence. Both are critical potential flashpoints for global political and economic instability.[2]

From global to inter-national

Flags reinforces conventional state-to-state relations. The world is not global, but emphatically inter-national. Sovereignty is opaque, in that events within a state's borders are held by governments to be entirely internal matters. The EU is an exception, as co-regulation has been practiced for half a century, notably since the "Europe 92" programme that transformed the 'common market' into an 'internal market'. But new progress is scarce, a number of barriers are reintroduced. States push their own national agendas at the expense of international multilateral organisations, the actions of which depend critically on the political compromises worked out between key member countries. Yet states are quite pragmatic in their global outlook and pursue a mix of multilateral deals, bilateral agreements and regional pacts. Although global institutions are weak, the politics of direct action is prominent, and is driven by transnational activist organisations.

In the Middle East, the danger that the CSIS envisaged materialises, in that *"every goal our country pursued in the region would be suspect... US commitments to promote reform and improve bilateral relations [are seen] simply as a smokescreen to obscure our country's inaction on the Palestinian–Israeli dispute."*[3]

The US turns isolationist, liberally using the "carrot" of market access and the "stick" of anti-dumping remedies and outright sanctions in its relations with other countries. Regional arrangements emerge as an alternative to global agreements, around which smaller states coalesce, resulting in regional "umbrella structures". China in particular capitalises on its domestic market to develop a three-tier trade policy rivalling that of the US. This policy brings together preferential bilateral agreements, a strong regional dimension (based on the "ASEAN+3" states—the 10 countries of the Association of Southeast Asian Nations plus China, Japan and South Korea), and a capacity to use the WTO to its advantage. Chinese–Japan relations however, remain tense.

Globalisation

1

Dani Rodrik, *Has Globalisation Gone Too Far?* Institute of International Economics, Washington, D.C., 1997.

2

As Kenneth Lieberthal notes in particular for Taiwan, where both sides are moving increasingly apart. See Kenneth Lieberthal, "Preventing a War Over Taiwan", *Foreign Affairs*, vol. 84 no. 2, March/April 2005, pp. 53 – 63.

3

From Conflict to Cooperation, CSIS, *op. cit.*, p.7.

Olivier Roy teaches Middle Eastern politics at the Centre d'Etudes et de Recherches Internationales (CERI), Fondation des Sciences Politiques, in Paris. He is the author most recently of *Globalised Islam: the Search for a New Ummah*, Hurst & Company, London, October 2004. Conversation with Albert Bressand, December 2004.

Salafism and the radicalisation of Muslims in the West: Olivier Roy's perspective

Is your book on globalised Islam about a crisis of Islam or of globalisation?

Olivier Roy: The book is about the unexpected consequences of globalisation for the Muslim world, stressing that they could lead to a welcome religious liberalism but also to new forms of fundamentalism based on Salafism, a strict interpretation of Islam which is now spreading among second generation Muslims in the West for reasons explored in the book.

Why has the Westernisation of Islam been a source of radicalisation, conflict and terrorism, after such a long history of cross-fertilisation between the two shores of the Mediterranean?

OR: Precisely, what we observe is not based on traditional Muslim cultures but reflects instead the recasting of traditional cultures through globalisation. Westernisation is both a source and a consequence of what I call "deculturation", the separation of Islam from Islamic cultures. New forms of religiosity among Muslims are a way to deal with this deculturation process and to recast Islam as a "mere" religion. Islam then becomes de-territorialised.

There have always been conflicts (crusades, colonialism, nationalism), but the previous conflicts were all "territorialised": about land, statehood or borders. In spite of their religious dimension, such conflicts were rooted in nationalism: Algeria in the 1950s, Palestine or now Chechnya. As a result, there was, and there is, something to negotiate, like the extent of a Palestinian state's territory. By contrast, conflicts linked with neo-fundamentalism are de-territorialised. What is at stake is the building of a "virtual ummah", a universal Muslim community, not linked with a given territory.

In this sense, there is nothing to negotiate. Conflict becomes an end in itself, not a means. Suicide action is a way to express that there is no accommodation with the existing world. And yet there could be a peaceful way to enact such a virtual ummah: the Internet.

Such a view appeals to an uprooted and disenfranchised youth, not only among second generation Muslims in the West but also among European rebels without a cause, who may convert to radical Islam to find such a cause. In this sense radical Islam has replaced the Marxist extreme left-wing in European campuses and under-privileged neighbourhoods.

The type of non-territorial, non-negotiable conflicts that you describe seem to rest on questions of principle that may never be settled. In your view, is it likely that we are facing a long wave of terrorist activities?

OR: The present crisis is transitional and generational, as was the revolutionary wave of the late 1960s and early 1970s. Second generation Muslims see neo-fundamentalism as a way to assert themselves through a religious universal Islamic identity against the cultural Islam of their parents (Moroccan Islam, Indonesian Islam) and against the learned tradition of the ulemmas. Even when they get involved in jihad in Afghanistan or Bosnia, they don't see themselves as fighters in these local wars but rather as fighters or martyrs in a fantasmatic "world jihad". Such a struggle, however, could be fuelled by a process of externalisation and de-territorialisation of existing conflicts, for instance, young Palestinians giving up the hope for a territory and a state.

If this is a transitional, generational phenomenon, how can the transition towards peaceful coexistence or cross-fertilisation be accelerated?

OR: By making room for Islam in the West and acknowledging that Islam is an integral part of Western societies. Suspicion about what is too obviously Muslim (like the veil in France today) should give way to an open approach. This is not a matter of two clear-cut religious-based cultures facing each other. Islam itself is no longer a holistic system of beliefs and behaviours, and what the West must adapt to are not religious dogmas but forms of religiosity emphasising values and ethics. This trend is clearly taking shape even among those with very orthodox and conservative views. We should address the Muslims in their diversity, and not through the prism of an organised community that does not exist.

How important would a peace settlement in the Middle East be in overcoming the feelings of hostility and hatred you describe?

OR: Although the resolution of the Israeli–Palestinian conflict would help to tame Islamic radicalism, it would be a mistake to think that there is a direct link between the two. The key lies precisely in acknowledging the globalisation of Islam, and the decoupling of Islam as a religion and the territories of the Middle East. We should similarly decouple Islam from the issue of immigration. Even if the Muslim population in the West originates from immigration, new generations see themselves less and less as "immigrants", even if they balk at assimilation. We must relate not to a homogeneous Muslim constituency, but to an increasingly individualised population. It is about Muslims, not Islam…

Part 2
The Three Global Scenarios

3 Low Trust Globalisation

4 Open Doors

5 Flags

6 Trilemmaps

Sand in the wheels of global mobility

Differing national rules and standards, as well as protectionist demands, restrict the global mobility of investment and capital, and diminish trade and migrant flows.

Efforts to further develop the global trade regime seldom succeed, and there is more support for the "Tobin tax" type of capital flow barriers.[1] Preferential trade occurs within economic "coalitions of the willing", coalitions which are established through regional and bilateral agreements. Capital is only lured across borders by the promise of significantly higher returns, while migration is tightly controlled, with major efforts being made by national governments to ensure most immigrants eventually return to their home countries.

Flags, therefore, presents particular challenges for multinational corporations. In many countries, environmental standards and other regulations may be used to mask protectionist intentions and to promote domestic companies. Weak international institutions, including an eviscerated WTO, provide little discipline to control the tendency of nationalistic governments to lean towards "beggar thy neighbour" policies. The US Congress systematically affirms its right to review international decisions that appear to put foreign interests above American ones—for example, WTO or NAFTA arbitration-panel rulings.

Not only are regulatory standards effectively used as hidden (or not-so-hidden) trade barriers, but international cooperation more generally becomes strained as states attend narrowly to their own self-interest. A loose coalition of European countries take the lead in allowing their national parliaments to modify or overrule European directives when it is felt that national interests are compromised.

Efforts to address global problems (such as climate change) collapse as a growing number of countries take the "free-riding" of the US as a signal to pull back on their own commitments to international cooperation. Across many realms where reciprocal action among nations is the key to success (e.g. in addressing international public health crises, capturing drug traffickers and protecting biodiversity), worldwide policy efforts flounder.

> **In many countries, environmental standards and other regulations may be used to mask protectionist intentions and to promote domestic companies.**

Globalisation

1

On the "Tobin tax", see note p. 76.

101

Insights
By Philip Bobbitt

Philip Bobbitt is author of
The War against Terror
to be published
in late 2005 by Knopf in New York
and Penguin in London.

Nuclear terrorism: the Berkshire Hathaway perspective, and catastrophic scenarios

On May 6, 2002, Warren Buffett addressed the annual meeting of Berkshire Hathaway, the holding company whose shares make him the world's second wealthiest person, with the following: *"We're going to have something in the way of a major nuclear event"* in the US. *"It will happen. Whether it will happen in 10 years or 10 minutes, or 50 years ... it's virtually a certainty."* Washington and New York would be the top two targets because terrorists want to traumatise the country and kill as many people as possible, Buffett said.

Buffett has holdings in Coca-Cola Co., American Express and The Washington Post, but his main business is insurance. Berkshire Hathaway's insurance companies—particularly General Re Corp.—took a USD 2.4 billion underwriting loss because of the 9.11 terrorist attacks. The companies are now writing policies on terrorism but limiting their liability in any nuclear, biological or chemical attack.

Three catastrophic scenarios

While at present the likeliest terrorist attacks are also the least dangerous, this will change over time. There are three scenarios often discussed. None of them contemplate a direct attack by a state upon the US, but all have something to do with the changing nature of states. A fourth scenario, the use of a radiological or dirty bomb, will remain a likely option, but the damage it can do falls short of the catastrophic.

• First is the possibility of Al Qaeda obtaining a nuclear bomb. The Baker-Cutler Commission reported to the US Congress that there have been a number of recorded attempts to steal nuclear devices from Russia since the collapse of the Soviet Union in 1991. The most vulnerable of these weapons is the ADM, a nuclear device used by engineers either as a mine or to move earth. While security around these devices has been lax, it is improving. Moreover, the shelf life of the tritium triggers on which they rely is not long.

• Second is the chance that Al Qaeda might build its own nuclear device. This would involve the procurement of highly enriched uranium, coupled with complicated engineering. There are approximately 130 nuclear research reactors in 40 countries, at least two dozen of which currently have enough enriched uranium for one or more nuclear bombs. A nuclear black market has sold comprehensive nuclear starter kits that included advanced centrifuge components, blueprints for nuclear warheads and some consulting services. The weapon would be large, about the size of an automobile, and would require precise detonation. Even if the weapon did not detonate properly—if it "fizzled"—the blast would be about 1 kt, or several hundred times the force of the Oklahoma City bombing. Successful detonation of a rudimentary nuclear bomb like that dropped on Hiroshima, however, would destroy every structure and life in a radius of a third of a mile, with an area ten times larger ravaged by fires and radiation.

• Third is the nightmare scenario in which terrorists seize a missile site or computer codes to bring off an unauthorised launch of a nuclear tipped intercontinental or submarine/sea-launched ballistic missile. This is at present the least likely possibility, because the information required to re-target weapons against the US, as well as the launch codes themselves, are closely held and missile sites are heavily guarded. It is, however, the most attractive option to Al Qaeda of all these, because it offers the possibility of triggering a war between the two great enemies of Islam in Al Qaeda's view: the US and Russia. This scenario grows in likelihood once states acquire nuclear warheads and develop ballistic missile technology, or once a market in proliferated weapons technology becomes more mature.

Thinking about the unthinkable: economic implications

The economic effects of any catastrophic nuclear attack would be incalculable but some conclusions can be drawn. Capital from Saudi Arabia and other Muslim states would be withdrawn in fear of being frozen by the US. Capital from the US that is at present exported would be diverted to homeland reconstruction and protection. Pension, medicare and other US government funds would be pillaged to provide insurance recovery funds. Foreign investment in US debt would sharply decrease, driving up interest rates to perhaps unprecedented levels. And the confidence of US consumers would collapse, at least for some time, shattering the psychological infrastructure of credit and investment.

3 Low Trust Globalisation

4 Open Doors

5 Flags

6 Trilemmaps

The Three Global Scenarios

Part 2

5.4
Economic growth in *Flags*

The economic environment of *Flags*, and the many hurdles it features, are not conducive to high growth. Trade barriers, both implicit and explicit, seriously slow down flows of goods. The mobility of labour and financial assets is significantly curtailed by security concerns. Innovation and knowledge sharing are also inhibited. All of these elements contribute to low productivity growth, which translates into global GDP growth of only 2.6%.

The US economy suffers badly in this scenario. Right after the recovery of 2004, growth levels plummet again, as a consequence of the gradual introduction of "grit"—barriers to trade and investment—in the global economic system. Although many countries raise such barriers, the US—spurred on by increasing security concerns—leads the way and sees growth rates average below 2% until the end of the decade. While under similar pressure, growth rates for the EU member countries do not have as far to fall as the US. Other factors also contribute to the curtailment of US investment and growth, such as high interest rate baselines: real bond yields average almost 4% over the period of analysis.

Thus, in *Flags* as in *Open Doors*, the rates of growth in Europe and the US converge, only in the former case convergence occurs at a lower rate—below 2% until the end of the decade. The economic connections between different regions of the world are weaker, enabling them to develop at their own pace. Local economic crises generally have less of a global impact as countries with little strategic importance are marginalised.

High risk premiums, lower BRICs growth
The reduced mobility of financial capital implies that emerging markets, even the most promising ones like Brazil, Russia, India and China (the BRICs as Goldman Sachs refers to them), receive considerably less foreign direct investment in *Flags* than in the other two scenarios. This has an additional negative impact on productivity levels and, consequently, on growth. China is forced onto a structurally different development path as a result of poor export demand, and growth rates average 6–7% for the period to 2015. Similarly, India sees its

ambition to become the world's software and offshoring powerhouse sharply curtailed (although this is effectively a return to the situation of the mid-1990s), and is subject to crises. This is reflected by high risk premiums in many emerging countries: on average the premium is 430 basis points over US Treasury Bill rates, considerably more than in *Low Trust Globalisation* and *Open Doors*. Ultimately, emerging markets are high risk, but offer high returns in a global economy that is not very boisterous otherwise.

The cost of macroeconomic misalignment
Perhaps the biggest economic threat in *Flags* is the lack of business cycle synchronisation between the different economic powers, combined with a loose and inefficient international financial architecture that is not conducive to proper coordination. Hence, considerable misalignments of exchange rates, deep trade imbalances and, given the interventionist nature of government, major fiscal imbalances. In this business climate crises will not be rare. Even though the crisis transmission mechanism is slower in *Flags* than in the two scenarios that are closer to the market incentives apex of the triangle—which implies greater market integration and globalisation—such crises can still be deep and disruptive.

The economic environment described above represents the baseline of the scenario. Crises can then be superimposed to generate a full volatility profile. In the case of *Flags*, crises such as an internal crisis in the EU, or increasing violence leading to the temporary halt of Saudi Arabia's oil production, could be particularly disruptive (see our discussion of macroeconomic crises in chapter 11).

Economic growth

5.5

The energy scene in *Flags*

In *Flags*, citizens look to their governments to ensure that the energy system meets their expectations, which are strongly driven by economic welfare considerations and by local environmental concerns. Concerns about future generations are also put forward by advocacy groups who emphasise the importance of pursuing indigenous resources and developing renewable energy sources. Meanwhile, governments harbour concerns of their own regarding energy security in relation to domestic and foreign policy. Last but not least, voters expect energy to be affordable. The market is not trusted to deliver this combination of objectives on its own, but economic efficiency is nevertheless a key consideration.

National resources and national champions

Emerging fears that access to oil and gas resources will become restricted, along with tough local environmental demands from citizens, lead governments to assert themselves in shaping the energy system. Governments allow for redundancies when they consider it beneficial for social cohesion or domestic economic and political stability. They embrace market forces when it is opportune, and monopolies coexist with liberalised markets.

Environmental concerns: broad horizons, but narrow decisions

Concern for the global environment, which a number of groups, coalitions and the media keep in the headlines, fails to manifest itself in a proper policy arena in which problems can be addressed in a coordinated manner. In practice, the policy debate tends to be centred on local air and water pollution issues, as in the US today. Pressure groups promote many different solutions and call for a radical change. Wind, hydro and nuclear power, as well as new fuels, all have their staunch supporters and resolute opponents.

A diverse energy mix

Policies aim to increase energy efficiency significantly, and strongly support the development of domestic energy sources, whether fossil fuels or renewables. Hydro is preferred if new capacity is required, while existing nuclear facilities are kept open for as long as possible.

France and China spearhead a global revitalisation of the nuclear industry around a new generation of power plants, with the Green movement divided as to whether the problem of climate change justifies a reassessment of their traditional opposition to nuclear power. As a result, a diverse energy mix emerges, with many different local and regional solutions.

A patchwork of heavy-handed regulations and taxes

Regulation is via legislation and *ad hoc* agreements. Ministries of energy are often all-powerful across the upstream and downstream environments. NGOs and the media play a role in the dialogue between government and the public, but ultimately the state takes the lead in looking after consumers and protecting national interests.

Consensus is difficult to find; however, in the transport sector, emission and efficiency standards are widely adopted in key countries and in a number of US states. This leads to the development of hybrid vehicles and further dieselisation in the short term, and the adoption of some fuel cells in the long run. Biofuels are developed more rapidly—of the alternative future fuels, they offer the most potential benefit in relation to the problem of greenhouse gases, when analysed on a source-to-sink basis (see box on p. 106).

Taxes are maintained at high levels to discourage energy consumption, while new energy technologies such as renewables are supported through "set-aside" obligations, with costs passed on to consumers. Carbon taxes are not implemented in a harmonised way across regions, while market-based instruments, such as internationally tradable carbon permits, are not trusted: they are considered to be complicated and vulnerable to deception. Nevertheless, progress on CO_2 abatement might yet be achieved as a side effect of efforts to reduce the growth in energy demand through efficiency gains, stimulating the development of renewables and, in the longer term, nuclear power. However, when governments need to choose, they prioritise energy security and employment over global environmental concerns.

National energy markets and social obligations

Full liberalisation of energy markets is increasingly questioned; this is prompted both by the apparent lack of end-consumer benefits, and

Part 2
The Three Global Scenarios

3 Low Trust Globalisation
4 Open Doors
5 Flags
6 Trilemmaps

by the politically unsettling nature of price volatility that results from liberalisation and seems to provide as much "noise" as signals to the market for new investments. There is also a lack of political will to break up incumbent gas and power strong holds. Governments never lose sight of social obligations—e.g. affordable energy prices, strategic, as well as energy security obligations; back up in the form of infrastructure redundancy and commercial stocks are insisted upon.

The markets are characterised by medium- and long-term bilateral supply contracts and by government support for those national companies that deliver on their policies. Governments create secure markets for renewables. Local taxation, designed to achieve objectives in environmental protection and to reduce energy demand, heavily influences end-consumer prices.

Governments play a critical role in securing long-term energy imports by enabling major cross-border projects, but these deals are often tied up in a wide range of political issues and pursued to secure supply by "direct connections".

IOCs between a rock and a hard place

NOCs are favoured and actively look for ventures with other NOCs. For IOCs, by contrast, access to national resources is difficult and the opportunities are generally fewer and smaller. Competition is tough and governments demand high performance from companies, although eagerness for technology transfer provides major incentives to work with IOCs. Once IOCs have been admitted through the national door, they can expect continuous pressure to renegotiate original terms, as host nations face budgetary pressures.

Assisted decoupling of energy and GDP growth

Below-trend world economic growth, and the strong focus on increasing energy efficiencies across all sectors, results in overall energy demand growth of around 1.6% per annum. With energy prices over the last five years—at approximately 4-5% of total world GDP, prices will have to rise significantly to have a major impact on energy intensity.[1] Government intervention is therefore necessary to reduce energy intensity.[2]

Coal demand increases considerably at 2% annually, as indigenous resources are mobilised, either directly or via conversion to liquid or gas. This is particularly true for Latin America and South Asia where coal demand rises by more than 5%.

With regard to alternatives, consensus on one solution is difficult to achieve. On the whole hydro is preferred to nuclear due to pressure group influence. The focus on renewables to address security of supply fears results in annual growth rates above 10%, particularly beyond 2015; their overall market share becomes around 8% by 2025. Wind is the fastest growing renewable, followed closely by solar. Unlike the other scenarios, biomass and geothermal grow relatively strongly as indigenous supplies. Solar provides robust distributed energy sources, with both photovoltaic (PV) and solar thermal growing significantly. Relative to the other scenarios, solar thermal grows more strongly relative to solar PV as it is aggressively pursued to deliver local heating solutions.

For regions like Europe, fearing lack of infrastructure development to deliver their energy needs, renewables are actively pursued, with rigorous local (and some Europe-wide) mandated supply levels rigorously implemented by government regulation. Local communities have a strong voice in keeping out locally polluting industries; however, planning regulation also discriminates locally against renewables.

Energy

1

This reflects past relationships between the affordability of energy, expressed as a percentage of total world GDP, and the growth of energy demand. Above a certain threshold, energy demand is reduced. This relationship is shifting over time: data over the last 35 years indicate that the point of "near zero" energy growth has moved recently from the long-term historical average of just over 10% of world GDP towards the region of 4–6%.

2

See chapter 12 for a comprehensive discussion of the energy intensity of growth and of energy security policies in the three scenarios.

Biofuels: a complex policy melting pot

Biofuels come in two categories: bio-esters and ethanol. Bio-esters are made from vegetable oils, such as rapeseed or soya oil, and are blended with diesel fuel. Ethanol is alcohol produced from the fermentation of sugars that are derived from plants, such as sugar cane, corn, wheat and barley, and is used as a gasoline component.

Bio-esters have mainly been used in Europe, primarily in France and Italy as 5% blends, and in undiluted form in Germany. A problem with bio-esters is that the availability of spare vegetable oil and recovered oils is limited, which makes them expensive and constrains their ultimate potential.

Ethanol has been used in large quantities in Brazil, where it is produced from sugar cane, and in the US, where it is produced from maize. The fuel potential of ethanol is greater than that of bio-esters.
Cellulose ethanol, in contrast to conventional ethanol, can be made from the non-food portion of crops (e.g. straw, corn stalks and corn cobs).

Brazil and the carbon credit boost

Brazil is expected to undergo a major resurgence as an ethanol producer, having signed a 10-year accord with Germany in which Germany has agreed to pay for carbon credits by funding the production of 100,000 new cars that run purely on ethanol. This arrangement will boost ethanol consumption in Brazil to 430 million litres a year. Export opportunities also beckon, which may provide an impetus for growth in the ethanol industry. For example, US ethanol demand is set to grow as the fuel additive methyl tertiary-butyl ether (MTBE)—originally used to enhance octane, and later in higher concentrations as an oxygenate to aid more complete combustion—is phased out, due to health concerns. Insufficient capacity in the US to cover this increased demand for ethanol could also provide export opportunities for Brazil.

Meanwhile, India and Thailand have imported Brazil's ethanol technology, to boost agricultural products and reduce oil dependency.

Agricultural policies and the 2003 EU Biofuels Directive

Yet despite the growing world demand for ethanol as a fuel additive, agricultural subsidies abroad could frustrate Brazil's efforts to penetrate other export markets. For example, in the EU, there will be a shift from crops-for-food to crops-for-fuel. This will be policy-driven in countries like Spain, Germany, France and the UK, to help farmers and reduce dependency on oil imports.

In April 2003, EU finance ministers agreed to the Biofuels Directive. This requires member states to set targets on the use of biofuels, which must constitute 2% of transport fuel by the end of 2005 and 5.75% by the end of 2010. Partial or full excise duty exemptions have been granted to make ethanol competitive as a fuel.

Environmentalists vs. farmers?

Some environmental groups are sceptical of the merits of biofuels, claiming the Directive will lead to environmentally destructive intensive farming and will inhibit incentives to build more environmentally friendly cars.

Currently, bio-components in fuels represented almost 1%, in volume terms, of the overall gasoline and middle distillates production worldwide. It is expected that by the end of the decade their share will have doubled. New technologies, able to convert cellulose materials, will develop and by 2020 it is anticipated that the share of bio-components may more than double again.

Part 2

The Three Global Scenarios

3 Low Trust Globalisation

4 Open Doors

5 Flags

6 Trilemmaps

Source: Shell estimates

Energy

Gas markets remain fragmented

Gas demand growth is 1.7% per annum, with growing market share in the power sector. In the US, the mounting challenge of meeting demand with indigenous supply pushes gas prices above prices for coal after 2015. This forces the opening of new areas for exploration and production in environmentally sensitive regions, despite—at times—huge public protests. Due to lower overall world demand growth, the regulatory process can keep up with market requirements for building new LNG import facilities, and at times there is excess capacity in re-gasification.

In the EU, the single European gas market does not materialise. Although national systems are interconnected and a degree of harmonisation is achieved, domestic markets remain under distinct regulatory regimes. In Russia, Gazprom preserves its monopoly power over all parts of the gas value chain. Gas export policy is an integral part of Russia's financial and foreign policy. The transition to market prices for gas in the Russian domestic market is slow—production costs can barely be recouped—and independent producers continue to struggle to achieve transparent access to pipelines.

China focuses on Central Asian pipeline gas and LNG, with the gas purchased and delivered within the framework of long-term bilateral contracts, preferably between NOCs. The LNG market is the only one in which IOCs can expect to benefit from a stable and encouraging framework.

Hard times for OPEC

Oil demand growth is weak in *Flags*—less than 1% per annum— as oil takes a double hit from low economic growth and energy conservation policies. Oil remains the dominant global fuel, but its market share wanes from the present 39% to 32% by 2025.

Up to 2010–2015, non-OPEC supply growth matches, on average, total world oil demand growth, despite modest oil prices. This is achieved because of both low demand and the success of government policies in maximising the recovery of indigenous resources.

Some countries, however, decide to extend the life span of their natural resources for the benefit of their domestic economies and

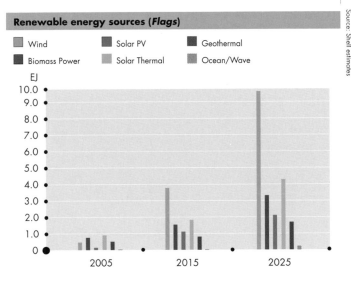

Renewable energy sources (*Flags*)

- Wind
- Biomass Power
- Solar PV
- Solar Thermal
- Geothermal
- Ocean/Wave

EJ

future generations, and non-OPEC supply levels off by 2015–2020. OPEC initially sees both a loss of market share and a fall in absolute production, and a turnaround is delayed till 2015.

OPEC countries remain strongly dependent on oil revenues, as they fail to diversify their economies. Geopolitical considerations and self-interest ensures that OPEC maintains sufficient spare capacity to absorb the frequent short-lived supply disruptions that occur due to sociopolitical unrest or demand surges.

In *Flags*, therefore, OPEC cohesion sees many ups and downs. Overall discipline is difficult to maintain as countries follow different strategies to maximise budget revenues. This results in the traditional "long-wave" oil price cycle, with alternating high and low volatility phases. Oil prices average the cost of non-OPEC supply with a margin to 2015 but increase thereafter, as OPEC's market share and therefore market power start increasing.

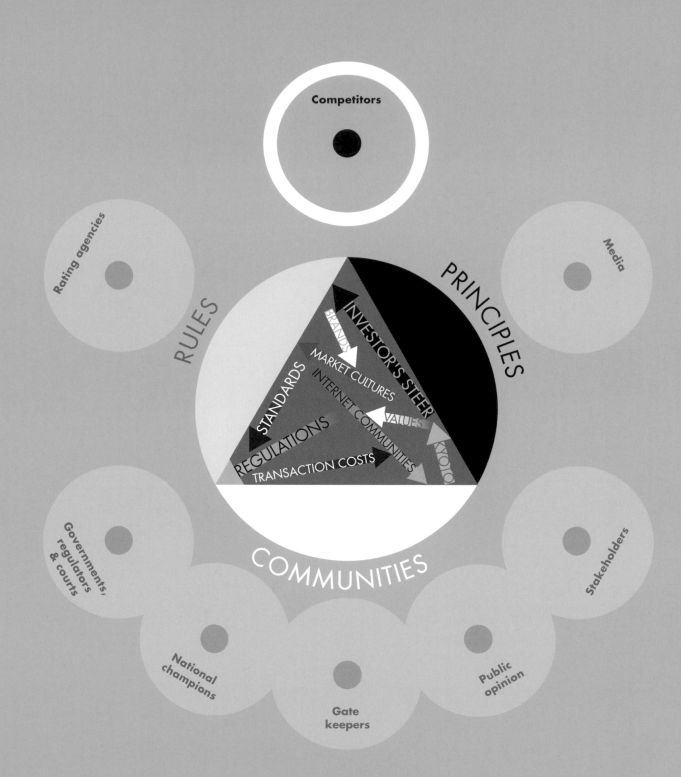

Part 2

The Three Global Scenarios

3 Low Trust Globalisation

4 Open Doors

5 Flags

6 Trilemmaps

Chapter 6

Trilemmaps on the three contrasted global business environments

While the three *Global Scenarios to 2025* may appear complex, as the forces behind them overlap, they capture essential policy trade-offs and defining features in the set of incentives, constraints and risks that will shape public and private strategies. The underlying framework is designed to allow this analysis to be pushed further, with respect to specific projects or challenges. The results of many such analyses have been summarised in the form of a *Trilemmap* matrix. Some important examples—concerning key dimensions of the business environment—are shared in the present chapter.

The selection covers:
• the sharply contrasted ways in which the dual crisis of security and trust is resolved:
• contrasted capital market cultures and investor attitudes;
• the regulatory environment and the relative importance of detailed rules, broader principles and national considerations;
• the nature of competitive advantages and their implications for integration and outsourcing;
• the nature of interactions between civil society, market participants and states.

On almost all of these dimensions, these three business environments are very distinct, and challenging.

Related perspectives on the impact of technological change are discussed in the form of a conversation with one of Japan's brightest Internet analysts and pioneers. Reflecting with him on how governance could evolve for the Internet—an essential global business/social/public infrastructure—we emphasise the way in which people's attitudes, a central focus in previous *Global Scenarios*, remain an essential influence on our business environment.

The important dimensions that we cover in this report are intended merely as illustrations. In all cases, the combination of forces in the *Trilemma Triangle* and the emphasis on policy trade-offs, coalitions and market cultures can be applied in a disciplined manner, whether at the global level or at market level.

6a

Contrasted resolutions of the dual crisis of security and trust

Market solutions, and how market failures are dealt with

Both the market and the state are called upon to resolve the crisis of security and trust. What can be achieved through the market, however, is far greater in *Open Doors* than in any scenario. While the state—notably through its regulatory function—deals quite successfully with this market failure in *Low Trust Globalisation*, civil society is left confronting much higher tensions in the less tamed environment of *Flags*. Hence the critical differences in the nature and production of public goods, in the importance of legal obstacles at the borders ("jurisdictional discontinuities") and in the nature and level of transaction costs.

"Built-in" versus "bolt-on" approaches

Security under *Low Trust Globalisation* cannot be provided by the market but is "bolt-on", as we saw in chapter 3, through intrusive checks and controls that are superimposed on existing processes. The Container Initiative, whereby the US wants the content of every container reaching its shores to have been screened for possible terrorist threats, is one example. Similarly, trust in the marketplace is provided through coercive intervention by regulators, in ways that are not necessarily well planned and coordinated. *Low Trust Globalisation* is a "prove it to me" world in which credentials are never taken at face value but must be tested systematically.

By contrast, in *Open Doors*, precautionary measures are favoured both to guarantee security and to support confidence in the marketplace. This is done through inclusive approaches in which people and organisations can be recognised on the basis of their past achievements, gaining access to built-in mechanisms that speed up controls. To find doors open to them, however, companies and even individuals must keep their own doors open to those who help them achieve the degree of understanding of their objectives, values and processes essential in this "know me" world.

Flags, not surprisingly, is a world in which defensive approaches lead nations and groups to protect themselves as "gated communities". Groups seek to protect their values by requiring strict adherence to them and by calling on the state to impose them upon others. This is a world in which companies and individuals often have to pick sides. Even enlightened causes are often promoted in a dogmatic manner in a "with us or against us" spirit. Conforming is key to being trusted, and foreigners, including foreign companies and even foreign concepts, are often seen as a threat.

Again, what we describe as distinct scenarios can also apply to different contemporary national environments.

Security and trust

Trilemm▲p 1

How is the dual crisis of security and trust dealt with?

Scenario	Resolving the security crisis	Resolving the crisis of trust
Low Trust Globalisation	*Ad hoc* crisis management. **Intrusive checks and controls.**	Rules-based mandatory standards. **"Prove it to me" world.**
Open Doors	Inclusive institutions and alliances. **Precautionary Principle.**	Principles-based standards and voluntary codes. Reputation premium. **"Know me" world.**
Flags	Reduced dependency, check points. **Gated communities.**	Affiliation, and community-based loyalty. **"Follow me" world.**

6b
Capital markets: the three cultures of "Exit", "Voice" and "Loyalty"

1

Albert O. Hirschman,

Exit, Voice and Loyalty:

Responses to Decline

in Firms, Organizations,

and States,

Harvard Business Press,

Cambridge, MA, 1970.

Investors' behaviours and the legal and regulatory environments translate into different capital market cultures in each of the *Global Scenarios*.

In particular the three scenarios contain quite different implications for the prioritising of risks and for risk management which we can summarise using the "Exit, Voice and Loyalty" trilogy. According to organisation theorist Albert Hirschman,[1] there are three fundamental ways in which people can react when they find themselves in conflict with an organisation or a community in which they belong: the first is to simply leave ("Exit"); the second is to stay but to voice their concerns or disagreements in the hope that a satisfactory solution can be found ("Voice"); and the third is to put loyalty before any other consideration and to remain silent, or at least fully within the limits of dissent that are acceptable (the traditional Japanese salaried man often being mentioned as a point of reference).

In a nutshell, *Low Trust Globalisation* is conducive to strategies shaped by the need for short-term optimisation and by the attractiveness of "Exit" as a central option when confronted with unwanted risks or returns. Investors vote with their feet and simply sell shares in companies that disappoint them.

By contrast, *Open Doors* is hospitable to strategies that rely more on the "Voice" option—beginning with intense dialogues between investors, companies and those stakeholders who have relational skills and clout. It is common for investors to seek higher returns over the long term through a process of strategic and operational adaptation in the firms in which they hold significant interests. Annual General Meetings are seen as important opportunities for such a dialogue.

Flags, as can be expected, sees major restrictions on capital flows and cross-border financial activity. Lack of transparency fosters investment in companies and instruments of one's own country, and staying relatively loyal to one's investment for lack of comparability.

Investors' expectations, cost of capital and foreign exchange markets

In *Low Trust Globalisation*, investors monitor companies closely and evaluate their performance against short-term benchmarks. Companies respond primarily to their shareholders. Longer-term strategic considerations play a minor role, and institutional investors are prepared to restructure their portfolios constantly. Risk aversion creates a home bias—in contrast to *Open Doors* where portfolios are globally structured and where companies pursue a broader stakeholder approach.

Fragmented capital markets have important implications for liquidity, which are reflected in higher interest rates, especially in *Flags*. In this scenario, banks play a particularly important role, not just as lenders but sometimes also as shareholders, with governments instructing banks—sometimes directly, sometimes through moral persuasion—to lend to strategically important industries. By contrast, *Open Doors* promotes an equity culture, where shareholdings are widely dispersed and where shareholders are also employees and consumers.

Foreign exchange markets also differ: whereas in *Flags*, many countries are likely to pursue a fixed exchange rate policy with inconvertible currencies, in *Open Doors* and *Low Trust Globalisation* capital movements are subject to few, if any, restrictions. In the latter, however, risks of short-term volatility and of longer-term misalignments are high, as the absence of market interventions lets cycles of "overshooting" and "undershooting" freely develop.

Part 2

The Three Global Scenarios

3 Low Trust Globalisation

4 Open Doors

5 Flags

6 *Trilemmaps*

What type of market culture?

Scenario	Investors	Cost of capital	Foreign exchange	Corporate finance
Low Trust Globalisation	**High scrutiny**; focus on short-term results measured by financial performance **benchmarks.** Underperformance results in frequent restructurings of portfolios. Shareholdings concentrated. Significant home bias.	Investors demand **higher risk premiums.** Less than full market integration limits liquidity in smaller markets and leads to **higher interest rates.**	High current and capital account convertibility. High **short-term volatility** and risk of long-term overshooting. Few official currency interventions.	**Fixed income** products serving as risk benchmarks. Private equity. **Credit ratings** absolutely critical. Investor relations a core competency.
Open Doors	Greater focus on long-term strategy and **sustainability.** Stakeholder and shareholder approach. Widely dispersed ownership. Investors are in for the long haul. Limited home bias.	Globally integrated and liquid markets. **Low risk premiums.**	**Fewer currencies**, several emerging markets adopt the dollar or the euro. Coordinated market **interventions** around exchange rate target-bands.	**Equity culture**, for both listed and private companies. High availability of **risk capital**. Private involvement in infrastructure financing.
Flags	**Fragmented** capital markets. National champions in financial markets with close ties to industries (*Keiretsu* style). Investors exert strong influence but only behind closed doors. Opacity results in **strong home bias**.	Interest rate differentials persist because of high transaction costs. Limited market integration creates **inefficiencies** and higher average interest rates.	Limited capital account convertibility. Fixed exchange rates and **currency unions** in many cases.	**Banks** as key intermediaries. Directed lending to strategic industries. "*Guanxi*" essential...

6c
Rules, principles and barriers: three regulatory cultures

As we have stressed already, and as the different aspects of the business environment reviewed in the preceding *Trilemmap*s further suggest, regulation takes quite different forms in the three *Global Scenarios*.

In the ***Low Trust Globalisation*** world, the pattern of corporate scandals and the public's distrust of the business world translate into renewed vigour among regulators. And new regulatory actors emerge at both the sub-national and the global scales. State authorities—local, state/provincial, national and global—can and do insist that companies meet demanding standards of both disclosure and performance. Enforcement against those companies whose activities are found in breach of such standards is swift and significant. New laws—building on the Sarbanes-Oxley requirements in the US—require CEOs and CFOs to take personal responsibility for the truthfulness and completeness of all reports issued by their companies.

The regulatory power of the state is reinforced by market pressures and legal actions. Continued emphasis on economic integration and trade liberalisation means that pressure for regulatory efficiency remains in place. Indeed, governments face "regulatory competition", with some jurisdictions promising a lighter regulatory touch as a way to attract new investment and jobs. Jurisdictions that regulate in ways that are perceived to be burdensome and inefficient have trouble maintaining a competitive edge, which does not mean that they do not answer in kind: blacklisting or penalising jurisdictions that opt for too lenient approaches, or that innovate too quickly, is widely supported.

Although regulatory competition is the rule, there is some limited cooperation on the international front, particularly where industry leaders insist on harmonisation of standards in support of trade.

In ***Open Doors***, corporate behaviour is determined less by governments than by the demands of the marketplace. Many companies adhere to voluntary standards that exceed legally mandated requirements. Failing to be seen as a "responsible corporate citizen" brings community pressure to bear and can cripple a company's ability to hire the top-quality workers. Business leaders are therefore very sensitive to public expectations, and "social context" determines practices in many spheres. Government regulation tends to reflect flexible approaches, as in emissions allowance trading systems. While jurisdictions still compete for new investment and jobs there is a substantial degree of cooperation among regulatory authorities. Regulatory competition is displaced by "regulatory co-opetition". From the International Accounting Standards Board (IASB) to the new Global Environmental Mechanism (GEM), regulators develop common (or, at least, baseline) standards and collaborative enforcement initiatives. Governments, NGOs and the business community are all committed to making international institutions work. The efforts of the OECD in the 1990s to establish pesticide standards, and the EU's commitment to common chemical testing protocols and other regulatory initiatives, blossom into worldwide efforts (often led by industry) to highlight "best practices" and promulgate highly protective standards. Mutual recognition of the regulatory rules and requirements of other jurisdictions is common.

In ***Flags***, national governments assert regulatory pre-eminence. Public insistence on safety and security translates into pressure for tough—and even inflexible—environment, health and other regulatory standards, no matter what the cost. "Command and control" mandates re-emerge as the dominant regulatory model. Efficiency falls by the wayside as a regulatory virtue.

On the international front, there is very little cooperation. Governments work together when they must, but largely set standards with an eye towards their own self-interest and domestic political pressures. In some circumstances, environmental rules are structured as hidden trade barriers. The WTO is hard-pressed to control the rise of this sort of protectionism as there is little support for international institutions within many countries. Trade suffers, with significant impact on smaller countries that are trade-dependent.

Part 2
The Three Global Scenarios

3 Low Trust Globalisation
4 Open Doors
5 Flags
6 Trilemmaps

Who regulates, and how?

Scenario	Regulatory authority	Regulatory style	International interaction
 **Low Trust Globalisation**	Regulators (local, state/province, **national and global**) and independent market watchdogs.	**Market mechanisms.** Full disclosure. **Private attorneys general**.	Interconnectivity and **regulatory competition**. Limited international cooperation (to support market access).
 **Open Doors**	Self-regulation and **consumer empowerment;** regulators; international bodies.	**Social contexts and values.** Transparency. Voluntary best practices. Market mechanisms (allowance trading).	Integration and **regulatory "co-opetition"**. Commitment to make international institutions work.
Flags	**States** (mostly national governments).	**"Command & control".** Inflexible, costly, inefficient. Non-disclosure.	Negotiated integration, **national regulatory dominance**, little international cooperation. Risk of protectionist standards.

What type of regulation?

Scenario	Regulatory foundations and principles
 **Low Trust Globalisation**	Security trumps everything, including market efficiency. **Compliance failures very costly**. High accountability of senior management. Box-ticking culture. Discretionary response to failures creates high regulatory risk and fosters risk aversion.
Open Doors	**Principles-based and predictable** regulations ensure level playing field. Protection of community of stakeholders, including consumers and employers. Compliance with spirit of regulations essential.
Flags	Nation-specific. **Complex webs of bilateral treaties**.

6d

Nature of transaction costs and of standardisation processes: the impact on competitive advantage

1

On transaction costs and the implications for industry structures and corporate organisations see the literature developed from notably Oliver E. Williamson, *Markets and Hierarchies: Analysis and Anti-trust Implications*, the Free Press, New York, 1975; and Oliver E. Williamson and Sidney G. Winters, eds., *The Nature of the Firm*, Oxford University Press, New York, 1993.

Transaction costs are a fundamental determinant of corporate organisation and industry structures, as they influence whether companies will tend to internalise activities or purchase ("outsource") them from the market.[1] As we emphasised, differences between legal and regulatory regimes ("jurisdictional discontinuities") can greatly add to the costs of transactions that take place across borders, as compared to transactions within the same country or jurisdiction. Similarly, the different requirements ("standards") that products or, increasingly, the production processes behind them must meet—for these products to be acceptable in a given market—have a strong influence on the cost of doing business, and on the manner in which companies can internationalise their activities.

Transaction costs vary considerably in the three scenarios and are especially high in **Low Trust Globalisation** as one is always exposed to legal risk that can be mitigated only by spelling out all liabilities clearly in any contract. Much time is spent, in that world, on identifying the "waiver clauses" that must be put in place for a transaction not to become a legal minefield.

Compliance with regulations is essential, with the focus being on the letter rather than the spirit of regulations, which adds, again, to transaction costs. Thus, in **Low Trust Globalisation**, few global standards emerge as there is intense competition and lack of trust among standard setters and companies. The US, EU and China use their market clout to try to make their national standards the global reference. The International Organisation for Standardisation (ISO) and other global standardisation arenas are used by strong players to keep weaker players at bay.

In **_Open Doors_**, transaction costs do involve an extra cost associated with rating activities—this is a world where the emphasis is more on filling out questionnaires—but companies with a good reputation find the cost acceptable. Efforts are made to simplify contracts. Standards that emerge from the marketplace and from society also continue to differ, but there is mutual recognition on a global scale and convergence towards best practices. Reaching consensus takes time, but is done under strict anti-trust disciplines.

In **_Flags_**, regulations reflect far more specific and contrasting agendas, under the direct influence of national politics. National preferences are often granted "between the lines", in the form of regulations that favour insiders or of standards that are set in large part by the national champions. This can be deliberate or simply due to the need to address problems with a long national history that foreign companies find harder to understand.

Transaction costs are about the local presence companies must build in order to play on a relatively even playing field. Connecting to the right local partners is essential, making it more difficult to operate corporate global structures around truly unified processes. Companies able to create global standards do so as part of their competitive strategy, often contradicting conclusions reached in industry forums. This is a world of conflicting proprietary "national" standards, of conclusive inter-governmental negotiations and of a few self-proclaimed "global" standards that powerful players attempt to impose extra-territorially.

Part 2
The Three Global Scenarios

3 Low Trust Globalisation
4 Open Doors
5 Flags
6 Trilemmaps

**Transaction costs
and standardisation**

Trilemm▲p7

What transaction costs, and what role for global standards?

Scenario	Transaction costs	Global standards
 **Low Trust Globalisation**	Reflect **jurisdictional discontinuities** and **distrust** among regulators. High legal costs.	ISO standards used as barriers to entry by oligopolies. **Extra-territorial** application of US and EU standards.
Open Doors	Include significant investment in reputation and a willingness to "keep one's door open". **Certifications** of all types have favourable net impact. Low barriers to cross-border cultures.	Active standardisation processes. Even when regulatory systems differ, **mutual recognition** and convergence of **best practices** facilitate seamless cross-border operations. Global anti-trust approach keeps standard-setting a level playing field.
Flags	Low within communities, very high across communities. Need for **costly local presence**.	**Extra-territorial** application of US and EU standards, and strong responses by countries in a position to do so. Global companies develop internal proprietary "global standards" as competitive assets".

6e
Towards a truly global civil society?

1

John Naughton,
"Contested Space: The
Internet and Global Civil
Society", in *Global Civil
Society 2001*, Helmut
Anheir, Marlies Glasius
and Mary Kalder, eds.,
Oxford University Press,
2001.

Developments in communication technology and globalisation have led to the proliferation of trans-boundary civil society organisations (CSOs). According to the Union of International Associations such organisations, which numbered less than 15,000 in the early 1980s and around 20,000 in 1990, are now close to 50,000. To explore what type of global civil society may emerge in the three *Global Scenarios*, four interelated dimensions are relevant which our *Trilemmap* 11 explores.

Role and legitimacy of civil society organisations

Cooperation with or co-opetition of civil society can be a power tool in the "soft power" arsenal of governments, international institutions and businesses. Many surveys show that the general public trust advocacy groups for information much more than they do the media or businesses. Yet some fear that attempts to outsource service provision to civil society will enable governments to dictate policy to civil society organisations. We see this playing out in the US, where the Church of Jesus Christ of Latter-day Saints (Mormon Church), a major provider of social services, has stated that it will not participate in state-funded faith-based social services provision programmes.

CSOs do not have the same public accountability as government bodies. They are private entities and are only accountable to any members they have for what they do. Some argue that these groups are as divorced from citizens' views as governments are and that their claims to legitimacy are weaker than those of democratic governments. Service provision organisations are at less risk from such a backlash. There are also questions about the representative nature of civil society groups, most recently focused on those that are increasingly able to influence national and global negotiations.

Organisation and types of coalitions

CSOs may define their agenda around single issues or broader objectives, and they can pursue it in isolation or within project-specific or long-term coalitions with other CSOs, governments and companies. Meanwhile, different types of organisational structures may develop, from the large international NGOs able to operate like multinational corporations to small and local CSOs.

The flow of information is critical to the health and strength of civil society which tends to assume that the Internet is a given and that the only challenge is to make effective use of it. John Naughton argues that this view is profoundly misguided: *"The Internet is the way it is, open, permissive, uncontrolled by governments and corporations, because of the values embodied in its technical architecture. These values resonate with those of global civil society. But there are powerful forces representing very different values, which are pressing to change the architecture to make the system much more closed and controllable."* [1]

Insider vs. outsider tactics in relations with companies

CSOs whose main objective is to influence decision makers (advocacy groups, interest-based organisations and social movements) have many different tactics. "Outsiders" see their role as stirring up public opinion, sometimes staging dramatic actions that place an issue on the public agenda. "Insiders" take advantage of public awareness, using it to work with governments and corporations to establish programmes for change. Often the two groups disparage each other: the insiders see the outsiders as obstructive, sometimes causing more harm than good; the outsiders dismiss the insiders as sell-outs.

North—South cooperation

Many North—South partnerships have sprung up in recent years and increasingly Northern CSOs are helping Southern CSOs to work for themselves. So perhaps we are not so much seeing the evolution of a transnational civil society as a strengthening of the capacity of local and national groups to tackle global issues. There seems to be a tacit agreement amongst Northern and Southern CSOs that democracy, broadly defined, is a good thing, as is a basic belief in human rights. However, beyond that it is difficult to find agreement on which priorities should be set. In particular, environmental groups of the developed world and development groups of the South often find that their priorities are in direct conflict with each other.

Part 2
The Three Global Scenarios

3 Low Trust Globalisation
4 Open Doors
5 Flags
6 Trilemmaps

Civil society

Trilemm▲p11

NGOs, CSOs, coalitions and the force of community: What type of civil society?

Scenario	Role of civil society	Organisation	Relations with companies	North–South links
Low Trust Globalisation	Expanding but constrained by states.	Regional and local CSOs (NGOs less legitimate). **Project-specific coalitions**.	**Mostly outsiders**. Cooperative or contesting, but always at a distance. Continuous negotiations of standards.	Larger role of NGOs in foreign aid, under strict conditionality.
Open Doors	Explosive growth in global and local CSOs (followed by consolidation). Using the power of communities to influence.	**Long-term coalitions** based on shared values among CSOs, NGOs, state agencies and market organisations.	**Mostly insiders**. Work with corporations.	Decentralised cooperation between CSOs and NGOs of North and South.
Flags	More extreme agendas, more use of violence.	NGOs are often **state-sponsored** or accredited.	Work less with corporations, more with (or against) **governments**.	*Ad hoc* international alliances with strong focus on national agendas.

Note: CSOs encompass all volunteer groups, trade unions, churches, cultural associations and single-person organisations as well as NGOs. The latter tend to be institutionalised organisations with fixed headquarters and paid staff.

6f

Internet "netizens" and the governance of the knowledge society of 2025: an Asian perspective

1

Izumi Aizu is
Deputy Director
of the Institute for
Hypernetwork Society
in Tokyo; a leading
participant in the UN
Working Group on
Internet Governance
and the World Summit
on Information Society;
and author of *Internet
Global Governance*,
NTT Publications, Tokyo,
November 2004.

2

Howard Rheingold,
*The Virtual Community,
Homesteading on the
Electronic Frontier*,
Addison Wesley, 1993.

3

Howard Rheingold,
*Smart Mobs: The Next
Social Revolution
Transforming Cultures and
Communities in the Age
of Instant Access*,
Basic Books,
New York, 2003.

4

Erez Kalir and Elliot E.
Maxwell, *Rethinking
Boundaries in
Cyberspace*, Aspen
Institute, Aspen,
CO, 2002.

Our assessment of our future business environment would not be complete if we did not cover how information and communication technology will shape the further development of globalisation. An essential aspect—probably the cornerstone—in the development of what is called the "global knowledge economy" or the "global networked society" is the Internet. How will *Trilemma* forces shape the evolution of the Internet and of the many processes for which it can serve as a foundation? We asked web pioneer Izumi Aizu:[1]

In his book *The Virtual Community*,[2] Howard Rheingold devotes a full chapter to the concepts that you and Professor Shumpei Kumon have put forward to make sense of the new political economy of the knowledge society, notably your description of "netizens" as key members of the global civil society. Who are "netizens"?

Izumi Aizu: Netizens are citizens who take advantage of global networks to position themselves as major actors of the information society. They do a lot of sharing online and they are happy to keep information free and unregulated. By exchanging and sharing, they enhance their mutual value or create new value.

Are there many netizens today, and where in Asia?
IA: Of all countries, Korea is the one where this notion is most readily embraced. Actually, most young Koreans understand the term "netizen" and apply it to themselves, and even their parents often recognise the term.

How does China fit in the picture?
IA: On the one hand, the Chinese government actively monitors the Internet traffic and carefully controls international connections through the seven authorised international gateways. But on the other hand, the population at large has made the Internet a part of its life. As in Korea, I can use the term "netizen" and be immediately understood by a Chinese audience. The Chinese character for netizen is a combination of the characters for network and people, and it is understood to refer to those who are very active in online forums. The Chinese "netizens" are not specially shy in criticising government policy, which is now well accepted at the local level if not above, but also in promoting causes that may take the government by surprise. A recent example is an intense anti-Japanese campaign that the leadership could not ignore as it was becoming an issue in relations between China and Japan. There are also thousands of "netizens" contributing their ideas to help the Deputy Chairman of the National Assembly, a national figure when it comes to the use of the Internet, to come up with proposals for new legislation in fields like pollution control. No less than 20 pieces of legislation have been influenced in that way, on subjects of interest in their daily life.

What do you see as the next major source of change for netizens worldwide?
IA: Mobile technology is a source of fundamental change, bringing forward what some call ubiquity—meaning the capacity to be connected whenever and wherever. This enables people to act immediately, either politically or socially. It is still too early to identify the full consequences of this phenomenon, but it can be a major source of changes in the relationship of people to each other. It already has a major impact on Islamic countries like Iran, Afghanistan and others.

Do you see the Internet as a catalyst for the *Open Doors Global Scenario*?
IA: The Internet is a platform for innovation in which anybody has the capability to be the innovator. This is changing the power of individuals very much in an *Open Doors* perspective. But states have not said their last word, and commercial trends like spam call for solutions that may take us into other scenarios....

Let me, in turn, quote Howard Rheingold, as he is asking whether what Shell calls the *Open Doors* approach will survive efforts by states to bring the Internet under closer scrutiny: *"Media cartels and government agencies are seeking to reimpose the regime of the broadcast era in which the customers of technology will be deprived of the power to create and left only with the power to consume. That power struggle is what the battles over file-sharing, copy protection, regulation of the radio spectrum are about."*[3] As he and other analysts suggest, there are also significant feelings of insecurity and distrust that can have an impact on Internet governance.[4]

Internet

Trilemm▲p 12

How is the global Internet governed?

Scenario	Business models for the web	Governing principles	Standards and governance of Internet
Low Trust Globalisation	**Free** content. **Controlled** traffic and **micro payments**.	**Regulations.**	**Tripartite** structure based on ILO model* bringing together states, companies and civil society.
Open Doors	Free enterprise. **"P2P"**, free music. "Intelprises". Public–Private Partnerships (PPPs). Spam.	Persuasion. **Self-regulation.**	**Bottom-up** process of standard-setting. Internet governance is seen as no more than an operational issue outside of government control.
Flags	Commercial-driven. "Free enterprise islands", and islands of **local freedom**. Filtering of cross-border flows.	**Sovereignty and coercion.**	Country regulation & standards, international coordination along **UN/ITU** processes.

Developed in cooperation with Izumi Aizu and Adam Peake, Institute for Hypernetwork Society/Glocom, Tokyo.
* ILO is the International Labour Organisation. It is governed by governments, employees and trade unions. ITU is the International Telecommunications Union.

BUSINESS

IRONMENT

Part 3 first explores major predetermined trends common to all scenarios before drawing implications for the energy industry.

Chapter 7 describes how the US and China are bound to be essential sources of change in the international order and how notably India and Europe endeavour to adapt or catch up. Tensions in trans-Atlantic relations receive special attention. Chapter 8 focuses on the one continent in risk of marginalisation in today's globalisation patterns, Africa.

Chapter 9 presents the adaptation of states to the role of market forces around the 'Market State' constitutional model in which the promise of the state is to maximise opportunities, not welfare.

Chapter 10 highlights key demographic trends, focusing on international migrations and their economic consequences. Chapter 11 presents the different patterns of economic growth.

Chapter 12 presents the triple discontinuity that will lead to a transformed energy system, and how energy security will be pursued in each scenario. Chapter 13 highlights implications of climate change for the energy-and-carbon industry of 2025.

Part 3

Our Global Business Environment

Part 3

Our Global Business Environment

7 Globalisation patterns

8 African futures

9 Market States

10 Demography and migrations

11 Patterns of economic growth

12 The search for energy security

13 The energy-and-carbon industry

Chapter 7
The US, China and changing globalisation patterns

In keeping with trends analysed in all *Shell Global Scenarios* of the 1990s, the *Global Scenarios to 2025* assume a high degree of globalisation, although a backlash against it is allowed for in *Flags*. Yet the observation that globalisation continues could be misleading if it were taken to refer to a process that affects almost all developed and developing countries equally.

Over the next two decades, an essential trend being played out across most of the *Trilemma Triangle* map will be globalisation strongly influenced by both the US (section 7.1) and China (section 7.2).

Not that other countries or regions will not play key roles in specific domains—with Europe, notably, being the second economic "superpower". Europe, however, as we discuss with C. Fred Bergsten (see box overleaf), is more of a *status quo* power, so much absorbed in the multi-faceted challenges of its continent-wide integration as to be inward looking. Similarly, India (section 7.3), while growing rapidly, will be preoccupied by domestic challenges: a diversity of communities with divergent, even conflicting perspectives will jostle for political influence—"mutiny" in Sir V.S. Naipaul's words. The capacity of Europe to implement structural reforms (section 7.4) and trans-Atlantic relations (section 7.5) will greatly influence how the world adapts to this new phase of globalisation.

7.1
The US as the world's innovation, financial and security hub

The differential in growth rates and in long-term growth potential between the US on the one hand, and Europe and Japan on the other (approximately 3% against 2% and 1%, respectively), means that trade with, and foreign direct investment into and out of, the US have become central to further integration patterns within the OECD.

We can see a striking illustration of this in Europe. For all its achievements in removing internal barriers and adopting an (almost) common currency, the EU has seen its level of trade and the extent of its economic integration with the US and Asia increase just as fast as its own internal integration, as a result of the faster growth of these regions. While key European countries have closed the gap with the US in productivity per hour, the preference Europeans give to leisure over higher incomes also explains that US standards of living are still a third higher, in purchasing parity terms, than those of the EU-15 (except if one values leisure at the same rate as hours worked, as argued by MIT professor Olivier Blanchard).[1] The US economy acts as the world's economic and financial centre of gravity.

This central role of the US economy is most likely to persist, even if one begins to worry that the US R&D effort will suffer from "*the government's shift of funding to defense and homeland security-related research*"[2] and that the US is no longer as hospitable to foreign students and migrants as it was.[3] A key reason for lasting differentials in growth rates is demographic. The US population is expected to increase by almost 50% during the first half of the 21st century, strongly contrasting with Europe, where a number of countries like Germany already have declining population and other countries are set to follow suit. Even in China, the one child policy—which the communist leadership has begun to reassess—has laid the ground for an ageing society and, eventually, a declining population.

In addition to its sheer economic and demographic importance, the US is also playing an increasingly central role in legal and regulatory terms. As we discuss in the next chapter, not only are US legal

1

Olivier Blanchard, "The Economic Future of Europe", *Journal of Economic Perspectives*, May 2004.

2

Adam Segal, "Is America Losing Its Edge?", *Foreign Affairs*, November/December 2004.

3

Global Intelligence: Starved for Talent, joint statement from Hewlett- Packard, Level (3) Communications, Micron Technology, Texas Instruments and Microsoft, *Washington Post*, November 17, 2004.

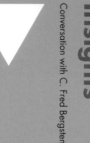

Insights

Conversation with C. Fred Bergsten

C. Fred Bergsten is Director of the Institute for International Economics in Washington D.C. and chairman of the G-8 Preparatory Conference that advises the annual G-8 Summits. He was Assistant Secretary of the US Treasury in the Carter administration. Discussion conducted by Albert Bressand at the IIE.

Overcoming US unilateralism and EU insularity: the G-2 perspective

Shell Scenarios emphasise the importance of China as the economic superpower in the making. Yet today, Europe is the world's other superpower on the side of the US. As you have written about the 21st century being "the trans-Atlantic century", how do you see the role of Europe and of the US–European relationship in our *Global Scenarios* time horizon?

C. Fred Bergsten: Presently, the EU and the US are the world's only economic superpowers. Japan, once a member of a putative G-3, has failed to position as a superpower when it could have done so, and will probably continue to fade away if only for demographic reasons. China is the rising power but is still a very poor country with an inconvertible currency, only halfway to being a market economy and probably even further away from political democracy. Yet I agree that the US–Europe relationship does not play the central role it could be playing, in spite of a billion dollars of daily trade and of over half a trillion dollars of corporate investment in both directions.

Why such a discrepancy?

CFB: Europe and the US currently have no conceptual foundation on which to base their relationship. A replacement for the foundation that the Cold War provided has still not been found, hence a constant risk of erosion or even of rupture of trans-Atlantic ties. The conflict over Iraq is only one example.

The US and Europe now see each other as inward-looking, highly egotistical entities. Europe views the US as wanting to run the world with other people's money and around US values, including the most parochial ones. Americans characterise Europeans as pontificating free-riders happy to hide behind America's leadership.

The type of US–EU relationship that you describe is a major contributor to the low-trust world explored in one of our scenarios. At the same time, you have been advocating the creation of a Group of Two (G-2) that would not only revitalise these relations but also contribute to a well functioning multilateral framework more reminiscent of our *Open Doors* scenario...

CFB: A G-2 would help counter the chief foreign policy shortcomings of each trans-Atlantic partner: America's tendency to unilateralism and Europe's tendency to insularity. To the extent that the G-2 could become an effective *de facto* steering committee, the existing international organisations, beginning with the G-7 or G-8, would indeed function more successfully. In this sense, one of the conditions for your *Open Doors* scenario would be fulfilled. Let me stress that the G-2 would not replace any of these institutional mechanisms but rather make them exercise their existing responsibilities more successfully by providing leadership within them from the only two entities, the EU and the US, presently able to do so. The G-2 would represent the innermost of a series of concentric consultation and decision-making circles.

As chairman of the Asia Pacific Economic Cooperation (APEC) Eminent Persons Group, you have played a prominent role in the Pacific Basin economic cooperation process. Is your present emphasis on G-2 an acknowledgement that APEC has not really succeeded in creating a genuine Pacific community with the US and China at the centre?

CFB: I believe rejuvenation of APEC can still happen under one of two states of affairs. One would be a sufficient faltering (or outright failure) of the Doha Round of trade negotiations that leads the member countries to seek a meaningful alternative for trade liberalisation. The other would be a serious movement towards creation of an East Asian Free Trade Area that leads the United States to again become concerned about initiatives by some Asian countries that could be "drawing a line down the middle of the Pacific". One can imagine the ASEAN countries developing their relations with China, Japan and India (the "10+3" framework of recent conferences) in ways that would elicit US reactions comparable to those of Secretary of State James Baker in 1989–90 regarding the proposals by the then Prime Minister of Malaysia, Mahathir Mohamad, for an East Asian Economic Group. I regard both of these as real possibilities, so I am doing my best to keep APEC alive as a possible contingency plan...

concepts and regulatory standards being increasingly adopted or imitated, but US long-arm jurisdiction is continuously extending its reach across borders. While the importance of the US culture in globalisation tends to be more noticeable—through Hollywood films, pop songs or "cool" trends—this less visible form of legal and regulatory influence from the US—in this case US courts, US regulators and US laws—may have a deeper impact on our global business environment.

Europe has an influence of its own, and does put forward novel approaches to cross-border regulatory integration. But European concepts like "mutual recognition" embody a more decentralised view of global integration. Europe can inspire, but the US is unsurpassed in terms of influence and control.

The SEC as securities markets regulator of last resort

One reason why the influence of states tended to be underemphasised in the 1990s was that many business gurus failed to understand the importance of regulation and regulators. A few efforts to the contrary notwithstanding, it is no longer the case that the state will intervene in, say, the telecoms or financial markets in the way the Japanese or French states used to under the heading of "industrial policy". Independent or semi-independent regulatory agencies now play an essential role in fulfilling the state's function of pursuing collective interests. The nature of those collective interests has also evolved and places a greater emphasis on the market and on a nation's "competitiveness". In this respect, US regulators play a central role, either because US practices are considered as the world's best and are emulated, or simply because compliance with US regulations happens to be a precondition for a company to operate globally.

In particular, access to US capital markets, or access to US investors, is increasingly important to a large number of companies, including companies that may not "operate" in the US in the traditional sense. In many ways, the US Securities and Exchange Commission (SEC) fulfils the role of head regulator for global capital markets just as the Fed acts as the world's *de facto* lender of last resort. International arenas such as the International Organisation of Securities Commissions (IOSCO) or the International Accounting Standard

> **Europe, the world's second economic superpower, has an influence of its own, but European concepts like "mutual recognition" embody a more decentralised view of global integration.**

Board (IASB) foster a gradual, often informal, process of integration among domestic jurisdictions, with the US always a key player. In some cases, Europe is able to leapfrog and adopt standards that build on US ones and, in doing so, correct some of their shortcomings: such is the case of the IFRS accounting standards that have been mandatory for listed companies in Europe since January 1, 2005 and are accepted (with mandatory reconciliation to USGAAP) for listing in US markets. Even then, the US has the capacity to stick to its own standards, and to make compliance with them a *de facto* precondition of seamless global operation for large companies.

127

By Adam Ward

Insights

Adam Ward is Senior Fellow for East Asian Security and the Editor of *Strategic Comments* at the International Institute for Strategic Studies (IISS), London.

China's global opportunity... and the Taiwan stumbling block

China's current grand strategy is founded on Beijing's sense that there is a unique "strategic opportunity" for it to seize over the next 20 years. This opportunity, which has been facilitated by globalisation trends, and which Beijing believes proceeds from the background of an essentially cooperative—though hardly tension-free—international relations framework, will give the government scope for pursuing its primary policy goal of economic development —the achievement of which is necessary in order to sustain social stability and Communist Party rule.

A fear of chaos

The Communist Party's powerful sense of political insecurity—which stems from the chaos of the Cultural Revolution, the fall of the Soviet bloc, the risk that China will end up as an anachronism in the international system, and the dangers associated with economic reform—exerts a significant influence on foreign policy.

A good relationship with the US is seen as crucial, even if this means temporary acceptance of American global primacy. Nonetheless, the suspicion that America is attempting to contain China provides Beijing with incentives to seek out new partners. China's diplomacy is directed towards expanding Beijing's international sway while seeking to avoid the impression of competition with the US. At a practical level, relations with Russia have at times been couched explicitly in terms of the need to dilute American power. Beijing has also made efforts to embrace Southeast Asian nations—to wean them away from US-centric foreign and defence policies—and to improve relations with India. In the trans-Atlantic divisions over the Iraq war, Beijing sensed a convergence in Sino-European perspectives.

A still limited diplomatic clout

And yet, China's scope for movement is limited. All of China's prospective partners in a multi-polar project—the usual term to describe alternatives to a unipolar world under US dominant influence—ultimately value their bilateral relationships with the US over their relations with lesser powers (including China). Even if this were not the case, China's particular political system makes a true convergence in strategic outlook between China and other countries, such as the liberal democracies of the European Union, difficult. Meanwhile, China's efforts to reassure its immediate neighbours that it is a constructive partner sit uneasily with an increasingly militaristic stance towards Taiwan.

The soft power of economic influence

For Beijing, capitalising on its "strategic opportunity" includes accumulating "comprehensive national power". Yet the structure of China's economy, which exhibits reliance on foreign demand and raw material supply as well as capital, highlights a significant degree of interdependence. In the modern global economy, states lack the means to accumulate and deploy economic power in pursuit of policy objectives, even if greater economic means enable the development of traditional forms of deployable power.

A more professional military

In recent years, Beijing has demonstrated a commitment to modernise the People's Liberation Army (PLA). In addition to the purchase of advanced equipment, largely from Russia, a higher degree of professionalism has been fostered and military exercises are increasingly sophisticated in integrating land, sea, air and asymmetrical (e.g. state *vs.* terrorist) dimensions. There is also a new clarity in China's military doctrine, which is no longer preoccupied with the protection of land borders, but rather by the need to prepare for the possibility of an intensive regional conflict on China's eastern and southern periphery—in practice, Taiwan and the East and South China Seas. In relation to Taiwan, the aim is to develop the means to coerce the island if this is required, and to deter or defeat outside intervention by the US, something which the Russian-made "kilo-class" submarines may come close to achieving. However, generational change has seen the gradual emergence of a new set of military leaders who are said to be less parochial in outlook and, recognising China's relative military weakness, may well have a greater tolerance for diplomacy.

A Chinese, and communist, dilemma

The prospect of a military crisis in the Taiwan Strait cannot be taken lightly. Although a Chinese military assault on Taiwan would entail enormous economic costs and a large risk of failure, such apprehensions might well be overridden in the heat of a crisis. The Communist Party's legitimacy is at stake: it is not clear that Party rule could survive inaction in the face of Taiwanese independence. Meanwhile, action could satisfy a nationalist goal but have a ruinous impact in Beijing's international relations: even in circumstances where a conflict was felt to have been triggered by Taiwanese brinkmanship and provocation, resorting to force would sweep away regional goodwill towards China and prompt states on its periphery to explore means of strengthening alliances and defensive capabilities in opposition to Beijing. Thus, China's window of opportunity might yet be slammed shut by the issue of Taiwan.

7.2
China as the world's manufacturing hub

The single most striking difference between globalisation at the end of the last century, and globalisation in the first quarter of the 21st century, is the speed at which China is assuming a spectacularly stronger role in international economic flows and in markets as distinct as the market for oil and the US Treasury Bills market. The fact that almost one-third of the world's cranes were located in and around Shanghai during the construction boom, or the importance of the Chinese automotive market—expected to grow from the present 20 million to 150 or 180 million cars before stabilising—highlight China's changing role as an engine for growth. More fundamentally, China's combination of currently cheap labour, market size and rapid technological modernisation is redefining the terms of global competition, with China the world's manufacturing hub.

In only a decade, from 1993 to 2003, China's share in world trade more than doubled from 2.2% to 5.2%, or about USD 500 billion. Trade as a percentage of GDP more than doubled in China between 1999 and 2003, while it contracted in Mexico, Korea, Malaysia and Taiwan. Indeed, countries of Eastern Europe and Eastern Asia that benefited from trade liberalisation and foreign direct investment (FDI) in the 1990s are already seeing a significant number of investors move to China. In the early 1990s, the Southeast Asian countries received 61% of the FDI flows going to Asia, and China only 18%. The situation has now completely reversed. As a result, the export industry of countries like Mexico (the *maquiladoras* plants close to the US border) is compelled to reinvent itself around capital and knowledge-intensive processes, or to close doors.

In 2003, according to the National Development Reform Commission, China accounted for a significant proportion of world consumption: 7% of crude oil, 25% of aluminium, 27% of steel products, 30% of iron ore, 31% of coal and 40% of the global consumption of cement. Such developments, as we discuss in chapter 12, have already significantly re-coupled GDP growth and energy consumption at the international level. In all scenarios, such trends will develop further.

Comparing China and competitor countries in terms of:

	Labour costs	Ratio of value added per unit of labour cost*
China/US	1/40	4/2.8
China/Japan	1/43	4/2.9
China/Germany	1/46	4/2.4
China/Singapore	1/29	4/1.9
China/Korea	1/15	4/3.8

* In 2001, a Chinese worker in the manufacturing sector cost, on average, USD 729, and generated added value of USD 2885 (hence the China VA multiplier of 4), against a USD 28,907 cost and a USD 81,353 value added for his or her US counterpart (VA multiplier of 2.8). Since this data was compiled, Chinese wages have begun to increase markedly.

1
Global Insight,
April 2005.

Not only are Chinese growth rates among the most impressive that the world economy has witnessed at any time in history but, after a decade of over-reporting by zealous bureaucrats, they are now widely assumed to be significantly under estimated. According to the Global Insight consultancy, which has conducted research on growth patterns at the provincial level, recent growth rates may have been as high as 14%, which would explain, in part, why market energy analysts and the IEA were so wrong in their energy import forecasts for China in 2004.[1]

This being said, the Chinese market itself is still fragmented, with many administrative barriers and provincial taxes creating obstacles to trade among provinces or even districts.

Insights
By Catherine Distler

Catherine Distler is managing director of the PROMETHEE think tank in Paris, working on globalisation, capital markets and the networked economy.

Can China price and manage risk?

The transformation of China into a fully-fledged market economy is well under way in the product and services markets, with WTO accession a key accelerator, but has only begun for financial services and capital markets. As a result, China is both the world's premier source of new growth opportunities, on a par with the US, and the world's largest source of improperly priced and managed risk. Modernising the financial system is essential to bringing this world-class risk under control, and the scenario period will not be too short for this process to run its course, as the habits of the centrally planned economy are dying hard...

Chinese financial markets still in their infancy

Equity and bond markets still play a relatively small role in risk pricing, transfer and management, and the question must be asked whether they can meet world standards within the next decade. Since its creation in 1990, China's stock market has developed to reach a market capitalisation of around USD 500 billion, enabling companies to raise some USD 100 billion. Yet the bearishness of the market since the end of 1990s is a sign among others that corporate governance issues and low dividend policies still stand in the way of efficient resource allocation. Market underperformance leads large

competitive Chinese companies to list abroad, which "entails some potentially dangerous outcomes," as emphasised recently by an executive of the Shanghai Stock Exchange.[1]

The creation of a properly functioning bond market open to foreign investors would be a critical step towards efficient risk pricing and credit rating. It would also reduce the uncertainty in business planning resulting from exclusive reliance on bank loans that often need to be rolled over the life of the funded project. As various funds now proliferate—Chinese pension or insurance funds, among others—being able to invest in bonds is key to ensuring that they can match their future payment obligations.

The Chinese banking system and its incipient risk-transfer function

The banking system, presently at the centre of risk transfer and management, it is itself a major source of risk. Non-performing loans (NPLs), estimated at around half a trillion dollars, make most Chinese banks technically insolvent. To begin redressing this situation, the Chinese government created four asset-management corporations (AMCs) in 1999 to manage USD 170 billion of NPLs. Yet hardly USD 81 billion had been sold at the end of 2004, of which USD 6 billion was to foreign investors. More worryingly, for each dollar of NPLs written off, more than one additional dollar of NPLs is still being created, as

most State-Owned Enterprises (SOEs) need new money to be kept alive. On the positive side, one presently witnesses the development of a secondary market in NPLs in which foreign investors are expected to acquire as much as USD 15 billion by the end of 2007.

The listing of state-owned commercial banks and most recently of the AMCs themselves is one way for regulators to promote organisational change. As foreign banks prepare to gain access to Chinese deposits, it is in China's interest to implement such changes before the end of the five-year WTO transitional period. At that juncture, China is required to open renminbi business to foreign-owned banks, which could pose enormous challenges to a still struggling financial system. WTO discipline could substitute for the lack of domestic consensus, saving years of step-by-step regulatory modernisation.

A currency risk bound to grow

NPLs are denominated in non-convertible renminbi and create no foreign currency exposure. On the contrary, foreign currency reserves, exceeding USD 610 billion in early 2005, have been used to the tune of USD 45 billion to recapitalise the Bank of China and China Construction Bank in preparation for listing. Yet China's further development will require the renminbi to become fully convertible. Therefore a challenge for China will be to properly

design, implement and sequence the convertibility of its currency for capital market operations.

Corporate governance as the ultimate risk management tool

Beyond the creation of bank- and market-based risk-transfer instruments, the fundamental challenge for China is the identification and pricing of economic risk. Corporate governance is the key lever in promoting this capacity on a countrywide scale.

As the Chinese state is still the largest shareholder, minority shareholders' rights are improperly protected. Improvements, though, are being made. China has begun to tackle what is an immense corporate governance agenda, passing in 1983, and modifying in 1999, the PRC Company Law. The latter now clearly articulates the rights and responsibilities of shareholders, boards, managers and supervisors. The Code of Corporate Governance has begun setting important disclosure requirements while the National Accounting Standards were improved considerably in 2003, as they are now largely patterned after International Accounting Standards (IAS/IFRS). Yet overregulation and underenforcement are common to most Asian corporate governance systems, and China is no exception. Listing and the outside pressure of institutional and foreign investors will be the best way to promote efficient corporate governance.

1

See "China needs its domestic capital market", Fang Xinghai (Deputy Chief Executive Officer of the Shanghai Stock Exchange), *Financial Times*, April 15, 2005.

Part 3

Our Global Business Environment

7 Globalisation patterns

8   African futures

9   Market States

10 Demography and migrations

11 Patterns of economic growth

12 The search for energy security

13 The energy-and-carbon industry

The ASEAN countries, India, Russia and the US adapting to the rise of China

The attractiveness of the Chinese market (which accounted for as much new demand in 2003 as the US market) and the role of China as an export market and as the hub for re-export to the US has found a diplomatic as well as an economic manifestation. China is actively developing a web of bilateral free-trade agreements (FTAs) with Southeast Asian countries. As a result Japan, Singapore and India are now being forced to compete by developing their own webs of bilateral FTAs or "partnership" agreements, with a Japan/China treaty the only major missing piece. The US, once the leading advocate of FTAs is not a party to the most important recent FTAs, as US diplomacy cannot contemplate an FTA with China.

The success of China is also a key factor behind India's efforts to accelerate its own opening-up (see section 7.3). In spite of a 68% increase over 2003, FDI into India, for instance, will have reached only USD 5 billion in 2004 as opposed to an estimated 70 billion for China, as foreign investors are attracted mostly to what is still a relatively protected Indian domestic market. Russia is also striving to double the size of its GDP by 2013: this is in part a reaction to the complete reversal of relative economic power between Russia and China, which gives rise to major dilemmas in resource-rich, but scarcely populated, Eastern Siberia.

Most interesting to watch, however, is the sophisticated US–China relationship, which is evolving beyond simple diplomatic and trade postures. Not only did China export USD 100 billion worth of goods to the US in 2003 (27% of its total exports) but, unlike Japan, China also plays its role of importer as a trump card, and skilfully draws on the domestic clout of US companies such as WalMart, GM and Motorola which have a substantial stake in China. WalMart is seen as having a favourable impact on prices in the US as a result of the importance of its low-cost imports from China (USD 30 billion in 2004), which represented a staggering one-eighth of Chinese exports to the US. Chinese authorities have been able to make the renminbi the second most important currency in an emerging dollar zone—and to achieve this status even before the renminbi is convertible. Indeed, the Chinese foreign exchange holdings, in excess of USD 610 billion at the end of 2004, are gradually giving China the type of financial clout *vis à vis* the US that only Japan enjoyed previously. New levels of interdependence will be reached as Chinese savings and trade surpluses continue to finance a rapidly expanding US public debt. Hence, the provocative statement by Deutsche Bank that the US and China can increasingly be considered as one economy.[1]

For all the talk of "pressures" being applied to China to revalue, the reality is that the only US groups campaigning actively for a revaluation of the Chinese renminbi are small supplying companies under pressure from large multinationals to cut their costs to Chinese levels, possibly by relocating to China. No surprise, therefore, that China sees no reason to unilaterally modify its administered exchange rate, the more so as there is wide disagreement as to the appropriate level (with a World Bank study advocating as high a rate as 2 renminbis for 1 dollar against 8 on PPP considerations, and the IIE a more modest 20% to 25% revaluation). Floating the renminbi might lead to a massive portfolio diversification by Chinese savers—and therefore depreciation of the renminbi!

Bad loans, political fragility and the Taiwan Straits

As Adam Ward of the IISS argues (see box p.128), China's ambitious development objectives could be derailed by war in the Taiwan Strait. Similarly, while the present "bad loans" overhang is skilfully managed,[2] a banking crisis resulting from continued "policy lending" to state-owned enterprises is still conceivable.

Such vulnerabilities notwithstanding, China does have the wherewithal to quadruple in size and power by 2025 (see charts pp.134 and 181). Resource constraints will increasingly matter, leading Chinese national companies to become savvy global players in commodities and energy markets or, possibly, to seek more inter-governmental deals to guarantee access to resources. Identifying, pricing and managing risk is, however, a far more encompassing challenge, and, as Catherine Distler suggests, Chinese capital and financial markets still have a long way to go before they can provide tools commensurate with "the Chinese risk" (see box). In addition to environmental risks, the key uncertainty, however, is of a political and legal nature.

1

Deutsche Bank Research,
March 25, 2004.

2

For a discussion of
corporate governance in
China, see conversation
with Liu Mingkang—then
Chairman of Bank of
China and presently
Chair of the China
Banking Regulatory
Commission—
in *Strategic
conversations on
business models @ the
financial frontier,* Albert
Bressand and Catherine
Distler, ed., PROMETHEE
in cooperation with
SWIFT, Paris, 2001.

131

Roderick MacFarquhar is the Leroy B. Williams Professor of History and Political Science in the Department of Government at Harvard University, and former Director of the John King Fairbank Center for East Asian Research. His publications include *The Origins of the Cultural Revolution*, 3 Volumes, Oxford University Press, 1997, and *The Politics of China : The Eras of Mao and Deng*, Cambridge University Press, 1997. Conversation with Albert Bressand.

From the "iron triangle" to the "competence mandate": political change in China

What leads you to look on the reform process, initiated by Deng Xiao Ping in 1979, as a watershed not only in the Communist era but in Chinese history?

Roderick MacFarquhar: The reforms Deng introduced marked a change from Confucian approaches as well as from Communist and Maoist ones. For the first time in Chinese history, profit and large-scale private enterprise were to be regarded not only as acceptable but as desirable. China would join the mainstream of nations and embrace international methods of development.

The way they embraced the market and capitalist methods would have been unthinkable before the thorough reappraisal that resulted from the Cultural Revolution, which was, strangely, in its essence, an immensely conservative undertaking. In line with Chinese efforts since the Opium War of 1839–42, Mao was trying to find a specific Chinese answer to the challenge of modernisation. Deng was able to say, in substance, that more than one century of search for a Chinese road had failed, and that the time had come to learn from successful countries, in East Asia and beyond—including America. He invited the Chinese Communist Party (CCP) to no longer fear that private wealth would stand in the way of central control, an obsession of Chinese rulers since the Han dynasty.

The failure of the Cultural Revolution led to new perceptions but not to a new political structure. Can economic development be pursued in a sustainable manner in the absence of political change?

RMF: The new economic ideas could not have flourished under the old system. The legacy of the Cultural Revolution was not an unchanged system but, rather, a greatly weakened political system. In no other Communist countries had the rulers unleashed upon themselves such a devastating process of criticism and punishment. Communist leaders at all levels in the hierarchy came under virulent attacks from Red Guards and society in general. As a result, the prestige of the CCP was greatly damaged and its legitimacy no longer unquestioned.

A second factor that made the existing structure less constraining was that the ideology was also undermined. Marxist–Leninism and Mao's Thought, which had replaced Confucianism as the glue binding state and society, had been taken to such extremes during the Cultural Revolution that Deng effectively abandoned it. Entrepreneurs and farmers could now go their own way, without fear of being labelled "rightists".

Third, the supreme leader himself no longer commanded the authority of an Emperor in the way Mao had still been able to do. Deng, to his credit, did not attempt to assume such absolute authority, but he had the standing to enlist the support of the leadership for reform. By contrast, with the Long March generation now gone, contemporary leaders are not in a position to impose a "grand vision" upon society. Ordinary people are now free to have their own ordinary "mini-visions". These three factors put an end to what could be called, in reference to your *Trilemma Triangle*, the "iron triangle" of Chinese political culture, a triangle in which the absolute ruler occupied the apex, with the CCP exercising unchallenged coercive power, and social cohesion achieved around an ideology—whether Confucian or Marxist—that tied the state and society together. Only the PLA has not seen its role directly challenged, but it is not certain it would still follow repressive orders in the face of mass protests.

With the "iron triangle" now gone, what transformations can further change the political landscape?

RMF: A major transformation is the growing role of religion, whether foreign religions or home-grown ones like Falun Gong. China, in effect, is a country with great emptiness at the centre, and this is very disturbing for the rulers. Yet, the Communist leadership can no longer recreate the state system that had been in place during the imperial age with a supreme ruler, a bureaucracy whose job was to carry out his instructions and an ideology that provided legitimacy to both. Ideology is now "on the shelf", which creates a space for people to try new ideas for change. Without ideological legitimacy, the Chinese leadership has to rely on its "competence mandate", a fragile source of power in any country, under any system. Pressures from farmers angry at corruption and arbitrariness will continue. The only way in which it can be defused—as it is, for instance, in India where such pressures are just as great—is by some democratic process that gives peasants a degree of control over their affairs and keeps leaders responsive to their concerns. Such change could come in at least three manners, although timing is very uncertain. The least plausible would be that the CCP embraced democratisation. A second possibility is gradual change beginning with the democratisation of CCP internal workings, to overcome the absence of any clear succession process. A third possibility is that economic setbacks followed by massive protests would force change.

In the long term, what strikes me is the importance that Chinese leaders attach to seeing China respected in the world. Many of them are bound to see that economic performance is one pillar for such respect. A political system that gives rights and dignity to all Chinese citizens is the other pillar.

> ' **The coastal elite and the modernised Communist Party will need to complete the transition to "a mature market economy governed by the rule of law".** '

The new Chinese long march towards a rules-based society

Importantly, the coastal elite and the modernised Communist Party will need to complete the transition to what Liu Guangsi, Vice Chairman of the Shanghai WTO Research Centre, calls "a mature market economy governed by the rule of law". The road is still a long one, but the way in which China has used its accession to the WTO to import comprehensive elements of the Western legal and regulatory framework is a telling illustration of what can be achieved. While China does not rush to make good on all its trade concessions, it does see the advantage of putting in place the hundreds of detailed rules that will accelerate the modernisation of its economic and business practices.

In assessing the sustainability of the Chinese development model, and the capacity of its coastal elite and Communist Party to lead the modernisation effort, we need also to have a sense of the political risks that globalisation implies from the Chinese point of view.

Chinese nationalism as an ingredient of political stability?

Chinese leaders interpret globalisation as an economic phenomenon, seeing it in terms of intensified participation in the world economy and the acceptance of its rules for international trade and investment. The Chinese people also see globalisation as a protection against the isolationist political nightmare of the Mao years. In this sense, globalisation for both the leadership and the people is part of China's "normalisation". However, each group has a different idea of what "normalisation" means.

The Chinese government's legitimacy rests largely on the country's economic growth. Yet it has never justified its rule only in economic terms but, fundamentally has claimed political authority on the basis of its ability to promote personal morality and social justice. Globalisation opens a window to undermine the moral authority of the state and to challenge its ability to provide a picture of order and continuity in a chaotic world. The government has responded to this political challenge by promoting "cultural nationalism".

133

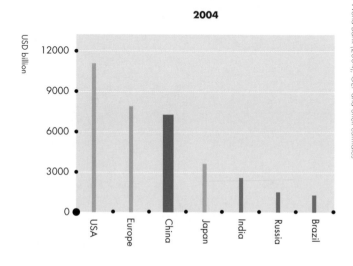

China as the world's largest economy (PPP terms) in 2025

Source: World Bank (2004), OEF and Shell estimates

2004

USD billion

12000
9000
6000
3000
0

USA | Europe | China | Japan | India | Russia | Brazil

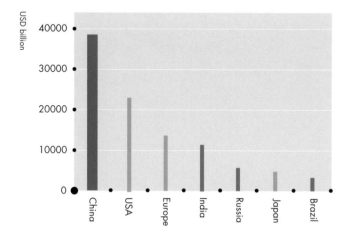

2025

USD billion

40000
30000
20000
10000
0

China | USA | Europe | India | Russia | Japan | Brazil

• Purchasing Power Parity (PPP) figures correct nominal figures for differences in domestic price levels between countries, so as to measure comparable "volumes" of consumption or production. In this graph PPP conversion weights are assumed constant over the scenario horizon, which is obviously a very crude assumption.

Here we need to understand that the term for nationalism, *minxu zhuyi*, is a recent import into Chinese, and has a racial tinge to it. The Chinese government has therefore preferred to emphasise *aiguo zhuyi*, or patriotism, as a term for nationalism. The difficulty with using this latter term is that it brings to the fore a number of ideas about cultural loss, the need to restore national self-respect, national unification and an assertion of traditional notions of sovereignty, and might imply a legitimisation of reinforced central control. Paradoxically, this may be the area where leadership and people come together. Both are united on the goal of making China a great power again. From the May 4th movement of 1919—which protested against the Treaty of Versailles' transfer of German territories in China to Japan—to today's fourth generation communist leadership, this is the one goal that has not changed.

This nationalist fervour raises troubling concerns for other countries, particularly within the neighbouring region where China is seen politically as challenging important aspects of the current *status quo*. China has a stake in the world system as it presently exists, and it is a *status quo* power in the sense of wishing to uphold the prevailing norms of the international economic game. Yet China's national interests will be pursued through a much broader spectrum of means, even if China is careful to play her cards in a patiently crafted sequence...

US–China relations
The US, as the global hegemon, is at the centre of China's strategic policy calculus, and will remain there over the period of our global scenarios. Both China's leaders and people believe that China rightfully belongs in the top league of great powers, or *da guo*, because of its civilisation, history, size, population and—now—increasing economic clout. In reaching for this position, they seek to overcome a "century of national humiliation", or *bainian guo chi*.

China stresses "great power diplomacy" or *da guo waijiao* as a key pillar of its foreign policy. But Beijing and Washington do not share a common understanding of each other's strategic presence in the Asian region. This could lead to an increasingly wary relationship between the two, complicated by the issue of Taiwan,

Part 3
Our Global Business Environment

7 Globalisation patterns
8 African futures
9 Market States
10 Demography and migrations
11 Patterns of economic growth
12 The search for energy security
13 The energy-and-carbon industry

which could grow in significance as the independence movement there strengthens, and by China's fear of strategic encirclement by the US, as the latter positions troops and bases around the Eurasian perimeter in its "war against terrorism".

In seeking to break out of this perceived containment by the US, China is actively seeking to strengthen relations with regional Asian states and to push regional integration. In doing so, China has managed to ameliorate the often palpable past anxiety of many South-East Asian states over its increasing strength; China is now seen to be behaving responsibly and both sides have grown increasingly economically interdependent on each other. China is actively involved in a host of regional initiatives, including the China–ASEAN Free Trade Agreement, the ASEAN+3 forum (including China, Japan and South Korea) and the Shanghai Cooperation Organisation bringing together China, Russia and the Central Asian countries. Yet there remains a latent suspicion within Southeast Asia over China's intentions. This extends to its doctrine of "peaceful rise" or *heping jiqi*; while intended to allay suspicions by promoting a vision of the region rising together, it may equally be compared with Japan's attempt in an earlier era to promulgate a "Greater East Asian Co-prosperity Sphere".

Meanwhile, underlying tensions with China's two key Northeast Asian neighbours continue to fester. Relations with Japan are friendly on the surface and cognisant of shared economic and business interests. But they remain rife with historically tense overtones, which strike a populist resonance on both sides and result in periodic nationalist demonstrations against each other. South Korea too, despite its growing economic dependence on China, remains wary under the surface, as the recent dispute over the extent of the ancient Korean Koguryo Kingdom (which China now claims was much smaller in power and scope) illustrates.

A further area of potential tension with the US is China's drive to achieve energy security by directly securing sources of energy supply with all the diplomatic resources at its disposal. China became a net oil importer in 1993. Today, China's oil import dependency is just short of 50% of consumption; it could rise to 75% by 2020. The energy interests within the Chinese regime are becoming an

increasingly important driver of China's foreign policy, fuelling discussion of the need for a national strategy for energy security, or *nengyuan anquan*, and even raising the possibility that China may have to go beyond diplomacy—using force, if necessary—to protect vital energy supplies. But as China moves abroad to secure energy supplies, it increasingly comes up against a US bent on the same objective; in the future the two may even collide.

While actively developing a regional Asian role, China is far less certain of what global role it should aim to play. Nevertheless, China is increasingly a global economic power in its own right. All other major powers agree that China's economic growth is fundamentally beneficial for the global market economy, even if China has found it difficult to secure the accolade of being labelled a market economy by the US. Some US strategic thinkers view China's growth as fundamentally threatening the US's hegemonic role. However, the legitimacy of the Chinese regime is predicated on economic growth. In an increasingly interdependent world, this reliance on growth translates into an increasing stake in the *status quo* of an existing international system—a system that provides benefits for China but also, as China is coming to realise, confers obligations and responsibilities on it.

China–US relations in the near future are therefore, for a number of reasons, potentially fraught. But, over the longer term, there also exists an equal potential for relations to become more constructive and more positively grounded, with a greater mutual awareness of a shared interest in global stability, provided China maintains a reasonable pace of economic growth.

The Chinese public and private governance challenge

Altogether, over the 2005–2025 scenario period, the fundamental challenge for China is, to use Minxin Pei's phrase, the governance challenge.[1] This is true, as we have seen, in the corporate and banking sector where "political lending" to SOEs and well connected firms still pre-empts the emergence of appropriate market discipline in banks, in the equity market and in the almost non-existent bond market. It is true also of public governance: as discussed with Harvard professor Roderick MacFarquhar, the "iron triangle" that kept China in the state-coercive, state-centric

1

Minxin Pei, "China's Governance Crisis", *Foreign Affairs*, September/October 2002

1

Andrew Nathan,
"China's Changing of
the Guard: Authoritarian
Resilience", *Journal of
Democracy*, v.14 n. 1,
January 2003, p. 16.

part of the *Trilemma* Triangle has largely disappeared (see box p.132). The Communist institutions that had developed from strong Confucian foundations are now fragilised, yet they have not been modernised.

Political modernisation may well happen. But as political observers such as Andrew Nathan have noted, China has made a transition from totalitarianism to a classic authoritarian regime, and one that appears increasingly stable. A political transition away from authoritarianism towards greater political liberalisation, while always possible, is neither inevitable nor for that matter apparently imminent. Of the two more likely possibilities that Roderick MacFarquhar identifies, one is violent—an economic crisis triggering higher levels of social unrest—and one is fairly constrained—a gradual democratisation of the Chinese Communist Party's internal processes (see box).

The ruling elite, realising that the greatest danger to the survival of the regime lies in public splits in the leadership (as were apparent during the Cultural Revolution, the Democracy Wall movement of 1978–79 and Tian An Men 1989), has moved to uphold unity and to narrow the effective range of policy debate within the party. Mindful of the rise of new social groups outside of the ruling establishment, with independent sources of power and wealth, the ruling regime has moved to co-opt successful business people into the party through "The Three Represents" doctrine put forward by Jiang Zemin in 2003. This creates corporatist-style links between the regime and the private sector, and keeps a check on the sorts of social groups that are allowed to organise themselves. To the extent that these groups flourish and even receive discreet official support, this may be a harbinger of further political reform. But if they are kept more firmly in line, this may suggest that the prospects for political liberalisation are quite limited.

Moreover, even if a transition away from authoritarian rule should take place, it is by no means certain that the successor regime to the current one will be more liberal and democratic. Much will depend on the context of the transition and the forces pushing change. The fear of many Chinese is of *luan* or chaos, that the successor regime could turn out not only authoritarian, but also much weaker and less able to govern effectively. How governance in China will evolve remains is indeed an essential question.

Part 3
Our Global Business Environment

7 Globalisation patterns

8 African futures

9 Market States

10 Demography and migrations

11 Patterns of economic growth

12 The search for energy security

13 The energy-and-carbon industry

7.3

India: Emerging out of China's shadow

For Europeans, India, like China, was a *"legendary seat of immense wealth and wisdom right up to the eighteenth century. Somewhere between the mid-eighteenth century and early nineteenth centuries, and well into the twentieth century, it became bywords for stagnant, archaic, weak nations."*[1] Yet perceptions seem to have come full circle—India now seems a future great power of the 21st century. Is such optimism underpinned by robust assumptions?

Economic development results from the interaction of economic fundamentals with what Dani Rodrik and Arvind Subramanian call "growth triggers" that allow the fundamentals to be mobilised beneficially.[2] In India, the fundamentals undeniably exist—a large and young population, pools of skilled human capital, and a vibrant domestic entrepreneurial spirit. It is the triggering mechanisms that raise issues, as they depend on lofty economic policies. Can India align economic reform from the top—espoused by an elite—with the ongoing political and social churning in society? This churning is occurring precisely because democracy and economic growth have stirred ambitions in various downtrodden ethnic and cultural groups. Unless economic policies and the aspirations of downtrodden groups are aligned, the former cannot be implemented effectively, and economic growth will never reach the heights achieved by China. Our prognosis over our scenario horizon is that a perfect alignment will not occur.

India's new found economic dynamism

Upon gaining independence in 1947, and under the stewardship of her first prime minister Nehru, India embarked on a journey of inward looking economic policies—at the time, the model to emulate was the Soviet Union. Economic growth remained stubbornly stuck to around 3% per annum—the infamous 'Hindu' rate of growth. In the 1980s, however, the government began to tentatively relax import licensing restrictions. In the wake of the 1991 financial crisis, reforms spread to the macroeconomic sphere, and the deregulation of large swathes of industry.

India's economic growth up to today can be described as one in which the government set out an explicit strategy to build up the manufacturing sector; however, given India's politics, the government did not follow the Soviet model to the hilt by wilfully neglecting the agricultural sector. Over the decades, the system ossified, so that manufacturing was caught in a web of regulation, while the agriculture sector remained stubbornly torpid. As a consequence, farmers were neither pulled in by the manufacturing sector, nor pushed out by the agricultural sector (and, when pushed, seem to have gone into the informal services sectors). Thus, as the graphics on the next spread illustrate, India did not trigger as strong a modernisation drive as China. While agriculture's share of GDP has steadily declined, the sector continues to hold the bulk of India's labour force—over 70% some decades ago, and still about 60% today.

The sector that has sparked excitement in India's regeneration is precisely one that the government had no explicit strategy for—i.e. the IT services sector. Outsiders began to take real notice of India when developed economies lost white collar jobs to faraway back offices in India. This success—in outsourcing—is driven by a number of factors: a large pool of technically skilled labour (a legacy of Nehruvian policies), a benign neglect from the government, a vibrant diaspora, and the rapidly declining cost of telecommunications. These factors have not only led to success in IT related services, but also in the outsourcing of other activities such as medical or financial research, and in the growth of a thriving domestic telecommunications and pharmaceutical industry.

Hence, the paradox of an economy where agriculture still occupies more than half the working population but only 22% of GDP, where the manufacturing success of the Asian tigers is largely absent, and where economic growth has been primarily generated by an informal services sector and a few corporate stars (Tata Consultancy Services, Bharti Telecom etc.) with clear yet limited momentum for other sectors.

1

Meghnad Desai,

"India and China: an

Essay in Comparative

Political Economy",

Paper for IMF

Conference on India/

China, Delhi,

November 2003.

2

Dani Rodrik and Arvind

Subramanian,

"Why India Can

Grow at 7% a Year or

More: Projections and

Reflections",

IMF Working Paper,

July 2004.

Insights

By Abraham Kozhipatt and Mattia Romani

China and India: Two qualitatively different development models

Manufacturing value added (real 2000 USD billion)

■ China ■ India

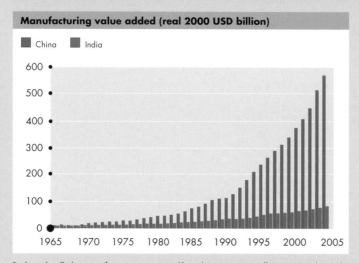

Rural population (% of total)

■ China ■ India

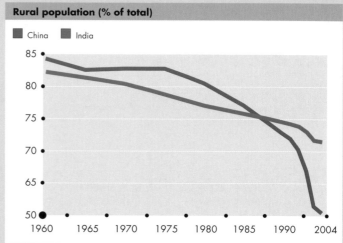

Push and pull: the manufacturing sector in China has grown rapidly, compared to India, and the rural Chinese are drawn to it.

IT and communications services exports (real 2000 USD billion)

■ China ■ India

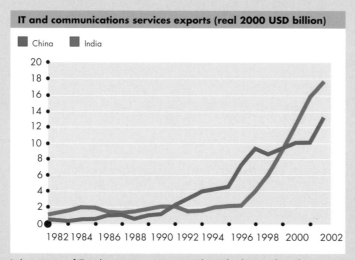

Number of computers (every 1000 people)

■ China ■ India

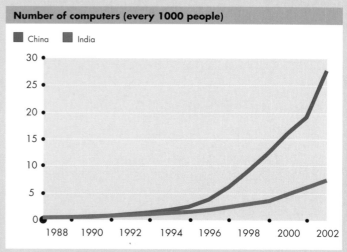

Indian exports of IT and communications services have clearly overtaken Chinese exports, but China is way ahead in applying IT to modernisation of domestic activities.

Growth of agricuture sector value added

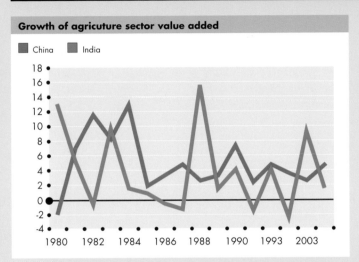

Compared to China's, Indian agriculture remains highly volatile, reflecting insufficient modernisation (as illustrated, for example, by fertiliser input), and a pronounced dependence on the weather.

Fertiliser consumption (100 gramme per hectare of arable land)

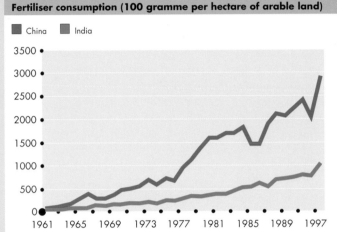

Sources:
WDI 2005,
World Bank,

National Bureau of
Statistics of China,
2004 Statistical
Survey,

The Economist,
March 3rd, 2005.

Value added in agriculture (real 2000 USD billion)

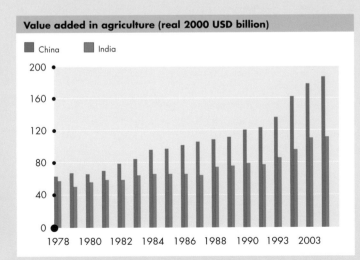

Rural China and rural India still hold more than 700 million people each. However, China has experienced a more rapid migration from its rural regions to its cities, while its agricultural sector has grown faster than India's over the same period.

Worker's remittances and FDI to China and India (real 2000 USD billion)

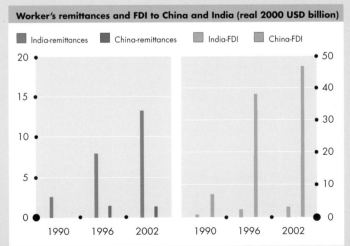

There are some 30 million ethnic Chinese in countries around the mainland—and 40% of Chinese FDI in 2003 originated from Macao, Hong Kong and Taiwan. In contrast, the Indian diaspora is scattered across more countries and professions—and has not yet displayed a similar vote of confidence in the Indian economy.

The much dicussed IT sector within services currently accounts for such a small share of GDP and employment that it cannot be a long-run source of growth. An India that is far more prosperous and equitable in 2025 than it is today must be one in which both the manufacturing (and especially) the agricultural sector have modernised.[1] In today's India, the heavy industry giant Tata has established a much heralded IT offshoot—Tata Consultancy Services. The prototypes along India's development path to 2025 may well be companies such as Bharti Telecom, which believes that the next big wave in India is in agriculture—specifically, in higher value products.[2]

Long-term structural change—India's institutional advantage

Crucially, a structural shift in agricultural output to higher value added items such as dairy products, the growth of manufacturing, and continued leadership in IT services all require further economic reform including in infrastructure investment. Thus, a critical uncertainty is whether India can implement economic policies that are dramatically different from currently accepted tenets.

The widely cited Goldman Sachs "BRICs" report on India's economic potential hinges on favourable demographics as a basis of strong growth. Based on their analysis, they suggest that India can sustain a 5% rate of growth to 2050. In a separate study, Dani Rodrik and Arvind Subramanian of the IMF use another model to suggest that in fact, India can sustain over 7% growth to 2025.

And there is more good news—India has been much more efficient than China at using capital. China has invested twice as much as India over ten years, and yet only achieved an average growth rate that is about 50% higher than India's. This suggests that India's growth, although lower than China's, can be partially attributed to more disciplined investment, and to the development of the less capital intensive services sector—contrasting with significant over investment in some sectors of the Chinese economy, notably in the state owned enterprises. Also, the quality of institutions—a point we stress again in our next chapter on Africa—is key to long-term success, and provides more good news to India. As Rodrik and Subramanian put it: *'India's growth in the near future will not*

need fundamental and difficult challenge of overcoming institutional backwardness, but can rely on the easier task of taking advantage of existing institutions. Contrast this, for example, with China which has grown extremely rapidly in the last quarter century, but which faces the inordinate challenge of large-scale institutional transformation. Another aspect of institutional quality is the resilience it creates to handling shocks. With strong institutions, a lot will have to happen to move India off its higher growth trajectory."[3]

This being said, economic projections such as those of Rodrik and Subramanian incorporate the impact of a number of social inefficiencies that are likely to keep India's growth below China's. Discussing these inefficiencies calls for a broader analysis of India's social and political fabric, with it's strengths and weaknesses.

The force of community and social cohesion in India

First, Indian democracy is a complex system, with little parallel to Western examples. There was no continual struggle against aristocratic privileges, nor a large scale industrial transformation. Hence, although democracy has taken strong root in India, it did not have the same organic growth as in the West. Instead, it was actively promoted by a benevolent state and, as a consequence, the growth of democracy in India is also associated with increased power for the state (rather than less, as in the Western case). And precisely because Indian democracy was not the outcome of organic social changes as in the West, it was not preceded by a revolutionary overturn of inequitable social customs such as the caste system. Simple regulations to abolish the caste system proved ineffective in the face of age-old attitudes and relationships. But democracy is changing all that—it has ignited the self-awareness of those on the lower rungs of the caste ladder. For these groups, who form political coalitions based on their ethnicity, caste and language, the state (which provided them with power through democracy) is naturally seen as a means of capturing economic surplus—via public sector jobs, and the dispensing of state largesse.[4]

Second, India is a grouping of multiple nationalities. India's federal system is more a 'holding-together' federalism than a 'coming-[to meet the] together' federalism like the US, where previously sovereign polities gave up part of their sovereignty in return for

1

Robert Cassen, Tim Dyson and Leela Visania (Editors), *21st Century India Population, Economy, Human Development and the Environment*, Oxford University Press, New Dehli, 2004.

2

By John Ridding, "Heard it on the grapevine", *Financial Times Weekend Magazine*, February 05, 2005.

3

Dani Rodrik and Arvind Subramanian, "Why India Can Grow at 7% a Year or More: Projections and Reflections", IMF Working Paper, July 2004.

4

Pranab K. Bardhan, "Political-Economy and Governance Issues in the Indian Economic Reform Process", University of California at Berkeley. Also see V.S. Naipaul, "India: A Million Mutinies Now", Minerva, London.

Part 3

Our Global Business Environment

7 Globalisation patterns

8 African futures

9 Market States

10 Demography and migrations

11 Patterns of economic growth

12 The search for energy security

13 The energy-and-carbon industry

shared economic gains. In contrast, in India, the state spends significant resources to keep the contending nationalities together, and economic integration remains a distant goal. As a consequence, the federal government in India is much more powerful than its US counterpart, but paradoxically, is also paralysed by the divergent aims and priorities of the various states.[1]

As a result of these social factors:
• Indian political life and bureaucracy will be increasingly populated by politicians and civil servants with regional and ethnic loyalties. This will impact on the quality of country-wide economic reform policy.
• Second, central government policies to promote economic growth through reform will be slower than in China. Policy will progress by gentle nudges (two steps forward, and one back), rather than through grand sweeps–because there has been no social revolution, and in its absence, social dissent is managed not through resolution, but through co-opetion and selective buyouts of various groups.
• Third, the economic disparities between various states will grow. With the liberalisation of the Indian economy, certain Western and Southern states with a better geographical location and social harmony have grown much faster than hinterland states in North India. This has profound implications for the cohesiveness of the federation over our scenario period.

The India of 2025: the reality of Indian economic growth

As a consequence of this sociopolitical reality, how high can India's growth rate be? In Meghnad Desai's view, India is incapable of the sustained growth rates that China has achieved. "*To stay a stable peaceful society, India has to be a muddle and mess. It is a miracle that proceeding in the way it has done, it has come as far as it has, trebling its per capita income. But there will not be growth convergence between China and India... China will again become a viable Great Power; India may become just a Great Democracy.*"[2]

While India may not be able to sustain growth rates at 8% and above as China has done, its growth rate will nevertheless be highly significant, as we discussed above. And as vast numbers of people emerge out of poverty over the next decades, the growth dynamic may well change to an even higher gear—taking on board more of the 'lost growth' due to poor policies and inefficiencies identified by

studies such as Rodrik and Subramanian's. But the harsh logic of compound growth will dictate that, over our scenario period, India will fall further behind China in economic power.

India as a *Jet Stream* player

India's international aspirations can be characterised as a 'soft' and pragmatic approach; on the international stage, to achieve influence through her economic, democratic and cultural achievements; but nevertheless, on the regional stage, to also be a military power, to maintain a 'balance' *vis à vis* China. In the spirit of the non-aligned approach that suffused foreign policy during the cold war, India will not allow herself to be used as a regional counterpoint to China, neither by the U.S., nor by her regional neighbours. Justifiably, she fears that this will draw her into a competitive and antagonistic relationship with her giant neighbour.

We have posited that the *Jet Stream* will be primarily influenced by the U.S. and China over our scenario horizon. Certainly, we do not expect India's influence to be fully felt over our scenario period —because she will still be resolving her internal tensions, especially between the forces of community and market incentives, as expressed in our *Trilemma Triangle*. Nevertheless, this very process of resolution will have a major impact on the *Jet Stream* by 2025; it is in contrast to that which we see in China—where the key issue is a resolution of the tension between the state and the market. Hence, the world in 2025 will see two new powers—China and India— that differ greatly politically and economically. This will be entirely befitting of a world that we posit will clearly shift over our scenario horizon from a western-centric to a far more heterogenous one.

Over the next two decades, India will be distinguished by her rapid economic growth and the consequent lifting of millions out of poverty, her experiments in democracy and pluralism, and last but not least, her desire for international influence and leadership born out of the sense of an ancient civilization restored to health. All these traits will make her a beacon to many other developing nations, thereby providing very significant variety in a world where the US and China are essential sources of change.

1

Pranab K. Bardhan,

op.cit.

2

Meghnad Desai,

op.cit.

Focus

Bollywood: broadcasting India's dreams and soft power

1

Bollywood stars get into a dance pose during the making of Indian movie *Aan* (Men At Work) about the Indian police force.

2

Activists belonging to Bajrang Sena, a Hindu hardline group, burn a poster of Bollywood film *Girlfriend* during a protest in the central Indian city of Bhopal, June 14, 2004. Hardline Hindus hurled stones at cinema halls in India and damaged property to stop the screening of the film, saying it violated the country's culture. *Girlfriend* is one of the first mainstream Indian films to address homosexuality.

On the set of Aan *in Bombay.*[1]

The Indian film industry—Bombay's mainstream 'Bollywood' studios, as well as independent and regional film makers—convey a striking picture of how one billion Indians react to globalisation and economic growth. Bollywood reveals three trends in Indian society. First, a two tier India—while the growing urban middle classes colourfully embrace globalisation, the rural and urban poor remain stubbornly poor. Second, a growing nationalist and religious sentiment in society and politics. Third, an awakening of regional and ethnic identities that increasingly splinters India.

Celluloid dreams

India's mainstream film industry clearly puts commercial interests over any concerns to portray realistic social environments and dilemmas —Bollywood caters explicitly to a domestic audience (and a diaspora) and therefore shows Indians the India they want to see. This is an India where heroes and heroines regularly change costumes over five times in a single dance sequence, and no helicopter is too expensive as an urban transport option. Thus, Bollywood suggests an India that is unapologetic about consuming and embracing globalisation.

The harsh reality

Yet, in spinning its web of dreams, Bollywood fails to capture the reality of 700 million rural Indians and the daily grind and chaos of India's cities. Bollywood's largest cinema studios and their most glamorous stars mostly focus on themes popular in urban India and to the prosperous diaspora. In contrast, only 'B' grade Bollywood films explicitly cater to film goers in rural spaces.

Globalisation on India's terms?

Through 'watching' Bollywood, the second trend that comes to prominence is the nationalist and religious element in society and politics. Bollywood suggests that India may be embracing globalisation, but it is doing so on its own assured terms —the picture of a vibrant and successfully adapting society that Bollywood paints is increasingly a nationalist and 'Hindu' society that is proud of its own flag and culture.

Challenging this portrayal with more testing reality is left mostly to independent film makers. They more openly portray changing social norms, but are often confronted by violently conservative groups intent on preserving their image and conception of Indian and Hindu society.

Regional cinema and awakening regional identities

Yet, across India, economic growth and democracy have also led to a flowering of linguistic and caste identities. This is mostly expressed through vibrant regional politics and documented in regional cinema.

Regional cinema, while following Bollywood's formulaic 'song and dance' formula, is more willing to portray rural themes. Regional film stars do not have a national following but are extremely popular within their provinces, whose linguistic and ethnic identities they better represent. Such regional film stars also wield political influence because their regional audiences greatly identify with them and blur the distinction between aspirations and reality.

India's soft power

Describing the substance of her cinema, and society's reaction to these works, provides a 'people's view from within India'. A largely unintended upshot of this flourishing cinema also connects to the *Jet Stream* agenda. This is the growing 'soft power' that India wields not only on her very successful diaspora across the globe, but amongst her wider neighbours and even beyond.

Bollywood and its music is not only wildly popular in the subcontinent and amongst the diaspora, but in regions as diverse as Southeast Asia and the Middle East. In countries such as Kuwait, at a time when the fundamentalist challenge is on the rise, people turn to Bollywood as a less threatening and culturally closer form of entertainment than Hollywood. Thus, emergent India also wields a softer and subtler influence on the *Jet Stream*—her 'soft power' through her films and music.

Activists protest against the film Girlfriend.[2]

Part 3
Our Global Business Environment

7 **Globalisation patterns**
8 African futures
9 Market States
10 Demography and migrations
11 Patterns of economic growth
12 The search for energy security
13 The energy-and-carbon industry

7.4
Europe's reactions to changes brought about by the US and China

Europe and the global adjustment process
Europe is the other economic superpower, with a GDP equivalent to that of the US—far above that of China. The euro is the only currency that could see its role rival that of the dollar. The euro bond market and electronic exchanges such as the Eurex derivatives market position Europe at the forefront of global finance. Boeing and Airbus have swapped roles as incumbent and challenger in the civilian aerospace sector. Conforming to European antitrust or environmental standards is essential for companies to compete globally, witness the global implications of EU decisions regarding the competitive behaviour of companies as important as Microsoft. Yet Europe is not a force for change on a scale comparable to the US or China, even if the adoption of the Kyoto Protocol does illustrate the role Europe can play on some important global issues. A feeling of estrangement is apparent, with the sense of trans-Atlantic community greatly weakened and Euro-Asian summits noticeable mostly for what they do not address and achieve.

The proposed European Constitution, and the risk of growing distrust
While the national ratification process may well falter, EU leaders were able to agree on a proposed Constitutional Treaty that would clarify the decision-making process, further extend the already wide scope of majority voting, and make visible the importance of common democratic values in the very definition of Europe. Euroscepticism notwithstanding, the EU model is an inspiring one for new or aspiring members like the Baltic countries, Turkey or Ukraine. The number of European soldiers deployed abroad, from Afghanistan to Liberia, has steadily increased, and the creation of a Minister of European Affairs (a member of the EU Commission also chairing the Foreign Affairs Council) can help Europe become a key player on global security issues. Yet these achievements may, or may not, unleash virtuous cycles beyond first order economic and diplomatic successes, depending on the *Jet Stream*. For one, Europe would not be marginalised as she often is if the US, presently in an arms race with itself, built on

its foreign policy tradition and expanded its concept of global security to include development and institutional dimensions. The stage would be set for cooperative governance in a globalised world of one military superpower and three economic and political global powers.

More generally Europe is built on a foundation of very high trust among member countries (e.g. trusting police officers at a Portuguese airport to open the doors not just to Portugal but to the territory of all "*Schengen*" countries up to the polar circle). As a result, Europe fares much better when the overall international context (the *Jet Stream*) is also one of high trust, as in *Open Doors*. Growing distrust on the world scene, however, can erode this very foundation of trust inside Europe. Observing that the US 'greenback' notes carry the words "in God we trust", the euro bank notes could very well carry the words "in one another we trust," to reflect how EU countries agree to share fundamental elements of sovereignty. By contrast, disagreements over the proposed Constitutional Treaty illustrate that a rising tide of trust may not be there to help deal with the challenges that are accumulating both around Europe and within Europe—where, for instance, an aging population will severely test the capacity of the so called "European social model" to provide the type of welfare that citizens have come to take for granted.

Two sets of issues stand out: the structural reforms known as the "Lisbon agenda", a subject we only briefly mention in this *Jet Stream* volume, and trans-Atlantic relations.

The Lisbon competitiveness[1] agenda
The example of Scandinavian and smaller EU countries shows that growth-fostering reforms are possible without dismantling social protection, yet the demographic and pension time bombs and high unemployment rates call for much more determined implementation of the Lisbon agenda of structural economic reforms, notably in labour markets.

Over the scenario period trans-Atlantic relations will be critical to setting the stage for further European integration, or for elements of disintegration, as well as to setting the *Jet Stream* context.

1

On the ways in which the EU 'social model' can be combined with, or create obstacles to EU competitiveness, see Martin Neil Baily and Jacob Funk Kirkegaard, *Transforming the European Economy*, Institute for International Economics, Washington, D.C., September 2004.

143

7.5
Will the EU and US drift apart?

1

Erik Jones, "Debating

the Transatlantic

Relationship: Rhetoric

and Reality",

International Affairs, vol.

80 no. 4, July 2004,

p.601.

2

Philip H. Gordon,

"Bridging the Atlantic

Divide", *Foreign Affairs*,

vol. 82 no. 1, January-

February 2003.

3

On this opposition

between processes

and results, see Dr

Eberhard Sandschneider,

"Reinventing trans-

Atlantic relations",

American Institute for

Contemporary Studies,

The Johns Hopkins

University, 2003,

www.aicgs.org/c/

sandschneider.pdf.

4

Charles Krauthammer,

"The Unipolar Moment",

Foreign Affairs, vol. 70

no. 1, Winter 1990-91,

p.25.

5

Robert Kagan, "The US-

EU divide", *Washington

Post*, May 26, 2002.

A paradoxical relationship

The image of a trans-Atlantic relationship more troubled than ever comes from the divergence about Iraq that occurred in the beginning of the year 2003 when France, Germany and Russia openly opposed US decision to attack Iraq. It also implies that this relationship has been "troubled" for a long time. Examples of past tensions are numerous, from the Suez crisis of 1956 to the Euro-missile crisis of the beginning of the 1980s, from Europe's farm subsidies to America's steel tariffs and tax subsidies for exports, from state direct and indirect subsidies in aeronautics to the ongoing debate around genetically modified foods, and from the Kyoto Protocol to the International Court of Justice.

However, none of the divergences that arose in the past years were important enough to undermine significantly the pre-eminence of the relationship between the partners on both sides of the Atlantic, whether on the economic, strategic or diplomatic level. While, as argued in the two first sections of this chapter, the US and China are unique in terms of the changes they can foster, the US and the EU are certainly unique in terms of the level of economic integration they have reached. NATO, which could have appeared as irrelevant after the end of the cold war, invoked Article V of its Charter for the first time after 9.11—treating the attack on the US as an attack on all its members—and reinvented itself in November 2002 by declaring that it is committed to defend its member's shared values. It has enlarged to a new set of countries, and added to its mission maintaining regional stability in Europe, addressing "*out of area*" threats and combating terrorism. Both sides of the Atlantic agree that the trans-Atlantic links are stronger when Europe is united, and that "*the US has no greater collection of friends in the world than is to be found on the other side of the Atlantic. Failure to heed that fact can only make the US weaker, not stronge*r." [1]

While media coverage and public opinion focus on conflicts, "*Americans and Europeans broadly share the same democratic, liberal aspirations for their societies and for the rest of the world. They have common interests in an open international trading and communication system, ready access to energy supplies, halting the proliferation of weapons of mass destruction, preventing humanitarian tragedies, and containing a small group of dangerous states that do not respect human rights and are hostile to these common values and interest.*"[2]

However, when pursuing those shared objectives and interests, Europeans and Americans adopt radically different approaches. First they do not have the same appreciation of the respective importance of processes and end results. As a set of independent states, the EU puts an emphasis on processes, even at the expense of efficiency, while the US as a federal system does not share this emphasis on processes and considers that solving problems is much more important.[3] Second, Europe views international affairs as founded on the centrality of international institutions and on the rule of law. It prefers to use its economic power ("soft power") to influence the behaviour of foreign government and considers the use of military force ("hard power") as the last resort of international diplomacy. By contrast, on the other side of the Atlantic, the combination of an exacerbated feeling of vulnerability with the reaffirmation of an overwhelming military superiority makes the US prone to seek military solutions to its problems. Third, the US considers itself to be at war, Europe not.

Those divergences will not vanish in the near future, and will nurture the debate on the respective merits of multilateralism *versus* unilateralism. The way the US is acting is criticised in Europe as being "pseudo-multilateralism" as described in 1990 by Charles Krauthammer: "*a dominant great power acts essentially alone, but, embarrassed at the idea and still worshipping at the shrine of collective security, recruits a ship here, a brigade there, and blessings all around to give its unilateral actions a multilateral sheen.*"[4] Many Americans see the European call for multilateralism as the reflection of "*Europe's relative weakness [that] has produced an aversion to force as a tool of international relations.*"[5]

An unparalleled far-reaching economic relationship

In economic terms, the trans-Atlantic relationship is highly and mutually profitable. Half a century of joint political efforts and reciprocal financial investments made possible the emergence

Part 3

Our Global Business Environment

7 Globalisation patterns

8 African futures

9 Market States

10 Demography and migrations

11 Patterns of economic growth

12 The search for energy security

13 The energy-and-carbon industry

of what can be considered as an integrated trans-Atlantic value chain, which exists today almost independently from the political sphere.

First, the EU and the US are each other's most important trading partner and are likely to remain so for the foreseeable future. In the year 2003, exports of EU goods to the US amounted to euro 220 billion (22.6% of total EU exports), while imports from the US amounted to euro 151 billion (15.3 % of total EU imports); exports of EU services amounted in 2003 to euro 115 billion, while EU imports of US services amounted to euro 109 billion.

Second, the EU and the US are each other's most important source and destination for FDI. The share of the US investment in EU FDI inflows (net of intra-EU25 investment) amounted to more than 60% over the period 2001–2003, while the US was the destination of 35% of EU FDI outflows over the same period.[1] In terms of FDI stocks, US FDI stocks in the European Union amounted to USD 708 billion at the end of 2002, while EU FDI stocks in the US were USD 964 billion.[2] This is by far the largest investment relationship in the world.

In total, trans-Atlantic commerce approaches USD 2.5 trillion per year, a figure that includes trade as well as total foreign affiliate sales, adjusted for double counting of affiliate sales and exports/imports.[3] Continuing bilateral efforts aim at reducing or eliminating remaining barriers to trade and investment notably through closer cooperation between regulators in fields like financial markets, cosmetics, automobile safety, nutritional labelling or metrology. Annual bilateral meetings allow reviews of progress still to be made.

There is no doubt that "*the trans-Atlantic bilateral economic relationship is the most important globally, and is both highly advanced and substantially balanced.*"[4] While its relative importance—in terms of trade, investment and share of global GDP—is likely to diminish as actors like China and India grow in importance, no similar relationship could be developed in less than a couple of decades.

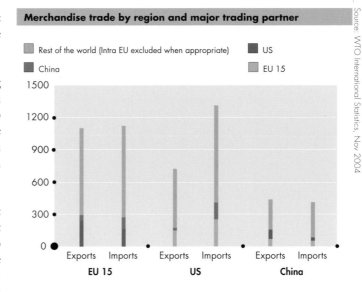

Merchandise trade by region and major trading partner

Rest of the world (Intra EU excluded when appropriate) ■ US
■ China ■ EU 15

Exports Imports | Exports Imports | Exports Imports
EU 15 | **US** | **China**

Source: WTO International Statistics, Nov 2004

1

Eurostat, "EU25 FDI: 2001–2003 data", *Statistics in focus*, 52/2004.

2

Raymond J. Ahearn, "US-EU trade relations: issues and policy challenges", Congressional Research Service, Library of Congress, February 10, 2005.

3

Joseph P Quinlan, *Drifting Apart or Growing Together?* Center for Transatlantic Relations, Washington, 2003.

4

European Union, "EU-US Bilateral Economic Relations", *Factsheet*, June 26, 2004.

1

Adam S. Posen,

"World Relations and

Transatlantic Relations",

American-German

Biennial Conference,

Institute for International

Economics, June 14-16,

2001.

2

Jeffrey Garten, "Why

the Airbus-Boeing Case

Could Wreck the WTO,

and How to Stop",

Newsweek International,

March 27, 2005.

3

Pascal Lamy,

"The emergence of

collective preferences

in international trade:

implications for

regulating globalisation",

Speech at the

Conference on Collective

Preferences and Global

Governance, What

Future for the Multilateral

Trading system, Brussels,

September 15, 2004.

4

Joseph Schumpeter,

*Capitalism, Socialism

and Democracy*, Harper

& Brothers, New York,

1942.

Focused but highly visable disputes

However, this mutually beneficial relationship does not prevent frequent trade disputes from arising. In Adam Posen's words, "*98% of EU–US trade just sort of goes on. It's this 2% we keep knocking about.*"[1] Conflicts between the US and the EU have a negative impact on the world trade climate. They could also derail critical negotiations like the Millennium Development Round and the Doha Round.

The Boeing–Airbus conflict is a major bone of contention in trans-Atlantic relations. In 1992, a first agreement was reached regarding how governments on both sides of the Atlantic granted subsidies to "their" aircraft company. In the autumn 2004, Boeing decided to file a complaint against Airbus before the WTO Dispute Settlement Body calling for an end to direct European subsidies to its super jumbo A380. Airbus countersued, arguing that Boeing receives indirect support for its 7E7 in the form of military and space contracts, as well as direct subsidies from the state of Washington and from the Japanese government through Japanese subcontractors.

Whether a new agreement is reached is of crucial importance for the global economy as such a dispute may well "wreck the WTO"[2]: whatever the ruling of the WTO arbitration panel, the US and the EU will ignore it for at least some time, as protectionist calls are mounting at the US Congress and as the EU is engaged in reinvigorating the Lisbon Agenda that aims at making the European economy the most competitive one through notably innovation and R&D spending. As a consequence, the WTO risks losing credibility, which will jeopardize its ability to resolve upcoming trade disputes—such as those over intellectual property rights and agricultural subsidies—and its efforts to further liberalise trade.

Diverging 'collective preferences'

Another tormented issue for the Doha Round could be related to what former EU Trade Commissioner Pascal Lamy[3] has labelled "collective preferences" by reference to the amalgamation of individual preferences through political debate and institutions within democratic societies as reflected in a body of fundamental principles, in regulations and standards. Collective preferences are the result of cultural values and also political experience. Three key divergences have substantial trade consequences, and could be solved differently in the three *Global Scenarios*, namely the "Precautionary Principle", and attitudes towards information.

Taking risk, prudently: the "Precautionary Principle"

The Precautionary Principle can be defined by reference to the 1992 Rio Declaration on Environment and Development: "*Where there are threats of serious or irreversible environmental damage, lack of full scientific certainty shall not be used as a reason for postponing cost effective measures to prevent environmental degradation*" and harm to human, animal or plant health. In Europe, this principle is applied in an extensive way through anticipative regulation when a risk may exist. In the US, the tendency is to strike the opposite balance between prudence and risk taking, accepting the "creative destruction" which Joseph Schumpeter saw as essential to capitalism.[4] It is accepted that one should wait until a prejudice can be proved before regulating. This divergence is behind the conflicts on hormone beef and GMO food, subjects on which European public opinion has been shocked by two scandals related to mad cow disease and contaminated blood. It also has major implications for the debate on global warming, even if some would say that the waiting period sometimes extends beyond the scientifically reasonable...

Information-age disagreements

Europe is also much more protective than the US when it comes to protecting consumers' personal data. Adopted in 1995, the EU Data Privacy Law forbids the transfer of private information to countries that lack equivalent privacy protection. This new law affected companies in the US where a self-regulatory approach prevails. A trans-Atlantic Safe Harbour Agreement was concluded in 2000 allowing data transfers to US companies that give EU residents adequate data-privacy protection. However, this agreement only applies to companies whose activities fall under the regulatory supervision of the Department of Commerce and the Department of Transportation: financial institutions—banks, securities firms and insurance companies—do not benefit from safe harbour protection at this time.

Part 3

Our Global Business Environment

7 Globalisation patterns

8 African futures

9 Market States

10 Demography and migrations

11 Patterns of economic growth

12 The search for energy security

13 The energy-and-carbon industry

In 2003, the US Department of Homeland Security (DHS) clashed with the European Union over airline passenger name recording as DHS required substantial data transfers—that would ordinarily violate EU data privacy laws—as a condition of US landing rights for European airlines. An agreement was announced in December 2003: 34 elements of personal data given at the time of check-in for trans-Atlantic flights are legally transmitted to the US Customs and Border Protection Bureau to allow screening of passengers for possible involvement in terrorist activities or other serious crimes. In a compromise move, the US agreed to reduce the length of data storage from 50 to 3.5 years. It also agreed to use the data only in fighting terrorism and related crimes and not for ordinary crimes as it had initially requested. However, the European Parliament is challenging this agreement before the European Court: the ruling may take years.

Addressing personal data protection at the world level is becoming even more pressing with the growing importance of e-commerce: it figures on the list of subjects to be addressed during the Doha Round.

Damage control, or coordinated bilateral initiatives
A likely medium-term scenario is one in which trans-Atlantic relations deteriorate as the euro ends up shouldering a disproportionate share of adjustment to the US trade deficit without stopping a new wave of trade conflicts and litigation. The danger would be a return to the late 1970s, when depreciation of the dollar, massive oil price increase and uncoordinated macroeconomic responses created trade frictions and "stagflation". Damage control would be the name of the game in trans-Atlantic relations and on the global scene. The world would clearly be then in *Low Trust Globalisation*, with risks that the fabric of international cooperation further unravels, leading to *Flags*.

Under *Low Trust Globalisation*, conflicts over "collective preferences" will linger and exacerbate. Some will be solved on a case-by-case basis around *ad hoc* solutions, like the Safe Harbour Agreement. WTO negotiations will have to deal with precaution particularities on the two sides of the Atlantic. Restrictions to trade will be the result of coercive intervention of regulators and "tit-for-tat" retaliations.

By contrast, in *Open Doors*, preventing stagflation and restoring the macroeconomic conditions of sustained growth could be a major common objective of the "G-8 plus China". Coordinated initiatives could set the stage for win–win approaches, whether in the framework of region-to-region "G-2" like policy dialogues or in a multilateral framework. The US would be expected to put the lid somewhat on its budget deficit and on its needs for capital imports, something which the capital markets may well come to expect in any case. China would certainly be asked to revalue the renminbi, something it could find advantageous to do without having to float its currency. Europe's contribution would also be in Europe's interest as it would lead towards achieving stronger growth. While seeking to achieve the "Lisbon competitiveness agenda", the European political class is clearly in need of external incentives to deal with the tougher part of the EU and national reform agendas covering liberalisation of public procurement and of labour markets.

AFRICA

Part 3
Our Global Business Environment

7   Globalisation patterns
8   African futures
9   Market States
10 Demography and migrations
11 Patterns of economic growth
12 The search for energy security
13 The energy-and-carbon industry

Chapter 8
African futures

As mentioned in the discussion on the 'resource curse' in chapter 1, the ample endowment of natural resources can create disincentives for economic and institutional development. The links between weak institutions, natural resource endowments, economic underperformance and civil conflict are becoming clearer. The role of the private sector in building or undermining institutional development in Africa will be an essential determinant of progress or failure.

Africa is the one continent at risk of being left behind in globalisation. Its international image is often characterised in terms of civil wars, the "curse of oil" and, more recently, for AIDS destroying what Africans create and aspire to. Yet Africa, a vast and diverse continent, is also home to 11% of global humanity, with a wealth of cultures, traditions and skills. It is richly endowed with natural resources, including oil and gas reserves. And the importance of Africa's mineral and ecological wealth to the rest of the world is expected to increase: for example, one in every five barrels of global oil capacity growth could come from West Africa in the next decade.

Africa's global importance is becoming more widely recognised: in terms of the global energy scene, for instance, in the US strategy to increase energy security; and in terms of the implications of globalisation for the broader international development agenda, as emphasised by the British Presidency of the G8 in 2005. Many African states have struggled to transform nature's endowments into sustained economic growth and widespread human development. As stressed by the Commission for Africa, a new partnership between Africa and the rest of the world is also needed: *"For its part, Africa must accelerate reform. And the developed world must increase and improve its aid and stop doing those things which hinder Africa's progress."*[1] Africa deserves our special attention.

In this chapter therefore, we first take note of the mixed signals of change coming from the continent (section 8.1). The following sections then take us successively through the three forces captured in the *Trilemma Triangle*: the force of community, the force of market incentives and globalisation and the force of cooercion by state and non-state actors. In section 8.2 we look at the evolving societal fabrics of Africa and the challenges of cohesion facing the fast-growing African populations. Section 8.3 highlights the risks of continuing to limit much of Africa's participation in the global economy to the natural resources and energy sector. Section 8.4 draws on recent scenarios that Shell helped UNAIDS[2] create to explore how AIDS in Africa might unfold and be addressed. Section 8.5 concludes on the implications of our *Jet Stream* context for Africa as a region.

Our purpose is not to provide detailed descriptions of African futures as we would in *Weather System* work but to highlight how different global contexts might influence how Africa can mobilise resources towards a better future. Institution building is a critical variable; this leads us to reflect on the role of transparency and good governance, before concluding with the implications of the three *Global Scenarios* for the type of institutional structure that would shape African and international policies and strategies.

1

Our Common Interest, Report of the Commission for Africa, March 2005, at www.commissionforafrica.org. Founded in 2004 to engage the international community in Africa's development path, the Commission for Africa was chaired by UK Prime Minister Tony Blair.

2

AIDS in Africa: Three Scenarios to 2025, work directed by Angela Wilkinson on secondment from the Shell scenarios team, available from www.unaids.org

1

First get the basics right, "A Survey of Sub-Saharan Africa", *The Economist*, January 2004, p.3. See also UNCTAD, 2004 and World Bank, WDI 2005.

2

Africa Environment Outlook, UNEP, 2004, and Office of US Foreign Disaster Assistance (OFDA), 2000.

3

For example, Angola beneficiaries have lost out in acquiring skills from foreign investors in the textile and garment industries, while the investors have benefited from favourable US import tariffs.

8.1

A context of diverse and mixed signals

Africa cannot be discussed without first stressing the substantial intra-continental differences that reflect different colonial legacies, economic structures, societal and religious contexts and international linkages—among African countries and with the rest of the world. Mixed signals of change must be interpreted when considering how domestic and international dynamics might unfold and interact.

Economic challenges

If Africa's share of global trade had stayed at 1980 levels, the continent's share of world exports would be double today's figure, and per capita income levels would be 50% higher.[1] Unfavourable trends in commodity prices ("terms of trade" halved over 40 years) have exacerbated this marginalisation process. Yet, despite being increasingly marginalised from global flows, Africa remains very dependent on trade: in 2004 trade constituted no less than 65% of sub-Saharan Africa GDP.

More poverty

Sub-Saharan Africa is the only region of the world to have grown poorer in the past 25 years: with half of its 700 million people surviving on USD 0.65 or less per day. Per capita income in 2004 was below the 1980 level in real terms. In a continent of 53 countries, 39 have been classified as low-income and 14 as middle-income countries. A significant portion of many countries' revenues is spent on servicing debt and much of sub-Saharan Africa has a high dependence on foreign aid, with the risk that this may sometimes hinder rather than stimulate domestic efforts.

Increasing environmental stresses

More than 20% of Africa's vegetated lands were classed as degraded—with 66% of this moderately to severely degraded—and 25 African countries are expected to experience water scarcity or stress over the next 20–30 years. There is some evidence that natural disasters have increased in frequency and severity over the past 30 years, particularly drought in the Sahel.[2]

Continuing conflicts

The spread of violence and war is of special concern in three areas: in West Africa (Guinea and Côte d'Ivoire), in Central Africa (the Democratic Republic of Congo and Great Lakes region, with massive involvement of neighbouring countries) and in the Horn of Africa (Sudan, Somalia, Eritrea, Ethiopia). The risk is that, in these areas, conflicts become perennial and intractable.

Drain of critical skills

A significant "brain drain" and "youth drain" is also taking place. The World Bank has estimated that some 80,000 highly qualified people leave the continent annually to work overseas. In South Africa it has been estimated that the emigration of skilled workers since 1997 has cost the country some USD 7.8 billion in lost capital, retarding economic growth. Many countries also fail to manage bilateral agreements with foreign investors to ensure the transfer of knowledge or skills to their local population.[3]

Democratisation and other success stories

At the same time, there are positive signals of change emerging from the Continent. Africa has gone through a decade of political transitions, including a move to multi-party competitive elections. Electoral transitions in Senegal, Ghana and Kenya have been watershed events. This has empowered civil society groups to challenge ruling elites and hold them accountable. A new generation of political leaders is emerging, many of whom voice a commitment to the common good of the people. For example, in Ghana the government, in its concern to be re-elected, has moved to invest in infrastructure—a development not unnoticed elsewhere in Africa. And some 24 countries, representing 75% of Africa's population, have so far signed up to the African Peer Review Mechanism, an initiative by the Africa Union's New Economic Partnership for Africa's Development (NEPAD) where a country puts itself forward for scrutiny by its peers to help identify actions needed to correct weaknesses. The pan-African parliament was established in 2004.

The introduction of new technologies, in particular the mobile phone, has also made a palpable impact on prospects for development, with the modernisation of telecommunications.

Part 3

Our Global Business Environment

7 Globalisation patterns

8 African futures

9 Market States

10 Demography and migrations

11 Patterns of economic growth

12 The search for energy security

13 The energy-and-carbon industry

8.2
Population and the force of community

In the next 20 years, although there may also be some localised population declines due to the impact of AIDS, the number of people living in the Continent is expected to increase, from 871 to 1242 million, with higher growth rates in Western Africa and a slowing of growth in Southern Africa.[1] However, the cultural diversity of Africa, of equal significance to the growth in population, is greater than in other world regions when measured on the basis of languages, ethnicity, international linkages or religions.[2] This rich tapestry of social fabrics means that religious beliefs, demographic trends, institutions and social norms will continue to call for diverse solutions, within Africa and beyond.

Religious trends and social cohesion

Religion has always been important in Africa and faith-based organisations (FBOs) are key providers of a range of essential services —including health, education and postal services—and a critical component in the physical and spiritual coping mechanisms of many African communities.

Religious affiliations and practices in Africa continue to evolve.[3] All across Africa, it has been noted that people are converting in large numbers to more evangelical forms of Christianity, e.g. Pentecostalism, and to the Wahhabi form of Islam. There has also been a resurgence in African traditional religions.

In the past, major conflicts have been fought between rival Muslim and Christian factions (Sudan, Chad, Nigeria). Discord caused by religious plurality is common in most parts of Africa. In North Africa, following the events of 9.11, there has been tension between governments and religious groups whom the government accuses of religious radicalism and terrorism. In Nigeria, religious fault lines between Muslims and Christians in some parts of the country have become further strained.

Recently, there have been many calls for multi-religious collaboration to deal with AIDS, so that religious bodies focus on the "90% that unites, rather than the 10% that separates". However, there are few collaborative relations in the form of operational networks—due to economic restraints, communication barriers, fundamentalism, and the politicisation of religion in some countries.

African communities are also characterised by clanship and respect for elders—in particular, older men. Whilst these relational bonds can help create social cohesion, patronage can also result in nepotism, promote gender inequality and manifest itself as the struggle for power between rival clans. Wider afield, it can weaken Africa's hand in dealing with failing and failed states.

Urbanisation

Africa's population is on the move. Under pressures of rapid population growth, rural resources and traditional methods of cultivating the land are less and less capable of providing subsistence farming for growing populations. As a result, more and more people have moved—either permanently or temporarily—to urban areas, mines, plantations and other centre of economic activity. Some 37% of African's now live in cities and urban identities abound, particularly amongst younger generations. The absence of widespread employment opportunities and of effective urban planning translates into huge slum cities, increasing rates of crime, and lack of access to clean water, electricity, sanitation and sewerage. If living conditions for the majority of urban dwellers continue to decline, or do not improve quickly enough, African cities could become a powder keg of political instability and social discontent.

Signals from beyond the continent

Internationally, the plight of Africa is increasingly recognised as a challenge for the global community. The Millennium Development Goals (MDGs), adopted in 2000 at the UN, provide a mechanism to address Africa's needs as part of a broader commitment to halve world poverty by 2015. 2005 is the year in which the Commission for Africa proposed an action plan reflecting wide consultation with African governments, the African Union and the African regional organisations, the civic sectors as well as the G8 countries and the market sector.[4]

1

US Bureau of Census Population Division

2

Alberto Alesina *et al.*, *Fractionalisation*, NBER Working Paper 9411, January 2003.

3

Wim van Binsbergen, *Challenges for the Sociology of Religion in the African Context —Prospects for the Next 50 years.* Paper read at the Social Compass 50th Anniversary Session, XXVIIth Conference of the International Society for the Sociology of Religion (ISSR), Torino, Italy, 21–25 July 2003.

4

Commission for Africa, *op.cit.*

8.3

Which economic and trade specialisations for African countries?

African governments face the challenges of needing to modernise and diversify their economies, of promoting more inclusive growth, of ensuring sufficient revenue growth to keep pace with the needs of their growing populations, and of securing a greater share of the opportunities offered by global trade. Trade is indispensable to African development strategies, and trade-related tariffs also form a significant part of many African government budgets (4.5% of GDP and 24% of government expenditure on average in sub-Saharan Africa, corresponding figures being 7.7% and 30.4% in North Africa and 2.8% of GDP and 11.0% of revenues in South Africa).

Diversify and integrate

As African countries "insert" themselves into the international division of labour, they must weigh in the balance the benefits of greater market access for their primary products and the costs of an undiversified export profile, e.g. less upward mobility in the world economy, greater exposure to external shocks, the increased likelihood of "export enclaves", etc. Whether the right balance can be struck is a major question for Africa's future.

Success stories like those of Mauritius and Botswana indicate that the right policies can deliver impressive results. Botswana is a landlocked country with only 4% cultivable land, extremely low levels of education and infrastructure, and large diamond mines. Mauritius—a nation built on one export (sugar), with high population growth, poor infrastructure, ethnic division and violent conflict—would also not have topped anyone's list of high-potential economies. Yet both countries have achieved high levels of economic growth, successfully leveraging international trade for their development strategies. Mauritius established an Export Processing Zone (EPZ) to diversify into manufacturing, while continuing to protect the import-substituting sugar industry to make trade reforms politically viable. Botswana has also diversified, but—most importantly—has delegated trade policy authority to a regional institution (the Southern Africa Customs Union), freeing the state from entrenched interests lobbying for protectionism.

The latter provide every incentive for African nations to remain primary product exporters. The development paths followed by Botswana and Mauritius, however, are at odds with current multilateral, regional and bilateral trade arrangements.

EU and US agricultural subsidies, and the reform of the global trade system

A plethora of bilateral trade arrangements exist with the US, EU and China, creating a complex and uneven landscape of trading linkages and opportunities. For example, some African textile exporting countries are able to compete with China, due to the benefits extended to them from the preferential arrangements of the US African Growth Opportunities Act (AGOA).

Reform of the multilateral trading system and reduction of US and EU agricultural subsidies have been highlighted as critical to reducing the constraints to Africa's development. In the words of the Commission for Africa: *"Rich nations must also dismantle the barriers they have erected against African goods…They must show this ambition by completing the current Doha Round of world trade talks in a way which does not demand reciprocal concessions from poor African nations."* Most poor African countries, however, are net importers of agricultural goods. Poor rural households tend to sell more food than they can eat in order to survive. For them, higher prices are welcome. Meanwhile, the urban poor often have to rely on their governments to keep food prices low. A repeal of farming subsidies in the EU or USA would benefit African exporting countries that compete with EU farmers, yet, in the short run, it would also increase the prices faced by net importers of food—until domestic production develops or while African consumers adopt Western food habits.

Coping effectively with the domestic impacts of global trade reform requires the effective capacity to plan and govern within individual countries and the willingness and capacity to negotiate and cooperate between African nations. The opportunities of trade for Africa will also continue to be shaped by the shared and differentiated interests of the US, China and the EU.

Part 3
Our Global Business Environment

7 Globalisation patterns
8 African futures
9 Market States
10 Demography and migrations
11 Patterns of economic growth
12 The search for energy security
13 The energy-and-carbon industry

Tackling poverty through enterprise and markets

The role of pro-poor enterprise—and pro-poor market growth—in eradicating poverty and enabling development have been recently highlighted. In the words of Management Professor Prahalad: *"We must stop thinking of the poor as victims or as a burden and start recognising them as resilient and creative entrepreneurs and value-conscious consumers."*[1]

A healthy small and medium-sized (SME) enterprise sector is also key to building economic stability and sustainability for future growth. In Africa, the development of the SME sector depends on creating a more enabling environment (e.g. political stability, property rights, rule of law, right investment climate, financial services and products) and addressing the shortage of business management skills. For example, private equity and venture capital are largely absent in Africa as a financing mechanism, but micro-finance (loans of 10 euro to 50,000 euro) and project finance (10 million euro and more) are more established.[2]

Addressing African energy needs

Despite producing 10% of the world's crude oil in 2002, only 36% of the African population has electricity and more than 80% of its rural population has none.[3] Traditional biomass continues to dominate the African energy scene, accounting for 39% of total energy demand in 2002 and contributing to a vicious cycle of continued poverty, environmental degradation and gender inequality. The IEA[3] estimates that—to reach the goals set out in the MDGs—USD 200 billion will need to be invested in the electricity sector and associated energy infrastructure, in Africa and South Asia. The World Bank estimates that meeting the relatively modest demand for electricity in sub-Saharan Africa and the Middle East up to 2010 will require USD 30 billion.

The influence of the African diaspora

In addition, as explored in chapter 11, the African diaspora will remain an important source of political influence overseas, as well as economic influence into the Continent: in 2002 USD 4 billion in remittances was received by countries in sub-Saharan Africa, representing some 4% of GDP, and North Africa attracted a further USD 14 billion (2.2% of GDP).[4]

8.4
AIDS undermining the foundation of development

Development in Africa is hostage to many security challenges. The wider and longer-term impact of AIDS has yet to be felt and will have a similar impact to civil wars—stripping away human lives in their adult prime, straining social cohesion, eroding the capacity to govern and spilling across borders.

Whilst Africa is not the only world region experiencing AIDS epidemics, it has been the hardest hit, with 60–70% of total global infections (25.5 million) occurring within the Continent. AIDS in Africa is far more than a health problem: over our scenario period, the impacts of AIDS in Africa have the potential to wipe out decades of development progress.

So far, more than 13 million Africans have already died from AIDS (2.2 million in 2003 alone), and 12 million children have lost one or both parents to the disease. HIV prevalence rates among young pregnant women (aged 15-24) in capital cities are greater than 10% in 11 African countries, and rates exceed 20% in five countries, all in the Southern region of the continent. In North Africa, over 91,000 people are living with the virus. In the worst-hit countries, AIDS is expected to wipe out 30% of the work force by 2020.

As documented in a major UNAIDS report, to which Shell contributed its scenario methodology and support (see Focus p.154), the root causes of the spread of AIDS are political, social and economic in nature. The associated impacts are widespread, touching individual households, communities, national economies, the health and education system and even the capacity of states to govern. And the impacts of AIDS are often not visible. For example, the impact of HIV/AIDS on small-scale farming is five-fold: loss of labour (e.g. weakened by ill-health, shifted to caring for sick, tied up in mourning rituals etc.); lower productivity and smaller areas under cultivation (e.g. spending shifts to healthcare, funerals, etc.); substituting tubers for cash crops (e.g. from coffee and bananas to cassava to save labour); loss of skills transfer, as adults die before they can pass on knowledge; less money to spend on educating children and children taken out of school to help with farming and care of sick adults.

1
C.K. Prahalad, *The Fortune at the Bottom of the Pyramid: Eradicating Poverty Through Profits,* Wharton School Publishing, Philadelphia, PA, 2005.

2
Sustainable Investment in Africa: Pipedream or Possibility? Report by the Forum for the Future and the Shell Foundation, 2005 (www.forumforthefuture.org.uk) and *Enterprise Solutions to Poverty,* A Report by the Shell Foundation, March 2005 (www.shellfoundation.org).

3
IEA, *World Energy Outlook,* Paris, 2004.

4
Global Development Finance – Striving for Stability in Development Finance, World Bank, 2003.

Focus

1

See www.unaids.org for further information on *AIDS in Africa: Three Scenarios for the Future*

AIDS in Africa: Three Scenarios to 2025

The recent launch and publication of a joint Shell/UNAIDS initiative marks the end of a three-year project which explored the possible directions and challenges of AIDS in Africa over the next 20 years.[1] The resulting three scenarios embody the first ever attempt to build the bigger picture, in terms of the deeper drivers and wider impacts of the epidemics in Africa

Tough Choices: Africa Takes a Stand

'Tough Choices' tells a story in which African leaders take tough measures to reduce the spread of HIV in the long term and protect the capacity to govern and generate income in the short term. This is not a time of abundance for much of Africa. There is an absence of sustained international interest in Africa's overall development. Skillful governance and social cohesion are of the utmost importance to effective mobilisation and the efficient use of resources. So is the development of regional and pan-Africa institutions. AIDS is perceived as one of many development challenges and one that must be tackled in recognition of the different socio-economic and religious contexts of Africa, as well as across borders. Choosing how to target scarce resources raises dilemmas and tensions, e.g. the need to focus on the skills and capacity of a minority essential for building and maintaining the functions of the state *versus* services for all and alleviating general poverty. There is the need to manage dissent. By 2025, those countries adopting a rigorous approach, which focuses on prevention, see eventual dividends in the prospect of an "AIDS-free" generation.

Traps and Legacies: The Whirlpool

'Traps and Legacies' sketches the dismal outcome if AIDS is divorced from its root social, economic and political causes and addressed primarily as an issue of individual behaviour change. AIDS deepens the traps of poverty, underdevelopment and Africa's marginalisation in a globalising world. Despite the good intentions of leaders and the initially substantial levels of aid from international donors, the emphasis on AIDS acts as a substitute for tackling more extensive and fundamental problems. A context of a domestic and regional fragmentation, national self-interest and lack of international unity unfolds. By 2025, the epidemic is still a real and present danger for many people across Africa.

Times of Transition: Africa Overcomes

In 'Times of Transition', AIDS serves as a metaphor for global crisis, resulting in a comprehensive and sustained response both nationally and internationally. There is global agreement that global stability and sustainability can only be achieved by enhancing human security and there is an emphasis on social justice and collective global responsibility. There is a doubling of aid flows to Africa, sustained for a generation, enabling investments in health systems, agriculture, education, electrification, water, roads, social development and institutional and governance capabilities. Increased debt relief and changes in the global trade regime combine with powerful changes in the ways African women and men relate to one another and to their communities. The focus on tackling HIV and AIDS does not detract from other health and development issues—for example, a new tuberculosis vaccine becomes widely available. By 2025 the end of the epidemic is in sight.

Part 3
Our Global Business Environment

7 Globalisation patterns
8 African futures
9 Market States
10 Demography and migrations
11 Patterns of economic growth
12 The search for energy security
13 The energy-and-carbon industry

8.5
Africa and the three *Jet Stream* contexts: instituition building as a critical variable

Mobilising commitment and resources towards better African futures requires a solid foundation. In addition to ensuring state capacity building and accountability within Africa, two other factors will play a key role in institutional development: a rejuvenated donor–recipient relationship, and a sea-change in the way the business community, both international and domestic, engages in the development process in Africa. Both factors are part of institution building, broadly defined (a dimension of development),[1] and will vary significantly depending on which *Global Scenario* prevails while Africa strives towards more promising development paths.

A discussion of institution building should start from Africa itself, where major efforts are already under way.

Transparency initiatives enable capacity building and accountability

In 2002, the African Union released figures asserting that corruption was costing Africa more than USD 148 billion a year and was causing the cost of goods to increase by as much as 20%, as well as deterring foreign investment and holding back development.[2] Obviously, corruption is not a problem confined to Africa, and "it takes two to tango"—the willingness to pay bribes matters as much as the readiness to take or demand payment.

Corruption, revenue transparency and accountability are now being tackled through a variety of national, sectoral and pan-African initiatives. For example, the Extractive Industries Transparency Initiative[3] (EITI) requires oil, gas and mining companies (including those that are state owned) to publicly disclose all payments they make to governments and the latter, in turn, report publicly on what they receive from companies.

Implementing national anti-corruption measures remains a challenge for many countries, however, as bodies charged with rooting out corruption are often underfunded. In the words of Transparency International, an NGO at the forefront of this action, African institutions responsible for implementing new anti-corruption measures "*face decreasing budgets, pressure for rationalisation, increased caseloads and other resource constraints.*"[4] Reform is difficult and reformers are marginalised.

The international community has also moved to support and reinforce such efforts. For example, with its Millennium Challenge Account, the US seeks to target its development aid to a small number of countries where it believes that aid will be most effective. Among the selection criteria are demonstrated results in reducing corruption.

The level and effectiveness of international assistance

Currently about half of African countries rely on official development assistant (ODA) for 10% or more of their gross national income,[5] and there are calls for rich countries to meet the commitments they pledged in 2000 (and in the 1970s), to raise ODA to 0.7% of GDP. The Commission for Africa, and the UK chancellor, have recommended 100% debt cancellation for the poor countries in sub-Saharan Africa.

Greater financial resources within the Continent could help in furthering human development, but the level and sources of financing are uncertain. Whilst new and innovative forms of financing for international development are sought, a key uncertainty is whether Africa will sustain international attention for the next 20 years, or will attention be distracted by development challenges in China and the Middle East?

Another uncertainty stems from the motivations at play in the provision and acceptance of international assistance for human development and whether the conditions placed on such assistance enable or constrain ownership and accountability.

1

X. Sala-I-Martin and A. Subramanian, "Addressing the Natural Resource Curse: An Illustration from Nigeria", *IMF Working Paper WP/03/139*, Washington, D.C., 2003.

2

http://news.bbc.co.uk/1/hi/world/africa/2265387.stm

3

The EITI brings together governments, international organisations, companies, NGOs and investors. www.eitransparency.org

4

Global Corruption Report, Transparency International, Berlin, 2004.

5

World Development Indicators, World Bank, 2004.

Focus

Forgiving debt, taxing jet fuel or selling IMF gold?

1

Jeffrey D. Sachs, *The End of Poverty*, Penguin Press, 2005.

Recent discussions on the way forward for Africa have tended to be organised around two perspectives that may or may not be compatible.

On the donors' side, the emphasis is often on achieving concrete objectives through targeted initiatives (such as "USD 2 billion to achieve primary schooling for all children in sub-Saharan Africa", "malaria prevention", "the fight against AIDS"…). The huge outpouring of generosity that followed the December 2004 tsunami, and the success of media-based collection efforts such as "telethons", illustrate the receptiveness of citizens in donor countries to such concrete proposals.

By contrast, African leaders emphasise the crippling burden that debt still represents, and ask

for immediate debt forgiveness. Their calls fall on receptive ears in a number of donor countries where debt forgiveness does not require fresh budgetary allocation. They are also supported by many NGOs taking part in the Make Poverty History campaign and by Professor Jeffrey D. Sachs at the Earth Institute.[1]

What role for debt and debt forgiveness?

In theory, a major initiative is already under way to reduce or cancel debt. The Highly-Indebted Poor Countries (HIPC) initiative, first canvassed by the IMF and World Bank in 1996 and implemented in 2002, has significantly increased the number of African countries with sustainable debts (i.e. the ratio of debt to export revenues is less than 150%). Yet debt servicing is still USD 15 billion per year for sub-Saharan Africa; and, as

UK Chancellor Gordon Brown has stated repeatedly, some countries still spend more on debt servicing than they do on health and education.

Two developments explain this situation. First, unlike bilateral donors, multilateral agencies have not cancelled the debt owed to them, as the discipline of project loan repayment was part of their traditional *modus operandi*. Secondly, as a number of governments have pointed out, the complex mechanisms of the HIPC initiative absorb scarce administrative resources; they call for debt relief to take the form of fresh grants.

Unconditional debt forgiveness for Africa is unlikely to be universally supported, even though former US President Clinton and Bill Gates are among the many people requesting help for Africa, and

despite UK Prime Minister Tony Blair's positioning of the July 2005 Gleneagles G8 summit as "the 100% debt relief summit". Donor countries may agree on objectives such as the 0.7% target for overseas development aid, and on additional efforts to strengthen the HIPC initiative. However, proposals for raising the necessary financing cover a large gamut—from off-market sales of IMF gold, to President Chirac's suggestion of an additional tax on jet fuel or air tickets. A British proposal aims "not only to drop the debt of yesterday but prevent debt from burdening countries well into the future" through the creation of an International Finance Facility that would mobilise future aid payments immediately.

Thus, debt relief has entered the mainstream of development assistance. However, the type of conditionality likely to prevail will vary considerably across the three *Global Scenarios*.

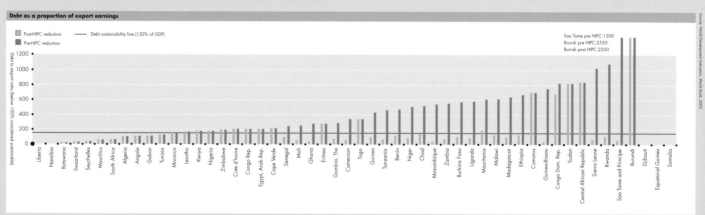

Debt as a proportion of export earnings

Source: World Development Indicators, World Bank, 2002

"If Africa is to take responsibility for its own development, it must be given greater influence in decision-making which affects it most directly and must be able to exert much greater pressure on the rich world to honour its commitments to the poor people of Africa."
(Recommendation by the Commission for Africa, March 2005)

Even well-intentioned, but conditional assistance, can produce some unintended consequences. For example, the latest wave of reforms by the international financial institutions (IFIs) saw calls for greater public participation, a renewed emphasis on poverty reduction (especially health and education), and more robust donor–recipient "partnerships". The resulting Poverty Reduction Strategy Paper (PRSP) process unfolded, whereby donors and recipients negotiate mutually agreeable macroeconomic, social and environmental goals that will reduce poverty and promote growth. On the face of it, these "softer" conditions are a welcome change for many from the previously imposed recipes for economic and institutional development; however, there remain serious questions. The ever-expanding list of conditions that poor nations must meet to qualify for development finance begs the troubling question: "If poor countries could meet every condition required by the IFIs, why would they be seeking external funding in the first place? Indeed, would they even be *developing* countries?"

As we look out over the next 20 years, how might institutional development in Africa be shaped by the different solutions to the crisis of trust and security we have outlined in our 2005 *Global Scenario* framework?

Institutional development in *Low Trust Globalisation*
In the world of *Low Trust Globalisation*, institutional development in Africa is influenced by the interests of the key global powers — the US, EU, China and Japan. Aid and investment are conditional and increasingly linked to notions of good governance rather than macroeconomic performance. Corruption within the public and private sectors is increasingly criminalised. African national budgets and revenues are managed under the scrutiny of the countries owning Africa's debts. The voices of the most powerful dominate.

Institutional development in *Open Doors*
As a voluntary initiative, forged from multi-stakeholder discussions reflecting transboundary concerns, the EITI is a prime example of an *Open Doors* approach to enhance transparency and accountability across the private and public sectors. The global media play an increasingly important role in providing a voice to the African peoples; accountability is built from the bottom up. Enhanced accountability stimulates a hardened sense of moral liability about corruption and there is a repatriation of monies to Africa. Concerted global interest and action, as part of a genuine effort to integrate Africa into the global economy and global society, enables the rapid development of effective pan-African institutions and promotes greater equity in the institutions of global governance. Greater public accountability is conducive to creating a more positive investment climate. An initially more massive, steady flow of international aid is used to better effect and displaced over time by greater flows of private equity, with aid coming in the form of matching funds.

Institutional development in *Flags*
Increasing bilateralism means that the EU, US and China linkages into Africa are increasingly competitive. Foreign powers (Western and non-Western) establish protectorates to safeguard their national strategic interests in Africa and, in doing so, nurture institutional development in African countries in their own image. Investors create oases of stability around specific projects and activities. However, outside of these fenced enclaves, there is limited international interest and, thus, limited influence on institutional development in Africa. In such cases, weak institutions continue to contribute to economic underperformance and fuel poverty and conflict. Pan-African cooperation is strained to breaking point. Faith-based and community organisations continue to weave a patchwork, but no quilt, of local institutions. Political, religious, cultural and clan-based power mechanisms and institutions abound but operate in parallel and in tension with one another.

MARKET
STATES

Chapter 9
From Nation States to Market States

Previous *Global Scenarios* have highlighted the importance of deregulation and the greatly diminished direct control that states have over the economy. We see this trend continuing. Yet a command and control approach is only one of the ways, and probably not the most sophisticated way, in which states can "intervene", or simply make their influence felt, in the economy and on the world scene. Indeed, in the pursuit of their own objectives, such as waging war in Iraq, limiting pollution or contributing to the fight against extreme poverty, states can use a range of tools that go well beyond command and control. Private contractors training Iraqi forces and protecting pipelines, the creation of state-regulated markets to trade pollution permits and the channelling of technical and financial assistance to micro-credit schemes—these are just a few examples of the new ways in which the state can exert its power.

Our *Global Scenarios* thoroughly challenge the view that states (which should refer to regulators as well as to governments) are becoming little more than referees in the global market arena. States adapt, transform and act.

States are also mindful of the "competitive advantage of nations"[1] that sets the stage for corporate strategies, and they play a role through education policies, research and development,

' In the pursuit of their own objectives, such as waging war in Iraq, limiting pollution or contributing to the fight against extreme poverty, states can use a range of tools that go well beyond command and control. '

1

Michael E. Porter,

The Competitive Advantage of Nations, Free Press,

New York, 1990.

international standard setting or complex trade and regulatory negotiations. Maximising opportunities for their citizens, companies, NGOs or faith-based organisations is a better description of what advanced states seek to achieve. The development of global legal forum shopping also gives the judicial branch of government—especially US courts—a significant role in relations between investors, companies and civil society groups.

By Philip Bobbitt

Insights

Philip Bobbitt, a member of the *Shell Global Scenario* team, is Professor of Constitutional Law at the University of Texas and author of *The Shield of Achilles: War, Peace, and the Course of History*, Alfred A. Knopf, New York, 2002.

The Market State, a long transition already under way

The state is not declining, nor is the nation dying, but the relationship between the two is changing and the particular version of the state that has dominated the developed world for more than a 100 years is undergoing a profound change.

Like earlier versions of the modern state stretching back to the Renaissance, the Nation State rests on its own unique premise for legitimacy: give us power and we will better the material well-being of the nation. Modern leaders—including figures as different as Roosevelt, Hitler and Stalin—all made this same promise although they had different ideas about how to achieve it. Indeed the great wars of the 20th century were fought in part to determine which of the three forms of the Nation State—communist, fascist, or parliamentarian—would accede to the axiomatic legitimacy of the Imperial States of the 19th century.

Now, at the moment of its greatest triumph, the parliamentary Nation State is increasingly unable to fulfil its legitimising premise: states are finding it more and more difficult to assure their public that their nations will enjoy increasing levels of equality, security and autonomy.

Five developments are chiefly responsible for this

First, the recognition of human rights as norms that require adherence within all states, regardless of their national laws. Second, the development of nuclear weapons and other weapons of mass destruction that render the defence of the state borders ineffectual for protecting the nation. Third, the proliferation of global and transnational threats such as AIDS or SARS, climate change and terrorism that no Nation State can hide from or control within its borders. Fourth, the growth of a world economic regime that ignores state borders in the movement of capital and thus curtails states in the management of their economic affairs, including the value of the national currency. Fifth, the creation of a global communications network that penetrates borders and threatens national languages, customs and cultures and from which no state can effectively cut itself off.

Widespread use of market incentives

A new constitutional order that reflects these five developments, and hails them as challenges that only it can meet, will eventually replace the Nation State. Indeed this is already happening. The deregulation of industry as well as the deregulation of women's reproductive choice, the replacement of conscription by all-volunteer forces, welfare reform that attempts to replace unemployment allowances with education and training to help the unemployed enter the labour market, and the use of NGOs and private companies as outsourced adjuncts to traditional government operations—all reflect the emerging Market State.

The legitimating premise of the Market State is: give us power and we will maximise your opportunities.

Different, yet stronger states?

There have been already half a dozen constitutional orders in the last 500 years (see box p.162). For more than a century at a time, the constitutional orders of the leading states remain stable. It happens, however, that we are entering one of those rare periods of seismic change—from the Nation State of the 20th century to the Market State of the 21st.

The Nation State is being challenged in a number of fundamental ways; by using market techniques as a supplement to legal regulation, states are gradually moving towards a Market State model. They will need to devolve power and institutions, adopting looser structures in the international context that will, perhaps paradoxically, ultimately strengthen the state.

Part 3

Our Global Business Environment

7 Globalisation patterns

8 African futures

9 Market States

10 Demography and migrations

11 Patterns of economic growth

12 The search for energy security

13 The energy-and-carbon industry

9.1

**Maximising a nation's opportunities:
the changing promises of the state**

Whereas past *Global Scenarios* tended to assume a withering away of the state, or resistance on its part to the forces of globalisation and market liberalisation, a third predetermined trend of fundamental importance in the new *Global Scenarios* is the gradual evolution away from a world where states follow a constitutional "Nation State" model to one where the dominant form of state organisation is the "Market State".

Power, law and identities

The transformation in the role and methods of the state is better understood as part of a longer trend in the way power, law and national identity transform over centuries. Power evolves in relation to military and economic techniques, with the US presently the world's sole superpower, and the power structure is reflected in the evolution of the legal order. "Constitutional orders" evolve, as the insights of our colleague Philip Bobbitt have made clear (see box). The "Nation State" was the latest such order in a much longer succession. What we document in this report is not a simplistic withering of the state, but the transformation of the Nation State into a new type of state—a type of state that is not only more at home with, but also quite effective in, a globalised market environment.

The most straightforward aspect of this change is that states in the advanced market democracies do not define their own success in terms of being able to resist market forces, as was still the case not long ago in Europe, but in terms of fostering market expansion in order to protect investors and, crucially, providing a wide range of public services or "public goods", such as defending the nation or providing high quality regulation. This has major implications for globalisation patterns as it implies both the continuation of trends highlighted in previous *Global Scenarios* under the "TINA" (There Is No Alternative) heading, and a much stronger role for states as they attempt to maximise opportunities for their citizens and companies, provide security, and restore trust in the marketplace.

States, indeed, are becoming increasingly skillful in enlisting the support of market forces to achieve their own objectives, to the point where government has redefined the nature of its fundamental promise to society. Such transformations have already happened in the past, when, for instance, State-Nations with imperial ambitions gave way to Nation States for which the welfare of the nation comes before expanding its territory (see box overleaf). Similarly, the promise of the Nation State—"give us power, and we shall maximise the nation's welfare"—is giving way to a new promise to maximise opportunities.

The use of market incentives by states

While retaining its power to coerce, notably on security-related matters, the state makes the fullest possible use of market incentives and mechanisms to transform behaviours and to implement strategies. Training programmes, for instance, are seen as more effective than unemployment compensation; voluntary armies, and even private security guards as military auxiliaries, are preferred to conscripts; and providing another reason for choice—like offering nuclear civilian technology to North Korea—is seen as a more powerful incentive than constraint. Hence the importance, in the three *Global Scenarios*, of the interplay between market forces, civil society and states.

States, regulators and hardliners

Such an analysis obviously requires that the notion of the "state" be defined broadly, to cover notably independent semi-autonomous regulatory agencies. Courts and the judicial system must also be included. Indeed, one of the key features of *Low Trust Globalisation*, the scenario presented in chapter 3, is the role of private legal actions—as part of the "private attorneys general" doctrine—in the fulfilment of the state's oversight and fraud-discovery process.

All countries do not undergo this transition in the same way. In Iran, for instance, hardliners *"shifted authority away from institutions accountable to elected bodies in favour of extragovernmental institutions under (their) firm control"*, such as various foundations.[1] Yet, overall, the transition towards Market States is under way, as the legal order adapts to the role of the market in redefining power.

1

Ray Takeyh and Nikolas K. Gvosdev, "Pragmatism in the Midst of Iranian Turmoil", *The Washington Quarterly*, Autumn 2004.

The transformation of the state

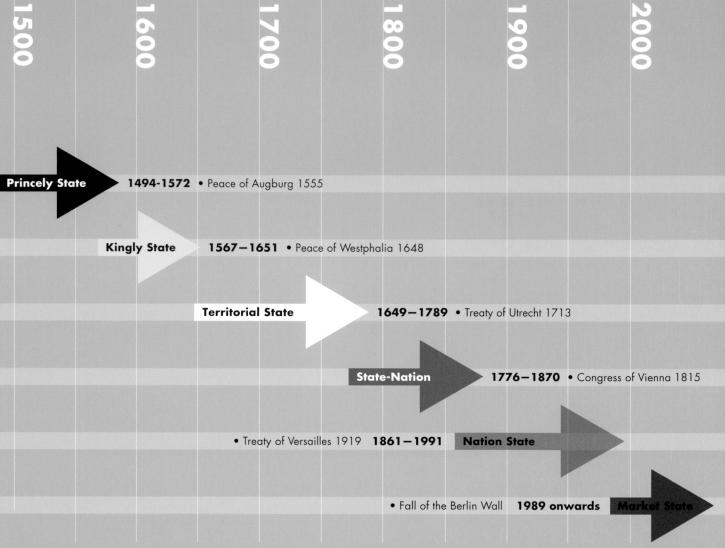

| | 1500 | 1600 | 1700 | 1800 | 1900 | 2000 |

Princely State — 1494-1572 • Peace of Augburg 1555

Kingly State — 1567–1651 • Peace of Westphalia 1648

Territorial State — 1649–1789 • Treaty of Utrecht 1713

State-Nation — 1776–1870 • Congress of Vienna 1815

• Treaty of Versailles 1919 — 1861–1991 — **Nation State**

• Fall of the Berlin Wall — 1989 onwards — **Market State**

The six constitutional orders of modern times

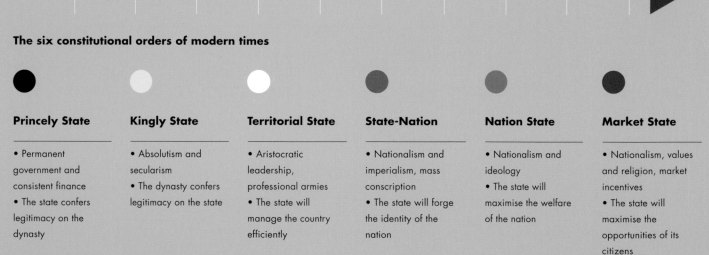

Princely State	Kingly State	Territorial State	State-Nation	Nation State	Market State
• Permanent government and consistent finance • The state confers legitimacy on the dynasty	• Absolutism and secularism • The dynasty confers legitimacy on the state	• Aristocratic leadership, professional armies • The state will manage the country efficiently	• Nationalism and imperialism, mass conscription • The state will forge the identity of the nation	• Nationalism and ideology • The state will maximise the welfare of the nation	• Nationalism, values and religion, market incentives • The state will maximise the opportunities of its citizens

Source: After Philip Bobbitt, *The Shield of Achilles: War, Peace and the Course of History.*

Part 3

Our Global Business Environment

7 Globalisation patterns

8 African futures

9 Market States

10 Demography and migrations

11 Patterns of economic growth

12 The search for energy security

13 The energy-and-carbon industry

9.2
The media as an agent of change

The transformation of the state and of the manner in which it pursues collective objectives has implications for how states relate to other states, to market participants but also to other actors, as captured in the *Trilemma Triangle*. Of particular importance, in this respect, are the new opportunities that this opens for "the fourth estate", namely the media.

The role of the news media has changed, in the last three periods of the state. In the late 18th and 19th century, the era of the State-Nation, the constitutional role of the press was foremost to transmit the political leadership's views: the *Federalist Papers*, first published as essentially op-ed pieces, and the journalism that powered the French Revolution are good examples. In the Nation State period, to this role was added the function of informing leaders about the public reaction as the public spoke back to government through the media. William Randolph Hearst's famous remark ("*You provide the pictures, I'll provide the war*") showed a shrewd appreciation of this, and so did the *Washington Post's* crucial exposure of Watergate felonies.

In the Market State, the news media have begun to act as primary shapers of perceptions, references and priorities, in direct competition with the government of the day. The media are well placed to succeed in this competition because they are trained to work in the marketplace, are quick to spot public trends, can call on huge capitalisations, and are the most capable users—far outpacing politicians—of the contemporary techniques of advertising and public relations. Communication then becomes critical to the fate of politicians, a sign of competence in the eyes of voters.

Indeed the competitive, critical function of the media in the Market State is similar to that of the political parties of the Left in the Nation State, hence the uneasiness of political analysts and intellectuals like Paul Virilio in France when they reflect on the role of CNN in shaping perceptions of the war in Iraq[1] or of Rupert Murdoch's news organisation in shaping British attitudes on European integration. The most formidable counter-power to US

power between Morocco and the western borders of Iran and India is not a government, not even a terrorist network, but Al-Jazeera, the small news organisation that operates out of Qatar.[2] This being said, according to Philip Bobbitt—whose work has shaped our exploration of the changing role of the state—*"the media are completely untrained in this task—ethically or politically"*.

Relations between the media and the other organs of government are further reshaped by the fact that, in the Market State, the public's attitude towards what can be accomplished by government changes (and thus also changes with respect to the scope of personal responsibility). In many countries, business activities and the activities of business leaders are replacing politics as the central source of news about the welfare of the people.

1

Paul Virilio,

L'écran du Désert,

Chroniques de Guerre,

Editions Galilée,

Paris, 1991.

2

Mohamed El-Nawawy,

Adel Iskandar,

Al-Jazeera: The Story

of the Network That Is

Rattling Governments

and Redefining Modern

Journalism,

Westview Press,

Cambridge, MA, 2002.

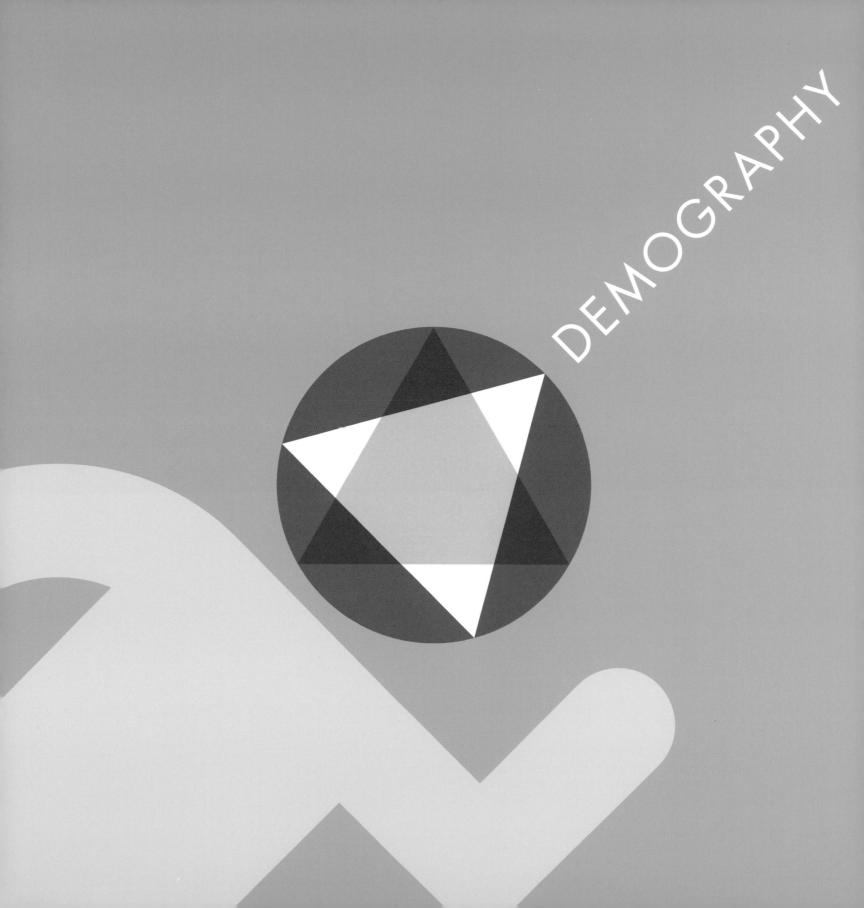

DEMOGRAPHY

Part 3
Our Global Business Environment

7 Globalisation patterns

8 African futures

9 Market States

10 Demography and migrations

11 Patterns of economic growth

12 The search for energy security

13 The energy-and-carbon industry

Chapter 10
Demography and migrations setting the stage

Before turning our attention to economic and energy outlooks, we need to complement the analysis presented so far with one set of essential variables that will affect not only aggregate consumption levels—notably energy consumption—but also the relative positioning of key countries or regions in terms of economic growth differentials, namely demographic variables. Demographics will also strongly shape the various types of demands on pension and health systems and, more generally, economic and social conditions including such intangibles as entrepreneurship, attitude toward authority and appetite for change.

The demographic transition...
A comprehensive review of the unfolding demographic transition would be beyond the scope of the present report, and excellent sources are available notably from the United Nations Population Division, the World Bank and OECD.[1] Simply as a way to highlight the importance of demographics, the present chapter begins with a brief summary of the main projections regarding the world population in 2025. Twenty years being a short period for demographic trends, we also look at the year 2050, a date when the world's population is likely to be close to reaching a peak according to the UN medium variant projections. This possibility for the world's population to stop increasing half a century from now stands in sharp contrast to the increase by 1.4 billion people—or more than one fifth of the present population—expected over our 2005—2025 scenario period (section 10.1).[2]

...and migration flows in each *Global Scenario*
Against this summarised background, we then turn our attention to the aspect of world population that can be expected to be most heavily influenced by the different contexts that could prevail under each of our three *Global Scenarios*, namely international migrations (section 10.2) and their implications for international financial transfers in the form of workers' remittances (section 10.3).

While migrations are often a highly divisive social and political issue, they tend to reflect temporary adjustments rather than permanent flows. The political and regulatory conditions that would prevail under each of our three *Global Scenarios* would have very distinct implications for the intensity and nature of the underlying transitory imbalances as well as for the type of barriers that could disrupt the adjustment mechanism (section 10.4).

1
See notably, *World Population Prospects: The 2002 Revision*, a three-volume set issued by the UN Population Division over the 2003–2004 period (see www.unpopulation.org); *Trends in Total Migrant Stock: The 2003 Revision*, UN Population Division; *Trends in International Migration*, OECD, SOPEMI 2002, Paris, 2003.

2
On the accuracy of demographic forecasts, see especially *World Economic Outlook*, International Monetary Fund, Washington, D.C., 2004.

10.1

2005–2050: completing the global demographic transition?

Assuming medium fertility and normal mortality rates, the United Nations Population Division, in its medium variant, projects a growth of the world population from 6.4 billion in 2005 to 7.9 billion in 2025, and 8.9 billion in 2050. The average growth rate during that period would be 0.77%, well below the growth rate experienced during the second half of the 20th century (1.76%) and recently (1.22% for 2000–2005). The world population would increase by 27% for 2005–2025 and by 39% for 2005–2050. By 2050, the world population would then be close to its peak before stabilising.

Yet the United Nations Population Division proposes other scenarios, including a high-growth and a low-growth scenario, according to which world population would reach respectively 10.6 billion and 7.4 billion by 2050. In the low-growth scenario, the world population would reach its peak (7.5 billion) in 2040 and then decline. In the high-growth scenario, by contrast, the world population would keep increasing during the whole 21st century and possibly well beyond.

One element that seems far more certain is that the population of the developed countries will reach its peak by the end of our scenario period, and these countries will see their share of the world population steadily declining, despite net annual migration of 2 million people. Much of the demographic change up to 2050 would take place in less developed countries, the population of which would increase, in relative terms, from 81% of the world population in 2005 to 84% in 2025 and 86% in 2050.

Among major areas, Africa and Europe are at opposite ends of the growth spectrum: their respective annual population growth rates would be 1.6% and -0.3%, respectively, over the 2005–2050 period. The other major areas would see an average growth rate around 0.7% over this period, including North America due to substantial immigration flows.

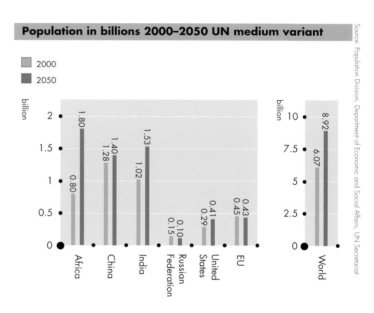

Population in billions 2000–2050 UN medium variant

- 2000
- 2050

Source: Population Division, Department of Economic and Social Affairs, UN Secretariat

In the medium variant scenario, while Asia would experience a population increase of 1.3 billion, the Asian share of worldwide population would nevertheless decline slightly between 2005 and 2050, from 60.7% to 58.6%. Meanwhile, the African population would more than double in absolute terms and, in spite of the impact of the HIV/AIDS epidemic on life expectancy, increase from 13.7% to 20.2% of the world population. Even in the Arabian Peninsula, national situations would contrast greatly: the population of the oil-producing countries of the Arabian Peninsula would double over the 2005–2050 period, while remaining modest in absolute terms (77 million); quite strikingly, however, the Yemenite population would have multiplied by no less than 4 in 2050, reaching 84 million.

Part 3

Our Global Business Environment

7   Globalisation patterns

8   African futures

9   Market States

10 Demography and migrations

11 Patterns of economic growth

12 The search for energy security

13 The energy-and-carbon industry

A rapidly urbanising developing world

The world's urban population will continues to grow faster than the total population, rising from 3.2 billion people in 2005 to 4.6 billion people in 2025, while the rural population will remain stable, around 3.3 billion people. Therefore, during the scenario period, urban areas will absorb all the growth of the world's total population…

The process of urbanisation is already advanced in the more developed regions, with 75% of the population living in urban areas in 2005, a proportion that is expected to increase to 80% by 2025. By contrast, developing countries' population living in urban areas will increase from 43% to 54%. This rapid urbanisation trend creates major challenges in term of housing, air pollution, water supply and sanitation, and infrastructure development. With a billion of the world's poor already living in urban slums in the developing world, the worst scenario is one in which the growth in world's population translates into an almost equivalent additional number of slum dwellers with little access to safe water, clean air, health care and education. Indeed, according to the UN, one of the main challenges of the new millennium is "our planet's transition to an urban world".

Among the 18 Millennium Development Goals (MDGs) are halving the number of people without sustainable access to drinking water and sanitation, and improving the lives of 100 million slum dwellers. The 2005 Annual Meeting of the World Economic Forum (WEF) in Davos saw a vibrant reaffirmation of the need to meet the MDGs,[1] and therefore of more than doubling aid to Africa to reach USD 33–38 billion per year (USD 13 billion today). Generating an effective consensus around such goals and implementing them would be a major step towards ***Open Doors***. By contrast, in ***Flags***, donors will slide to a patchwork of bilateral approaches intended to maximise security and trade links. In ***Low Trust Globalisation***, a global approach is not infeasible, but agreeing on the necessary reforms of the UN, of aid policies and of developing countries' governance is a challenge that may not be met.

10.2
Migrations and labour market globalisation

Migrations have increased rapidly during recent decades. They have given, and are likely to continue to give, rise to burning social and political issues in many host countries.

The worldwide migrant population grew by 130% between 1965 and 2000, yet migrants still only represented 2.3% of the world's population in 1990. In the 1990s, the dismantling of the former Soviet Union triggered important migrations from Eastern to Western Europe and made millions of ethnic Russians foreigners in newly independent states. Meanwhile, Chinese borders opened, and some 410,000 Chinese workers were allowed to go abroad according to the International Migration Organisation. In 2000, 175 million persons had their residence outside their country of birth, of which 60% lived in developed countries. One person out of 10 in developed countries is an international migrant (only 1 out of 70 in developing countries). Since 1990, the number of migrants in developed countries has increased on average by 2.3 million every year while decreasing slightly in developing countries. This trend is likely to persist.

Migrant population is quite concentrated already, with the US, Russia and Germany being host to almost one-third of the total.

An important lesson to consider, looking towards 2025, is that migrations tend to reflect temporary adjustment flows rather than permanent ones: how long will it take then for the broader demographic and economic transition to run its course, and what are the new factors that could influence it in each of the *Global Scenarios*?

Barring major unforeseen shocks, the sources on which the present analysis is based suggest that this demographic, economic and migration transition will have largely run its course by 2025, except in the Arabian Peninsula, which will experience major problems not covered here, and in India.

1

See notably, *Global Governance Initiative Report 2005*, World Economic Forum, 2005. Available at www.weforum.org/ globalgovernance.

Predetermined migration trends

Steady migration flows

For the next 20 years, the UN and the OECD estimate that migration flows will continue at a relatively stable level, with 2 million people migrating every year from developing to developed countries. Two-thirds of the migrant population (1.3 million per year) will enter North America, while most others will enter a European country (650,000 per year). 90,000 per year will go to Australia and New Zealand.

The Middle East countries

These absolute numbers, however, do not correlate with pressures on host countries. Compared to national populations, the higher proportions of migrants can be found in the Middle East: in the United Arab Emirates (74%), Kuwait (58 %), Jordan (40%), Israel (37%), Singapore (34%), Oman (27%), Estonia (26%) and Saudi Arabia (26%).

Refugees and asylum seekers

The flows of refugees and asylum seekers are affected by conflicts. On average, 500,000 people have been seeking asylum in developed countries every year since the beginning of the 1990s. These flows have no reason to decrease rapidly due to geopolitical instability, and the number of undemocratic governments.

Growing importance of qualified and student flows

"Migrations" are the result of four types of flows: family related, work related, refugees and students. Migration flows are still dominated by family-related migration. However, the 1990s saw a rapid increase of the proportion of labour-related migration as well as its feminisation. Women now outnumber men among international migrants in developed countries and represented nearly 49% of the migrants in 2000.

Qualifications, or the acquisition of qualifications as a student, is an increasingly important criterion for admittance into developed countries. Family reunion, by contrast, is likely to be a less common factor, even for women. Many OECD countries have put in place selective measures to facilitate the recruitment of highly skilled foreign workers, as well as of health workers, household workers and seasonal agricultural workers. This trend is likely to be reinforced by the needs of ageing populations in Europe.

Education level is increasingly taken into consideration as a key characteristic by host countries. It has long been the case in countries like Australia, Canada, New Zealand and the US but, since the mid-1990s, many European countries have enacted legislation with emphasis on migrants' skills. Five countries—the US, the UK, Germany, France and Australia— attract most foreign students.

In the US, between one-third and one-half of Masters in Computer Science and Mathematics are now awarded to foreigners. This may indicate a disaffection of US students for science, or possibly awareness that some high-tech jobs such as those of software engineering are increasingly being "off-shored" to countries like India.

Part 3

Our Global Business Environment

7 Globalisation patterns

8 African futures

9 Market States

10 Demography and migrations

11 Patterns of economic growth

12 The search for energy security

13 The energy-and-carbon industry

Source: UN Population Division 2002

Migrations occur in stages: people first "migrate" within their home country from rural to urban areas, and then possibly follow established patterns of migration towards foreign lands as made possible by networks of previous migrants. In this respect, China appears as the country that could experience the most destabilising flows if its huge internal migration from Western provinces towards the coastal areas, for lack of local opportunities, gave rise to foreign migrations, facilitated by what is already a large Chinese diaspora.

More divisive views on immigration policies

At present, most OECD countries are implementing or considering stricter immigration controls, a trend that should remain valid in the next 20 years, as immigration is moving to the fore of the political debate in most host countries. Yet deeper causes are at work that should keep immigration flows high. As observed by President Bush in his January 7, 2004 speech on immigration reform, "*some of the jobs being generated in America's growing economy are jobs American citizens are not filling.*" Between 2000 and 2010, the US Bureau of Labour Statistics projects an increase by 47% in science and technology jobs and by 90–100% in computer software engineering (against 15% for all occupations), and the situation in the student population suggests that many of the job seekers will not be US nationals.

Selection process for qualified job are already being put in place by some host countries in the sending countries; such cooperation at the source is likely to be increasingly included in broader agreements between host and sending countries.

In regions that try to promote free movement of people—as the European Union does—immigration is generating tensions, and putting social cohesion under strain. Willy Buschak, Acting Director of the European Foundation for the Improvement of Living and Working Conditions, summarises the situation in the following terms: "*the dilemma of (intra-EU) migrations is that while labour mobility may be good for economic growth and cohesion across the EU regions as a whole, it may put pressure on social cohesion at the local level if not accompanied by a holistic approach to integration.*"[1]

On March 22–23, 2005, the EU Council formally reviewed progress made under the Lisbon Agenda. While the Council agreed that, halfway

Main immigration countries

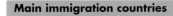

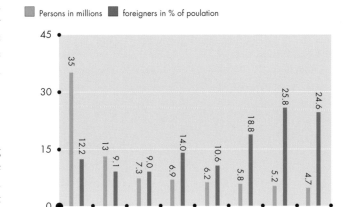

through, the achievements under the Lisbon strategy were mixed at best, member countries were unable to agree on the Commission's proposals to speed up the reform process. The most controversial issue turned out to the proposed creation of an internal market for services based on the country-of-origin principle. Reflecting the fear that the free cross-border flow of services would threaten social protection standards in the core economies, member countries decided to radically revise the EU's proposal. Even Eastern European leaders who stood to benefit from the EU's proposal went along, fearing a greater crisis if French voters vote down a constitution for the newly expanded union in their May 29 referendum. In the event, the conclusions of the summit of the EU Council remained rather vague, calling for instance for the need to "refocus priorities on growth and employment."

Open Doors is the scenario in which this holistic approach is most likely to be pursued by governments and companies and not simply by a number of militant groups in civil society. While the latter will be actively pursuing pro-integration causes in all scenarios, they are likely to be perceived as fringe groups in ***Low Trust Globalisation*** and as one set among many other advocacy groups in the divisive politics characteristic of ***Flags***.

1

See *Migration Trends in an Enlarged Europe*, European Foundation for the Improvement of Living and Working Conditions, February 2004.

Focus

Migrations into, out of, and within the BRICs

Brazil: limited movements of people both ways

Brazil, once a country of immigration, turned into a country of emigration during the second half of the 20th century.

The Northeastern part of Brazil is a region under severe environmental stress, with harsh droughts and desertification. Hunger has led 70% of the *Nordestino* population to migrate towards the Southeast of Brazil, contributing massively to the growth of the Rio and Sao Paulo metropolises. Sao Paulo is now the third largest city in the world. As for the remaining 30%, they are actively encouraged to settle in Western Brazil as part of a policy to develop the under-populated Amazonian heartland.

The number of Brazilians emigrating abroad remains limited. Key destinations are North America, Europe and Japan. At the end of 2000, Japan had 1.7 million registered foreign residents (persons who were in Japan for 90 or more days), among them some 250,000 migrants from Brazil. Most of them are *Nikkeijin*, descendents of Japanese who migrated to Brazil at the beginning of the 20th century.

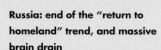

Russia: end of the "return to homeland" trend, and massive brain drain

With declining health standards and a fertility rate down to the 1.2 level, Russia has a shrinking population that would further decline from 145 million in 2000 to 114 million in 2050 in the absence of net migration flows. For its population to stabilise, Russia would need an average net flow of 500,000 migrants per year. Yet the flow of Russians returning from Baltic and CIS countries is rapidly dwindling, from 910,000 in 1994 to only 237,000 in 1999.

Beyond net migration figures, one dimension needs to be underlined: Russia experienced a large brain drain during the 1990s mainly through immigration towards Israel, the US and, to a lesser extent, Germany. The average level of education of ethnic Russians returning to the Russian homeland is higher than that of Russians on average, but much lower than the educational level of Russian emigrants. Russian specialists will continue to leave the country, as neither the Russian state nor Russian businesses can finance adequate levels of R&D and science-based activities at global market rate wages.

India: a relatively limited source of migrants, externally and even internally

Some 15 million Indians live abroad, 90% of them in Middle Eastern countries. The number of Indian natives in the US is around one million while 315,000 live in Canada and 150,000 in the UK. The number of Indian workers arriving in the US under H-1B visas has increased ten-fold during the 1992–2001 decade, reaching close to 60,000 per year. Security concerns, as could be expected to persist in *Low Trust Globalisation* and *Flags,* can have a very chilling effect in these already limited flows. According to NASSCOM, one-tenth of the 350,000 Indian IT specialists in the US have already returned to India as a result of the post-9.11 strengthening of US security procedures. India has now begun to tap more directly into the potential of its diaspora, and tries to emulate China's success in harnessing the support of non-residence for domestic economic development and entrepreneurship.

China: the world's great reservoir of potential migrants

No transition to a market economy has been undergone without a massive displacement of people from rural to urban areas and, on numerous cases, a large fraction of these people end up migrating abroad.

The number of Chinese internal migrants, the so-called floating population, ranges from 100 million to 200 million, according to diverse conflicting estimates, making them almost as numerous as international migrants worldwide. The South Eastern coastal provinces of Fujian, Zhejiang and Guangdong, among China's wealthiest and fastest-growing regions, attract the largest number of migrants from rural areas. Remittances from these "migrants" provide 40% of incomes in many farming areas.

Chinese migrants are mostly moving to South Korea or Japan, where they account for respectively 31% and 21% of the stock of foreign population, then either staying or travelling on to North America and Europe. Fewer than 200,000 nationals from PRC were legally living in Europe in 2000, a figure quite small when compared with migration flows to Canada of 40,000, to the US of 56,000, and to Japan of 86,000 in 2001.

Part 3
Our Global Business Environment

7 Globalisation patterns
8 African futures
9 Market States
10 Demography and migrations
11 Patterns of economic growth
12 The search for energy security
13 The energy-and-carbon industry

10.3
Remittances and economic development

Remittances—migrant workers' earnings sent back from the country of employment to the country of origin—play a central role in the economies of many labour-sending developing countries. They are now second only to foreign direct investment as a source of capital flows into developing countries, and represent the equivalent of around 150% of official aid flows, according to the IMF. Moreover, compared to declining and increasingly conditional aid flows and to volatile private lending, remittances are a stable, steadily increasing, source of financing more comparable to foreign direct investment.

According to the World Bank, "official" workers' remittances received by developing countries amounted to USD 93 billion in 2003, and should reach USD 100 billion in 2005. Total figures including remittances sent by irregular workers or through informal transfers may be twice as high. As remittances go hand in hand with migration, the US is the largest source of remittances with USD 28.4 billion in 2002 (official flows only), followed by Saudi Arabia (USD 15.1 billion) and Germany (USD 8.2 billion).

On the receiving side, Mexico has overtaken India as the largest recipient since the year 2000 (see graphic). China and India report substantial differences in remittances with, surprisingly, China receiving comparatively little remittances (USD 2.4 billion). The lower Chinese figure reflects differences in incentives and economic opportunities in the two countries. Indeed, if remittances and diaspora FDI are combined, financial inflows from emigrants into China are estimated at between two and four times more than into India.

Since 9.11, remittances have come under close scrutiny as part of international efforts to counteract terrorism. A large part of remittances transit through Hawala systems, namely compensation systems that do not flow through regular banking channels. They are thought to have played a part in funding Al Qaeda. Under the auspices of the Financial Action Task Force, developed countries have introduced more stringent regulations and supervision. The application of the "know your customer" principle has created difficulties for many undocumented migrants, as well as for people originating from regions perceived as a possible breeding ground for terrorism.

In ***Open Doors***, official figures for remittances can be expected to grow at a yearly rate of 15% against 7–8% during the last ten years. This would reflect a steady flow of migrants from developing to developed countries as well as the availability of more reliable data as banks provide more efficient services—with extended outreach and transparency—and lower fees to migrants willing to send money back home. In ***Low Trust Globalisation***, restriction on immigration for the sake of social cohesion is likely to limit the growth of remittances over the long run. Nevertheless, official figures should rise significantly during the initial five-year period as a result of better recording ratios reflecting more stringent application of regulations on money transfers. In ***Flags***, remitting countries, and some remittance-receiving countries, would resort to some form of taxation to finance social protection, leading migrants to favour unofficial financial circuits. Combined with restrictions on migration flows, this will translate into smaller growth of official remittances.

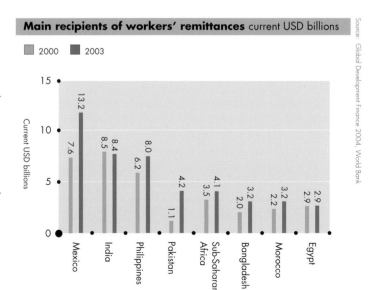

Main recipients of workers' remittances current USD billions

Source: Global Development Finance 2004, World Bank

10.4
Migrations in the three *Global Scenarios*

Open Doors: integration-driven immigration patterns

In ***Open Doors***, immigration is channelled in part through "civil society networks" that new migrants establish to settle and integrate in the host countries. The higher growth characteristic of this scenario tends to limit restrictions to inflows of migrant populations. It also eases the economic transition in source countries, thereby limiting the number of candidates to immigration. Hence a better balance is reached between the aspired and the potential levels of migration flows.

Open Doors is also the most favourable scenario in socio-economic and cultural terms as it provides a richer and denser web of mechanisms to recognise and address the tensions created by the presence of large migrant communities, a consideration especially relevant in Europe.

The importance of precautionary measures and the search for "built-in" solutions to the crisis of trust and security foster a number of pro-integration policies within host countries as well as across host and source countries. The notion of civil society is seen in a cross-border perspective that facilitates coordinated action against crime, trafficking in human beings and other important impediments to harmonious migrations.

In addition, communitarian values, including Islamic and Christian values, are affirmed less in opposition to other values and more as contributions to the emergence or strengthening of multicultural societies. While US and European approaches continue to differ, they have in common that they treat cultural diversity as an asset and they use market incentives as a mechanism for the creation of win–win perspectives. European governments will seek political integration of the various communities and work towards cultural assimilation. Reopening the debate on the separation of church and state, they may have to affirm the compatibility between religious revelation and rationalism...

Low Trust Globalisation: a labour-market driven logic

The general philosophy in ***Low Trust Globalisation*** is one of limiting migrations to what the labour market actually needs. Current US policies toward undocumented immigration combine a keener awareness of what the US economy needs with measures to keep such flows temporary. In proposing a "temporary worker programme" that would cover undocumented immigrants already living in the US, President Bush hoped to lay the foundation for this stricter approach in future decade(s). The H-1B visas now accessible to migrants are conditional to being offered a job, and their validity is limited to three years renewable only once. The ceiling for H-1B visas has been lowered to 65,000 from October 2003 onward, putting an end to several years of increased ceilings (195,000 in FY 2001–2003) to satisfy the needs of a growing economy. This measure takes into account both post-9.11 security concerns and the lower labour market requirements due to the slowing down of the IT sector.

The question in the EU will be more complex, however, as this logic cannot apply to intra-EU migrations (including from the Eastern European countries after what is after all only a transitory period of restrictions). Adopting US-style policies toward Turkey, Africa and Latin America would be a clear sign that the EU is shifting from its present ***Open Doors*** aspirations to ***Low Trust Globalisation*** ones.

Flags: the logic of distrust

Flags is a world more in tune with the traditional economic argument describing migrants as "stealing jobs" from nationals aspiring to them. Restrictive immigration policies can be expected to be more lenient for those occupations that serve the needs of ageing populations in developed regions, notably in terms of health care. Measures would be taken to limit family-related migration and to prevent migrants from settling in host countries. Highly skilled workers would also remain accepted on a temporary basis.

"Off-shoring" jobs to countries like India will be seen positively, as developed countries seek access to low-cost labour pools without having to incur the risks that Western governments associate, in this scenario, with movements of people into their territory.

What contribution will migrations make to development in host countries and source countries?

Scenario	Immigration policy in developed countries	Impact on labour-sending countries
Low Trust Globalisation	Immigration restricted to **labour market needs** (highly qualified migrants or specific segments). Students welcome in scientific departments.	Risk of "**youth and brain drain**". Mid-level remittance flows.
 **Open Doors**	Market incentives as a mechanism for the creation of win–win perspectives. **Diversity** considered as an asset. Student mobility encouraged. Lenient behaviour toward immigrants and **asylum seekers.**	Developing countries benefit from **two-way flows** (exporting labour and importing off-shored work). Easier cross-border knowledge sharing and co-production. Higher remittance flows.
Flags	Migrants caricatured as "stealing jobs". Migration limited to selected labour market segments (e.g. healthcare). Selective **visa policies** favouring trusted source countries. Family-related immigration restricted; asylum seekers discouraged on security grounds.	Low official remittances. Migrants pushed towards **black market solutions** on all fronts. Economic development constrained by reduced inward flows of knowledge, finance and off-shored work.

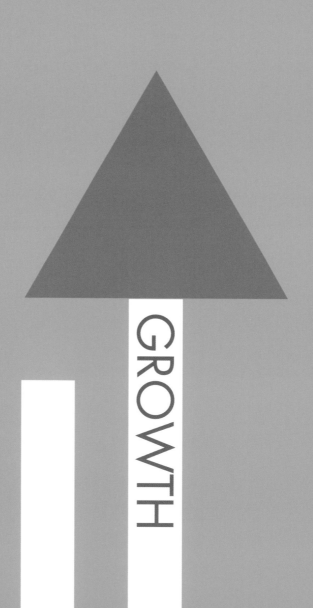

Part 3
Our Global Business Environment

7 Globalisation patterns
8 African futures
9 Market States
10 Demography and migrations
11 Patterns of economic growth
12 The search for energy security
13 The energy-and-carbon industry

Chapter 11
Patterns of economic growth in the three *Global Scenarios*

Long-term economic prospects vary substantially across the three *Global Scenarios to 2025* reflecting differing sets of incentives, market structures, geopolitical trends and degrees of global integration. Having provided some description of economic policy and growth in each of the *Global Scenarios to 2025*, we now outline (section 11.1) baseline long-term growth prospects including some regional breakdown, (section 11.2), with a distinct growth trajectory for each of them that reflects, notably, different levels of trade and investment flows we conclude with a brief analysis of current account inbalances (section 11.3).

Baselines, crises and volatility stories
These trajectories do not represent economic forecasts, as such forecasts tend to become increasingly meaningless with longer time horizons. To study how volatility may be superimposed on our baselines, some possible crises and the impact of these crises on economic growth and oil prices can be modelled separately. In our view, integrating crises and volatility stories in each scenario is better done as part of customised applications, which can be informed by the specific risks and opportunities at stake.

Average GDP growth rates (2005–2025)
projections for the three *Global Scenarios**

Low Trust Globalisation	US		3.1
	Eurozone		2.1
	Japan		1.1
	China		7.4
	India		6.7
	World total		**3.1**

Open Doors	US	3.8
	Eurozone	2.8
	Japan	1.5
	China	8.4
	India	7.5
	World total	**3.8**

Flags	US	2.3
	Eurozone	1.8
	Japan	0.9
	China	6.7
	India	6.5
	World total	**2.6**

* at market exchange rates, USD

Modelling was carried out in close cooperation with Oxford Economic Forecasting. The plausibility of the results was tested in two workshops with the Institute for International Economics (IIE) in Washington (see notably pp. 182–183).

11.1

Economic growth in the three *Global Scenarios*

1

Jennifer Blanke
and Xavier Sala-I-Martin,
"The Growth
Competitiveness Index:
Assessing Countries
Potential for Sustained
Economic Growth,"
in Michael Porter,
Augusto Lopez-Claros,
Xavier Sala-I-Martin and
Klaus Schwab,
*The Global
Competitiveness Report
2003–2004,*
Oxford University Press,
New York, 2004.

The *Global Scenarios* are characterised by significantly different global economic growth rates, ranging from 2.6% per annum in ***Flags*** to 3.8% in ***Open Doors***. By 2025, the level of global economic prosperity is 40% higher in ***Open Doors*** than in ***Flags*** and around 17% higher than in ***Low Trust Globalisation***.

While output expansion in ***Low Trust Globalisation*** is largely in line with the level of global economic growth achieved between 1965 and 2000, ***Flags*** entails a considerably flatter growth trajectory. By contrast, ***Open Doors*** implies a marked acceleration in economic growth that is sustained over a long period. This is not implausible, as the global expansion in the 1990s produced growth rates comparable to those implicit in ***Open Doors***.

Differing rates of productivity growth and different patterns of knowledge sharing

Global growth differentials between the three scenarios are largely explained by differing levels of *productivity growth*.

In ***Open Doors***, technological progress is particularly rapid thanks to substantial R&D efforts both in the private and public sectors. Closer collaboration through international research networks helps push forward the global technology frontier, while the faster diffusion of new ideas allows developing countries to catch up more rapidly. Some of them might even become "core innovators"—a group of countries that today essentially comprise the OECD area.[1]

In ***Flags***, by contrast, national barriers undermine collaborative research efforts across borders and impede the wider distribution of technological innovations. Knowledge spillovers are comparatively limited, which has two consequences. First, greater productivity differentials persist across countries and might even widen, and, second, global productivity growth remains below its potential.

Differing degrees of trade openness and trade specialisation

With trade barriers being progressively dismantled, and the importance of cross-border institutional discontinuities diminishing, foreign trade expands rapidly in ***Open Doors***. Goods and services markets become increasingly integrated, allowing countries to allocate their productive resources more efficiently. Arguably, the developing world benefits most. Reducing their own trade barriers, they gain greater access to OECD markets. In ***Low Trust Globalisation***, trade integration also increases, albeit along a significantly flatter path due to security concerns and continuing institutional differences across borders. As a result, countries are still unable to exploit fully their competitive advantages, which undermines their growth potential. This effect is, of course, much larger in ***Flags*** where markets for goods and services remain considerably fragmented.

Differing degrees of capital market integration, crisis transmission and inflation

Also, financial markets are more integrated in ***Open Doors***, fostering a more efficient allocation of capital on a global scale. As countries have better access to foreign savings thanks to the elimination of institutional or other barriers, capital deepening (an increase in the quantity of capital per worker)—a prerequisite for faster economic growth—is no longer constrained by the lack of domestic savings. Institutional convergence, mutual recognition and greater transparency reduce the home market bias among both institutional and retail investors.

Greater capital market integration in ***Open Doors*** encompasses integration in sovereign and corporate bond markets, in equity markets as well as in bank lending and in markets for venture capital. It also stimulates capital market integration through foreign direct investment flows. While the gains from capital flows depend on what type of capital is moving, the overall benefits of greater integration are large. According to a study by the Institute for International Economics, developing countries alone have notably gained as much as USD 350 billion a

Determination of growth

Scenario	Trade integration	Productivity growth	Access funds
Low Trust Globalisation	**Medium – High.** Jurisdictional discontinuities.	**Medium – High.** Security concerns put a lid on sharing knowledge and innovation.	**Good.** Need to comply to strict transparency rules.
Open Doors	**High.** Seamless cross-border flows.	**High.** Global knowledge base and workforce.	**Excellent.** Global pool of savings.
Flags	**Low.** Grit in the global trade systems.	**Low.** Restricted knowledge sharing.	**Constrained.** Strong home bias.

Innovation and flows of knowledge

Scenario	Fundamental research funding	Cross boarder flows and networking	Industry R&D
Low Trust Globalisation	**Government funded.**	Limited to a few trusted partners. Travelling restrictions hinder networks. Some key networks continue to exist.	Expensive, as limited sharing among companies within the industry. Strong protection of intellectual property rights.
Open Doors	**International private–public networks.**	Fluid networks and development of new "core innovators" in India and China.	Efficient and shared. Industry finances key partnerships with research institutes. International property rights used sparingly.
Flags	**Governments fund research on security–related issues only.**	Weak networks and duplication of research within each country.	Sensitivity on sharing information with peers makes R&D very compartmentalised. Regulation makes technology and intellectual property transfers across boarders more difficult.

1

Wendy Dobson and
Gary C. Hufbauer,
*World Capital Markets:
Challenge to the G10*,
Institute for International
Economics,
Washington, D.C., 2003.

year in additional GDP up to 2000, by increasing their openness to capital flows;[1] as a result, GDP was approximately 5% higher than it would have been otherwise. These gains look set to multiply in ***Open Doors*** where remaining barriers to capital flows, including institutional discontinuities, are removed progressively.

A very different pattern develops in ***Flags***. With capital markets remaining highly fragmented, rapid economic growth requires high domestic savings in order to finance investments. In the US, where domestic savings are traditionally very low, growth could be significantly impeded. By contrast, in countries with high savings rates, especially in Asia, there is a risk of overinvestment and of persistent "bad loans" problems. Thus, on a global scale, capital is misallocated, undermining economic growth.

The benefits of greater capital market integration do not come without some negative side effects. As markets become more integrated, asset prices may become more volatile. Financial crises are transmitted more rapidly and, when they occur, the toll on incomes can be significant. This is well recognised in ***Open Doors*** where a new international financial architecture is put in place in order to prevent and contain financial crises. In ***Flags***, but also in ***Low Trust Globalisation***, closer policy coordination and crisis management is much harder to achieve; although global capital markets remain comparatively less integrated, the risk of financial contagion may be higher than in ***Open Doors***.

Inflation

Inflation remains relatively benign. In ***Open Doors***, consumer price inflation in the OECD area averages approximately 2.5%, with Japan managing to overcome its prolonged period of deflation. Consistent with this, both short-term and long-term interest rates in the US hover around 4.5%, implying real rates of around 1.5%. Slightly higher real rates persist in the Eurozone and Japan. In ***Flags***, by contrast, OECD inflation is only about 1.5% due to considerable slack in the economy. Real bond rates are comparatively higher and hover around 4% and 3.5% in the US and the Eurozone respectively.

'

Developing countries alone have notably gained as much as USD 350 billlion a year in additional GDP up to 2000, by increasing their openness to capital flows.

,

Part 3
Our Global Business Environment

7 Globalisation patterns
8 African futures
9 Market States
10 Demography and migrations
11 Patterns of economic growth
12 The search for energy security
13 The energy-and-carbon industry

Fragmentation and integration in product, labour and capital markets

Scenario	Goods and services markets	Labour markets	Capital markets
Low Trust Globalisation	International trade is high, but below potential. Security provisions as invisible trade barriers. Codes and standards hinder trade with non-compliant countries (ISO certification).	**Visa requirements** curtail labour mobility. Qualification discrepancies deter cross-border labour moves. Companies outsource non-critical functions.	Differences in standards lead to preference for **FDI** and **short-term capital flows**. Some home bias in equity investments. "Savings-rich" countries give access to their private savings pool only to trusted partners.
Open Doors	Goods move freely across borders. Companies take the lead to harmonise goods and services standards. Strong global trade.	Strong labour **mobility**, virtual companies and outsourcing.	Integration markets lead to **efficient capital allocation**. Less home bias. Accessible pool of international savings.
Flags	The international trade system is clogged. Implicit and explicit barriers to trade.	Labour flows limited by escalation of reciprocal **retaliation** on visa requirements. Little outsourcing due to concerns over **security** of sensitive information.	Many capital markets remain closed. Strong **home bias for** fixed income assets. **Domestic savings** finance national bonds issues.

1

The policy implications
are discussed in detail in
The United States and the
World Economy: Foreign
Economic Policy for the
Next Decade, C. Fred
Bergsten, ed., Institute for
International Economics,
Washington, D.C., 2005.

2

In the modelling
exercise, we assume
that membership in the
Eurozone will remain
unchanged.

It is likely, however,
that the common
currency area will
expand over the next
two decades and
encompass further parts
of the EU, including
the new member
countries.

3

World Economic Outlook,
International Monetary
Fund, September 2004,
Washington, D.C.,
p. 148.

11.2
Regional patterns of growth and development

US primacy, an ageing Japanese society, rapid growth in China and India

In each of the *Global Scenarios* considerable growth differentials persist across countries and regions. As far as the industrialised countries are concerned, the US continues to outperform the Eurozone and Japan, regardless of the individual scenario. This performance is largely due to superior demographics and structural factors.[1] However, whereas in *Open Doors* trend growth in the US accelerates from the current level of around 3.5%, it slows in *Low Trust Globalisation* and falls drastically in *Flags*.

In the Eurozone,[2] the long-term growth spectrum ranges from 1.8% in *Flags* to 2.8% in *Open Doors*. Cumulatively, this difference amounts to 35 percentage points in terms of economic prosperity, highlighting the importance of implementing the policy agenda the European heads of government agreed upon in Lisbon in 2000. Important growth differentials persist within the Eurozone itself. Taking into account demographic factors, output in Germany and Italy (where potential growth is currently estimated at approximately 1.7%) is not likely to expand on average by more than 2.5%, even in *Open Doors*. However, these countries' growth performance may be considerably worse—in *Flags*, their output may grow at just 1.5%.

Meanwhile, Japan, which has a rapidly greying society, economically stagnates. In 2000, 17% of Japan's population was 65 years or older, the world's highest percentage. Population ageing tends to depress growth, an effect the International Monetary Fund estimates at -0.8% in terms of Japan's lower real GDP per capita growth for the period 2000–2050.[3] According to the IMF, this impact is higher than in any other country. Furthermore, faster-ageing countries are likely to experience a reduction in their current account balances as the elderly run down their assets during retirement. In the case of Japan, this effect is estimated to amount to almost 3% of GDP. Thus, even in *Open Doors*, Japanese long-term economic growth averages only 1.5%; in *Flags*, output expands by less than 1%. It is important to note, however, that population projections are subject to substantial uncertainty and, to the extent that our assumptions turn out to be too pessimistic, potential output growth would be higher in all three scenarios.

Also in all three scenarios, substantial contributions to global output growth come from China and India, the world's two most populous countries. In *Open Doors*, these two economies grow by 8.4% and 7.5% pa respectively between 2004 and 2025, and even in *Flags* they still enjoy an expansion of real output of around 6.5% pa. Although impressive, these growth rates need to be put into perspective. Based on market exchange rates, both China's and India's level of GDP remains substantially below that of the US and the Eurozone to 2025, even in the high growth context of *Open Doors*. Indeed, in this scenario the GDP gap between the US and China would almost double over the next two decades in absolute terms.

Important contributions to global economic growth also come from Brazil and Russia. Benefiting from increased global integration, their output expands by more than 4.5% and 6.5% pa respectively in *Open Doors*. A more inward-oriented policy stance, resulting in less trade and foreign investment, would shave off about 2 percentage points, however. In the case of Brazil, this implies that in a *Flags* scenario GDP per capita would stagnate over the next two decades.

The renminbi riddle

The long-term economic outlook under the three scenarios and its implications with regard to the relative contributions to global growth of individual economies is based on market exchange rates, as is shown by the charts next page. Using market exchange rates can be misleading, however. This seems to be the case especially with China, whose authorities have kept the exchange rate pegged to the dollar since 1994 and left the renminbi largely inconvertible with regard to capital transactions. According to World Bank estimates, the misalignment is so large that, based on purchasing power parity (PPP), China would already be the third largest economy in the world after the US and the Eurozone. Indeed, if member countries of the Eurozone were considered individually rather than as a bloc, China would be the world's second largest economy in PPP terms.

Part 3
Our Global Business Environment

7 Globalisation patterns
8 African futures
9 Market States
10 Demography and migrations
11 Patterns of economic growth
12 The search for energy security
13 The energy-and-carbon industry

Source: World Bank (2004), OEF and Shell estimates

Total GDP in three scenarios (USD billion)

— USA   — Eurozone   — Japan   — China   — India

In market rates[1]

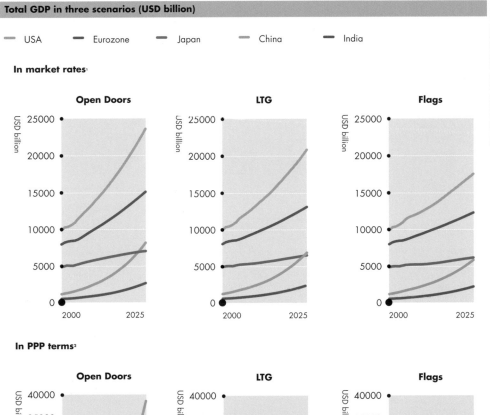

In PPP terms[2]

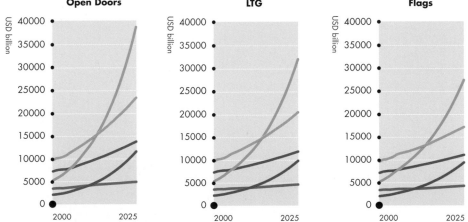

1. In this model the Chinese renminbi is only allowed to float within a narrow band over the scenario horizon.

2. Purchasing Power Parity weights are assumed fixed over the scenario horizon.

Four strongly correlated forces could create major macroeconomic imbalances over the medium and long term:
1. The US Current Account deficit, estimated to reach 6% of GDP by the end of 2005, and possibly USD 1 trillion or more by the end of the decade;
2. The US fiscal deficit of 3% of GDP;
3. The dollar's depreciation already of 35% against the euro but only of 14% on a trade-adjusted basis;
4. The tensions around the peg of her currency to the dollar by China.

How these tensions could lead to crises was discussed by the Shell Scenario team and IIE senior experts in March 2005 in Washington.

In attendance were Director C. Fred Bergsten; Michael Mussa, former Director of the IMF research department and member of the US Council of Economic Advisers during the Reagan administration; Morris Goldstein, former deputy director of the IMF research department;

Bill Cline, previously Chief Economist at the Institute for International Finance; Martin Baily, former Chairman of the Council of Economic Advisers during the Clinton administration; and Adam Posen, who has been a visiting scholar and a consultant at central banks worldwide.

The Shell participants were Peter Cornelius, Cho Khong, Mattia Romani, Wim Thomas and Albert Bressand.

The US twin deficit, dollar depreciation and the power of China: what route to stability?

In its recent analysis of the 'twin deficit', the IIE expresses concern at the simplistic view that links current account deficit and fiscal deficit. Yet the two deficits are quickly increasing: to what extent is this sustainable?

Michael Mussa: The US has shifted, over the last 30 years, from being the world's largest creditor (with net foreign assets exceeding 25% of GDP) to being the world's largest debtor (with net foreign debt now in the 25% range). On current trends the external liabilities will exceed 100% of GDP within the next 25 years. No modern economy has ever experienced such fundamentals in a sustained manner. Some form of adjustment will need to occur. Already private foreign asset holders have become less enthusiastic to hold the dollar, contributing to its depreciation—this is the first sign that a process of correction is operating. Such depreciation will over time bring the current account deficit down. But there is good reason to believe that further correction will occur. Three complementary elements will need to be in place for the adjustment to happen:
1. depreciation of the US dollar;
2. US demand growth that is slower than output growth, allowing net exports to go up; and
3. higher rates of world demand growth.

Does this imply that reducing the fiscal deficit is not an important step in the adjustment process?

Michael Mussa: The current account deficit and the fiscal deficit are not twins—they are linked by a complex relationship. Nonetheless, in some cases reducing one will help reduce the other.

Bill Cline: Over the last two decades the current account and the fiscal deficit moved in the same direction in only six out of 20 years. People used to think that a unit adjustment in the fiscal deficit implied automatically a unit improvement of the current account: now the consensus is that the elasticity appears to be much lower.

Michael Mussa: Reducing the deficit has an intrinsic value as an important step towards creating a sustainable macroeconomic environment in the US. There have been, recently, some encouraging signals. That being said, beyond 2010 the federal deficit and debt situation will begin to look much more bleak. Demographics imply that the federal outlay on Social Security and Medicare benefits will rise from 6% of GDP in 2004 to more than 15% by 2050. My view is that significant fiscal consolidation is desirable to put us on a sound and sustainable path for the longer term. Such adjustment would also bring some benefits in terms of current

account correction, both through a real-economy mechanism and through a financial one. On the real economy side, a fiscal adjustment will contribute to reducing the growth of domestic demand relative to domestic production, hence improving the external position. On the financial side, a smaller deficit reduces the huge gap between national savings and investment, which means that the US becomes less dependent on imports of foreign capital. Smaller foreign capital inflow also implies diminished interest abroad to acquire dollar-denominated assets, and hence a downward pressure on the dollar. This would be the advantage of using fiscal policies as a major adjustment tool, rather than relying only on monetary policy. The higher interest rates that would result from the excessive reliance on monetary policy, in fact, are likely to lead to an appreciation of the dollar, and put further pressure on the current account by making US exports less competitive.

But adjustment, especially if it involves a fiscal element, is usually a very long process. How many years would it take to have an effect on the current account?

Michael Mussa: The only way of adjusting without creating inflation is to decrease domestic consumption relative to potential output growth. Ideally

each year demand growth should be at least 1 percentage point below output growth. This implies a halving in the growth of domestic consumption compared with 2004 when it went up 4.5 %! Such adjustment cannot happen overnight, as it involves the contraction of some sectors, notably residential construction, and movement of resources into the US industries that are either exporting or competing with imports. Flexible though the US economy is, such changes do not happen instantaneously and may cause the economy to lose forward momentum.

Martin Baily: The IIE recently developed a scenario looking at the depreciation of the dollar necessary to bring the current account deficit down to 2.5 % of GDP by 2015. The results were quite worrisome, and this without any additional assumption of a worsening fiscal deficit: they included double-digit interest rates, plus significant reduction in domestic consumption, investment and, naturally, in growth rates. The dollar, in this scenario, would depreciate very quickly. However, this may not lead to a reduction of the current account deficit as large as one would hope because a large share of the US trade deficit reflects intra-firm trading by 'affiliates', i.e. American companies abroad or foreign companies in the US. Companies exporting to the US will squeeze their margins before losing market share to domestic goods or before moving plants back to the US or changing their suppliers. This means that a devalued dollar may take a while to create the necessary improvements in the current account.

The outlook you describe implies a slow and gradual adjustment, led by a combination of structural changes in the components and size of domestic demand and a weaker dollar. The latter reflects a lower appetite for the US dollar in the international markets, particularly in Asia. Are you worried that things may not work out in such an orderly manner?

Michael Mussa: Yes, I am. Foreigners may continue to accumulate US assets at the same spectacular rate as they have done in the past. But while 'more of the same' is possible, I think it is not desirable. Eventually inflationary pressure will increase and the Fed will forcefully slow growth in demand by raising interest rates. If they don't do it promptly and gradually, technically they will 'fall behind the curve', and then the rise will need to be sudden and sharp, with interest rates up to 7%: this is perhaps the fastest channel to decelerate domestic consumption, deflate the housing

market and the construction sector. But the other side of the coin is a substantial slow down in growth rates. The consequences would be felt in the stock exchange as well: the Dow Jones could easily fall back to 8000 or 7000. This 'worst case scenario' would be similar to what happened in 1979–80: at that time, the positive inflation and negative output effects of a surge in world oil prices combined with a loss of confidence in US economic policies. A similar crisis may not even solve completely the current account problem as quickly as in the previous case: higher interest rates would in fact imply a strengthening of the dollar against the euro, with Asian currencies probably maintaining their peg to the dollar.

Fred Bergsten: In addition to devaluation and an economic slump, another real danger is protectionism. A paper by Marcus Noland indicates that the most accurate determinant of bilateral trade barriers is the bilateral trade deficit.[1] A possible reaction to the mounting trade deficit could be a re-emergence of trade barriers with the countries mainly responsible for the trade deficit. There are historical precedents worth bearing in mind: the Reagan administration in the early 1990s imposed substantial trade barriers with Japan on automobiles, steel, machine tools and numerous other products, and before that we

had the 'Nixon shock' of 1971 when the US applied an across-the-board import surcharge and Japan was forced to restrain its textile exports to the US. Policymakers concerned with addressing the current account deficit should remember that what really triggered a US decision to seek major declines of the dollar, in the past, has never been the reluctance of foreigners to buy US dollars but rather the risk of new trade restrictions.

Whether these crises will materialise depends also on the behaviour of other key players. China's bilateral trade surplus already soared beyond USD 150 billion last year. This puts China in a crucial position: what role can it have in the adjustment process, especially as far as the management of its exchange rate policy is concerned?

Morris Goldstein: 2005 is the year when the Chinese Current Account surplus could reach a staggering 8% of GDP. If this happened more pressure would be put on the government to appreciate the renminbi and bring down the surplus—pressure that up to now has not materialised. Some Asian currencies, like the Korean won and the Singapore dollar (historically pegged to the dollar and hence to the renminbi) have started appreciating recently. This, together with the fact

that the Chinese economy does not seem to be decelerating as had been hoped, makes the appreciation of the currency a desirable way of cooling the economy—especially given the fact that all the administrative measures adopted before are coming off. This would, of course, contribute greatly to the adjustment process in the United States, 'exporting' some of the burden of the adjustment back to China. But this is exactly what the Chinese authorities are very cautious about—they want to use a more controllable variable, as it is very difficult to establish the extent of the revaluation that would slow down the economy without stopping it. Employment and social stability are what the Chinese leaders are most concerned about, yet I would offer the view that the current system is not going to buy them social stability forever.

Fred Bergsten: If the currency was freed to float and the capital controls were lifted, the renminbi might not appreciate and hence slow down the Chinese economy! Look at the experience of Japan when it removed capital controls in the 1980s: the immediate reaction was capital flight and portfolio diversification. This implies that, if the Chinese authorities were to let investors take their funds abroad, the upward and downward pressures on the currency could ultimately cancel each other out.

1
Marcus Noland, "US–China Economic Relations", in *After the Cold War: Domestic Factors and US–China Relations*, Robert S. Ross, ed. M.E. Sharpe, Armonk, New York, 1998.

183

The charts on p.181 also report, therefore, the contributions of different countries to global growth using PPP conversion factors. Arguably, this comparison, based on constant weights over the 25-year period, has its own weaknesses, since the gap between market-based and PPP rates is likely to narrow over time as the cost of living increases in line with rising living standards. In South Korea, for example, the gap between PPP exchange rates and market exchange rates fell from almost 50% to 7% over the high growth period of 1980 to 1996. These caveats notwithstanding, using the PPP conversion factor China catches up quickly with Europe and the US, becoming the biggest economy before 2015 in all three scenarios. India, with its much lower starting level, grows rapidly as well—in *Open Doors* it finds itself in a similar position by 2015 to that of China in 2005.

Africa, Latin America and Eastern Europe: highlights

Open Doors provides by far the most favourable environment for other developing countries as well. Africa achieves a growth rate of 4.8% pa between 2004 and 2025, implying a considerable acceleration of output growth compared with the preceding two decades. Nevertheless, living standards improve rather gradually as the continent's population, hit though it is by the AIDS epidemic, will have doubled by 2025. Thus, poverty and underdevelopment will still define the environment with which most African countries, notably in sub-Saharan Africa, will have to struggle. In *Flags*, per capita incomes in Africa essentially stagnate, and in some countries even decline. With fewer public resources and less development assistance under this scenario, HIV/AIDS threatens to get out of control.

While a more outward-looking policy stance and deeper economic integration would allow Latin America to grow at about 4.5% pa in the more favourable scenarios, in *Flags* per capita incomes rise only very gradually. As in Africa, a number of individual countries actually experience a decline in per capita incomes in absolute terms.

While Eastern Europe benefits from its accession to the EU, these benefits are substantially larger in *Open Doors* as Eastern Europe outperforms the member countries of the EU-15 by a wide margin and grows at 4.8% pa in this scenario, thus becoming an increasingly important driver for economic growth in the wider economic space of Europe.

Notwithstanding rapid growth in some countries, especially in the BRICs, the US remains the richest economy in the world in per capita terms. Regardless of scenario and the methodology used to aggregate global output, its economy looks set to remain the global powerhouse even as the rapid development of China becomes a major aspect of globalisation under almost any scenario.

Part 3
Our Global Business Environment

7 Globalisation patterns
8 African futures
9 Market States
10 Demography and migrations
11 Patterns of economic growth
12 The search for energy security
13 The energy-and-carbon industry

11.3
Current account imbalances

Persistent growth differentials will have important implications for global current account imbalances and exchange rates. In 2004, the US current account deficit is estimated to have amounted to close to 6% of GDP; unlike in the late 1990s when a US investment boom led to a widening external gap, this has been driven primarily by lack of saving. With America's net national savings rate amounting to less than 2% of GDP, around USD 2.6 billion of capital inflows are needed each business day to fund America's saving shortfall. Importantly, this shortfall reflects both low private saving and a substantial budget deficit of more than 3.5% of GDP.

Can the US economy grow its way out of the existing imbalance? Only if it can hold to the elevated 3% annualised trend that has been in place since 1995. Will the Federal Reserve be able to maintain its pro-growth policy bias and hold interest rates lower than might otherwise be the case for a rapidly growing economy? Rapid productivity growth is also critically important for the US economy to continue to attract foreign savings to finance its current account. These two assumptions are consistent with **_Open Doors_**, a scenario where the US current account deficit remains manageable. Under this scenario, the burden of adjustment is expected to be shouldered by an increasing number of countries (including China) which move to more flexible rate regimes.

A US deficit growing by 1% of GDP every year?

Over the medium to long term, the adjustment process is facilitated by a more responsible fiscal policy stance in the US and pro-growth structural policies in the Eurozone, which increase the absorptive capacity in the common currency area. Things may turn out quite differently, however. Further fiscal shortfalls in the US, which would further reduce national savings, would promote further increases in the current account deficit and intensify the need for foreign capital. Taking into account that America's net foreign debt has already reached USD 2.5 trillion, Catherine Mann of the Institute for International Economics projects that the US current account deficit could be rising by a full percentage point of the economy per year, resulting in a deficit of USD 1 trillion per year and 10% of GDP

by 2010.[1] In her simulations, she assumes that the dollar depreciates by 15% in effective terms and then remains unchanged for a sustained period.

A situation where ever-wider deficits are accompanied by ever-increasing debt burdens is clearly unsustainable. Could a continuous dollar depreciation do the job? In a separate experiment Mann shows that a steadily depreciating real dollar, at about 10% per year, would be needed to keep the current account from widening as a share of GDP.

But what if foreign investors lost confidence in the more fragmented world described in **_Flags_**? There are several serious implications. To begin with, shortfalls in foreign financing would lead to higher interest rates in the US, less investment and hence less economic growth. Although lower economic growth dampens US import demand, an even greater exchange rate depreciation might be needed to achieve the required adjustment in the current account. However, the greater the need for a further dollar depreciation, the greater the risk that this occurs in a disorderly fashion. In **_Flags_**, but also in **_Low Trust Globalisation_**, a Plaza-type accord seems unlikely, however, raising the risk of a sudden and sharp fall in the dollar.[2] A dollar crash would no doubt have severe consequences. With interest rates rising sharply in this scenario, companies—but also the highly indebted household sector—would be hurt badly. Foreign companies' competitiveness would suffer from a collapse of their price competitiveness, causing the financial crisis to radiate increasingly widely.

Clearly, there is a strong incentive for policy makers to avoid this outcome. However, unless the necessary policy adjustments are made—a more responsible fiscal policy stance in the US, continued structural reforms in Europe and a more flexible exchange rate policy in Asia, i.e. key ingredients for a move towards **_Open Doors_**—there is substantial risk of rising protectionism. Should this happen, global economic growth could be substantially lower in the future, as envisioned in **_Flags_**. On this matter as on many others the critical 'branching points' between our _Global Scenarios_ will reflect policy decisions and behaviours. May the present work contribute to the many debates that will arise as we approach some of these branching points.

1
See Catherine Mann, "Managing Exchange Rates: Achievement of Global Re-Balancing or Evidence of Global Co-Dependency?" _Business Economics_, July 2004, pp. 20–29.

2
Peter Bernstein, "The World Needs Another Plaza Accord," _Financial Times_, November 17, 2004. See also note p. 78.

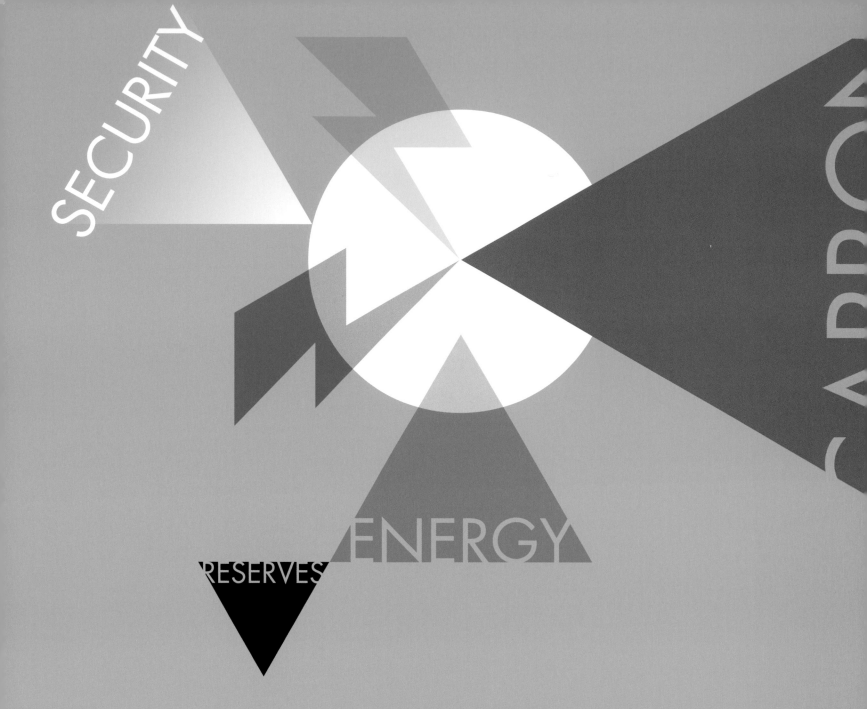

Chapter 12
The triple discontinuity and the search for energy security

The 2004 energy watershed

The energy sector appears to have entered a new era, as renewed worries are increasingly expressed about the long-term balance between energy demand and supply.[1] The short-term price impact of an unforeseen steep rise in oil demand, most notably from China, was exacerbated by the military intervention in Iraq, social tensions in Ven-ezuela, Nigeria and Iran, terrorist attacks in Saudi Arabia and the renewed assertiveness of state insti-tutions in Russia's business environment. Financial markets have provided long-term signals that do not point to a return to the *status quo*. Discounted cash flow analysis suggests that global equity markets are valuing the oil sector at medium-term oil prices well over USD 30/bbl[2], up from USD 25/bbl in the summer of 2004 and USD 18/bbl a couple of years ago.

The upstream industry itself has adjusted price expectations upward for acquisition decisions. Implied proved reserve values in North America, for example, increased year-on-year by nearly 15% in 2003 and nearly 30% in 2004, and more than 25% in the first quarter of 2005 compared to the full year 2004. Since 2003, North American implied proved reserve values have even outpaced the escalation in blended commodity prices over the same period.[3]

In a similar vein, in January 2005, India signed an LNG supply contract with Iran for a price which was 38% higher than the price offered by Iran and declined by India only a few months earlier.

Are the short-term price signals blips on the radar screen, reflecting temporary tensions that will disappear when the cycle runs its course? Or do they point to deeper structural changes? The concomitance of three major discontinuities points to the second answer. They are:
• the relinking of global economic growth and energy consumption,
• concerns over energy security reflecting worries about reserves as well as political tensions,
• the emergence of carbon as a commodity in its own right, even if its price is a negative one (i.e. with carbon-emission credits the positively valued commodity).

Having provided a succinct description of the development of the energy systems in each of the scenarios, we now outline in greater detail fundamental trends and critical uncertainties for overall energy usage and the energy mix.

In section 12.1, we present the potential impact of these three discontinuities on the energy system in general. Section 12.2 then focuses on the impact of rapid development in the third world, most notably in China 'relinking' economic growth and energy consumption. Section 12.3 presents the different dimensions of energy security, from availability of oil and gas reserves to access to producing regions, with an emphasis on the role of investment. Section 12.4 then considers how responses to security of supply concerns would differ in the three scenarios as a result of different geopolitical, policy and regulatory environments. The third discontinuity—carbon—is discussed in our concluding chapter.

1

Deutsche Bank (*Current Issues*, December 2, 2004) calls for massive investment to close the emerging structural supply gap. The IMF (*World Economic Outlook*, April 2005) suggests prices as high as USD 56 in real terms by 2030. ECB President Jean-Claude Trichet on April 8, 2005, indicates that the ECB is increasingly concerned about future energy prices.

2

Global Oil and Gas Sector Review, CSFB Equity Research, April 7, 2005.

3

Herold M&A Upstream Transaction Review, Statistical Snapshot, John S. Herold, Inc., Norwalk, CT, Year End 2004 and First Quarter 2005.

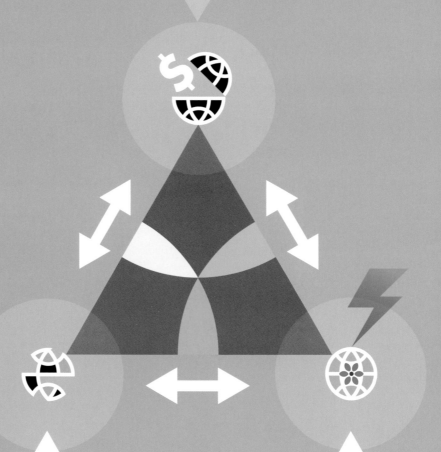

Three underlying discontinuities

Relinking

Fast, energy-intensive global growth

Remove barriers to investment?

Energy Security

Concerns over long-term energy supplies and accessibility

Which way towards energy security?

Carbon

Carbon emissions monitored and priced

Promote low-carbon economy?

Part 3

Our Global Business Environment

7 Globalisation patterns

8 African futures

9 Market States

10 Demography and migrations

11 Patterns of economic growth

12 The search for energy security

13 The energy-and-carbon industry

12.1
The triple discontinuity, and the 21st century energy agenda

The triple discontinuity can be summarised in three words: "relinking", "energy security" and "carbon". It introduces significant changes in the nature of demand, supply conditions and the working of the price mechanism itself. Its impact could be exacerbated in specific circumstances ranging from episodes of overheated demand in China to creeping yet irreversible climate change that could make this planet a hostile one within the lifetime of today's children.

• **Relinking**: If the year 2004 goes down in history as a watershed year for the global energy system, it will be because of the new relationship between oil demand and economic growth which the IMF did not hesitate to describe by referring to the state of "permanent oil shock" into which the world may therefore fall.[1] Global economic growth has once again become more dependent on energy as a result, notably, of the rapid development of China and India. A "global middle class" is now knocking on the door of prosperity, with energy a fundamental enabler. With China the world's manufacturing hub, global economic growth as a whole has become more energy-intensive again.

• **Energy security**: A second source of strain is energy security, a concept rooted in geology and technology as well as in politics and international relations. The reserves debate took on a new impetus as markets were confronted: with inconsistencies in reserves categorisations by companies; with unease about longer-term access and supply reliability from some important non-OECD regions; and even with some observers expressing doubts about the state and nature of the vast reserves bases in the Middle East. Production of conventional oil and gas in non-OPEC countries appears about to plateau within a decade or so. A number of producer countries, within and outside of OPEC, may also find it in their interests to keep production at a lower plateau for a longer period, as their concerns for future generations may outweigh pressures for immediate revenue maximisation. The notion that supplies are flexible enough to meet demand in almost any foreseeable circumstance can no longer taken for granted. It is clear that

massive investment must be made—and protected—in very challenging regions for the energy consumer to carry on turning the car key or switching on the light without even thinking about where the gasoline, or electricity, comes from. The IEA called attention at its May 2005 Ministerial meeting to the risk that the necessary investments are not being made at the pace needed.

One remark on terminology: in this book, the word "reserves" is generally applied in its commonly-used form, to describe "expected producible oil and gas resources", rather than the more narrow definitions used by industry professionals and in Company reporting, to classify petroleum resources.

• **Carbon**: The third major discontinuity is the one introduced by regulatory and market developments that make carbon a commodity in its own right, even though the price of that commodity is negative (i.e. the price to dispose of it is positive). The energy system will therefore be operating, to an unprecedented extent, as an energy-and-carbon system. The public—in Europe but also in many parts of the US, and in developing countries most at risk—expect this system to deliver both high growth and a low-carbon economy. In all scenarios, the "carbon" discontinuity makes its impact felt by influencing legislation and regulation of markets, by fostering the development of alternative fuels, and by affecting the whole structure of relative prices throughout the value chain.

To meet the many challenges implied by a low-carbon economy, a number of reforms will be contemplated, if not implemented. Some will be energy specific. Others will raise broader issues such as attitudes towards nuclear energy, or towards application of new technology (e.g. genetically modified energy crops). Social innovation as manifested in behaviours towards energy use and sharing will be a major variable. Efforts to reduce the GHG emissions associated with the production and use of energy are likely to trigger far-reaching transformations. These are important enough to warrant more in-depth assessment, as presented below in chapter 13.

1

IMF, *World Economic Outlook: Globalization and External Imbalances*, Washington, D.C., April 2005. For alternative forecasts, see notably International Energy Agency, *World Energy Outlook 2004*, Paris, 2004; US Department of Energy, *Annual Energy Outlook 2004*, Washington, D.C., 2004; European Commission, *World Energy, Technology and Climate Policy Outlook (WETO 2030)*, Brussels, 2003; Institute of Energy Economics Japan, *Asia/World Energy Outlook 2004*, Institute of Energy Economics, Tokyo, 2004.

Focus

1

Noureddine Krichene.
"World crude oil and
natural gas: a demand
and supply model",
Energy Economics, vol.
24, 2002, pp 557-576,
New York.

Economic development and energy demand: the need to consider income elasticity, price elasticity and structural change

Economic development raises the income per capita of countries like China and India, and therefore their energy consumption per capita as they move up "the energy ladder". The increase of energy consumption triggered by an incremental increase in income is called income elasticity: it is the percentage change in energy demand associated with a 1% change in its GDP. It reflects the complex process of development and change in the nature of economic growth in a given country at a given time. Predicting how the characteristics of energy demand in China and India will affect global demand requires that this complexity be taken into account.

	Average annual oil demand growth (%) (1)	Average annual GDP growth (%) (2)	Ratio (oil) (2/1)
1965-1973	7.7	4.7	1.62
1974-1994	0.9	3.1	0.30
1995-2003	1.5	3.6	0.43

Source: IMF and Shell

Most forecasters tend to use the ratio between energy demand growth and economic growth as a proxy for income elasticity. This ratio is simply observable and has decreased substantially after the 1973 energy crisis. Since the mid 1990s, the ratio has increased again (see tables below and graph on page 191).

Virtually all forecasters agree that income elasticity will remain below 1.0 and, therefore, that oil intensity will continue to fall. But how much of this is due to a change in the income elasticity and how much to price elasticity? While the IEA, DOE and OPEC all implicitly assume in their models GDP growth to energy demand ratios between 0.43 and 0.55, it is not clear what the underlying assumptions for key emerging markets are.

Income elasticity, price elasticity and structural change

Energy demand is determined by the complex interaction of a number of variables besides economic growth such as access to technology, consumer choices and, crucially, prices. Using the simple ratio between energy demand and GDP as an estimate of elasticity is equivalent to assuming that all determinants of demand other than GDP growth—notably prices—will remain constant, which can be highly misleading. Estimating the simultaneous impact of changes in prices and income over time is necessary if one wants to estimate accurate elasticities and forecast future demand correctly. A number of econometric studies try to do this, by using multivariate energy demand models to estimate the role of income and prices simultaneously.

Two conclusions stand out:
First, prices do matter, even if with a time lag, and their impact can hide part of the impact of economic growth itself if historic data are used indiscriminately. True, in the short term, the demand for energy is quite inelastic to changes in prices; but, in the longer term, price elasticity goes up as people change their habits and countries modify their infrastructures to reflect new preferences. Some of the decrease in energy intensity observed on the basis of historic data is the reflection of price increases of the past and not of the "energy ladder" itself.

	Econometric approach -long term Income elasticity	Ratio approach oil demand/GDP ratio
Pre-1973	1.80	1.62
Post-1973	1.20	0.34

Source: IMF and Shell

Second, econometric results differ significantly depending on the estimation techniques and the time frame they take into account. Income elasticity estimates ranges from 0.53 to 1.38, price elasticity between -0.05 and -1.01.

A study recently published by an IMF staff member indicates how conclusions can differ once the more comprehensive view of demand elasticity is adopted (see table). Prior to the 1973 crisis, an increase in world GDP by 4.7% per annum led to a rise in oil consumption by 7.7% per annum. Higher oil prices triggered substantial improvement in energy efficiency: less oil was needed to produce one extra unit of output. While both the econometric result and the ratio decrease substantially in the post-1973 period, the "ratio" approach would suggest that demand elasticity fell more strongly than is suggested by the estimates including the impact of prices.

While neither the econometric approach nor the simple "ratio" approach are fully satisfactory, this analysis indicates that prices and other key variables need to be considered when assessing the impact of emerging markets, above all India and China, on future energy demand. Some characteristics of these countries, such as their low starting point in energy efficiency, excellent access to technology, fast population growth, and low per capita disposable income, suggest that historic patterns cannot be relied upon to predict future demand: China and India may achieve energy efficiency more quickly than we expect. But the historical patterns also unequivocally indicate that a higher price level is instrumental to change consumer attitudes to energy demand and hence 'step up' energy efficiency, contributing to a satisfactory balance between global demand and supply.

Part 3

Our Global Business Environment

7 Globalisation patterns

8 African futures

9 Market States

10 Demography and migrations

11 Patterns of economic growth

12 The search for energy security

13 The energy-and-carbon industry

12.2

"Relinking": energy for the developing world

The correlation between overall primary energy growth and GDP growth had decreased from 1.2 in the mid-1960s to a low of 0.3 by 2000, as the oil price shocks of the 1970s fostered higher efficiency, technological change and diversification of supply. Since 2000, however, this long-term trend of reducing energy content per unit GDP growth has reversed, and the correlation more than doubled from around 0.3 to 0.7. This relationship can be further analysed as a combination of income elasticity and price elasticity (see box).

With global economic growth fuelled, in large part, by the development of Asia and the "BRICs", the energy ladder becomes an essential consideration for the global energy markets. However, the intensity of energy usage at each stage of development, including on the high-income "plateaux", differs widely across countries. While Japan and some European countries have per capita income levels similar to US ones, their per capita energy consumption is only about half of the US level. This reflects different geographical and climatic conditions, but also the cumulative impact of policies directed at improving energy conservation (whether to reduce trade imbalances or, increasingly, to protect the environment).

A critical uncertainty for the world's energy outlook is which of the two paths—the American or the Euro-Japanese one—China, India and other emerging markets will now follow.

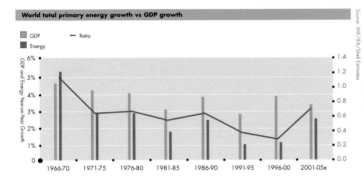

Source: IMF/IEA/Shell Estimates

The energy ladder

Econometric studies[1] indicate that, in general:

• Low-income countries are highly dependent on traditional energy sources (with the risk that deforestation makes their needs increasingly hard to satisfy);

• Once countries reach the threshold of about USD 3000 per capita GDP (in PPP terms), energy demand explodes as industrialisation and personal mobility take off;

• From around USD 15,000, demand grows more slowly as services begin to dominate;

• Beyond USD 25,000, it is possible for economic growth to continue without significant energy increases (although the true picture may differ if one corrects for the relocation of energy-intensive industries to lower-income countries).

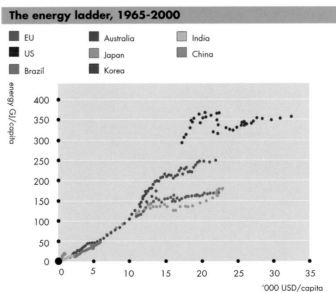

Source: IMF/BP

[1]
Strictly speaking, estimating the elasticity of demand for crude oil with respect to changes in income requires that the oil price be held constant. Krichene, who estimates income and price elasticities jointly in a global demand and supply model, finds the demand for crude oil to be more income-elastic than implied when directly comparing GDP growth and energy demand. However, his findings confirm that the demand for oil has become substantially less income-elastic in the post-1973 period. See box.

1

Energy Research
Institute of the National
Development Reform
Commission, People's
Republic of China,
October 2003.

Whither China's energy demand?

China's energy efficiency has remained substantially lower than the world average. Whereas the Chinese economy requires almost 1.5 barrels of oil to produce USD 1000 of output, the global economy needs only half that amount.

This is of critical importance because, having doubled its oil demand over the last ten years to 6.4 million bbl/d, of which around 3 million bbl/d is now imported, China is now the world's second largest oil consumer. Even more strikingly, China accounted for no less than 40% of the new demand for oil in the 2001–2004 period. This rapid growth will continue: "*depending on how demand for energy services are met, China could quadruple its domestic product between 1998 and 2020 with energy use rising by 70–130%.*"[1]

By contrast, the OECD's share of global oil demand dropped from around 75% in the mid-1960s to slightly more than 60% in the early 2000s.

In terms of total primary energy demand, stressing that few governments in the world are as determined as the Chinese one to promote higher energy efficiency, the IEA forecasts that it will be sufficient for China's energy consumption to rise by 2.2% pa in 2002–2030 in order for China's economy to expand by 5% pa during this period. Oil demand growth would be considerably more rapid

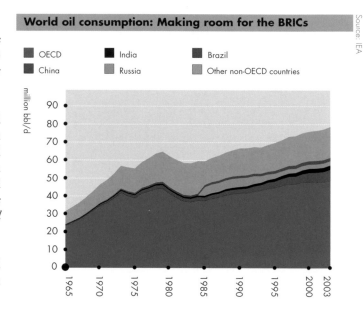

World oil consumption: Making room for the BRICs

OECD · India · Brazil · China · Russia · Other non-OECD countries

Source: IEA

at 3.7% pa, however. The fastest increase is forecast for gas, whose demand would rise by 4.6% pa. The IEA projections imply therefore that China's demand elasticity with respect to income is falling below the world average. As a result, the energy intensity of the Chinese economy will decline and gradually approach that of the world economy. However, if this occurs at a slow pace, tensions in global energy markets will not be removed, or might even be increased if Chinese growth is stronger than the projected 5%, or if energy-efficiency policies face difficulties when implemented at the local level. China was, not long ago, the land of bicycles and village-level energy-inefficient metal workshops. Bicycles are now giving way to cars and SUVs, while energy efficiency remains low in small production units as well as State Owned Enterprises. Even following the IEA forecast, the energy intensity of total Chinese economic output would still be around 1 barrel of oil equivalent for each USD 1000 of output, 50% more than the world average by the middle of the next decade.

Making room for the BRICs in world energy consumption will therefore imply much higher levels of energy investment worldwide. As discussed below, it will also compound the CO_2 emission challenge to a degree unforeseen when the Kyoto Protocol was signed in 1992.

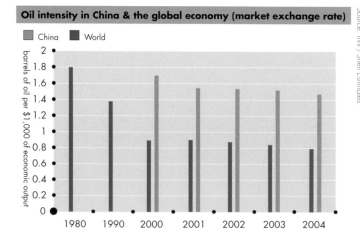

Oil intensity in China & the global economy (market exchange rate)

China · World

Source: IMF/Shell Estimates

Part 3

Our Global Business Environment

7 Globalisation patterns

8 African futures

9 Market States

10 Demography and migrations

11 Patterns of economic growth

12 The search for energy security

13 The energy-and-carbon industry

12.3

Reserves and energy security as an investment issue

The second discontinuity is concerns—whether for geological and technological reasons or for political ones—over security of energy supplies.

The increased risk of reaching a peak in oil supplies in the relatively near future has been debated for decades. However, the failure of previous warnings to materialise is no reason to dismiss the new ones. Whether one is concerned about conventional oil and gas or about energy supply in general, the essential question is the extent to which the price mechanism can be trusted to generate the appropriate signals, investments and technological developments in time for economic growth and development to proceed smoothly.

The static image of reserves has long since given way to a dynamic relationship between needs and capacities in which the key is investment—whether in exploration, in alternative technologies, or in new distribution and organisational infrastructures. Energy investments in producing countries with high export dependency are increasingly accompanied by diplomatic, military and human development assistance from importing countries, concerned about their security of supply.

We thus look at resources, first with a geologist's and technologist's eye—considering conventional oil and gas, recovery rates, and unconventionals—and then with the political economy of security in mind. We conclude with the overall investment scene.

Loch Ness monster or Cassandra: the oil peak debate

The most visible component of the debate concerns expected ultimate recoverable reserves. The "Hubbert peak" debate, named after the Shell Oil geophysicist who predicted in 1956 that US oil production would peak in the early 1970s, is again in full swing, albeit now globally.

Whether this is merely the resurgence of a mythical monster born of innate pessimism, or whether Cassandra will be proven right after being several times dismissed, is still an open question for many. Uncertainties in statistical and geological data have potentially huge implications: a sensitivity study by the US Department of Energy indicated timings for oil production to plateau as divergent as 2040 and 2015, depending on the resource base assumptions at the optimistic (USGS) and pessimistic (Campbell)[1] ends of the range.

1

Colin Campbell, "Forecasting Global Oil Supply", Submission to H.M. Government Consultation on Energy Policy, 2003.

"Futures of the past": 60 years of estimates of world ultimate oil recovery

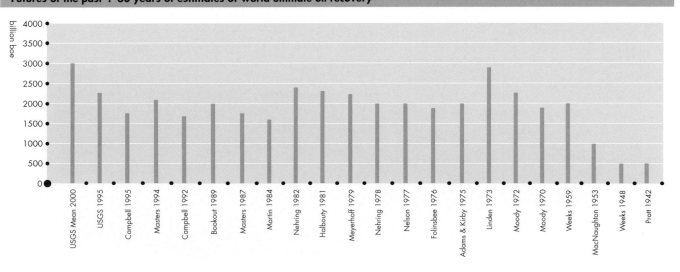

Source: IHS Energy/Shell

Annual discovered volumes, 1900-2000/2040*

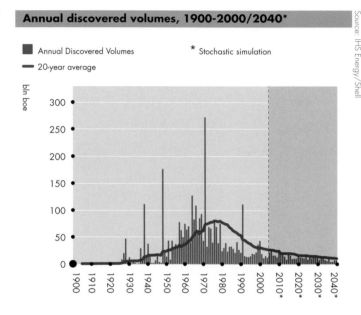

■ Annual Discovered Volumes   * Stochastic simulation

— 20-year average

1

The figures are a
compilation of publicly
available data which
may use different
definitions.

Gas: large reserves, but less scope for new finds?

The presently known conventional gas reserves are equivalent to about 85% of known oil reserves, but only a quarter has so far been produced. Gas reserves increased on average at a rate of 3.3% pa over the last two decades, and discoveries more than replaced produced volumes.

Overall, the gas supply outlook is generally reported to be robust. However, significant efforts and investment will be needed in developing infrastructure to move gas to major consuming markets. The environment in each of the scenarios would present different challenges to the timeliness and adequacy of such infrastructure. This would in turn entail challenges before the end of the scenario period on the availability of adequate supplies to gas to some markets—especially in *Open Doors*.

Geographic concentration of gas reserves creates other types of challenges for importing countries. Russia, Iran and Qatar together contain over 55% of the world's proved reserves.[1] Reserves in North America and Europe, 4% and 3% respectively of the world's proved reserves,[1] are in decline. It seems unlikely that significant new conventional gas volumes will be discovered so gas supply sources will remain highly concentrated.

Scope to expand the recovery from the existing conventional resource base

Enhanced recovery of resources has been a key feature of the oil and gas industry from its inception, prolonging the life of many fields well beyond initial expectations. The present average oil recovery factor is nearly 30%, but technological progress could still increase the recovery factor by 10–15%. This would lift the available reserves by about 530 billion barrels, or 17 years of consumption at present levels. For gas, there seems to be less scope, with an expected recovery factor of around 70% of the conventional resource base.

While major new finds cannot be ruled out, recent statistics do provide worrisome signals. Reserves estimates have increased over time but the annual average increase in proven oil reserves,[1] which stood at 4.5% in the 1980s, has slowed down considerably since the early 1990s to around 1%. Discoveries only replaced some 45% of production since 1999. In addition, the number of discoveries is increasing but discoveries are getting smaller in size. The 25 biggest fields hold some 33% of discovered reserves and the top 100 fields 53%: all but two of the giant fields were discovered before 1970.

A simple extrapolation of the volumes discovered annually suggests that volumes to be found between now and 2050 could be as low as 500 billion boe. However, this magnitude of undiscovered potential is considered conservative by some, who believe it is influenced too much by the declining exploration successes of late and by cautious views about the commercial viability of future finds. Limiting the discussion to conventional hydrocarbons would give an increasingly incomplete picture as unconventionals become more important.

Part 3

Our Global Business Environment

7 Globalisation patterns

8 African futures

9 Market States

10 Demography and migrations

11 Patterns of economic growth

12 The search for energy security

13 The energy-and-carbon industry

Optimal production: the resource holders' perspective

Production levels by OPEC member countries will be an increasingly important variable, both for price formation and for security of supply. OPEC's announced growth aspirations to 2010 outstrip expected total market growth; indeed, in all three of our scenarios, OPEC's "market share" is set to increase.

The growing domestic consumption of energy by OPEC countries and the paths they follow to development are increasingly important considerations. Most OPEC countries remain dependent on oil revenues and many face rapid demographic growth. Their energy consumption is bound to rise steeply, and they will need increasingly higher oil prices to balance their national budgets and to keep their social expenditure per capita at least constant. Insufficiently diversified economies, such as those of the Middle East and Russia, often have a preference for many years of stable revenues over short-term oil production and revenue maximisation. Alternatively, countries may produce more and ring-fence a part of their revenues in a fund for future generations, as Kuwait and Norway have done.

The trends we have described suggest that, if they remain cohesive in the low-growth scenario, OPEC members can defend a floor-price for their oil. By contrast, maintaining a ceiling-price in periods of high demand will be more elusive, especially if spare capacity will be expanded only in ways that make commercial sense for the individual cartel member. Indeed, 2004–2005 events challenge the traditional assumption that OPEC will be able to balance the world's oil markets over the longer term without major price increases.

The steep rise in reserves declared by all OPEC countries in the early 1980s, and the few revisions since then, suggest that oil production has been replaced by new reserves although there is little discussion of these matters. Political considerations, resulting in opposition to investment by foreign companies, may alter the pace of exploration and production from country to country. Altogether, as we dicuss below (see p. 200), a new balance must be found between the producer ("resource-holder") countries' perspective in which economic diversification and job creation matter immensely, and the need for higher levels of investment—including international investment—at a time when the IEA is beginning to worry that the world is falling behind in this respect.

> **The combination of the currently known conventional resource base, the infrastructure bottlenecks stemming from the concentration of gas resources in Russia and the Middle East, and the investment challenge suggests a tightening gas supply/demand balance in scenarios with high demand growth.**

What future for unconventional hydrocarbons?

The resource base of unconventional hydrocarbons dwarfs that of the conventional resource. Leaving aside methane hydrates which still present a major technological challenge, unconventional deposits are about three times the size of conventional oil and gas on a barrel of oil equivalent basis. Meanwhile, coal deposits are more than 2.5 times the size of conventional and unconventional oil and gas resources together.

However, the recovery factor of unconventional resources to date has been not much over 10%, and only so in certain places. Promising technologies, like *in situ* conversion, may improve the recovery from oil shales, heavy oil and bitumen deposits dramatically. If only 50% of the unconventional oil is accessible, and if the recovery factor can be improved by 10–20%, the total liquids reserves base would be doubled.

For gas only some 250–500 billion boe could be added, a meagre 15–30% increase of present reserves. If, however, extraction of methane hydrates became possible, a 1% recovery would be enough to more than double the present gas reserves.

A transition towards unconventional hydrocarbons to supplement conventional resources is a common feature of all our scenarios, at

a speed depending on technical, commercial and environmental considerations, as well as on sustained higher energy prices.

Will societies allow the development of unconventional hydrocarbons in the absence of carbon abatement? Will capital be available for investments much larger than in the case of conventional oil?

Unconventional resource potential (volumes in place)

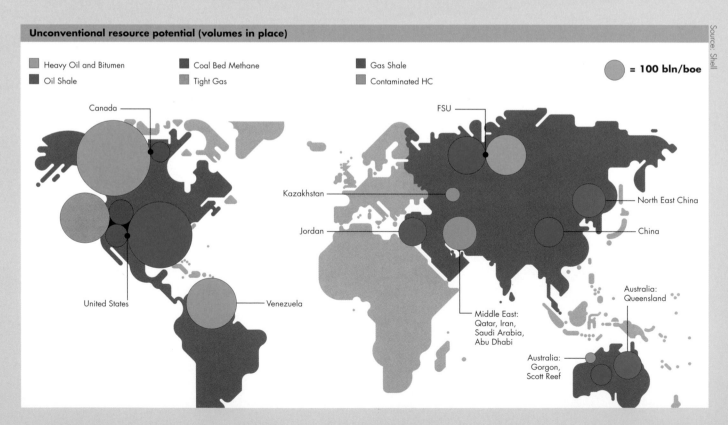

196

Part 3

Our Global Business Environment

7 Globalisation patterns

8 African futures

9 Market States

10 Demography and migrations

11 Patterns of economic growth

12 The search for energy security

13 The energy-and-carbon industry

The USD 16 trillion energy investment challenge

Whether it implies increased exploration, development of alternative energy sources, construction of pipelines and gas terminals or making the energy system more resilient and flexible, energy security is, first and foremost, an investment issue.

According to the IEA, global investment needs in the energy sector total USD 16 trillion from 2003 to 2030. Required investment in the oil and gas sectors alone is estimated to total more than USD 6 trillion, with nearly 75% of this amount in exploration and production. To offset the underlying decline in existing supply sources and to support long-term growth, it is estimated that capital investment needs to be raised from currently around USD 150 billion per year to about USD 240 billion by 2025.

At current savings rates, around 7% of global savings (or around 1.6% of world GDP) would be needed to finance energy investments. But the investment challenge is much tougher to meet for certain regions. As far as its domestic resources are concerned, North America should easily finance what is, by far, the greatest investment need in absolute terms (USD 3.5 trillion over the 20-year scenario period) as this represents less than 0.5% of US GDP per year. Requirements in developing countries, many of which have only limited access to foreign capital, are more difficult to meet. Huge investment requirements in Africa and the Middle East require resources amounting to 4% and 3% of their regional economic output, respectively. This is around eight times higher, as a proportion of GDP, than the investment requirements in the OECD area.

In Russia, investment needs in the energy sector are estimated at around USD 1 trillion over the next three decades—equivalent to 5.5% of GDP per year and more than five times the global average. Of this, investment needs in the oil sector are estimated at around USD 330 billion, or about USD 11 billion a year on average. Interestingly, the Russian government's Energy Strategy for the next 15 years put required investments in the oil sector at USD 14 billion, more than twice the current level and significantly higher than the IEA projections.

A combination of competing budget priorities, the limited size of the domestic capital market, and relatively low sovereign-debt credit ratings, suggests that the major producing countries would need to attract foreign direct investment (FDI) to fund these large investment needs. However, in many producing countries FDI in oil and gas remains restricted. More than one-third of the world's reserves of oil is entirely closed to FDI and access to another 22% is severely limited.

After years of neglect, promoting a more trusting relationship between producer and consumer countries should be considered a high priority, and would be especially beneficial to the energy-poor developing countries, a point explored in the context of our scenarios.

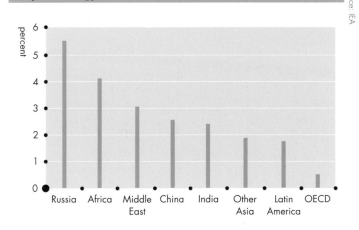

Required energy investment as a share of GDP, 2001–2030

Source: IEA

197

1

"IEA urges a swift end to subsidies", *Financial Times*, April 4, 2005.

2

North American Natural Gas Vision: January 2005, North American Energy Working Group, Experts Group on Natural Gas Trade and Interconnections, http://www.pi.energy.gov/pdf/library/NAEWGGasVision2005.pdf

3

IEA, forthcoming.

12.4

Three contrasted approaches to energy security

Energy security will remain a key consideration during the scenario time span, potentially leading to far more politicised energy relations and creating new sources of tensions among countries as well as new opportunities for entrepreneurship and cooperation. Ambiguity will persist as to what the term "energy security" covers: physical supplies can be threatened by rising international insecurity as well as by depletion of supply sources. Insecurity can also result from the lack of investment in enhanced recovery of existing sources, in new energy sources and/or in infrastructures.

Depending on the scenario, importing countries will worry more or less about a wide range of events: the relatively slow pace of investment in new infrastructure in the Middle East, intense competition among major importing countries for scarce resources, and more. Similarly, as we shall now discuss, they will put their trust in very different measures, from self-reliance policies to international dialogue on investments and opening markets to free trade.

A. Energy security in *Low Trust Globalisation*

In *Low Trust Globalisation*, energy security is achieved in large part through proactive policies seeking to diversify supply and to reduce vulnerability to external shocks. Government policies encourage geographical diversity of sources, reducing dependence on regions with high geopolitical risk, and diversity of primary sources and fuels, as well as strategic and commercial stockpiles, interconnection of infrastructures and "rapid response" mechanisms. Regulation can be heavy-handed, and departures from pure economic efficiency are accepted when they contribute to higher levels of energy security. Indeed, this trade-off between economic efficiency and security plays the defining role in this scenario (by contrast, for instance, to the trade-off between economic efficiency and environmental efficiency central in *Open Doors*).

Renewable and unconventional energy sources are encouraged through tax credits or R&D support. A number of governments "pick winners" by launching national or cooperative programmes in support of specific technologies; these may include the fourth generation of nuclear power plants, including the type of Pebble Bed Modular Reactors (PBMR) recently selected for industrial development by China. They do so, however, with a view to accelerating market development (e.g. by authorising competitors to pool R&D efforts) and not as the fully-fledged national programmes that may flourish in *Flags*.

To reduce vulnerability to external shocks, government policies will also have to include demand-side initiatives. A good example of the logic involved is the approach that the IEA put forward in April 2005. On the one hand the IEA recommends letting market forces do their job more effectively by removing the fuel subsidies that hide true energy costs from consumers. In the words of Claude Mandil, IEA Executive Director, "*the oil market is not functioning well because there is no significant demand response to price signals*".[1] On the other hand, in its papers "*Saving Oil in a Hurry*" and "*Saving Electricity in a Hurry*",[3] the IEA asks governments to stand ready to intervene at short notice before a crisis grows out of proportion to rein in demand through coeercive administrative measures such as driving bans or shorter working weeks.

Concerns for energy security may create indirect support for carbon taxation and for cap-and-trade schemes for carbon emissions such as Kyoto, even if the "K" word is not actually used.

International cooperation tends to be limited to ensuring interconnection between energy transmission systems. Energy security tends to be defined, therefore, at the European, North American and possibly East Asian level. In this scenario, the future of NAFTA and of the EU "Near Abroad" policy *vis à vis* Russia and the FSU countries tends to revolve largely around energy relations. In the context of NAFTA, the US promotes tighter integration of the gas industries along the lines of the "*Vision to 2025*" recently advocated by the North American Energy Working Group (NAEWG).[2] Geographic proximity does not guarantee, however, that barriers to integration can be overcome, and the Working Group limits its ambitions to encouraging parallel developments ("conscious parallelism"), their hope being that regulatory concepts and energy prices, although not energy policies themselves, will continue to converge.

How is energy security pursued?

Scenario	Mechanism	Demand policies	Supply policies
Low Trust Globalisation	Diversity of supply. Indigenous sources encouraged.	Removal of import subsidies. Fuel and carbon **taxation**, congestion charging and some other fees. Emergency rationing.	Focus on indigenous regional resources. **Interconnection** of networks.
Open Doors	Open markets. Global standards and rules. Global investment facilitation.	Prices **internalise** environmental costs. Consumer pull for sustainability. **Hybrid vehicles**.	**Consumer–producer dialogue** to manage stocks and spare capacities and to promote investment. **Global infrastructures**.
Flags	Bilateral agreements, self-reliance.	Fuel taxation. Energy **conservation**. **Coercive** regulations.	Preference for indigenous resources. **Point-to-point connections**.

Insights

Conversation between Albert Bressand and C. Fred Bergsten

As part of the cooperation between Shell and the Institute for International Economics that contributed to these *Global Scenarios*, the Shell scenario team and the IIE senior experts discussed, in March 2005, how the agenda for US foreign economic policy under the second Bush administration—put forward by the IIE in 2005—would play out within the three Shell scenario contexts.

A consumer–producer dialogue to begin decartelising oil markets

Albert Bressand: The IIE stresses that the world economy pays a high price for cartelised oil markets.[1] You advocate a two-tier policy to, on the one hand, put a lid on US oil demand through serious conservation measures (such as a carbon or gasoline taxes) and, on the other hand, reduce OPEC's cartel power through the use of strategic reserves and commercial stocks to keep oil prices within an agreed band. These two measures would probably fit best in the *Open Doors* scenario…

C. Fred Bergsten: Absolutely. It might even be that putting forward such policies would be one important initiative to bring the world back into what you call an *"Open Doors"* world. I think the US and China, as the world's largest and most inefficient oil consumers, could consult one another on how they could cooperate to prevent oil prices from reaching levels, such as USD 70 per barrel, that would be highly detrimental to the two economies and to the world.

The US could first consult China and propose to coordinate use of strategic reserves and commercial stocks in the event that the US is able to convince its IEA partners to adopt such a reserve management policy. With positive signals coming from Beijing, and possibly New Delhi, the US would find it easier to achieve consensus within

the IEA on a comprehensive package of more responsive domestic policies, coordinated use of oil reserves and invitation to far-reaching dialogue with producing countries. The stage would then be set for a cooperative approach bringing together oil-importing and OPEC (or exporting countries) in support of world economic growth, development of the poorer countries and energy security. With strategic reserves already in the order of 1.5 billion barrels, a mutually advantageous oil price management framework could be put in place, as was done to a more limited but successful extent in 1991.

AB: What if this consensual approach fails to materialise? How would the US and key consumer countries attempt to somehow "decartelise" oil markets in *Low Trust Globalisation*?

CFB: In line with the role of legal actions that you highlight in this scenario, a first signal could be for the US Government to join several cases brought against OPEC under the Sherman antitrust act in the US. The IEA would be the organisation the US would turn to in order to create a "coalition of the willing" that could be extended to India and to China, even if very informally. The IEA could then agree on changing its rules regarding the conditions under which member countries can sell oil from their strategic

reserves, deciding to do so in order to prevent an excessive rise in prices and not just supply disruptions.

OPEC countries might then try to counteract such moves through their usual quota system as well as by removing export capacities from the market, in the name (for instance) of "installation maintenance". Determined action on the part of consumer countries would be likely to prevail over the medium term, especially if backed by strong measures to discourage demand and encourage alternative energy sources. OPEC countries would probably find it in their interest to discourage major energy substitution programmes by entering into an agreement with the IEA on the desirable price band.

AB: My own feeling is that, in this scenario, the US and the IEA countries would be using their economic and political power to "get a seat at the table" of OPEC meetings. This would indeed be very much in line with the type of *realpolitik* that is the hallmark of *Low Trust Globalisation*. China could effectively contribute to this agreement, without having to enter into the type of formal alliance or understanding that you describe for *Open Doors*. Speaking as a European, I can also imagine that the IEA would be the appropriate forum for Europe—and Japan—to encourage US initiatives of

energy conservation on the demand side.

CFB: Well, this could indeed be an important aspect of a better working trans-Atlantic relationship. Note, as a precedent, that the US finally abolished price controls for oil and gas as part of a G-5 deal at the Bonn summit in 1978…

AB: Would the agreement then go as far as to induce, if not participate in, at least some coordination by the US with the Kyoto mechanism?

CFB: Well, this is doubtful, as it is seen in the US as a separate issue. But climate change policies deserve a separate conversation.

AB: How might the type of initiative that IIE calls for play out in a *Flags* world? Imagine that the IEA countries cannot agree on what policies to pursue, what sort of a unilateral initiative do you think the US could take?

CFB: The US could still try unilateral variants of the same approach. Surely such an initiative would not go unnoticed and would have substantial impact, but it would be much less likely to succeed.

1

The United States and the World Economy—Foreign Economic Policy for the Next Decade, C. Fred Bergsten and IIE, Washington, D.C., 2005

Part 3

Our Global Business Environment

7 Globalisation patterns

8 African futures

9 Market States

10 Demography and migrations

11 Patterns of economic growth

12 The search for energy security

13 The energy-and-carbon industry

OPEC, Saudi Arabia, Russia and strategic petroleum reserves

In *Low Trust Globalisation*, OPEC continues to follow the strategy that it seems to be pursuing today—supporting prices at a high level by somewhat constraining production and restricting investment in new productive capacity. This strategy maximises short-term revenues. Critically, such a strategy assumes a steady global oil demand over the long term, a realistic assumption in *Low Trust Globalisation*. Saudi Arabia is the lynchpin of OPEC and bears the brunt of day-to-day management. It can be expected to implement the OPEC strategy successfully.

Revenues in OPEC countries are spent on social programmes, possibly putting a lid on energy investment. Nevertheless, many large exporting countries shun foreign investment, resulting in continued low spare capacity and a tight supply–demand balance. Low spare capacity leaves the world vulnerable to supply disruptions and increases both price volatility and peak prices. A mix of commercial market stocks and strategic stocks are held by consumers, and are released via market forces or government intervention, depending on the course of high-price episodes. OPEC sees this as a "fair" way to distribute the pain of maintaining essential spare capacity; however, even though strategic reserves may be used more flexibly by IEA countries, no coordination develops between OPEC and IEA in the form that we suggest in *Open Doors*.

Natural gas—key to energy security in *Low Trust Globalisation*

Natural gas is critical to energy security.

• In Europe, the key issue is the region's heavy dependence on Russia, which accounts for around 40% of its gas imports. A competitive market develops, with harmonised regulation for cross-border trade. This framework recognises the need to unbundle the ownership of infrastructure, such as pipelines, from the rest of the value chain for competition and investment to develop. While strong regulation is likely to increase the cost of gas market development, regulatory relaxation for specific "strategic" investments is possible. Diversity of supply drives simultaneous development of LNG and pipeline supply. LNG is a price-taker as it competes for market share with long-term contract pipeline gas.

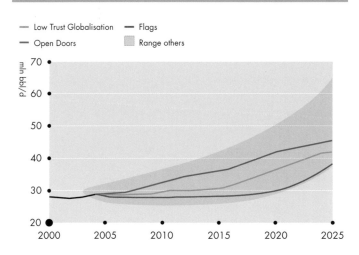

Call on OPEC (crude)

— Low Trust Globalisation — Flags
— Open Doors ▨ Range others

mln bbl/d: 70, 60, 50, 40, 30, 20
2000, 2005, 2010, 2015, 2020, 2025

• In the US, there is growing realisation that the indigenous resource base is under pressure. Even maintaining production near current levels probably requires sustained high prices; this concern is compounded by the fear that significant increases in gas imports from outside North America may increase global gas prices. NGOs voice strong opposition to the opening of federal lands. Concerns about physical security and regulatory hurdles delay the development of import infrastructure.

• In Asia, China and India emerge as the new growth poles for LNG demand, and shop for the best overall value (price, infrastructure, upstream share). Iran and Qatar target Asia as the main market to unlock resources and revenues.

Coal, renewables and nuclear

Coal dominates and maintains its share of the global power market. For China, this alleviates energy security concerns while also raising major logistical problems—coal already represents 60% of Chinese rail freight traffic. New clean technologies (e.g. Integrated Gasification Combined Cycle (IGCC) and CO_2 sequestration) enhance its use in the power sector, while Coal-to-Liquids (CTL) technology does so in the transport sector.

201

Renewables and indigenous energy sources are stimulated by government policy, particularly in Europe. Renewables grow by more than 10% per annum and gradually achieve close to 5% market share by 2025. Wind is the fastest growing non-hydro renewable, followed by solar. Solar photovoltaic (PV) rapidly develops, at a rate of almost four times that of solar thermal, as PV provides extensive distributed and centralised power generation solutions. Ocean energy, predominantly from waves and tidal flows, sees increased installed capacity over this period.

Nuclear energy faces public opposition in Europe and North America, but the example of China and the concerns about the impact of coal lead to a gradual reassessment. The next generations of power plants may therefore achieve the levels of support needed for politicians to take the risk of launching new construction programmes in a number of European countries and in the US.

B. Energy security in *Open Doors*
In *Open Doors*, the essential trade-off in energy policies is between, on the one hand, fostering the provision of sufficient energy at affordable prices to end-users, and, on the other hand, working towards the clean and safe environment that global and local communities tend to widely support.

Internationally, consumers and producers are inclined to seek "win–win" approaches that come more naturally in this scenario where international cooperation is a key feature. In *Open Doors*, countries join forces to reduce tensions, promote development and create room for pure market interactions. Energy security then is largely about security of investment, an issue that is at present addressed mainly through bilateral tax and investment treaties but in which the OECD and WTO might play a stronger role.

The consumer–producer energy dialogue in *Open Doors*
OPEC does not wane away in *Open Doors* as new oil and gas production come increasingly from non-OECD countries. This is not the pure market-centric world described in the *Shell 2001 Business Class* scenario. Rather, consumer countries look for a way to strike "win–win" deals with producers. This (along with tighter links between the EU and Russia) applies a non-threatening

counterweight to OPEC's increasing market power. OPEC member countries, meanwhile, have an interest in limiting price rises below the thresholds that would significantly accelerate the long-term evolution of the energy system. The two sets of interests are reconcilable, partly depending on the speed at which OPEC economies diversify. To keep prices within what is then a mutually agreed broad band—as opposed to an OPEC-imposed one—it makes sense to "share the burden". Coordinating spare capacity expansion by OPEC with management of strategic and commercial stockpiles by consumer countries is the way to do it. As described in the insert by C. Fred Bergsten and Albert Bressand, it is possible, in this context, for the IEA and OPEC to develop the type of consumer–producer dialogue needed to move away from a cartelised oil market while giving producing countries assistance in the diversification of their economies.

C. Energy security in *Flags*
Energy security in *Flags* might be seen as less of a problem in light of the lower growth in demand. Yet this is a world where a large number of producing countries may opt to pursue a set of national or populist goals that keep energy markets fragmented and often prone to unpleasant surprises. Policymakers do worry therefore about security of supply and access to resources; so governments strike bilateral deals and push towards alternative and indigenous energy sources while also looking for alternative ways of using fossil fuels (e.g. CTL).

Local solutions proliferate in an environment where global integration stalls and competition is limited. Technical progress and innovation are slow. There are few one-size-fits-all technical solutions as some countries opt for high levels of renewables growth (where the traditional utility industry can evolve to provide this capability) while others adopt advanced coal technologies where indigenous supply abounds. The US government is a strong voice in promoting domestic gas, coal, nuclear and renewable energy sources, even when governmental incentives are needed to encourage investment. This is the scenario in which legislators go the farthest in lifting restrictions on drilling for gas in the areas where access is currently limited. The Arctic pipeline is encouraged with favourable regulatory and fiscal terms.

Part 3

Our Global Business Environment

7 Globalisation patterns

8 African futures

9 Market States

10 Demography and migrations

11 Patterns of economic growth

12 The search for energy security

13 The energy-and-carbon industry

In their effort to increase self-reliance, governments also attempt to reduce imports of oil and gas through regulatory and fiscal means, encouraging substitution (e.g. nuclear power generation) as well as end-use efficiency through coercive measures going beyond the temporary emergency initiatives envisioned in *Low Trust Globalisation*. These measures dampen the demand for energy further, which is already lower than in the alternative scenarios due to sluggish economic growth.

The role of national energy companies ("NOCs") in *Flags*

Concerns about energy security revive the "'old order'" of bilateral long-term contracts, point-to-point connections and political horse-trading to secure imports. Consumer countries encourage their national energy companies to trade "security of demand" (i.e. long-term purchase agreements) for security of supply. Indian and Chinese energy companies, strongly backed by their governments, pursue national policy objectives as well as commercial ones. Competition among and with national companies to access oil and gas resources may not result in delivery of greater volumes onto world markets, but in capture of resources to meet domestic demand in their home countries.

Flags, therefore, is the scenario where energy security becomes an almost routine part of diplomatic and military relations. Regional approaches are favoured, even though the US may discover again that being located in the same hemisphere does not necessarily make Latin American countries more prone to accept large US investments in their natural resources sector. OPEC struggles too in *Flags* because of lack of quota discipline and because of recession periods in which prices fall abruptly.

Unconventional resources are far less attractive to develop in this more challenging environment. Yet a significant number of projects are supported for the sake of long-term energy security.

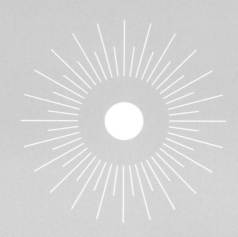

CLIMATECHANGE

Chapter 13
The energy–and–carbon industry of 2025

Can the type of economic growth discussed in the three scenarios be sustainable? While the worries expressed by the Club of Rome[1] have been largely discarded as Malthusian, and while environmental policies have developed considerably since those early days, the rapid growth of the "BRIC" countries and the relinking of economic growth and energy consumption have brought to the fore a new set of far-reaching environmental concerns. How these concerns are addressed, and whether companies, new market mechanisms and/or regulators will be trusted to provide appropriate solutions, will be an important aspect of the resolution—or lack thereof—of the dual crisis of security and trust in each scenario.

The impact of human activity on the planet will reflect the demographic and economic trends analysed in our previous chapters. It will span the full spectrum of issues from local to global in ways that this report can only sketch, leaving detailed discussions for more specialised work. We focus here on two interrelated issues illustrating this diversity of considerations, at very different levels of political priority: namely, the risks of detrimental climate change (section 13.1), how this is taken into consideration through the Kyoto Protocol and other policies (section 13.2), and threats to biodiversity (section 13.3). In each case, the type of policy response that can be expected is strikingly different across the three *Global Scenarios*.

> ' **National decisions made now and in the longer-term future will influence the extent of any damage suffered by vulnerable population and ecosystems later in the century.**
>
> US National Research Council[2]

1

Donella H. Meadows, Dennis L. Meadows, Jorgen Randers and William W. Behrens III, *The Limit to Growth: A Report for the Club of Rome's Project on the Predicament of Mankind*, University Books, New York, 1972.

2

Climate Change Science: an analysis of some key questions, Committee on the Science of Climate Change, National Research Council, National Academy Press, Washington, 2001.

Focus

O' ice and men: unfreezing Kyoto politics

Humanity may be living in the age of 'globalisation'; yet views on climate change continue to reflect national perspectives and histories. Two main controversies crystallise opposition between national views: the first, about the reality and course of climate change; the second, about whether the newly industrialising countries have the same right as Western nations enjoyed previously to follow carbon-intensive paths to prosperity and happiness.

Behind these controversies are three schools of thought.
• Advocates of the precautionary principle—who tend to come from Europe, New England or California—point to a 'natural climate' disturbed by the industrial revolution from the 19th century onward.
• Meanwhile, believers in human ingenuity and its ability to keep technology frontiers advancing relentlessly, question the causal relationship linking industry to environmental deterioration; they see industry as part of the solution, some even stressing the beneficial impact of carbon (e.g. in the form of more abundant crops and timber).
• The third school of thought, those who speak for emerging countries' right to develop, wait for the other two schools to neutralise each others' arguments, while constantly reminding global public opinion that Western nations have no right to close the door after themselves.

Underlying all three schools of thought is the same concept of the 'natural climate'; their differences lie mainly in whether and by how much it has been affected by human activity. But what if the 'natural climate' that all three point to were itself not as natural as it is assumed to be?

Research into the three cycles through which the earth's climate moves—100,000, 41,000 and 22,000 years in length respectively—has led to the conclusion that glaciers should have begun to reoccupy parts of Northern Europe and Canada some thousands of years ago. The earth should be well on its way into another long ice age.

Why is it not?

To understand this finding, we have to look more closely at the earth's climatic cycles. Over the last million years, the earth has progressed through a series of long ice ages separated by shorter warm 'interglacial periods'. These cycles are marked by variations of up to 10% in the light received in the Northern hemisphere in summer, and variations in atmosphere gases; both types of variation have left their mark in a range of ways (e.g. tree rings, sediments, ice cores) that scientists have analysed to great depth.

In 2003, William Ruddiman[1] was thus able to identify a major discontinuity in the cycles of CO_2 and methane. After the earth had passed the peak in Northern hemisphere summer sunlight 10,000 years ago, CO_2 concentrations did start to decrease from their peak of 275 ppm towards 240 ppm—but they stopped their decline six thousand years ago. Similarly, methane concentrations stopped their normal decline (from about 0.7 ppm towards 0.45 ppm) about 5000 years ago.

The cause lies most probably, argues William Ruddimann, in the development of farming. CO_2 concentrations significantly started to go 'off cycle' when late Stone Age Europeans began to clear and burn forests to grow wheat, barley, peas and other crops. Disruption in the methane cycle 3000 years later coincided with the action of farmers in Southern China, and then farmers in the Ganges delta, flooding lowlands to grow rice and thereby triggering greatly increased fermentation of organic material. Could a relatively sparse human population trigger such changes in land use? The 11th century survey of Southern England commissioned by William the Conqueror, captured in the *Domesday Book*, does show that, scarce as the population was at the time, most of natural forest cover had been cleared. In the words of Ruddiman, if man had not injected billions of tons of carbon into the atmosphere through deforestation and flooding, "current temperatures would be well on the way toward typical glacial temperatures." Instead, human activity up to the 20th century managed to establish a kind of forced equilibrium, keeping temperatures at roughly the same levels.

This equilibrium is now seriously at risk. The impact of expanding farming and deforestation, of massive industrial GHG emissions, both linked with expanding human population is pushing climate into a different set of feedback loops—and may take the planet well beyond the type of changes we are used to dealing with.

1
William F. Ruddiman, "The Anthropogenic Greenhouse Era Began Thousands of Years Ago", *Climatic Change*, vol. 61 no. 3, 2003, pp. 261-293; and "How Did Humans First Alter Global Climate?", *Scientific American*, March 2005, pp. 46–53.

Part 3

Our Global Business Environment

7   Globalisation patterns

8   African futures

9   Market States

10 Demography and migrations

11 Patterns of economic growth

12 The search for energy security

13 The energy-and-carbon industry

13.1
Climate change and the fate of Kyoto

While the film *The Day After Tomorrow* was viewed sceptically by many, a quick look at reports by leading insurers and re-insurers[1] shows clearly that climate change has become a significant risk on the balance sheet of companies. While political stances remain widely divergent, notably on either side of the Atlantic, a quiet revolution has indeed begun in company boardrooms and in the marketplace.

Compared with a pre-industrial level of around 280 ppm, CO_2 concentration in the atmosphere is now at 380 ppm. After years of intense controversy, it is generally accepted that this reflects largely the impact of human activities and that this "anthropogenic" change has been a key driver in the rise of average temperatures in recent decades. It is also accepted that levels in the range of 700–1000 ppm would lead to very damaging impacts, possibly calling for the relocation of millions of people, as described notably in scenarios developed by the Intergovernmental Panel on Climate Change (IPCC). A level of 500–550 ppm is expected to help avoid the worst calamities.[2] Containing the increase in CO_2 concentration within 500–550 ppm will require considerable effort: according to the most recent IPCC assessment, such a level could already be reached by 2050 with further increases throughout the 21st century unless precautionary action is taken.[3]

Such action should be considered a matter of some urgency, in light of recent changes in our understanding of climate history. The earth's natural cycles—highly predictable variations in sunlight due to three types of orbital movement—are well researched and are often invoked as alternative explanations for any warming trend beyond short-term oscillation. However, far from providing alternative explanations of the present, they have had the effect of cooling the earth and have offset man-induced global warming. Indeed, ice cores in Antarctica show that CO_2 oscillated during a long sequence of ice ages and interglacial periods between 240 and 275 ppm. Anthropogenic warming is more than likely to have begun as early as 6000 years ago, as a result of changes in land use resulting from neolithic agricultural revolution and, later, flooding in large areas for rice cultivation in China and India (see box).

Carbon emissions can be reduced through qualitatively different changes. Key options are to:
1. Impose efficiency gains, to reduce demand growth,
2. Consider alternatives that are cleaner, or
3. Add "tailpipe solutions" such as sequestration, which solve the problem after the event, quite often at high cost.

Different combinations of such policies can be expected to prevail in different regions, with the US more inclined to support technology-based solutions and the EU favouring a precautionary approach, through taxes and standards.

A number of critical uncertainties
While the importance of carbon in the overall policy, strategy and market environment can be considered as a "predetermined trend", key uncertainties include: the extent to which the US or a significant number of US states adopt policies aiming at carbon reduction objectives; the prices that carbon emission rights will fetch; the type of support that will be available for the development of new technologies; the effectiveness of the new market mechanisms in reducing carbon emission growth; the level of global integration and reach of the off-set mechanisms; and how fair the carbon reduction objectives are perceived to be by developing economies and their willingness to accede these.

While added costs will be immediately visible, active carbon management will also create major new opportunities at three levels: within company operations, within specific regions and globally. Energy companies can generate emission credits through their own operations, as part of projects with other companies and governments (e.g. by providing CO_2 to be re-injected in not too distant oil fields or depleted gas fields), or as participants in international programmes and markets around the Clean Development Mechanism (CDM) and the emissions trading markets (see box p. 90). The relative attractiveness of these various strategies differs significantly across the three scenarios, with local considerations critical in *Flags* and a more systemic approach conceivable in *Open Doors*.

1
See notably Swiss Re, *Sigma*, No.1/2004.

2
For an opposite, minority view see Peter R. Odell, *Why Carbon Fuels will Dominate the 21st Century's Global Energy Economy*, Multi-Science Publishing Ltd, Brentwood, England 2004. Professor Peter Odell is professor Emeritus of International Energy Studies at Erasmus University, Rotterdam.

3
Nebojša Nakićenović and Rob Swart, eds., *A Special Report of Working Group III of the IPCC, Emissions Scenarios*, Cambridge University Press, 2000.

1

John Browne, "Beyond
Kyoto", *Foreign Affairs*,
July/August 2004, p.20

2

Carbon dioxide
(CO_2), methane (CH_4),
nitrous oxide (NO_2),
hydrofluorcarbons (HFC),
perfluorocarbons (PFC),
sulphur hexafluoride (SF_6).
Commitments concerning
limitations or reductions
in GHG emissions vary
on a per-country basis
and are expressed
as a percentage of
emissions during the base
year – 1990 for CO_2 and
N_2O, and 1990 or 1995
for the rest.

Cap-and-trade policy options

The Kyoto Protocol, ratified by 127 countries representing 55% of total CO_2 emissions in 1990, came into force on February 16, 2005. Its essential feature is the combination of a discretionary political and administrative decision—to cap carbon emissions—with a set of market mechanisms (trading schemes) in order to achieve that political objective in a cost-effective manner. In addition, the Kyoto process is open-ended: progress achieved in one period is expected to drive more ambitious objectives in terms of emission capping and in terms of the range of participating countries. How this happens in Kyoto can be compared, if not to the EU integration process, at least to the process of global trade liberalisation.[1] Under the first commitment period from 2008 to 2012, industrialised countries are the only ones to face binding targets regarding the emission of the main greenhouse gases (GHGs),[2] including CO_2. These targets reflect underlying national differences in emissions, wealth and capacity. They now apply to all developed countries, except Australia (which vowed to stick to the agreed targets) and the US.

The US exception matters immensely, as the country accounted for 36% of GHG emissions in 1990, against 30% for the EU, 17% for Russia and 9% for Japan. Yet, while the US is likely to stay out of the Protocol, states such as New York and California are coming up with schemes of their own. Efforts to reduce other pollutants—notably in power generation—may also provide other channels through which Kyoto-like cap-and-trade schemes could materialise in the US.

Kyoto signatories can resort to four policy options that encourage a broader view of ecosystem management and that give an essential role to market pricing mechanisms through "cap-and-trade" instruments:

• First, remembering that about 20% of present carbon emissions are due to deforestation, countries are allowed to subtract from their industrial carbon emissions certain increases in carbon sequestered in "sinks" such as forests.
• Second, the Protocol recognises emissions trading, which allows countries to buy allowances from other countries that reduce their emissions beyond their commitment.

• Third, under the *Joint Implementation* scheme, an investor from a country with a commitment may obtain carbon credits from the implementation of a project in another country member of the Protocol.
• Fourth, while the *Clean Development Mechanism* (CDM) is also project related, it involves countries that have not adopted commitments, thereby potentially expanding the ways in which credits can be claimed.

The "pricing-in" of carbon in the economy

2005 may well be remembered as the year when what is known as "the energy industry" became "the energy-and-carbon industry". While a genuine "hydrogen economy" may take decades to materialise—if it ever does—economists can make the case that we have already moved from the age of hydrocarbons to that of hydrogen and carbon, as both commodities now carry a price tag. Atoms of carbon are convenient "vehicles" to deliver hydrogen into the world's billions of combustion chambers. Until Kyoto, what happened to the atoms of carbon was of concern to ecologists but not to economists. This is no longer the case.

The price discovery mechanism behind the carbon emissions schemes—notably the European Emissions Trading Scheme (EU ETS)—has been patterned after similar markets for nitrogen oxide and sulphur oxide set up in the US to achieve efficient pollution abatement. As a result of the EU ETS, a whole new set of markets can be expected to develop to help companies, investors and speculators to unbundle the rights and liabilities attached to the carbon part of hydrocarbons from those attached to the hydrogen part. These markets can develop before engineers have put in place the capacities and systems needed to manage carbon separately from hydrogen, e.g. through various forms of sequestration and processing. In this sense, the economy is ahead of the energy infrastructure.

Even in the absence of US participation, the price signals coming from the European ETS will serve as "shadow prices" that economists and investors will use to shed light on major energy and industrial projects as well as on a company's balance sheet and long-term liabilities. A major "cognitive threshold" has now been crossed: having to monitor and measure emissions that, unlike "pollution", cannot otherwise be

Part 3

Our Global Business Environment

7 Globalisation patterns

8 African futures

9 Market States

10 Demography and migrations

11 Patterns of economic growth

12 The search for energy security

13 The energy-and-carbon industry

seen is much more than an administrative process. Putting a price on emissions, even a small one, further compels the analysis of the chain of causalities that link the "carbon side" and the "hydrogen side" of energy activities. And investors are well aware of the significance of this change, irrespective of political doubts on the Kyoto Protocol. As observed by McKinsey, *"emitting carbon... will become more expensive and shareholders want to know how executives plan to manage these costs... companies should set up new tracking and reporting processes to keep shareholders informed... and weight the trade-offs of maintaining their current emissions, buying allowances and credits, or reducing their carbon output and selling their allotted credits."* [1]

Crossing the economic and cognitive Rubicon

This crossing of the economic and cognitive Rubicon towards the carbon economy coincides with other major scientific and legal developments that all concur to make the carbon and hydrogen economy a reality in politics as well as in society.

A number of important studies have reinforced the fundamental findings behind the IPCC consensus.[2] A study of the world's oceans and carbon released in February 2005 has further reduced doubts about climate change that were due to the limitations and uncertainties inherent in considering only atmospheric temperatures to see whether global temperatures are rising. The eight-country study of the Arctic has vividly demonstrated how the impact of climate change is far more pronounced in the polar region similar findings on Antarctica (where 87% of glaciers are receding) also concur with this. This has special relevance as the Arctic ice cap, twice thinner now than 30 years ago, and fresh water flow play a fundamental role in the earth's "cooling system" and in the Atlantic Basin circulation patterns.

A number of major law firms are preparing to petition the Inter-American Commission on Human Rights (IACHR) on behalf of the Inuit Arctic community *"to find against the United States, the world's leading producer of greenhouse gasses, for causing global warming and threatening the Inuit's existence"*.[3] Meanwhile on July 21, 2004, 8 US states and the city of New York sought an injunction against the production of GHGs by a number of power companies, leading to Peter Roderick, director of the Climate Justice Programme, to welcome *"this historic moment—the world's first legal action to stop greenhouse gas emissions"*.[4]

World energy demand and CO₂ emissions: an EU abatement case

Source: EU Commission

	1990	Ref 2030	Carbon abatement	% Diff
CO$_2$ emissions (GtCO$_2$)	20.8	44.5	35.3	-21%
Total consumption (Gtoe)	8.7	17.1	15.2	-11%
Coal	2.2	4.7	2.7	-42%
Oil	3.1	5.9	5.4	-8%
Natural Gas	1.7	4.3	4.3	0%
Nuclear	0.5	0.9	1.2	36%
Renewables	1.1	1.4	1.8	35%

Implications of a stable 550 ppm world for the energy mix

There are many paths to a lower carbon world but they all require step-change evolutions. A further shift to natural gas, nuclear energy, renewables and bio products will all need to be a critical part of a comprehensive approach to keep CO$_2$ concentrations below 550 ppm; so will carbon capture and storage, and advanced vehicle technologies. Taking into account existing commitments for the Kyoto period and assuming a carbon price of euro 13.5/ tonne CO$_2$ the European Commission has simulated a carbon-abatement case in which a 21% reduction in world CO$_2$ emissions compared to the reference case comes from both reduction in energy demand and decrease in the carbon intensity of the energy mix. The biggest loser is projected to be coal, followed by oil.

Natural gas, by contrast, is not affected as the downward pressure on gas consumption is compensated by coal-to-gas substitutions. The market shares lost by coal and oil are taken up by nuclear and renewable energies.

Within the renewables category, the Commission's model foresees a 20-fold increase in wind, solar and small hydro. Clearly, different paths to a lower carbon world are possible; an alternative one has been outlined, for example, by the World Business Council for Sustainable Development (WBCSD). All forecasts have in common, however, a decline in the income elasticity of energy demand and rapid development of nuclear and renewables.

1

Christoph Grobbel *et al.*, "Preparing for a Low-Carbon Future," *The McKinsey Quarterly*, no. 4, 2004.

2

"Evaluating Climate Impacts with Intermediate Complexity Models", Presentation by Reto Knutti (National Center for Atmospheric Research, USA), IPCC Expert Meeting on Emission Scenarios, 12–14 January 2005, Washington, D.C.

3

"Inuit to take on the US?" *Eco*, Climate Negotiations NGO Newsletter, Milan, December 13, 2003.

4

See www.climatelaw. org, or www.foe.co.uk

13.2

Implications for climate change policies: the fate of the Kyoto Protocol in the three *Global Scenarios*

Efforts to bring the world community together to address the threat of climate change fare quite differently in the three scenarios, with implications that differ from the EU and WBCSD projections summarised above. The key differences reflect the different incentives and constraints that shape policies, regulations and strategies in the three scenarios.

Kyoto in *Low Trust Globalisation*

In *Low Trust Globalisation*, coercive regulations coexist with successful efforts by the business community to promote market-friendly frameworks and policies. As the Kyoto Protocol bumps along with the US and China on the sidelines, the lack of a coherent approach to the problem of climate change emerges as a source of international tension and a deterrent to further trade liberalisation and economic integration. The EU endeavours to incentivise a number of countries, including China, through trade concessions and carbon credit purchases, as well as encouraging its own domestic industries to abide by what is a binding, yet not truly global, treaty. Led by California and New York, a number of US states become party to trading schemes that the US does not endorse at federal level.

European industry is at a disadvantage. Together with the US government, which is suspicious of international instruments but under some pressure from US environmental groups, it seeks to promote a reinterpretation of Kyoto that gives each country considerable flexibility in how it implements the accord. Technology programmes are counted as credit-creating activities, even if their impact on reduction of GHG emissions is only a virtual possibility. While the industrialised countries lead the way, developing countries are required to join the trading-scheme regime as the price for continued access to open markets. Even though a global framework emerges, actual GHG reductions do not occur during the period. Developed world emissions remain flat at best, with emissions in the developing world continuing to grow—albeit with proponents of the regime claiming that the rate of growth is below "business as usual".

Carbon taxes are favoured over the trading of carbon-emission credits,

as this leaves the state with a higher degree of control. Such taxes are not fully transparent to end-consumers, and may arouse opposition.

"Carbon markets" and Kyoto in *Open Doors*

Open Doors is the scenario in which carbon management will be treated as an integral part of hydrocarbon resource development, to achieve high levels of sustainable growth. Although regulators in *Open Doors* primarily aim at ensuring that energy markets are highly competitive as we have seen in chapter 12, policy makers also address "market failures", namely situations where markets fail to price for externalities (e.g. pollution, global warming). They can do so by encouraging the development of market-based instruments such as carbon-emission credits. In *Open Doors*, this tends to be the preferred approach, and policy makers endeavour to make these markets global in scope through the setting of common emission standards and of global rules for cross-border offsets as in the Kyoto CDM.

Under *Open Doors*, the Kyoto Protocol rises like a phoenix from the ashes. Governments, working with environmental NGOs and business leaders, commit to a "Beyond Kyoto" agreement that slowly but steadily ramps up GHG controls over two decades. The emphasis is on a global emissions-allowance trading regime. Developing countries are induced into participating by the promise of subsidised projects to reduce GHG emissions—projects that often deliver other benefits as well, such as reduced local air pollution and increased energy efficiency. The German decision of 2004 to subsidise the production of Brazilian cars running on biofuels is a good example.

A new mechanism would help to supervise treaty implementation by monitoring performance, benchmarking results, and providing a clearing house for data and information on climate change policies and technologies.

According to our preliminary analysis, in spite of these developments but under "normal" policy conditions, CO_2 concentration in *Open Doors* would cross the "550 ppm trajectory", in the second decade of the scenarios period. *Open Doors*, however, is the scenario in which more radical policy changes are conceivable—for instance, as part of the Kyoto revision process—if a consensus were reached that highly detrimental changes are on the way.

Part 3

Our Global Business Environment

7 Globalisation patterns

8 African futures

9 Market States

10 Demography and migrations

11 Patterns of economic growth

12 The search for energy security

13 The energy-and-carbon industry

Planet

Trilemm ▲ p19

What happens to the Kyoto Protocol?

Scenario	Scope and implementation	Developing countries
Low Trust Globalisation	Kyoto implemented with **flexibility**. Concerns about impact on competitiveness. **Insurers** and **negatively impacted** groups use their business and legal influence to protect against climate change impact.	Participation in Kyoto and "burden sharing" preconditions of some trade concessions under the "fair trade doctrine". **China** incentivised to join.
Open Doors	**"Beyond Kyoto"** agreement; a global mechanism is created to supervise implementation.	Sales of carbon credits an important source of development assistance and funds.
Flags	**Kyoto unravels** as free-riding is pervasive. Companies and countries opt out.	Free-riding by developing countries, some boycotts and extra-territorial lawsuits.

Focus

Biomass

Biomass resources are potentially the world's largest energy resource base, equivalent to 2.1 billion boe/d. However, only a fraction of this is available on a commercial basis and biomass is still burdened by low combustion efficiency, negative health associations (e.g. particulates) and limited range (due to costs of transport). Bio-fuels compete with the power sector for biomass resource. Of all the alternative future fuels, bio-fuels offer the most potential greenhouse gas benefit, and can be easily blended into the diesel or gasoline currently sold and used in unmodified vehicles.

Hydropower

The International Journal of Hydropower & Dams indicates that over 8000 TWh/yr of global hydropower capacity is considered to be economically feasible for development, two-thirds of which has yet to be developed. Unlike many other renewables sources, hydropower has the advantage of peak load capability; it also has lower operating costs and longer plant life than most other large-scale generating options.

Wind

Wind energy capacity has doubled every three years for the last decade. Although costs have declined as utilisation has increased via larger units, development has depended largely on government support. Significant growth in Denmark, Spain and Germany is expected to be followed by rapid development in the Americas and the Far East.

Solar

Solar energy is made up of two components: photovoltaic (PV) and solar thermal, with PV having higher costs than solar thermal. Hence, it is expected that PV will primarily be applied more as a distributed solution.

Energy from the sea and the land

Geothermal has potential where fluids exist above 200°C at depths that can be reached economically. However, realising that potential depends on the development of suitable technology. Geothermal has a potential resource base of 45 TWh globally. The areas with most potential are Iceland, East Africa, Japan, the Americas and the Far East.

Tidal schemes offer localised solutions since the potential of these schemes varies with location. However, in areas such as the UK, Canada, South America and China, tidal schemes do offer a solution that is highly predictable in terms of volume and timing.

Remote communities

Renewables may continue to achieve double-digit annual growth rates. Two factors help to drive this growth: renewables are seen as providing alternative solutions to energy diversification and environmental issues; and also as providing remote communities with a solution that avoids the need to develop infrastructure for connection to central generation locations.

Altogether, as discussed in the three scenarios, policies, regulations and behaviours, as well as relative costs, will set the real limits for the use of renewable energy sources.

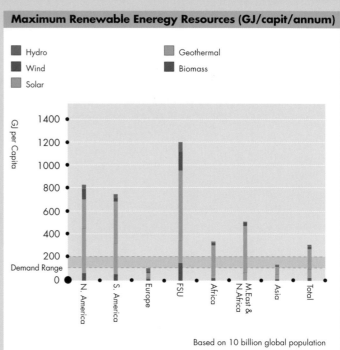

Maximum Renewable Eneregy Resources (GJ/capit/annum)

Legend: Hydro, Wind, Solar, Geothermal, Biomass

GJ per Capita — values: 1400, 1200, 1000, 800, 600, 400, 200, 0

Demand Range

Categories: N. America, S. America, Europe, FSU, Africa, M.East & N.Africa, Asia, Total

Based on 10 billion global population

Source: adapted from UN 2000, WEC 1994, and ABB 1998.

Part 3

Our Global Business Environment

7 Globalisation patterns

8 African futures

9 Market States

10 Demography and migrations

11 Patterns of economic growth

12 The search for energy security

13 The energy-and-carbon industry

Hence, the work we have begun to analyse how a second variant of *Open Doors* could unfold, in which the diffusion of state-of-the-art technologies is accelerated, and carbon sequestration is promoted aggressively, becoming mandatory for all new coal-based power plants. Determined policies of that type, according to our preliminary estimates, could keep carbon emissions within the "550 ppm long-term trajectory".

A feature of energy markets in *Open Doors*, therefore, is that the final price of energy products includes a significant element of carbon-emission credits. Groups of leading companies undertake voluntary emission reductions. They recognise that trading these obligations can dramatically lower costs. Carbon pricing is transparent, and low-carbon influences consumer choices through lower prices and not simply through environmental ethos. Governments promote new technologies of carbon capture and sequestration. A major industry develops, within or on the side of the energy industry.

Energy efficiency without Kyoto in *Flags*

In a world of *Flags*, cooperation is much harder to achieve. The Kyoto Protocol unravels as one country after another follows the US lead and bails out. Without any sense of reciprocity, governments go their own way on the issue of climate change. While the EU tries to put on a brave front and insists that controls on GHG emissions will be implemented across its 30-country zone, "free-riding" by other nations soon makes this policy untenable. A number of countries, for instance, will accept payments for carbon credits while not really pursuing environmentally sound policies. With its competitiveness eroding in the face of products coming into the global marketplace from other jurisdictions where companies bear no climate-change-related regulatory costs, Brussels eventually abandons its GHG control programme.

Those parties who have not signed up to the Protocol may nevertheless promote higher efficiency in the use of hydrocarbon fuels as part of their energy security and environmental agendas. Societal pressure will in fact lead states, such as China, to stimulate cleaner technologies to address the impact of burning coal or of vehicle emissions. Reductions in GHG emissions, however, are largely incidental to these local pressures.

A lower-carbon economy develops therefore in *Flags*, reflecting not so much the consumer's choice but rather lower global economic growth, national aspirations to self-sufficiency as well as concerns over local pollution.

As a result, according to our preliminary analysis, CO_2 concentration in *Flags* would be still below the long-term 550 ppm trajectory in 2025.

13.3

Biodiversity and protected areas in the three *Global Scenarios*[1]

1

This section reflects discussions at the Biodiversity Workshop organised by David Hone, Sachin Kapila and Richard Sykes (Shell) with IUCN and other other organisations, London, March 8–9, 2005.

2

Our Common Future, The World Commission on Environment and Development, Oxford University Press, 1987. This book is also known as the Brundtland Report from the name of the Chair of the Commission.

Biodiversity has emerged as a crucial consideration for groups concerned with sustainable development. Recognition of its importance continues to rise as awareness grows of how profoundly interconnected the different natural subsystems on our planet are. Energy companies are confronted with important biodiversity issues every time they conduct a major project, especially in fragile regions. Yet these issues are still far from featuring highly in the policy debate. The term biodiversity itself sounds slightly abstract, and is not as easily defined as "climate change" or "pollution". It can be used to refer to specific ecosystems, to endangered species present in different regions simultaneously, or to the global pool of genetic resources available to mankind for uses ranging from agriculture to pharmaceutical. Evidence is gradually emerging, however, that the destruction of natural habitats has reached such proportions as to create a genuine challenge to the diversity of life forms—a diversity on which our global ecosystem is increasingly understood to depend.

Both energy production and energy consumption can have very significant impacts on specific sites and on larger ecosystems, and regulators will take this into account in ways that the *Global Scenarios* can help analyse. This being said, no single company or organisation can be the sole custodian of biodiversity, as this requires major and coordinated adaptations or precautions in land use and many other activities. As they proceed with care in their own operations, companies must also be involved in forums and other forms of cooperative action, in order to be able to relate specific site issues with the broader agenda. In this spirit, for instance, Shell collaborates with the International Union for the Conservation of Nature and Natural Resources (IUCN) and other organisations.

The Convention on Biological Diversity

Modern as it may sound, concerns for biodiversity were already present in India in the 3rd century BC when Emperor Asoka established protected areas for mammals, birds, fish and forests; and in Sumatra in the 7th century AD, when the first nature reserve attested in history was created. Closer to the present day, the imperative to protect certain sites has gained increasing recognition through the establishment of the Yellowstone National Park in 1872 and the Kruger National Park in 1926; through the creation of the first biosphere reserves (now numbering 425 in 95 countries) as part of the 1968 Man and the Biosphere Programme; and through the 1972 World Heritage Convention leading to the recognition of 149 natural World Heritage sites by 2003. The 1992 Earth Summit in Rio approved the Convention on Biological Diversity and the Framework Convention on Climate Change. These two conventions go beyond previous instruments that were limited to specific species; they make the protection of biodiversity in general a legally binding objective for signatories. In this context, Shell has committed not to explore for resources in World Heritage sites.

Within our scenario time horizon, issues of biodiversity and protected areas (PAs) can be expected to assume increasing importance, in connection notably with the Millennium Development Goals (of which Goal 7 calls for environmental sustainability) and with the 2010 Biodiversity Target agreed among the parties of the Convention on Biological Diversity. Critical issues include:
• How to define 'high biodiversity value', and with what linkages to other environmental issues (e.g. pollution),
• How to value biodiversity, and for whom,
• The role of Environmental Impact Statements and alternative tools,
• The development of partnerships enabling companies, NGOs and governments to share resources and commitments.

How protected are "protected areas"?

The number of protected areas (PAs) has increased rapidly, reaching 20,000 at the end of the 1960s and more than 100,000 in 2003. The Brundtland Report envisioned that as much as 12% of native ecosystem needed to be protected. The notion of PA has therefore outgrown the initial concept of special areas that could be managed almost entirely outside of the normal economic realm. The key challenge for companies is then to identify which voluntary or mandatory standards they should abide by when operating in the various types of PAs.[2]

How is 'biodiversity' treated and defined in the three *Global Scenarios*?

Scenario	Level of priority	Drivers	Key trade-offs and objectives
Low Trust Globalisation	**Low**.	Long-term liabilities, mandatory rules	**Local** environmental and specific **global NGO** concerns more important.
Open Doors	**High**, as part of policy agenda.	Valuation of benefits. Partnering.	"**Ecosystems services**" become central reference.
Flags	**Case-by-case** assessment.	Militant campaigns, local causes.	Protection of **specific sites and species**.

Peter Schwartz, who headed the Shell Scenario team in the 1980s, is co-founder and Chairman of Global Business Network, a scenario/strategy consulting network now part of the Monitor Group. Active in venture capital, he helped Steven Spielberg with the *Minority Report* film on our high-tech future and published *The Art of the Long View* (Doubleday Currency, 1990) and *Inevitable Surprises* (Gotham Books, 2003). Conversation with Albert Bressand in Davos, 2005.

Preparing for the unexpected: concluding words with Peter Schwartz

Albert Bressand: When I think of how you help major organisations look beyond the familiar challenges, the first theme that comes to my mind is that of climate change. Have your views changed since you first described, in *Inevitable Surprises*, how non-linear developments could wreak havoc on the planet as we know it?

Peter Schwartz: There are three new data points since *Inevitable Surprises* was published. Some very deep ice cores from the Antarctic ice shelf indicate that the stable interglacial period we are in could last much longer than we fear. Secondly, there is growing evidence in the North Atlantic and North Pacific that the salinity and temperature may be changing at an accelerating rate. Finally, while we have been focusing on a new stable state in which the Northern Hemisphere would be on the whole colder, drier and windier (similar to 8200 years ago), there is now evidence that the earth could stabilise at a much warmer point, quite inhospitable to humanity. The current evidence suggests that a period of rapid climate change is unlikely before 2020 but the odds are quite substantial by mid-century.

Based on analogies with other fields such as International Accounting Standards, I would suggest that the US will never be reconciled to the Kyoto Protocol because of its very nature as an international binding treaty. Do you agree this is the key obstacle, or are there other aspects that make Kyoto undesirable?

PS: The Bush Administration and Congress are opposed to the Kyoto Treaty for three main reasons. It is true that they see it as an intrusion on US sovereignty, although if they really believed it was in the US interest they would care less about sovereignty. President Bush and Vice-President Dick Cheney take seriously the views of the few sceptics who continue to question the validity of the scientific understanding of climate change. They also believe that US automakers will be hurt disproportionately and that there is a high risk of costly premature action.

You are a key advisor to the Chairman of the California Environmental Protection Agency. How much can California contribute to the reduction of greenhouse gases? And how decentralised can action against risks of detrimental climate change be?

PS: Ideally leadership on these issues would come from Washington. There is little doubt that one national standard would be far more efficient. However, the Bush Administration is not deeply engaged so the states have taken steps to respond. California was given the right to set its own emission standards in the early 1970s because of the magnitude of its pollution problems. As the seventh largest economy in the world and a huge car market, California can have an impact by itself. In addition, many other big states have elected to follow its lead.

Beyond those you could see in 2003, are there some new 'inevitable surprises' that you think we should we be paying attention to?

PS: I can see at least four new surprises:

1) The possibility of an Arab Spring. The death of Arafat, the Syrian withdrawal from Lebanon and the elections in Iraq could all be early signals of movement toward relative peace, stability and the prospect of economic progress in the Middle East.

2) Looking at Venezuela, Brazil, Chile and the Andean nations, and even Mexico, we are seeing the early stages of a dramatic swing to the left and towards an anti-US coalition in Latin America. The US could find itself deeply re-engaged in the nexus of Latin politics, drug wars and China's newly found interest in the resources of this rich continent.

3) There is a demographic collapse under way in Russia. In addition to the well-known dramatic increase in the death rate of older men, we are now seeing a dramatic decline in the fertility rate of young women which means not only fewer older workers, but soon fewer younger workers as well.

4) Advances in quantum information systems are creating the basis for a whole new era of IT using the quantum properties of matter and energy. The power of IT will continue to grow at an exponential pace even as we reach the limits of conventional silicon technology. The productivity impacts will be enormous, including a fall in costs by several orders of magnitude.

Part 3
Our Global Business Environment

7 Globalisation patterns

8 African futures

9 Market States

10 Demography and migrations

11 Patterns of economic growth

12 The search for energy security

13 The energy-and-carbon industry

IUCN distinguishes between six types of area depending on the reason for their protection (I: scientific and wilderness protection, II: ecosystems, III: specific natural features, IV: habitat and species management, V: landscape and aesthetics, VI: renewable resources management). The last two types are seeing the most rapid increase in number of PAs. Each of the three *Global Scenarios* would envisage a different relationship between economic activities and protection of these various types of PA.

In *Open Doors*, the win–win spirit that is the hallmark of this scenario would probably see, to quote Jeffrey A. McNeely of IUCN, *"biodiversity replaced by ecosystems services as the driving metaphor for conservation"*.[1] The IUCN has identified four types of ecosystem service:
(1) the provision of specific resources such as fresh water, fuel wood or genetic resources;
(2) the regulation of key processes such as climate, disease and flood;
(3) cultural benefits of a spiritual, recreational or aesthetic nature; and
(4) more general supporting services.

The nature of *Open Doors* is such that, for important PA sites, a value would be systematically placed on the benefit that local communities and the global community derive from all four types of service, irrespective of whether they are market or non-market services.

In *Low Trust Globalisation*, complying with a patchwork of local and national rules defines the agenda, the more so as liabilities are defined and redefined in ways holding companies accountable for past and future consequences of their activities. When protection is provided in this scenario, it tends to be in the form of stringent interdictions. Examples can be seen in some aspects of the EU's *Natura 2000* programme which seeks to exclude large parts of national territories from the sphere of economic activities, even if at the cost of other desirable objectives (e.g. when dead trees may not be gathered up but must be left to rot back naturally into the soil, hampering fire prevention efforts even in areas at high risk of forest fire).

In *Flags*, the "Not In My Backyard" syndrome is very strong, yet a number of groups and communities also protect specific areas or species in ways reminiscent of the most aggressive animal rights activists. Biodiversity as such is unlikely to lend itself to the type of campaigns that are the hallmark of *Flags*, but more focused causes will be embraced relentlessly.

Our scenarios could be further enriched in light of more specific scenarios presented by IUCN at the World Parks Congress in 2003,[1] the more so as two of these scenarios presuppose policy developments and attitudes quite in line with, respectively, *Open Doors* (the "Triple Bottom Line" IUCN scenario in which "economic growth, social well-being, and environmental sustainability are three intertwined goals"), and with *Flags* (the "Rainbow" IUCN scenario in which a globalisation backlash happens with PAs managed for the benefit of local communities). By contrast, the third IUCN scenario, "Buy Your Eden", is better understood in light of the attitudes and policies that would prevail in the top part of the *Trilemma Triangle* (a region explored by Shell in the *2001 Business Class scenario*) as it would see monetary considerations prevail over almost any other consideration.

Environmental protection, biodiversity and climate change—the issues of this concluding chapter—illustrate how complex the interactions can be between market incentives, the force of community ("values") and the power of the state to regulate or to coerce, nationally or through international treaties like Kyoto. Our goal would be met if the *Shell Global Scenarios to 2025*, and the *Trilemma Triangle* methodology behind them, help to move beyond the limitations of utopia thinking to highlight what trends, trade-offs and choices are likely to shape the global business environment in which communities are served and value created.

1

Jeffrey A. McNeely and Frederik Schutyser, "Contemplating an Uncertain Future: Scenarios for Protected Areas", World Parks Congress, September 2003.

A - Z

Absolute poverty term proposed in 1973 by Robert S. McNamara, then President of the World bank, as a "condition of deprivation that falls below any rational definition of human decency." One USD a day represents the absolute poverty line according to the World Bank.

ADM Atomic Demolition Munitions

ADRs American Depository Receipts. These stocks issued by a US bank and listed on either the NYSE, AMEX, or Nasdaq, are representing a specified number of shares of a foreign corporation. ADRs are an indirect way for foreign companies to trade on American exchanges.

AGM Annual General Meeting

APEC Asia Pacific Economic Cooperation. APEC, created in 1989, has evolved from an informal dialogue group to a forum for facilitating economic growth, cooperation, trade and investment in the Asia-Pacific region. APEC has 21 members: Australia, Brunei Darussalam, Canada, Chile, People's Republic of China, Hong Kong, China, Indonesia, Japan, Republic of Korea, Malaysia, Mexico, New Zealand, Papua New Guinea, Peru, The Republic of the Philippines, The Russian Federation, Singapore, Chinese Taipei, Thailand, United States of America, Viet Nam.

ASEAN Association of South East Asian Nations. Established in 1967 by Indonesia, Malaysia, Philippines, Singapore, and Thailand, it now includes also Brunei Darussalam, Cambodia, Laos, Myanmar, and Vietnam. Its purposes are to accelerate the economic growth, social progress and cultural development, as well as to promote regional peace and stability.

ASEAN+3 ASEAN+China, South Korea and Japan: this forum met for the first time at the Kuala Lumpur East Asian Summit in December 1997 to address the Asian financial crisis. It aims at accelerating trade, investments and technology transfers in East Asia.

Basis point one-hundredth of a percentage point (used in the context of interest rates).

BINGOs Business Initiated Non-Governmental Organisations

BIS Bank for International Settlement. It has two missions: the promotion of non-inflationary growth and the stability of the international financial system.

BRICs Brazil, Russia, India and China. An acronym coined by Goldman Sachs in its Global Economics Paper, in October 2003 ("Dreaming with BRICs: The Path to 2050"); it supports the idea that "over 50 years, Brazil, Russia, India and China – the BRICs economies – could become a much larger force in the world economy."

BTL Biomass-to-Liquid

CDM Clean Development Mechanism. A mechanism established by the Kyoto Protocol for project-based emission reduction activities in developing countries.

CCP Chinese Communist Party

Chiang Mai swap arrangements in May 2000, the Finance Ministers of ASEAN + 3 agreed to establish a regional financing arrangement called the "Chiang Mai Initiative" or CMI. CMI has two components: an expanded ASEAN swap arrangement and a network of bilateral swap arrangements among ASEAN +3 countries.

CG Corporate Governance

CSOs Civil Society Organisations

CTL Coal-to-Liquids

ECB European Central Bank. The ECB is the central bank for the euro. Its mission is to maintain the euro purchasing power and price stability in the eurozone that comprises the 12 following countries: Austria, Belgium, Finland, France, Germany, Greece, Ireland, Italy, Luxemburg, Netherlands, Portugal, Spain.

ECOWAS Economic Community of West African States. This regional organisation of 15 West African nations formed in 1975–Benin, Burkina Faso, Cape Verde, Ivory Coast, Gambia, Ghana, Guinea, Guinea-Bissau, Liberia, Mali, Niger, Nigeria, Senegal, Sierra Leone and Togo—aims at achieving economic integration and shared development so as to form a unified economic zone in West Africa.

E & P	Exploration & Production
ETS	Emission Trading Scheme. Emissions trading gives companies the flexibility to meet emission reduction targets either by reducing emissions on site or by buying allowances from other companies who have excess allowances.
FBO	Faith-Based Organisation
FDI	Foreign Direct Investment. It is investment of foreign assets into domestic structures, equipment, and organisations. It does not include foreign investment into the stock markets.
FSU	Former Soviet Union
G-2	Group of Two. Consultative mechanism proposed by C. Fred Bergsten (see page 82) through which the European Union and the United States would manage their own economic (and possibly some security) relations and informally steer the world economy
G-8	Group of Eight. Coalition of eight of the world leading nations: Canada, France, Germany, Italy, Japan, Russia (since 1998), United Kingdom, and United States. The hallmark of the G-8 is an annual economic and political summit of the heads of states and governments (a representative of the European Union also attends the summit).
GDP	Gross Domestic Product. The total market value of all final goods and services produced in a country in a given year.
GHGs	Greenhouse gases: atmospheric gases which warm the lower atmosphere by absorbing thermal radiation—the six gases listed in the Kyoto Protocol are the following carbon dioxide (CO_2); methane (CH_4); nitrous oxide (N_2O); hydrofluorocarbons (HFCs); perfluorocarbons (PFCs); and sulphur hexafluoride (SF_6)
GRI	Global Reporting Initiative. Multi-stakeholder process and independent institution whose mission is to develop and disseminate globally applicable Sustainability Reporting Guidelines. These Guidelines are for voluntary use by organisations for reporting on the economic, environmental, and social dimensions of their activities, products, and services.
GRINGOs	Government-related NGOs
GTL	Gas-to-Liquids
Hubbert peak	point at which the curb of global oil production reaches its maximum
IASB	International Accounting Standards Board. It is an independent, privately-funded accounting standard-setter based in London developing a set of high quality, global accounting standards. The IASB co-operates also with national accounting standard-setters to promote convergence in accounting standards around the world.
IEA	International Energy Agency. It is the energy forum for 26 industrialised countries committed to taking joint measures to meet oil supply emergencies.
ICBM	Inter-Continental Ballistic Missile
IGCC	Integrated Gasification Combined Cycle
ILO	International Labour Organisation. It is a UN specialised agency which seeks the promotion of social justice and internationally recognised human and labour rights
IMF	International Monetary Fund. This international organisation of 184 member countries has been established to promote international monetary cooperation and exchange stability, to foster economic growth and to provide temporary financial assistance to countries to help ease balance of payments adjustment.
IOCs	International Oil (and energy) Companies
IOSCO	International Organisation of Securities Commissions. Its members cooperate to promote high standards of regulation in order to maintain efficient and sound securities markets.

IP	Intellectual Property
IPCC	Intergovernmental Panel on Climate Change. The role of the IPCC is to assess the scientific, technical and socio-economic information relevant to the understanding of the risk of human-induced climate change.
IPO	Initial Public Offering. First sale of stocks by a company to the public.
ISO	International Organisation for Standardisation. This NGO is a network of the standardisation bodies from 150 countries and of other organisations set up by national partnership and industry associations.
ITU	International Telecommunication Union is an international organisation within the United Nations system where governments and the private sector coordinate global telecom networks and services.
IUCN	World Conservation Union (formerly International Union for Conservation of Nature and Natural Resources). It is a network of states, governmental agencies and NGOs whose mission is "to influence, encourage and assist societies throughout the world to conserve the integrity and diversity of nature and to ensure that any use of natural resources is equitable and ecologically sustainable."
jurisdictional discontinuities	differences in regulations between jurisdictions
keiretsu	Japanese term describing a loose conglomeration of companies organised around a single bank for their mutual benefit
"Know your customer"	policy that banks need to implement in order to reduce the likelihood to become unwitting participants in illicit activities conducted or attempted by their customers.
Kyoto Protocol	the formal name of the agreement is the Kyoto Protocol to the United Nations Framework Convention on Climate Change. This agreement on global warming, reached during the United Nations Conference on Climate Change in Kyoto in 1997 came into force on February 16, 2005 following its official ratification by Russia on November 18, 2004 (the 122 countries that had previously ratified the Protocol accounted for 44% of carbon dioxide and other gas emissions; Russia emitting 17% of carbon dioxide, Russian ratification allowed to reach the threshold of 55% needed for the Kyoto Protocol to come into force).
LAFTA	Latin-American Free Trade Association (LAFTA) created in 1960. The Latin American Integration Association, an intergovernmental organisation that promotes regional integration, has replaced it in 1980. It has twelve member countries: Argentina, Bolivia, Brazil, Chile, Colombia, Cuba, Ecuador, Mexico, Paraguay, Peru, Uruguay and Venezuela.
legal forum shopping	the attempt by a litigant to find the best jurisdiction, or court, globally so as to try a case more favourably
LNG	Liquefied Natural Gas
M&As	Mergers and Acquisitions
Millennium Development Goals	adopted at the Millennium Summit of the United Nations in September 2000, it sets 8 goals to be reached by 2015: eradicate extreme poverty; achieve universal primary education; promote gender equality and empower women; reduce child mortality; improve maternal health; combat HIV/AIDS, malaria and other diseases; ensure environmental sustainability; develop a global partnership for development.
Mutual recognition	principle of international law whereby States party to an agreement decide that they will recognise and uphold legal decisions taken by competent authorities in another Member State.
NAFTA	North American Free Trade Association. This comprehensive trade agreement links Canada, the US and Mexico in a free trade area. NAFTA went into effect on January 1, 1994.
NATO	North Atlantic Treaty Organisation: alliance of 26 countries from North America and Europe – Belgium, Bulgaria, Canada, Czech Republic, Denmark, Estonia, France, Germany, Greece, Hungary, Iceland, Italy, Latvia, Lithuania, Luxembourg, The Netherlands, Norway, Poland, Portugal, Romania, Slovakia, Slovenia, Spain, Turkey, United Kingdom and United States – to safeguard the freedom and security of its member countries by political and military means.

netizen	a citizen taking advantage of global networks to position himself/herself as an actor of the information society
NGOs	Non-Governmental Organisations
NOCs	National Oil (or energy) Companies
NPLs	Non-Performing Loans. They refer to loan accounts whose principal and/or interest is unpaid.
OECD	Organisation for Economic Co-operation and Development: This forum of 30 member countries – Australia, Austria, Belgium, Canada, Czech Republic, Denmark, Finland, France, Germany, Greece, Hungary, Iceland, Ireland, Italy, Japan, Korea, Luxembourg, Mexico, Netherlands, New Zealand, Norway, Poland, Portugal, Slovak Republic, Spain, Sweden, Switzerland, Turkey, United Kingdom and United States – develop and refine economic and social policies. The OECD is also known for "soft law" – non-binding instruments – on difficult issues such as its Guidelines for multinational enterprises.
OTEC	Ocean Thermal Energy Conversion
OPEC	Organisation of Petroleum Exporting Countries. Created in 1960, it has 11 members: Algeria, Kuwait, Libya, Indonesia, Iran, Iran, Nigeria, Qatar, Saudi Arabia, United Arab Emirates, Venezuela.
PAs	Protected Areas. According to the IUCN definition, a PA is "an area of land and/or sea especially dedicated to the protection and maintenance of biological diversity, and of natural and associated cultural resources, and managed through legal or other effective means."
PPP	Purchasing Power Parity
PPPs	Public-Private Partnerships
precautionary principle	regulatory tool designed to protect the safety of the environment and consumers, allowing risk managers to take measures to avoid a potential hazard without waiting until all the necessary scientific knowledge is available. The precautionary principle was enshrined on an international level during the 1992 Rio Conference on the Environment and Development.
public goods	an exception to the free-market system marked by two characteristics: first, if one person consumes public goods the amount available remains the same; second, once public goods are available, no one can be stopped from consuming them for free.
SADC	Southern African Development Community: its aims at promoting regional cooperation in economic development among its members – Angola, Botswana, Lesotho, Malawi, Mauritius, Mozambique, Namibia, South Africa, Swaziland, Tanzania, Zambia, and Zimbabwe.
SEC	Securities and Exchange Commission: US regulatory agency created in 1934 to protect American investors and maintain the integrity of the US securities markets.
SLBM	Submarine-Launched Ballistic Missile
soft power	the ability to co-opt support rather than coerce
Tabaksblat corporate governance code	this code, drawn up by a committee, headed by former Unilever CEO Morris Tabaksblat, has been designed to strengthen the past structure of checks and balance in Dutch listed companies.
triple bottom line	economic performance, sustainable development, and social responsibility.
ubiquity	capacity to be connected whenever and wherever
USD	US dollar
US GAAP	US Generally Accepted Accounting Principles comprising a massive volume of standards, interpretations, opinions and bulletins developed by the FASB (Financial Accounting Standards Board).
USGS	US Geological Survey

virtual community	a term commonly used to describe various forms of computer-mediated communication among large group of people.
WMDs	Weapons of Mass Destruction
Wolfsberg Principles	principles signed on October 30, 2000, by the Wolfsberg Group – an association of twelve global banks – and covering "know your customer", anti-money laundering and counter terrorist financing policies.
WBCSD	World Business Council for Sustainable Development
WTO	World Trade Organisation: global international organisation created in 1995 and dealing with the rules of trade between its 148 members.

bbl:	**barrel**
bbl/d:	**barrel per day**
boe:	**barrel of oil equivalent**
EJ:	10^{18} **Joule**
GJ:	10^{9} **joule**
GW:	10^{9} **watt**
KW:	10^{3} **watt**
ppm:	**particle per million**
USD:	**US dollar**
trillion:	10^{12}
tWh:	10^{12} **watt/hour**

**Part 1
Forces of
Change and
Analytical
Framework**

**Chapter 1
The dual
crisis of
security
and trust**

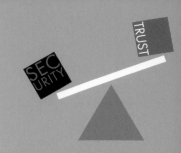

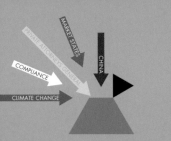

**Chapter 2
Mapping
complex
trade-offs:
the *Trilemma*
dynamics**

**Part 2
The Three
*Global
Scenarios***

**Chapter 3
*Low Trust
Globalisation***

**Chapter 4
*Open Doors***

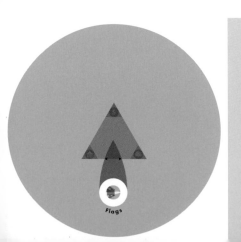

**Chapter 5
*Flags***

**Chapter 6
Trilemmaps
on the three
contrasted glob
business
environments**

Part 1
Forces of Change and Analytical Framework

Part 2
The Three *Global Scenarios*

Part 3
Our Global Business Environment

Chapter 7
The US, China and changing globalisation patterns

Chapter 8
African futures

Chapter 9
From Nation States to Market States

Chapter 10
Demography and migration setting the stage

Chapter 11
Patterns of economic growth in the three *Global Scenarios*

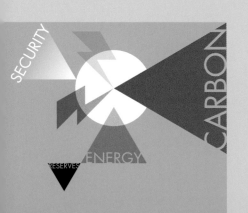

Chapter 12
The triple discontinuity and the search for energy security

Chapter 13
The energy-and-carbon industry of 2025

Part 3
Our Global Business Environment

by **Albert Bressand Ph.D.**,
Vice President,
Global Business Environment,
Royal Dutch/Shell Group

Global Scenarios **have been part of the Shell corporate culture for more than three decades. Having joined Shell only recently— even if after many years of close interactions with the scenario team— I can still be excused for acknowledging by name our debt and gratitude to present and past Shell colleagues, and to distinguished external experts. Since the pioneering work of Pierre Wack—who coined the term 'scenario' to describe the method he designed to help Shell anticipate change— scenarios have been continuously improved** **and adapted to Shell's needs. Admiration for his work and that of his successors—Peter Schwartz—a long time inspirer—Joop de Vries, Kees van der Heijden, Joseph Jaworski, Roger Rainbow and Ged Davis—is widely shared well beyond Shell. The scenario team also wants to acknowledge two professional communities without which the present report would not exist.**

Leading edge users

The first community are the "scenario users" within Shell. Their demand for challenging perspectives on their business environment is the *raison d'être* of this work. Interacting with them— whether they are in Houston, Moscow, Port Harcourt, Mexico City, Rio, Oslo, Singapore, Beijing, Brunei or The Hague—is what has led us to experiment with new approaches that put the user at the centre —whether a country Chair, strategist, planner or project manager—. The *Trilemma Triangle* has therefore been designed for customised uses, across contexts and time horizons. To serve the needs of these demanding users in shorter times and at higher levels of analytical sophistication is the reason why we developed it. Special gratitude goes to those who oversaw scenario exercises and to those who took part in the scenario exercises, notably John Barry, Jeremy Bentham, Tim Bertels, Ed Cadena, Mark Carne, John Crocker—and his colleagues in the International Directorate—, David Easterfield, David Freedman, Tony Heggs, John Hofmeister, Peter Kidd, Kees Langeveld, Erik Nijdam, Tzu-Yang Lee, Doug McKay, Martin Poletto, Alan Simpson, Ian Smith, Martin Solomon, Hans Vlemmings, Mark Weintraub and Andy Wood among others.

Centres of excellence

The second community without which this work would not have been possible is a global network of centres of excellence and of insightful individuals whom we would like to thank for their generous contributions. Stressing that any shortcoming is ours, we want to emphasise how much we are indebted to these eminent experts. Some have worked so closely with the scenario team that we consider them as colleagues rather than advisers. Such is the case with Professor Philip Bobbitt from the University of Texas—who reminds us that the state has transformed rather than withered away, several times since the Renaissance—and with Stilpon Nestor, whose understanding of corporate governance issues is reflected in no less than the OECD Guidelines on this essential aspect of business leadership and value creation. Catherine Distler, Managing Director of Promethee in Paris, contributed notably to the analysis of social cohesion, European and Asian integration and trans-Atlantic issues. Others are members of leading institutions with which relations have been strengthened.

C. Fred Bergsten and his colleagues at the Institute for International Economics (IIE) in Washington have been very close partners in this endeavour. Martin Baily, a former Chairman of the Council of Economic Advisers, William Cline, respected for his work on international debt, Gary Hufbauer and Jeffrey Schott, who know the international trade scene like few trade negotiators do, Michael Mussa, a former Economic Counselor and Director of the Department of Research at the International Monetary Fund, Nicholas Lardy, Morris Goldstein, Catherine Mann, and Adam Posen, who kindly challenged a number of our political and economic policy assumptions, John Williamson, who has helped to understand and look beyond the "Washington consensus" which he coined, and their IIE colleagues have spared no effort to help us seek analytical clarity and integrity. May they accept our gratitude.

Thane Gustafson—of Georgetown University and CERA—has, as always, provided state-of-the-art understanding of the Russian perspective, as did Lilia Shevtsova who is with the Carnegie Endowment in Moscow. Minxin Pei, also from the Carnegie Endowment, has provided insights on China that will continue to inspire.

Daniel Esty from the Center for Environmental Law and Policy at Yale University was of great help on environmental regulatory matters.

As in previous scenario rounds, John Gray at the London School of Economics and Steve Tsang at St. Antony's College, University of Oxford have been generous in sharing insights that helped prioritise and structure our work.

Our cooperation with the International Institute for Strategic Studies (IISS) is well illustrated in this volume, as Rodney Craig, Tim Huxley and Adam Ward help us address security issues. Special gratitude is owed to John Chipman, who heads IISS and made this productive relationship possible. Our relations with the Centre for Strategic and International Studies (CSIS) in Washington are gathering momentum around notably regional analyses. Shireen Hunter on Islamic issues, Bob Ebel, Frank Verrastro and Al Hegburg on energy matters, Stephen Morrison on African matters, Jon Alterman and Tony Cordesman on Middle Eastern affairs, Sidney Weintraub and his colleagues Lowell R. Fleischer and Phil McLean on Latin America—all have begun to help us navigate complex agendas in ways we look forward to developing further.

Technology issues, while less explicitly discussed here than in previous *Global Scenarios* play a major role in our overall analysis. Special thanks are owed to Vince Kasten and Ralph Welborn at Unisys and to Izumi Aizu, Adam Peake and Shumpei Kumon at the HyperNetwork Institute in Tokyo. Contacts with the Institute for Policy Studies (IPS) in Singapore, as catalysed by Tzu Yang Lee and IPS chairman Tommy Koh, are of special importance in light of the use the Singapore authorities make of scenario analysis.

Other contributors to our work have included Jonathan Story and Bruce Kogut from INSEAD, Peter Oppenheimer of Christchurch College, University of Oxford, Anupam Khanna from the World Bank, Doug Miller, the President of GlobeScan, Helmut Anheier from the University of California, Mark Valencia, Senior Fellow at the East-West Center in Hawaii and Simon Commander from the London Business School. Econometric work has been conducted with Oxford Economic Forecasting.

Professor Klaus Schwab and Ged Davis, now heading the Centre for Strategic Insight at the World Economic Forum made possible an extremely fruitful dialogue at Davos in January 2005 with the

WEF members and with the Forum of Young Global Leaders.

Intellectual exchanges often bring together the personal and the professional, and it is a special pleasure to acknowledge Gilles Kepel as well as Olivier Roy, and the Harvard and Boston community—as illustrated in conversations with Roderick MacFarquhar, Jenny White and long-time mentor Joseph S. Nye.

Again, the final report and its shortcomings are ours, but the hopes we have to build on this work rest on this network of demanding yet generous and friendly cooperations.

Shell Global Scenarios team

In the world of ideas and creativity, one receives in proportion to what one gives, and the *Shell Global Scenarios* team has spared no effort to be worthy of these generous contributions. Peter Cornelius, the Group's Chief Economist, Wim Thomas, the Head of the Energy team, Cho Khong, the Group's Chief Political Analyst, and Angela Wilkinson who also led the pace-setting scenario work on AIDS in Africa with UNAIDS, the Scenario Managers formerly Gerard Drenth and presently Norbert Roelofs, have all led this work collaboratively. Their task has been made easier and more rewarding by the professionalism and dedication of outstanding colleagues: Kamran Agasi, Simon

Jeroen van der Veer
Chief Executive
Royal Dutch/Shell Group

'

Energy companies, more than most businesses, need to take a long-term view. That is why Shell has been producing *Global Scenarios* **for more than 30 years. These scenarios are different from forecasts in that they provide a tool that helps us to explore the many complex business environments in which we work and the factors that drive changes and developments in those environments.**

This information plays a vital part in the judgements and decisions we make about our business and its future, decisions which typically are about complex projects developed and operated over several decades.

Clarity and simplicity

In my view, the new *Global Scenarios to 2025* bring clarity and simplicity on matters of high complexity.

In the 1990s, the Shell *Global Scenarios* explored a world of globalisation, new technology and market liberalisation, and an alternative model where emphasis was placed on social and community aspirations. In this spirit, the *2001 Global Scenarios* set out two different worlds, *Business Class* driven by efficiency, economic integration and declining power of nation states, and *Prism* that highlighted the power of cultural values and cohesion. While these themes are still very relevant, the events of September 11, 2001 and the crisis of trust in the market arising from corporate scandals have brought

profound changes in our business environment, which the *Global Scenarios to 2025* also explore. In particular, the feelings of insecurity and mistrust that have arisen in the light of these events have led to new barriers to free movement of people, goods and capital, as well as a stronger role for the state both in protecting national security and in restoring trust in the market.

These changes make the interactions between market participants, states and society more complex. The scenarios provide a way of navigating through that complexity by outlining three sets of forces—market incentives, the force of community, and coercion and regulation—and how these drive towards three different objectives—efficiency, social cohesion and security.

These objectives are, at times, incompatible and the scenarios explore the resulting trade-offs that are needed to reconcile them, setting out what is called a *Trilemma Triangle*. The *Trilemmaps* that the scenarios team develops also provide insights on the kinds of strategy different groups may adopt in different strategic contexts.

That framework has led to the breaking of a time-honoured tradition in *Shell Global Scenarios*—that the analysis should lead to two alternatives. The new analytical framework has shown that three *Global Scenarios* offer the best way to capture the interactions between the three sets of forces and the subsequent trade-offs and choices that shape the business environment over the long term.

Introducing our Global Business Environment

● To use the metaphor of air navigation, the work of the Shell Scenarios team is designed to help charter routes across three interrelated levels: the *Jet Stream* level of long-term predetermined trends, uncertainties, and forces; the *Weather Systems* that reflect specific features of key regions as influenced by the *Jet Stream* context; and market-level trends and turbulences. This report presents *Jet Stream* contexts that will impact the Royal Dutch/Shell Group as a whole, through predetermined trends and through long-term equilibria captured in *Global Scenarios to 2025*. The analytical framework developed for this report can also shed light on *Weather Systems* and market-level risks and opportunities, something done separately in customised *Navigation* applications.

Cotton, Paul Domjan, Abraham Kozhipatt, Mattia Romani, Peter Snowdon and Andrew Slaughter. Le-Hoa Thieu and Helen Stapleton have spared no effort to keep this complex process properly organised in the most professional and friendly manner.

It was very rewarding to work with Peter Grundy, the lead graphic designer, from Grundy & Northedge in London, Denis Allard and the BRIEF Studio in Paris as well as Shell Visual Media Services, notably Martin Juniper and Daniel Tillett whose creativity and professionalism ensured that our analytical work is communicated through concise and effective graphic imagery.

Anne St. John-Hall has been of tremendous help in achieving the editorial quality we strive for.

Our colleagues in Group Strategy and Planning—Karl Rose, Chris Ellins, Shaun McCarthy, Ahmed Mouti and Petra Schruth, under the leadership of previously David Lawrence and currently Haw-Kuang Lin— have contributed significantly. Climate change and biodiversity issues have been addressed in close cooperation with David Hone and Sachin Kapila.

Discretely, but surely, PX Corporate Centre management Robin Aram, Lex Holst and Mary Jo Jacobi have set benchmarks to aspire to, while Adrian Loader, and Jeroen van der Veer, created the space, intellectual freedom, attention span and demanding expectations that inspired.

To all, within and outside of Shell, our gratitude and, even more importantly, our determination to keep improving on a work that they made possible.

Designed by
Grundy & Northedge, London

Artworked by
BRIEF, Paris and
Visual Media Services

Print managed by
Visual Media Services